# Essays in Management and Administration

# Essays in Management and Administration

Edited by Andrew F. Sikula
*University of Illinois at Chicago Circle*

CHARLES E. MERRILL PUBLISHING CO.
*A BELL & HOWELL COMPANY*
COLUMBUS, OHIO

Published by
Charles E. Merrill Publishing Co.
*A Bell & Howell Company*
Columbus, Ohio 43216



International Standard Book Number: 0–675–08928–X
Library of Congress Catalog Card Number: 72–95933

1 2 3 4 5 6 7 —79 78 77 76 75 74 73

Printed in the United States of America

*Dedicated to my relatives and friends*
*in Mogadore and Akron*

# PREFACE

This book of essays is designed to be used in conjunction with the text *Management and Administration,* by Andrew F. Sikula (Columbus, Ohio: Charles E. Merrill Publishing Company, 1973). However, this volume of readings could also be utilized separately or in conjunction with a different text in any introductory course in management, organization theory, and/or administration. Furthermore, this collection of writings could additionally and appropriately be used to supplement and complement materials in many other self-study, extension, undergraduate, graduate, or even post-graduate courses which attempt to envision management and administration from a broad overview systems perspective.

This volume is divided into five parts and twelve major sections chronologically and respectively corresponding to the five parts and twelve chapters in *Management and Administration.* Each section contains two contemporary essays pertaining to the chapter subject matter. The contained twenty-four essays represent a unique collection of pertinent articles authored generally by well-known experts in the discipline of management and related fields. These readings portray current and advanced thinking within the key administrative areas of: (1) management: an overview, (2) basic administrative terminology and concepts, (3) planning, (4) organizing, (5) controlling, (6) leading, (7) staffing, (8) motivating, (9) decision making, (10) communicating, (11) external environments, and (12) management principles and transferability.

This author is, of course, indebted to the authors, journals, and/or publishers who granted permission to him for inclusion of these essays in this volume.

*Andrew F. Sikula*

*Chicago, Illinois*

# CONTENTS


## PART I. SETTING AND BACKGROUND 1

*Chapter 1. Management: An Overview* *2*

**Andrew F. Sikula:** A Set-Systems Model of the Management-Administrative Processes 3

**Harold Koontz:** The Management Theory Jungle 13

*Chapter 2. Basic Administrative Terminology and Concepts* *31*

**William G. Scott:** Organization Theory: An Overview and an Appraisal 32

**Hall H. Logan:** Line and Staff: An Obsolete Concept? 56

## PART II. TRADITIONAL PROCESSES 65

*Chapter 3. Planning* *66*

**Stewart Thompson:** What Planning Involves 67

**William F. Pounds:** The Process of Problem Finding 83

*Chapter 4. Organizing* *104*

**Andre L. Delbecq:** How Informal Organization Evolves: Interpersonal Choice and Subgroup Formation 105

**Warren G. Bennis:** Organizational Developments and the Fate of the Bureaucracy 114

*Chapter 5. Controlling* *140*

**John Leslie Livingstone:** Management Controls and Organizational Performance 141

**William C. Pyle:** Monitoring Human Resources—"On Line" 154

**PART III. BEHAVIORAL PROCESSES 177**

*Chapter 6. Leading* *178*

**Robert C. Albrook:** Participative Management: Time for a Second Look 179

**W. J. Reddin:** The 3-D Management Style Theory: A Typology Based on Task and Relationships Orientations 195

*Chapter 7. Staffing* *208*

**Winston Oberg:** Make Performance Appraisal Relevant 209

**George S. Odiorne and Edwin L. Miller:** Selection by Objectives: A New Approach to Managerial Selection 222

*Chapter 8. Motivating* *242*

**J. G. Hunt and J .W. Hill:** The New Look in Motivation Theory for Organizational Research 243

**Melvin Sorcher and Herbert H. Meyer:** Motivating Factory Employees 260

**PART IV. COORDINATING PROCESSES 267**

*Chapter 9. Decision Making* *268*

**Peer O. Soelberg:** Unprogrammed Decision Making 269

***Rex. V. Brown:*** Do Managers Find Decision Theory Useful? 285

*Chapter 10. Communicating* *305*

***George W. Porter:*** Nonverbal Communications 306
***William S. Howell:*** A Model as an Approach to Interpersonal Communication 317

**PART V. ENVIRONMENTS AND IMPLICATIONS 329**

*Chapter 11. External Environments* *330*

***Leon C. Megginson and Kae H. Chung:*** Human Ecology in the Twenty-First Century 331

***Endel J. Kolde:*** The International Business System 346

*Chapter 12. Management Principles and Transferability* *357*

***Harold Koontz:*** A Model for Analyzing the Universality and Transferability of Management 358

***Rollin H. Simonds:*** Are Organizational Principles a Thing of the Past? 376

# Essays in Management and Administration

# Part I. Setting and Background

# Chapter 1. Management: An Overview

*Andrew F. Sikula*

# *A SET-SYSTEMS MODEL OF THE MANAGEMENT-ADMINISTRATIVE PROCESSES*

## INTRODUCTION

Debate continues to exist among business practitioners and academicians concerning the activities, operations, functions, and processes performed by managers. Historically, "traditional" processes of planning, organizing, and controlling were initially identified. However, modern human relations oriented businessmen and authors are currently emphasizing "behavioral" processes such as staffing, leading, and motivating. Many misconceptions currently exist pertaining to these managerial processes. The most common misinterpretation exists when individuals interpret any one process to be succinctly and distinctly different from the remaining managerial processes. Another frequent fallacy is to envision any such process as an area consisting of precise, commonly accepted procedures and methodologies. This article points out that the managerial-administrative processes are integrative and overlapping in nature, that such processes are as much an intuitive-subjective approach or frame of reference as they are precise, predetermined procedures, and that such processes exist within and thus are partially determined by various factors comprising any organization's external environments.

---

Used by permission of the author.

## TRADITIONAL PROCESSES

Managers have been studied in terms of the functions that they perform. Initial descriptions of such functions identified the processes of planning, organizing, controlling, and so on depending upon who was doing the identifying. Early management authors when identifying the functions of managers always seemed to come up with slightly different classifications; but usually part of any such categorization were the processes of planning, organizing, and controlling. The management literature today has evolved to the point where the phrase "traditional processes" refers to the earliest-to-be-identified administrative functions of planning, organizing, and controlling.

Virtually all management textbooks, old and new, in attempting to describe the planning, organizing, and controlling processes treat each function as a unique, distinct activity, and accordingly usually designate separate chapters and/or sections of texts as explanations of such activities. Thus, the misconception of envisioning the managerial activities of planning, organizing, and controlling as separate processes began and today still prevails. A more realistic interpretation of the traditional processes is shown in Exhibit I. Planning, organizing, and controlling are not separate and distinct managerial processes. As an illustration, budgets, reports, organization charts, and the like are unquestionably devices which are used for planning, organizing, *and* controlling purposes. Traditional functions overlap considerably but the degree of overlap is a question that many managers and academicians do not agree on. The key point is to beware of the extremes. Planning, organizing, and controlling are not totally distinct functions nor are they processes which are so similar that the terms can be considered to be synonymous. There are both unique and integrative aspects of the traditional processes.

Some readers may quarrel with this author's inclusion of only the planning, organizing, and controlling processes as components of the "traditional" processes. Others might include activities such as directing, leading, actuating, et cetera. The author chose only the previously mentioned three functions because they are the most commonly accepted traditional functions.

Not only is there nonconsensus about the number of traditional processes and their degree of similarity, but there is also disagreement as to the importance of each such process. Some authors insist that planning is the heart of all administrative processes, while others argue vehemently that either organizing, controlling, or some other process is the focal point from which all other administrative processes evolve or revolve. This phenomenon can be illustrated visually by simply varying the size of the

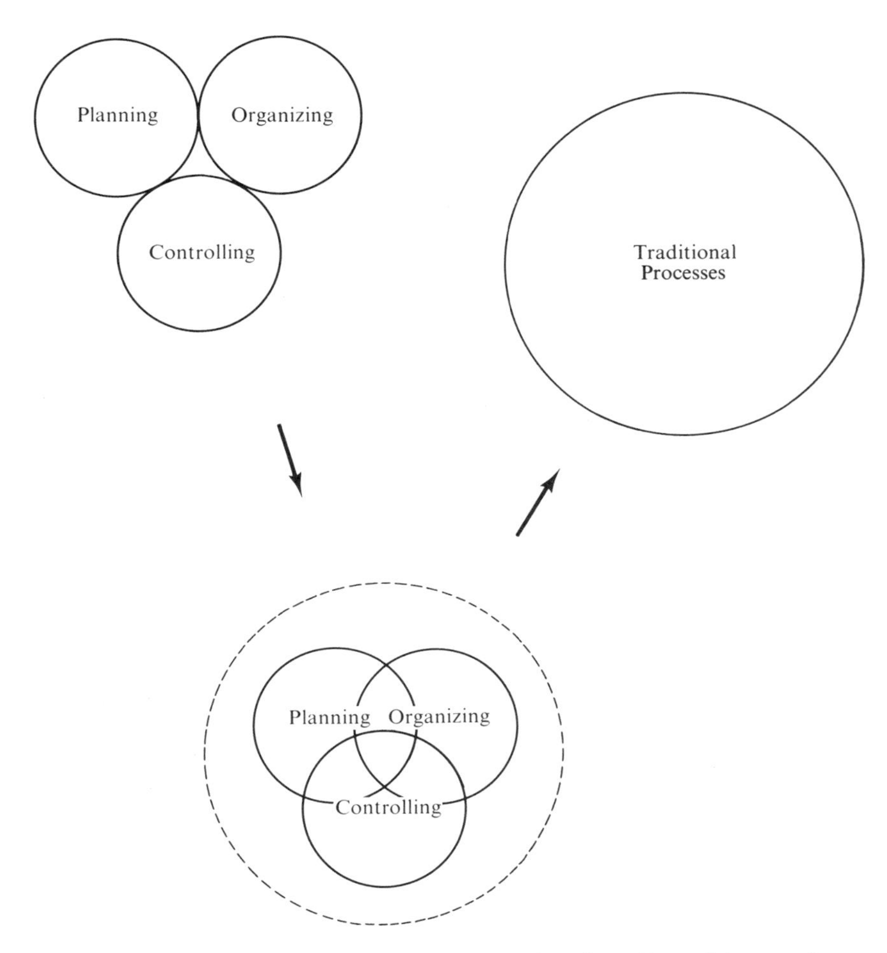


*EXHIBIT I* The Traditional Processes: Planning, Organizing, and Controlling

three circles contained within the traditional processes in Exhibit I. The respective importance of the individual processes contained within the traditional processes is a debatable and situational issue. The author has assumed that the three processes are equally important as indicated by equal-sized circles in Exhibit I.

One final fallacy pertaining to the traditional processes should also be noted at this time. There exists a mistaken notion that there are set procedures, methodologies, and techniques associated individually and collectively with the traditional processes. Unquestionably, management and administration careers are becoming more professional and scientific; but such occupations will always remain at least to some degree an art. Traditional processes may employ the scientific method, a problem solving approach, and numerous principles of management, accounting, and the like. However, always and also important are any manager's intuition, frame of reference, and subjective approach to matters as well as any predetermined procedure for or methodology of attacking problems.

## BEHAVIORAL PROCESSES

Authors and practitioners during Frederick Taylor's "scientific management" era popularized the "traditional" processes. With the advent of the "human relations" movement initially authors and later practitioners began to emphasize "behavioral processes." The behavioral processes emphasize the role of human beings in the managerial-administrative process. Good managers were now seen as individuals who could work well with people, thus enabling others to more fully utilize their human capabilities. Administrative processes such as those shown in Exhibit II began to be emphasized.

Again, controversies exist over issues such as those shown in Exhibit II. Why the functions of staffing, leading, and motivating rather than other functions? What behavioral process is the most and least important? To what degree do the behavioral processes overlap? These and other legitimate questions can be raised and debated concerning Exhibit II.

Even more so than the traditional processes, the behavioral processes should realistically be envisioned as a combination of objective procedures and subjective approaches. For example, effective leadership techniques and motivational methods are usually said to be "situational" depending upon environmental factors. Under such conditions subjective-intuitive considerations prevail rather than rigid procedural methods.

## COORDINATING PROCESSES

Many students of administration and organization theory have spent many long hours trying to understand how large (and small) organizations seem to be molded together to form operative, on-going institutions. What are the tangible and intangible linking components which tie together all the individual parts and permit the existence of a productive enterprise? Again some controversy over the specific identification of such factors no doubt exists, but, as shown in Exhibit III, activities and processes such as problem solving, decision making, and communications are usually agreed to be key coordinating and linking processes.

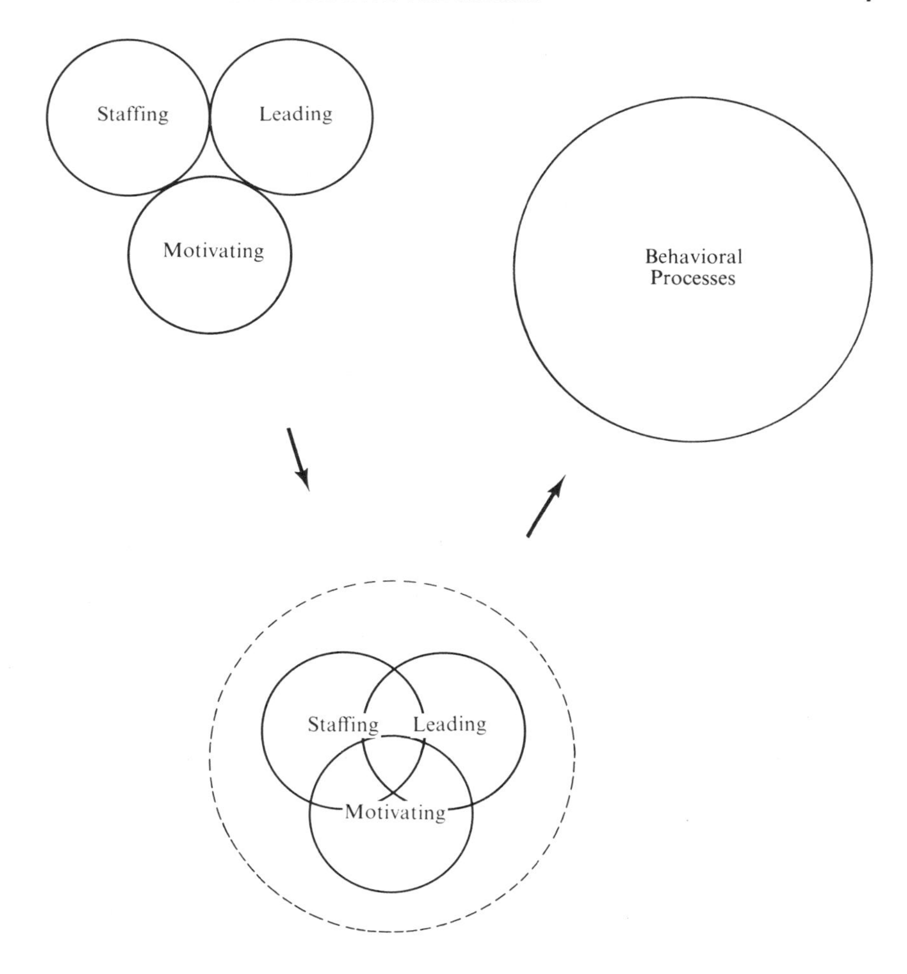


*EXHIBIT II* The Behavioral Processes: Staffing, Leading, and Motivating

The number of coordinating activities, the relative importance of any such activity, the degree of overlap of various linking processes, and the amount of subjectivity incorporated within such processes, are all issues upon which general managerial consensus has not yet been reached.

## SET-SYSTEMS MODEL OF THE MANAGERIAL-ADMINISTRATIVE PROCESSES

Just as individual managerial processes within the traditional, behavioral, and coordinating processes have mistakenly not been envisioned as being

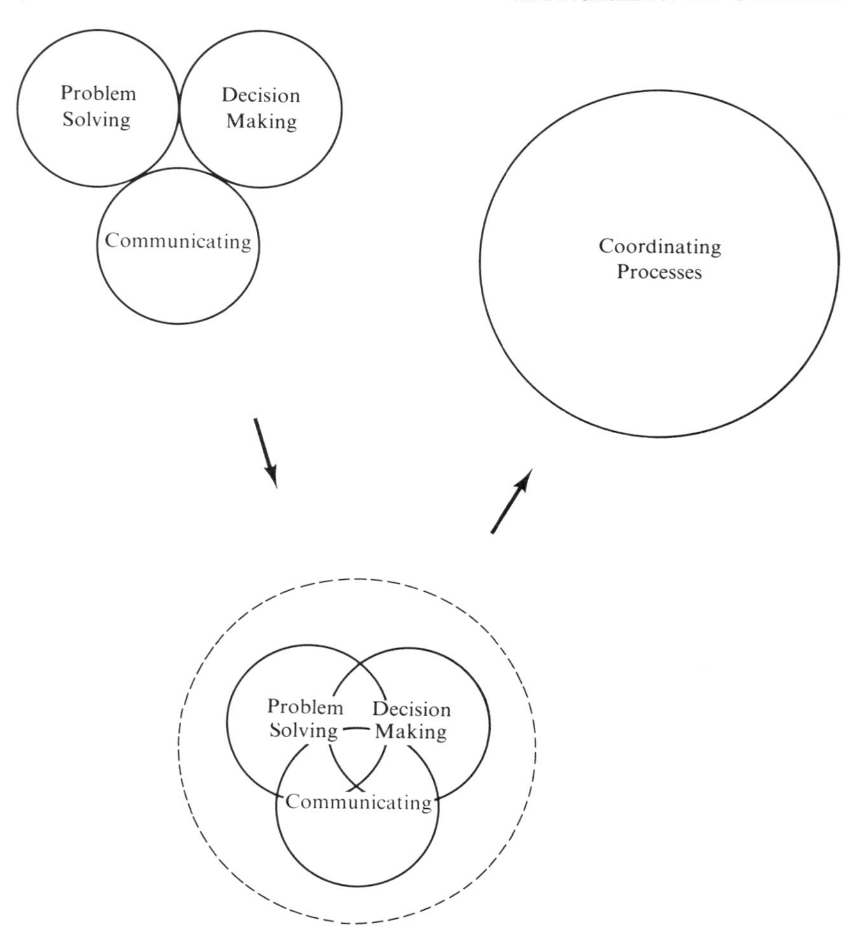


*EXHIBIT III* The Coordinating Processes: Problem Solving, Decision Making, and Communicating

overlapping in nature, the same misconception is also true of these processes taken collectively. Exhibit IV indicates that traditional processes and behavioral processes are not somehow mysteriously linked together by the coordinating processes, but that instead such processes are part and parcel of each other. The amount of overlap again may serve as a point of discussion and dissention among readers.

## THE ENVIRONMENT

Managerial-administrative processes do not exist within a vacuum. Every organization and institution is part of a larger environment. The environ-

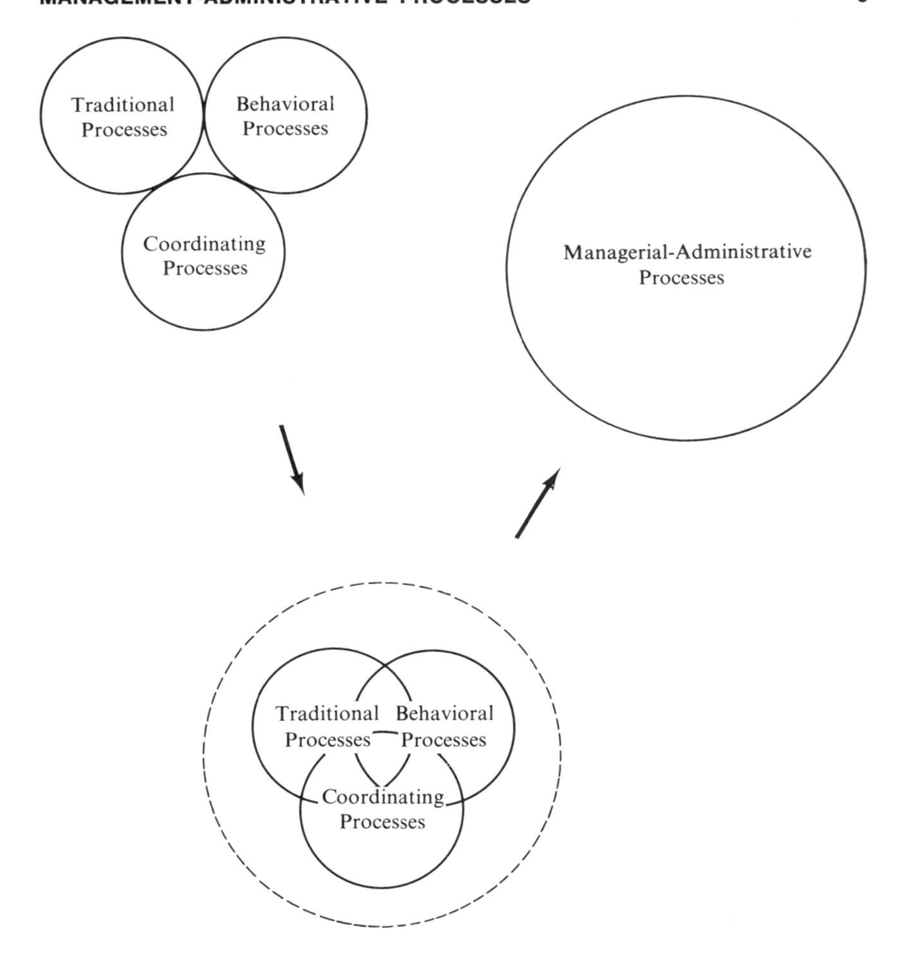


*EXHIBIT IV* The Set-Systems Model of the Managerial-Administrative Processes

ment consists of a number of factors usually classified as social, economic, political, and technological in nature. Such factors also can be represented by set theory as shown in Exhibit V. A more comprehensive listing of environmental factors might include spiritual, ethical, physical, cultural, and other factors.

In actuality, any organization or institution exists within numerous external environments each of which contains social, economic, political, and technological factors. Geographically, such environments are usually labeled as local, regional, national, and/or international in scope. In general, the more distant the external environment is geographically, the less immediate is the influence exerted by such an environment upon the or-

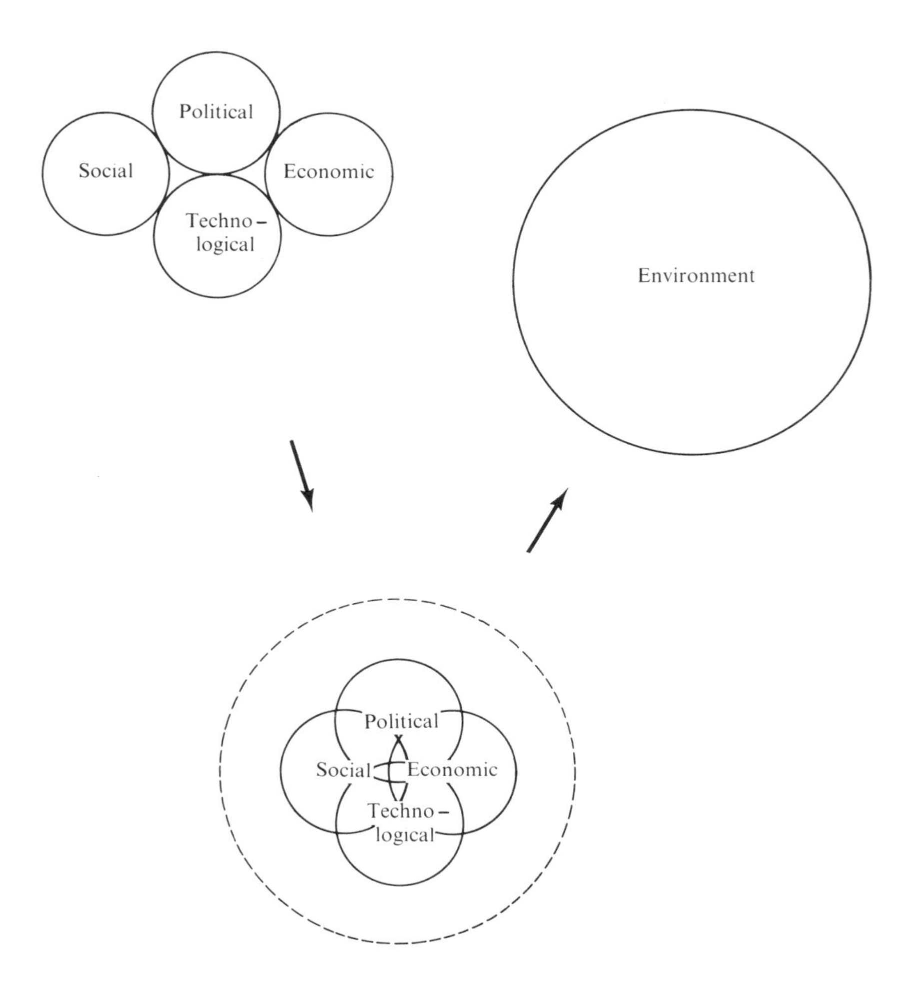


*EXHIBIT V* The Environment: Social, Political, Economic, and Technological Factors

ganization. Readers should easily be able to illustrate how local-technological, national-economic, international-political, and other such environmental factors affect not only the implementation but also the formulation of managerial-administrative processes.

## THE MANAGERIAL-ADMINISTRATIVE PROCESSES AND THE EXTERNAL ENVIRONMENTS

The final exhibit, Exhibit VI, integrates materials from the previous five exhibits. The traditional, behavioral, and coordinating processes merge

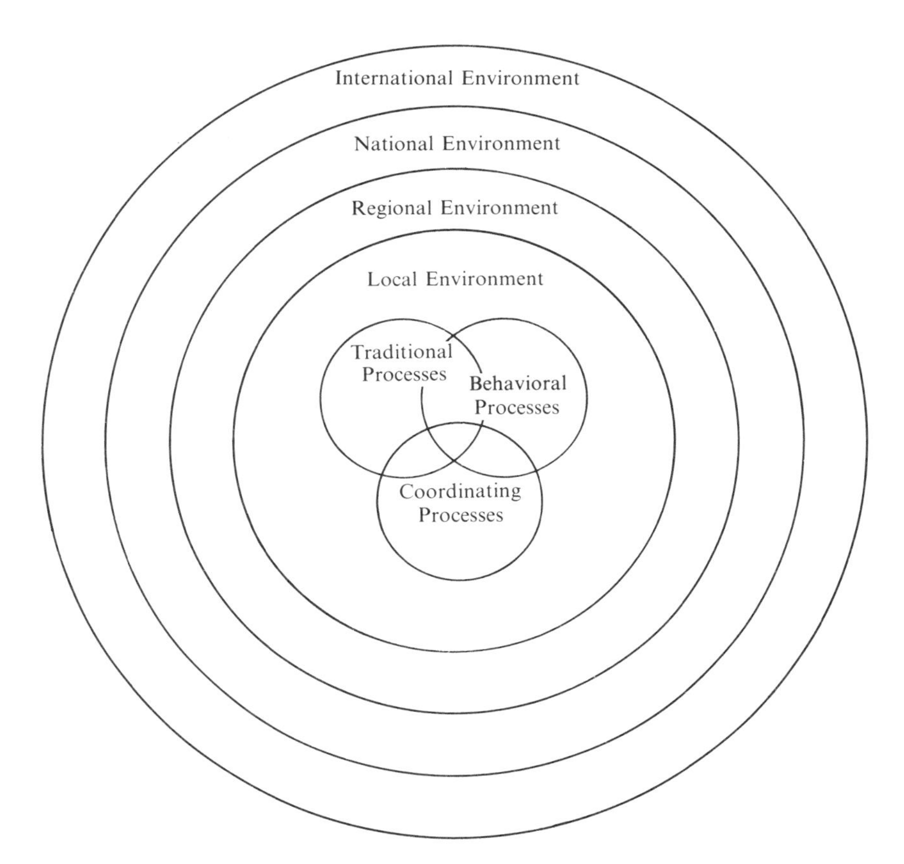


*EXHIBIT VI* The Managerial-Administrative Processes and the External Environments

to form the managerial-administrative processes which exist in a setting consisting of local, regional, national, and international environments. This model emphasizes the integrative nature of the managerial processes and the interaction of the managerial processes with the external environments.

## CONCLUSIONS

The preceding discussion has attempted to illustrate the following points:

1. The study of management and administration usually takes the form of identifying various managerial functions, activities, or processes.
2. There is no common agreement as to the exact nature or labeling of such processes.

3. The relative importance (individually and collectively) of various managerial processes (traditional, behavioral, and coordinating) is debatable and situational.

4. Managerial-administrative processes are best envisioned as integrative and overlapping rather than as succinct and distinct entities.

5. Managerial-administrative processes similarly are a combination of methodological procedures and techniques plus intuitive-subjective approaches applied to various problem areas and subject matters.

6. Managerial-administrative processes exist within and are partially determined by various social, political, economic, and technological factors of the local, regional, national, and international environments.

7. Many misconceptions and controversies currently exist within both management theory and practice. Set-systems thinking can help integrate administrative theories and practices both internally and externally.

*Harold Koontz*

# *THE MANAGEMENT THEORY JUNGLE*

Although students of management would readily agree that there have been problems of management since the dawn of organized life, most would also agree that systematic examination of management, with few exceptions, is the product of the present century and more especially of the past two decades. Moreover, until recent years almost all of those who have attempted to analyze the management process and look for some theoretical underpinnings to help improve research, teaching, and practice were alert and perceptive practitioners of the art who reflected on many years of experience. Thus, at least in looking at *general* management as an intellectually based art, the earliest meaningful writing came from such experienced practitioners as Fayol, Mooney, Alvin Brown, Sheldon, Barnard, and Urwick. Certainly not even the most academic worshipper of empirical research can overlook the empiricism involved in distilling fundamentals from decades of experience by such discerning practitioners as these. Admittedly done without questionnaires, controlled interviews, or mathematics, observations by such men can hardly be accurately regarded as *a priori* or "armchair."

---

Used by permission of the author and of the publisher. *Journal of the Academy of Management,* vol. 4, no. 3, pp. 174–188, December, 1961.

The noteworthy absence of academic writing and research in the formative years of modern management theory is now more than atoned for by a deluge of research and writing from the academic halls. What is interesting and perhaps nothing more than a sign of the unsophisticated adolescence of management theory is how the current flood has brought with it a wave of great differences and apparent confusion. From the orderly analysis of management at the shop-room level by Frederick Taylor and the reflective distillation of experience from the general management point of view of Henri Fayol, we now see these and other early beginnings overgrown and entangled by a jungle of approaches and approachers to management theory.

There are the behavioralists, born of the Hawthorne experiments and the awakened interest in human relations during the 1930's and 1940's, who see management as a complex of interpersonal relationships and the basis of management theory the tentative tenets of the new and undeveloped science of psychology. There are also those who see management theory as simply a manifestation of the institutional and cultural aspects of sociology. Still others, observing that the central core of management is decision-making, branch in all directions from this core to encompass everything in organization life. Then, there are mathematicians who think of management primarily as an exercise in logical relationships expressed in symbols and the omnipresent and ever revered model. But the entanglement of growth reaches its ultimate when the study of management is regarded as a study of one of a number of systems and subsystems, with an understandable tendency for the reasearcher to be dissatisfied until he has encompassed the entire physical and cultural universe as a management system.

With the recent discovery of an ages-old problem area by social, physical, and biological scientists, and with the supersonic increase in interest by all types of enterprise managers, the apparent impenetrability of the present thicket which we call management theory is not difficult to comprehend. One can hardly be surprised that psychologists, sociologists, anthropologists, sociometricists, economists, mathematicians, physicists, biologists, political scientists, business administration scholars, and even practicing managers, should hop on this interesting, challenging, and profitable band wagon.

This welling of interest from every academic and practicing corner should not upset anyone concerned with seeing the frontiers of knowledge pushed back and the intellectual base of practice broadened. But what is rather upsetting to the practitioner and the observer, who sees great social potential from improved management, is that the variety of approaches to management theory has led to a kind of confused and destructive jungle warfare. Particularly among academic disciplines and their disciples, the primary interests of many would-be cult leaders seem to be to carve out a distinct (and hence "original") approach to management. And to defend this originality, and thereby gain a place in posterity (or at least to gain a publication which will justify academic status or promotion), it seems to have become too much the current style to downgrade, and sometimes misrepresent, what anyone else has said, or thought, or done.

In order to cut through this jungle and bring to light some of the issues and problems involved in the present management theory area so that the tremendous interest, intelligence, and research results may become more meaningful, it is my purpose here to classify the various "schools" of management theory, to identify briefly what I believe to be the major source of differences, and to offer some suggestions for disentangling the jungle. It is hoped that a movement for clarification can be started so at least we in the field will not be a group of blind men identifying the same elephant with our widely varying and sometimes viciously argumentative theses.

## THE MAJOR "SCHOOLS" OF MANAGEMENT THEORY

In attempting to classify the major schools of management theory into six main groups, I am aware that I may overlook certain approaches and cannot deal with all the nuances of each approach. But it does seem that most of the approaches to management theory can be classified in one of these so-called "schools."

### The Management Process School

This approach to management theory perceives management as a process of getting things done through and with people operating in organized groups. It aims to analyze the process, to establish a conceptual framework for it, to identify principles underlying it, and to build up a theory of management from them. It regards management as a universal process, regardless of the type of enterprise, or the level in a given enterprise, although recognizing, obviously, that the environment of management differs widely between enterprises and levels. It looks upon management theory as a way of organizing experience so that practice can be improved through research, empirical testing of principles, and teaching of fundamentals involved in the management process.[1]

Often referred to, especially by its critics, as the "traditional" or "universalist" school, this school can be said to have been fathered by Henri Fayol, although many of his offspring did not know of their parent, since Fayol's work was eclipsed by the bright light of his contemporary, Frederick Taylor, and clouded by the lack of a widely available English translation until 1949. Other than Fayol, most of the early contributors to this school dealt only with the organization portion of the management process, largely because of their greater experience with this facet of management and the simple fact that planning and control, as well as the function of staffing, were given little attention by managers before 1940.

This school bases its approach to management theory on several fundamental beliefs:

1. that managing is a process and can best be dissected intellectually by analyzing the functions of the manager;
2. that long experience with management in a variety of enterprise situations can be grounds for distillation of certain fundamental truths or generalizations—usually referred to as principles—which have a clarifying and predictive value in the understanding and improvement of managing;
3. that these fundamental truths can become focal points for useful research both to ascertain their validity and to improve their meaning and applicability in practice;
4. that such truths can furnish elements, at least until disproved, and certainly until sharpened, of a useful theory of management;
5. that managing is an art, but one like medicine or engineering, which can be improved by reliance on the light and understanding of principles;
6. that principles in management, like principles in the biological and physical sciences, are nonetheless true even if a prescribed treatment or design by a practitioner in a given case situation chooses to ignore a principle and the costs involved, or attempts to do something else to offset the costs incurred (this is, of course, not new in medicine, engineering, or any other art, for art is the creative task of compromising fundamentals to attain a desired result); and
7. that, while the totality of culture and of the physical and biological universe has varying effects on the manager's environment and subjects, as indeed they do in every other field of science and art, the theory of management does not need to encompass the field of all knowledge in order for it to serve as a scientific or theoretical foundation.

The basic approach of this school, then, is to look, first, to the functions of managers. As a second step in this approach, many of us have taken the functions of managers and further dissected them by distilling what we see as fundamental truths in the understandably complicated practice of management. I have found it useful to classify my analysis of these functions around the essentials involved in the following questions:

1. What is the nature of the function?
2. What is the purpose of the function?
3. What explains the structure of the function?
4. What explains the process of the function?

Perhaps there are other more useful approaches, but I have found that I can place everything pertaining to management (even some of the rather remote research and concepts) in this framework.

Also, purely to make the area of management theory intellectually manageable, those who subscribe to this school do not usually attempt to include in the theory the entire areas of sociology, economics, biology, psychology, physics, chemistry, or others. This is done not because these other areas of knowledge are unimportant and have no bearing on management, but merely because no real progress has ever been made in science or art without significant partitioning of knowledge. Yet, anyone would be foolish not to realize that a function which deals with people in their various activities of producing and marketing anything from money to religion and education is completely independent of the physical, biological, and cultural universe in which we live. And, are there not such relationships in other "compartments" of knowledge and theory?

### The Empirical School

A second approach to management I refer to as the "empirical" school. In this, I include those scholars who identify management as a study of experience, sometimes with intent to draw generalizations but usually merely as a means of teaching experience and transferring it to the practitioner or student. Typical of this school are those who see management or "policy" as the study and analysis of cases and those with such approaches as Ernest Dale's "comparative approach."[2]

This approach seems to be based upon the premise that, if we study the experience of successful managers, or the mistakes made in management, or if we attempt to solve management problems, we will somehow understand and learn to apply the most effective kinds of management techniques. This approach, as often applied, assumes that, by finding out what worked or did not work in individual circumstances, the student or the practitioner will be able to do the same in comparable situations.

No one can deny the importance of studying experience through such study, or of analyzing the "how-it-was-done" of management. But management, unlike law, is not a science based on precedent, and situations in the future exactly comparable to the past are exceedingly unlikely to occur. Indeed, there is a positive danger of relying too much on past experience and on undistilled history of managerial problem-solving for the simple reason that a technique or approach found "right" in the past may not fit a situation of the future.

Those advocating the empirical approach are likely to say that what they really do in analyzing cases or history is to draw from certain generalizations which can be applied as useful guides to thought or action in future case situations. As a matter of fact, Ernest Dale, after claiming to find "so little practical value" from the principles enunciated by the "universalists," curiously drew certain "generalizations" or "criteria" from his valuable study of a number of great practitioners of management.[3] There is some question as to whether Dale's "comparative" approach is not really the same as the "universalist" approach he decries, except with a different distiller of basic truths.

By the emphasis of the empirical school on study of experience, it does appear that the research and thought so engendered may assist in hastening the day for verification of principles. It is also possible that the proponents of this school may come up with a more useful framework of principles than that of the management process school. But, to the extent that the empirical school draws generalizations from its research, and it would seem to be a necessity to do so unless its members are satisfied to exchange meaningless and structureless experience, this approach tends to be and do the same as the management process school.

## The Human Behavior School

This approach to the analysis of management is based on the central thesis that, since managing involves getting things done with and through people, the study of management must be centered on interpersonal relations. Variously called the "human relations," "leadership," or "behavioral sciences" approach, this school brings to bear "existing and newly developed theories, methods, and techniques of the relevant social sciences upon the study of inter- and intrapersonal phenomena, ranging fully from the personality dynamics of individuals at one extreme to the relations of cultures at the other."[4] In other words, this school concentrates on the "people" part of management and rests on the principle that, where people work together as groups in order to accomplish objectives, "people should understand people."

The scholars in this school have a heavy orientation to psychology and social psychology. Their primary focus is the individual as a socio-psychological being and what motivates him. The members of this school vary from those who see it as a portion of the manager's job, a tool to help him understand and get the best from people by meeting their needs and responding to their motivations, to those who see the psychological behavior of individuals and groups as the total of management.

In this school are those who emphasize human relations as an art that the manager should advantageously understand and practice. There are those who focus attention on the manager as a leader and sometimes equate management to leadership, thus, in effect, tending to treat all group activities as "managed" situations. There are those who see the study of group dynamics and interpersonal relationships as simply a study of socio-psychological relationships and seem, therefore, merely to be attaching the term "management" to the field of social psychology.

That management must deal with human behavior can hardly be denied. That the study of human interactions, whether in the environment of management or in unmanaged situations, is important and useful one could not dispute. And it would be a serious mistake to regard good leadership as unimportant to good managership. But whether the field of human behavior is the equivalent of the field of management is quite another thing. Perhaps it is like calling the study of the human body the field of cardiology.

### The Social System School

Closely related to the human behavior school and often confused or intertwined with it is one which might be labeled the social system school. This includes those researchers who look upon management as a social system, that is, a system of cultural interrelationships. Sometimes, as in the case of March and Simon,[5] the system is limited to formal organizations, using the term "organization" as equivalent to enterprise, rather than the authority-activity concept used most often in management. In other cases, the approach is not to distinguish the formal organization, but rather to encompass any kind of system of human relationships.

Heavily sociological in flavor, this approach to management does essentially what any study of sociology does. It identifies the nature of the cultural relationships of various social groups and attempts to show these as a related, and usually an integrated, system.

Perhaps the spiritual father of this ardent and vocal school of management theorists is Chester Barnard.[6] In searching for an answer to fundamental explanations underlying the managing process, this thoughtful business executive developed a theory of cooperation grounded in the needs of the individual to solve, through cooperation, the biological, physical, and social limitations of himself and his environment. Barnard then carved from the total of cooperative systems so engendered one set of interrelationships which he defines as "formal organization." His formal organization concept, quite unlike that usually held by management practitioners, is any cooperative system in which there are persons able to communicate with each other and who are willing to contribute action toward a conscious common purpose.

The Barnard concept of cooperative system pervades the work of many contributors to the social system school of management. For example, Herbert Simon at one time defined the subject of organization theory and the nature of human organizations as "systems of interdependent activity, encompassing at least several primary groups and usually characterized, at the level of consciousness of participants, by a high degree of rational direction of behavior toward ends that are objects of common knowledge."[7] Simon and others have subsequently seemed to have expanded this concept of social systems to include any cooperative and purposeful group interrelationship or behavior.

This school has made many noteworthy contributions to management. The recognition of organized enterprise as a social organism, subject to all the pressures and conflicts of the cultural environment, has been helpful to the management theorist and the practitioner alike. Among some of the more helpful aspects are the awareness of the institutional foundation of organization authority, the influence of informal organization, and such social factors as those Wight Bakke has called the "bonds of organization."[8] Likewise, many of Barnard's helpful insights, such as his economy of incentives and his theory of opportunism, have brought the power of sociological understanding into the realm of management practice.

Basic sociology, analysis of concepts of social behavior, and the study of group behavior in the framework of social systems do have great value in the field of management. But one may well ask the question whether this is management. Is the field of management coterminous with the field of sociology? Or is sociology an important underpinning like language, psychology, physiology, mathematics, and other fields of knowledge? Must management be defined in terms of the universe of knowledge?

## The Decision Theory School

Another approach to management theory, undertaken by a growing and scholarly group, might be referred to as the decision theory school. This group concentrates on rational approach to decision—the selection from among possible alternatives of a course of action or of an idea. The approach of this school may be to deal with the decision itself, or to the persons or organizational group making the decision, or to an analysis of the decision process. Some limit themselves fairly much to the economic rationale of the decision, while others regard anything which happens in an enterprise the subject of their analysis, and still others expand decision theory to cover the psychological and sociological aspect and environment of decisions and decision-makers.

The decision-making school is apparently an outgrowth of the theory of consumer's choice with which economists have been concerned since the days of Jeremy Bentham early in the nineteenth century. It has arisen out of such economic problems and analyses as utility maximization, indifference curves, marginal utility, and economic behavior under risks and uncertainties. It is, therefore, no surprise that one finds most of the members of this school to be economic theorists. It is likewise no surprise to find the content of this school to be heavily oriented to model construction and mathematics.

The decision theory school has tended to expand its horizon considerably beyond the process of evaluating alternatives. That point has become for many only a springboard for examination of the entire sphere of human activity, including the nature of the organization structure, psychological and social reactions of individuals and groups, the development of basic information for decisions, an analysis of values and particularly value considerations with respect to goals, communications networks, and incentives. As one would expect, when the decision theorists study the small, but central, area of decision *making,* they are led by this keyhole look at management to consider the entire field of enterprise operation and its environment. The result is that decision theory becomes no longer a neat and narrow concentration on decision, but rather a broad view of the enterprise as a social system.

There are those who believe that, since management is characterized by its concentration on decisions, the future development of management theory will tend to use the decision as its central focus and the rest of management theory will be hung on this structural center. This may occur and certainly the study of the decision, the decision process, and the decision maker can be extended to cover the entire field of management as anyone might conceive it. Nevertheless, one wonders whether this focus cannot also be used to build around it the entire area of human knowledge. For, as most decision theorists recognize, the problem of choice is individual, as well as organizational, and most of what has been said that is pure decision theory can be applied to the existence and thinking of a Robinson Crusoe.

## The Mathematical School

Although mathematical methods can be used by any school of management theory, and have been, I have chosen to group under a school those theorists who see management as a system of mathematical models and processes. Perhaps the most widely known group I arbitrarily so lump are the operations researchers or operations analysts, who have sometimes anointed themselves with the rather pretentious name of "management scientists." The abiding belief of this group is that, if management, or organization, or planning, or decision making is a logical process, it can be expressed in terms of mathematical symbols and relationships. The central approach of this school is the model, for it is through these devices that the problem is expressed in its basic relationships and in terms of selected goals or objectives.

There can be no doubt of the great usefulness of mathematical approaches to any field of inquiry. It forces upon the researcher the definition of a problem or problem area, it conveniently allows the insertion of symbols for unknown data, and its logical methodology, developed by years of scientific application and abstraction, furnishes a powerful tool for solving or simplifying complex phenomena.

But it is hard to see mathematics as a truly separate school of management theory, any more than it is a separate "school" in physics, chemistry, engineering, or medicine. I only deal with it here as such because there has appeared to have developed a kind of cult around mathematical analysts who have subsumed to themselves the area of management.

In pointing out that mathematics is a tool, rather than a school, it is not my intention to underestimate the impact of mathematics on the science and practice of management. By bringing to this immensely important and complex field the tools and techniques of the physical sciences, the mathematicians have already made an immense contribution to orderly thinking. They have forced on people in management the means and desirability of seeing many problems more clearly, they have pressed on scholars and practitioners the need for establishing goals and measures of effectiveness, they have been extremely helpful in getting the management area seen as a logical system of relationships, and they have caused people in management to review and occasionally reorganize information sources and systems so that mathematics can be given sensible quantitative meaning. But with all this meaningful contribution and the greater sharpness and sophistication of planning which is resulting, I cannot see that mathematics is management theory any more than it is astronomy.

## THE MAJOR SOURCES OF MENTAL ENTANGLEMENT IN THE JUNGLE

In outlining the various schools, or approaches, of management theory, it becomes clear that these intellectual cults are not drawing greatly different inferences from the physical and cultural environment surrounding us. Why, then, have there been so many differences between them and why such a struggle, particularly among our academic brethren to obtain a place in the sun by denying the approaches of others? Like the widely differing and often contentious denominations of the Christian religion, all have essentially the same goals and deal with essentially the same world.

While there are many sources of the mental entanglement in the management theory jungle, the major ones are the following:

### The Semantics Jungle

As is so often true when intelligent men argue about basic problems, some of the trouble lies in the meaning of key words. The semantics problem is particularly severe in the field of management. There is even a difference in the meaning of the word "management." Most people would agree that it means getting things done through and with people, but is it people in formal organizations, or in all group activities? Is it governing, leading, or teaching?

Perhaps the greatest single semantics confusion lies in the word "organization." Most members of the management process school use it to define the activity-authority structure of an enterprise and certainly most practitioners believe that they are "organizing" when they establish a framework of activity groupings and authority relationships. In this case, organization represents the formal framework within an enterprise that furnishes the environment in which people perform. Yet a large number of "organization" theorists conceive of organization as the sum total of human relationships in any group activity; they thus seem to make it equivalent to *social* structure. And some use "organization" to mean "enterprise."

If the meaning of organization cannot be clarified and a standard use of the term adopted by management theorists, understanding and criticism should not be based on this difference. It hardly seems to me to be accurate for March and Simon, for example, to criticize the organization theories of the management process, or "universalist," school for not considering the management planning function as part of organizing, when they have chosen to treat it separately. Nor should those who choose to treat the training, selecting, guiding or leading of people under staffing and direction be criticized for a tendency to "view the employee as an inert instrument" or a "given rather than a variable."[9] Such accusations, proceeding from false premises, are clearly erroneous.

Other semantic entanglements might be mentioned. By some, decision-making is regarded as a process of choosing from among alternatives; by others, the total managerial task and environment. Leadership is often made synonymous with managership and is analytically separated by others. Communications may mean everything from a written or oral report to a vast network of formal and informal relationships. Human relations to some implies a psychiatric manipulation of people, but to others the study and art of understanding people and interpersonal relationships.

### Differences in Definition of Management as a Body of Knowledge

As was indicated in the discussion of semantics, "management" has far from a standard meaning, although most agree that it at least involves getting things done through and with people. But, does it mean the dealing with all human relationships? Is a street peddler a manager? Is a parent a manager? Is a leader of a disorganized mob a manager? Does the field of management equal the fields of sociology and social psychology combined? Is it the equivalent of the entire system of social relationships?

While I recognize that sharp lines cannot be drawn in management any more than they are in medicine or engineering, there surely can be a sharper distinction drawn than at present. With the plethora of management writing and experts, calling almost everything under the sun "management," can one expect management theory to be regarded as very useful or scientific to the practitioner?

### The *a priori* Assumption

Confusion in management theory has also been heightened by the tendency for many newcomers in the field to cast aside significant observations and analyses of the past on the grounds that they are *a priori* in nature. This is an often-met accusation made by those who wish to cast aside the work of Fayol, Mooney, Brown, Urwick, Gulick, and others who are branded as "universalists." To make the assumption that the distilled experiences of men such as these represent *a priori* reasoning is to forget that experience in and with managing *is* empirical. While the conclusions that perceptive and experienced practitioners of the art of management are not infallible, they represent an experience which is certainly real and not "armchair." No one could deny, I feel sure, that the ultimate test of accuracy of management theory must be practice and management theory and science must be developed from reality.

### The Misunderstanding of Principles

Those who feel that they gain caste or a clean slate for advancing a particular notion or approach often delight in casting away anything which smacks of management principles. Some have referred to them as platitudes, forgetting that a platitude is still a truism and a truth does not become worthless because it is familiar. (As Robert Frost has written, "Most of the changes we think we see in life are merely truths going in or out of favor.") Others cast away principles of Fayol and other practitioners, only to draw apparently different generalizations from their study of management; but many of the generalizations so discovered are often the same fundamental truths in different words that certain criticized "universalists" have discovered.

One of the favorite tricks of the managerial theory trade is to disprove a whole framework of principles by reference to one principle which the observer sees disregarded in practice. Thus, many critics of the universalists point to the well-known cases of dual subordination in organized enterprise, coming to the erroneous conclusion that there is no substance to the principle of unity of command. But this does not prove that there is no cost to the enterprise by designing around, or disregarding, the principle of unity of command; nor does it prove that there were not other advantages which offset the costs, as there often are in cases of establishing functional authorities in organization.

Perhaps the almost hackneyed stand-by for those who would disprove the validity of all principles by referring to a single one is the misunderstanding around the principle of span of management (or span of control). The usual source of authority quoted by those who criticize is Sir Ian Hamilton, who never intended to state a universal principle, but rather to make a personal observation in a book of reflections on his Army experience, and who did say, offhand, that he found it wise to limit his span to 3 to 6 subordinates. No modern universalist relies on this single observation, and, indeed, few can or will state an absolute or universal numerical ceiling. Since Sir Ian was not a management theorist and did not intend to be, let us hope that the ghost of his innocent remark may be laid to deserved rest!

What concerns those who feel that a recognition of fundamental truths, or generalizations, may help in the diagnosis and study of management, and who know from managerial experience that such truths or principles do serve an extremely valuable use, is the tendency for some researchers to prove the wrong things through either misstatement or misapplication of principles. A classic case of such misunderstanding and misapplication is in Chris Argyris' interesting book on *Personality and Organization.*[10] This author, who in this book and his other works has made many noteworthy contributions to management, concludes that "formal organization principles make demands on relatively healthy individuals that are incongruent with their needs," and that "frustration, conflict, failure, and short-time perspective are predicted as results of this basic incongruency."[11] This startling conclusion—the exact opposite of what "good" formal organization based on "sound" organization principles should cause, is explained when one notes that, of four "principles" Argyris quotes, one is not an organization principle at all but the economic principle of specialization and three other "principles" are quoted incorrectly.[12] With such a postulate, and with no attempt to recognize, correctly or incorrectly, any other organization and management principles, Argyris has simply proved that wrong principles badly applied will lead to frustration; and every management practitioner knows this to be true!

### The Inability or Unwillingness of Management Theorists to Understand Each Other

What has been said above leads one to the conclusion that much of the management theory jungle is caused by the unwillingness or inability of the management theorists to understand each other. Doubting that it is inability, because one must assume that a person interested in management theory is able to comprehend, at least in concept and framework, the approaches of the various "schools," I can only come to the conclusion that the roadblock to understanding is unwillingness.

Perhaps this unwillingness comes from the professional "walls" developed by learned disciplines. Perhaps the unwillingness stems from a fear that someone or some new discovery will encroach on professional and academic status. Perhaps it is fear of professional or intellectual obsolescence. But whatever the cause, it seems that these walls will not be torn down until it is realized that they exist, until all cultists are willing to look at the approach and content of other schools, and until, through exchange and understanding of ideas some order may be brought from the present chaos.

## DISENTANGLING THE MANAGEMENT THEORY JUNGLE

It is important that steps be taken to disentangle the management theory jungle. Perhaps, it is too soon and we must expect more years of wandering through a thicket of approaches, semantics, thrusts, and counterthrusts. But in any field as important to society where the many blunders of an unscientifically based managerial art can be so costly, I hope that this will not be long.

There do appear to be some things that can be done. Clearly, meeting what I see to be the major sources of the entanglement should remove much of it. The following considerations are important:

1. *The need for definition of a body of knowledge.* Certainly, if a field of knowledge is not to get bogged down in a quagmire of misunderstandings,

the first need is for definition of the field. Not that it need be defined in sharp, detailed, inflexible lines, but rather along lines which will give it fairly specific content. Because management is reality, life, practice, my suggestion would be that it be defined in the light of the able and discerning practitioner's frame of reference. A science unrelated to the art for which it is to serve is not likely to be a very productive one.

Although the study of managements in various enterprises, in various countries, and at various levels made by many persons, including myself, may neither be representative nor adequate, I have come to the conclusion that management is the art of getting things done through and with people in *formally organized groups,* the art of creating an environment in such an organized group where people can perform as individuals and yet cooperate toward attainment of group goals, the art of removing blocks to such performance, the art of optimizing efficiency in effectively reaching goals. If this kind of definition of the field is unsatisfactory, I suggest at least an agreement that the area should be defined to reflect the field of the practitioner and that further research and study of practice be done to this end.

In defining the field, too, it seems to me imperative to draw some limits for purposes of analysis and research. If we are to call the entire cultural, biological, and physical universe the field of management, we can no more make progress than could have been done if chemistry or geology had not carved out a fairly specific area and had, instead, studied all knowledge.

In defining the body of knowledge, too, care must be taken to distinguish between tools and content. Thus mathematics, operations research, accounting, economic theory, sociometry, and psychology, to mention a few, are significant *tools* of management but are not, in themselves, a part of the *content* of the field. This is not to mean that they are unimportant or that the practicing manager should not have them available to him, nor does it mean that they may not be the means of pushing back the frontiers of knowledge of management. But they should not be confused with the basic content of the field.

This is not to say that fruitful study should not continue on the underlying disciplines affecting management. Certainly knowledge of sociology, social systems, psychology, economics, political science, mathematics, and other areas, pointed toward contributing to the field of management, should be continued and encouraged. And significant findings in these and other fields of knowledge might well cast important light on, or change concepts in, the field of management. This has certainly happened in other sciences and in every other art based upon significant science.

2. *Integration of management and other disciplines.* If recognition of the proper content of the field were made, I believe that the present cross-

fire of misunderstanding might tend to disappear. Management would be regarded as a specific discipline and other disciplines would be looked upon as important bases of the field. Under these circumstances, the allied and underlying disciplines would be welcomed by the business and public administration schools, as well as by practitioners, as loyal and helpful associates. Integration of management and other disciplines would then not be difficult.

3. *The clarification of management semantics.* While I would expect the need for clarification and uniformity of management semantics would largely be satisfied by definition of the field as a body of knowledge, semantics problems might require more special attention. There are not too many places where semantics are important enough to cause difficulty. Here again, I would suggest the adoption of the semantics of the intelligent practitioners, unless words are used by them so inexactly as to require special clarification. At least, we should not complicate an already complex field by developing a scientific or academic jargon which would build a language barrier between the theorist and the practitioner.

Perhaps the most expeditious way out of this problem is to establish a commission representing academic societies immediately concerned and associations of practicing managers. This would not seem to be difficult to do. And even if it were, the results would be worth the efforts.

4. *Willingness to distill and test fundamentals.* Certainly, the test of maturity and usefulness of a science is the sharpness and validity of the principles underlying it. No science, now regarded as mature, started out with a complete statement of incontrovertibly valid principles. Even the oldest sciences, such as physics, keep revising their underlying laws and discovering new principles. Yet any science has proceeded, and more than that has been useful, for centuries on the basis of generalizations, some laws, some principles, and some hypotheses.

One of the understandable sources of inferiority of the social sciences is the recognition that they are inexact sciences. On the other hand, even the so-called exact sciences are subject to a great deal of inexactness, have principles which are not completely proved, and use art in the design of practical systems and components. The often-encountered defeatist attitude of the social sciences, of which management is one, overlooks the fact that management may be explained, practice may be improved, and the goals of research may be more meaningful if we encourage attempts at perceptive distillation of experience by stating principles (or generalizations) and placing them in a logical framework. As two scientists recently said on this subject:

> The reason for this defeatist point of view regarding the social sciences may be traceable to a basic misunderstanding of the nature of scientific

> endeavor. What matters is not whether or to what extent inexactitudes in procedures and predictive capability can eventually be removed . . .: rather it is *objectivity,* i.e., the intersubjectivity of findings independent of any one person's intuitive judgment, which distinguishes science from intuitive guesswork however brilliant. . . . But once a new fact or a new idea has been conjectured, no matter how intuitive a foundation, it must be capable of objective test and confirmation by anyone. And it is this crucial standard of scientific objectivity rather than any purported criterion of exactitude to which the social sciences must conform.[13]

In approaching the clarification of management theory, then, we should not forget a few criteria:

1. The theory should deal with an area of knowledge and inquiry that is "manageable"; no great advances in knowledge were made so long as man contemplated the whole universe;
2. The theory should be *useful* in improving practice and the task and person of the practitioner should not be overlooked;
3. The theory should not be lost in semantics, especially useless jargon not understandable to the practitioner;
4. The theory should give direction and efficiency to research and teaching; and
5. The theory must recognize that it is a part of a larger universe of knowledge and theory.

## REFERENCE LIST

1. It is interesting that one of the scholars strongly oriented to human relations and behavioral approaches to management has recently noted that "theory can be viewed as a way of organizing experience" and that "once initial sense is made out of experienced environment, the way is cleared for an even more adequate organization of this experience." See Robert Dubin in "Psyche, Sensitivity, and Social Structure," critical comment in Robert Tannenbaum, I. R. Weschler, and Fred Massarik, *Leadership and Organization: A Behavioral Science Approach,* McGraw-Hill Book Company, New York, 1961, p. 401.

2. Ernest Dale, *The Great Organizers: Theory and Practice of Organization,* McGraw-Hill Book Company, New York, 1960, pp. 11–28.

3. *Ibid.,* pp. 11, 26–28, 62–66.

4. Tannenbaum, Weschler, and Massarik, *op. cit.,* p. 9.

5. J. G. March and H. A. Simon, *Organizations,* John Wiley & Sons, Inc., New York, 1958.

6. Chester Barnard, *The Functions of the Executive,* Harvard University Press, Cambridge, Mass., 1938.

7. "Comments on the Theory of Organizations," *American Political Science Review,* vol. 46, no. 4, p. 1130, December, 1952.

8. Wight Bakke, *Bonds of Organization,* Harper & Row, Publishers, Incorporated. New York, 1950. These "bonds" or "devices" of organization are identified by Bakke as (1) the functional specifications system (a system of teamwork arising from job specifications and arrangements for associations); (2) the status system (a vertical hierarchy of authority); (3) the communications system; (4) the reward and penalty system; and (5) the organization charter (ideas and means which give character and individuality to the organization, or enterprise).

9. March and Simon, *op. cit.,* pp. 29–33.

10. Chris Argyris, *Personality and Organization,* Harper & Row, Publishers, Incorporated, New York, 1957.

11. *Ibid.,* p. 74.

12. *Ibid.,* pp. 58–66.

13. O. Helmer and N. Rescher, "On the Epistemology of the Inexact Sciences." The Rand Corporation, P–1513, Santa Monica, Calif., pp. 4–5.

## DISCUSSION QUESTIONS

1. What are the "traditional processes" of management? What is the meaning of the term "traditional"?
2. Explain how set systems can be used to describe and portray the managerial processes.
3. Illustrate how the environment can be portrayed in terms of set diagrams.
4. List and briefly describe the six "schools of thought" within the "management theory jungle" according to Professor Koontz.
5. Identify and briefly explain some of the major sources of mental entanglement in the Koontz "management theory jungle."
6. Compare the similarities and differences between the Sikula and Koontz interpretations of the overview of the management discipline.

# Chapter 2. Basic Administrative Terminology and Concepts

*William G. Scott*

# *ORGANIZATION THEORY: AN OVERVIEW AND AN APPRAISAL*

Man is intent on drawing himself into a web of collectivized patterns. "Modern man has learned to accommodate himself to a world increasingly organized. The trend toward ever more explicit and consciously drawn relationships is profound and sweeping; it is marked by depth no less than by extension."[1] This comment by Seidenberg nicely summarizes the pervasive influence of organization in many forms of human activity.

Some of the reasons for intense organizational activity are found in the fundamental transitions which revolutionized our society, changing it from a rural culture, to a culture based on technology, industry, and the city. From these changes, a way of life emerged characterized by the *proximity* and *dependency* of people on each other. Proximity and dependency, as conditions of social life, harbor the threats of human conflict, capricious antisocial behavior, instability of human relationships, and uncertainty about the nature of the social structure with its concomitant roles.

Of course, these threats to social integrity are present to some degree in all societies, ranging from the primitive to the modern. But, these threats become dangerous when the harmonious functioning of a society rests on the maintenance of a highly intricate, delicately balanced form of human

---

Used by permission of the author and of the publisher. *Journal of the Academy of Management,* vol. 4, no. 1, pp. 7–26, 1961.

collaboration. The civilization we have created depends on the preservation of a precarious balance. Hence, disrupting forces impinging on this shaky form of collaboration must be eliminated or minimized.

Traditionally, organization is viewed as a vehicle for accomplishing goals and objectives. While this approach is useful, it tends to obscure the inner workings and internal purposes of organization itself. Another fruitful way of treating organization is as a mechanism having the ultimate purpose of offsetting those forces which undermine human collaboration. In this sense, organization tends to minimize conflict, and to lessen the significance of individual behavior which deviates from values that the organization has established as worthwhile. Further, organization increases stability in human relationships by reducing uncertainty regarding the nature of the system's structure and the human roles which are inherent to it. Corollary to this ponit, organization enhances the predictability of human action, because it limits the number of behavioral alternatives available to an individual. As Presthus points out:

> Organization is defined as a system of structural interpersonal relations . . . individuals are differentiated in terms of authority, status, and role with the result that personal interaction is prescribed. . . . Anticipated reactions tend to occur, while ambiguity and spontaneity are decreased.[2]

In addition to all of this, organization has built-in safeguards. Besides prescribing acceptable forms of behavior for those who elect to submit to it, organization is also able to counterbalance the influence of human action which transcends its establishment patterns.[3]

Few segments of society have engaged in organizing more intensively than business.[4] The reason is clear. Business depends on what organization offers. Business needs a system of relationships among functions; it needs stability, continuity, and predictability in its internal activities and external contacts. Business also appears to need harmonious relationships among the people and processes which make it up. Put another way, a business organization has to be free, relatively, from destructive tendencies which may be caused by divergent interests.

As a foundation for meeting these needs rests administrative science. A major element of this science is organization theory, which provides the grounds for management activities in a number of significant areas of business endeavor. Organization theory, however, is not a homogeneous science based on generally accepted principles. Various theories of organization have been, and are being evolved. For example, something called "modern organization theory" has recently emerged, raising the wrath of some traditionalists, but also capturing the imagination of a rather elite *avant-garde*.

The thesis of this paper is that modern organization theory, when stripped of its irrelevancies, redundancies, and "speech defects," is a logical and vital evolution in management thought. In order for this thesis to be supported, the reader must endure a review and appraisal of more traditional forms of organization theory which may seem elementary to him.

In any event, three theories of organization are having considerable influence on management thought and practice. They are arbitrarily labeled in this paper as the classical, the neo-classical, and the modern. Each of these is fairly distinct; but they are not unrelated. Also, these theories are on-going, being actively supported by several schools of management thought.

## THE CLASSICAL DOCTRINE

For lack of a better method of identification, it will be said that the classical doctrine deals almost exclusively with the *anatomy of formal organization*. This doctrine can be traced back to Frederick W. Taylor's interest in functional foremanship and planning staffs. But most students of management thoughts would agree that in the United States, the first systematic approach to organization, and the first comprehensive attempt to find organizational universals, is dated 1931 when Mooney and Reiley published *Onward Industry*.[5] Subsequently, numerous books, following the classical vein, have appeared. Two of the more recent are Brech's, *Organization*,[6] and Allen's, *Management and Organization*.[7]

Classical organization theory is built around four key pillars. They are the division of labor, the scalar and functional processes, structure, and span of control. Given these major elements just about all of classical organization theory can be derived.

(1) *The division of labor* is without doubt the cornerstone among the four elements.[8] From it the other elements flow as corollaries. For example, *scalar* and *functional* growth requires specialization and departmentalization of functions. Organization *structure* is naturally dependent upon the direction which specialization of activities travels in company development. Finally, *span of control* problems result from the number of specialized functions under the jurisdiction of a manager.

(2) *The scalar and functional processes* deal with the vertical and horizontal growth of the organization, respectively.[9] The scalar process refers to the growth of the chain of command, the delegation of authority and responsibility, unity of command, and the obligation to report.

The division of the organization into specialized parts and the regrouping of the parts into compatible units are matters pertaining to the functional process. This process focuses on the horizontal evolution of the line and staff in a formal organization.

(3) *Structure* is the logical relationships of functions in an organization, arranged to accomplish the objectives of the company efficiently. Structure implies system and pattern. Classical organization theory usually works with two basic structures, the line and the staff. However, such activities as committee and liaison functions fall quite readily into the purview of structural considerations. Again, structure is the vehicle for introducing logical and consistent relationships among the diverse functions which comprise the organization.[10]

(4) *The span of control* concept relates to the number of subordinates a manager can effectively supervise. Graicunas has been credited with first elaborating the point that there are numerical limitations to the subordinates one man can control.[11] In a recent statement on the subject, Brech points out, "span" refers to ". . . the number of persons, themselves carrying managerial and supervisory responsibilities, for whom the senior manager retains his over-embracing responsibility of direction and planning, co-ordination, motivation, and control."[12] Regardless of interpretation, span of control has significance, in part, for the shape of the organization which evolves through growth. Wide span yields a flat structure; short span results in a tall structure. Further, the span concept directs attention to the complexity of human and functional interrelationships in an organization.

It would not be fair to say that the classical school is unaware of the day-to-day administrative problems of the organization. Paramount among these problems are those stemming from human interactions. But the interplay of individual personality, informal groups, intraorganizational conflict, and the decision-making processes in the formal structure appears largely to be neglected by classical organization theory. Additionally, the classical theory overlooks the contributions of the behavioral sciences by failing to incorporate them in its doctrine in any systematic way. In summary, classical organization theory has relevant insights into the nature of organization, but the value of this theory is limited by its narrow concentration on the formal anatomy of organization.

## NEOCLASSICAL THEORY OF ORGANIZATION

The neoclassical theory of organization embarked on the task of compensating for some of the deficiencies in classical doctrine. The neoclassical school is commonly identified with the human relations movement. Generally, the neoclassical approach takes the postulates of the classical school, regarding the pillars of organization as givens. But these postulates are regarded as modified by people, acting independently or within the context of the informal organization.

One of the main contributions of the neoclassical school is the introduction of behavioral sciences in an integrated fashion into the theory of organization. Through the use of these sciences, the human relationists demonstrate how the pillars of the classical doctrine are affected by the impact of human actions. Further, the neoclassical approach includes a systematic treatment of the informal organization, showing its influence on the formal structure.

Thus the neoclassical approach to organization theory gives evidence of accepting classical doctrine, but superimposing on it modifications resulting from individual behavior, and the influence of the informal group. The inspiration of the neoclassical school were the Hawthorne studies.[13] Current examples of the neoclassical approach are found in human relations books like Gardner and Moore, *Human Relations in Industry*,[14] and Davis, *Human Relations in Business*.[15] To a more limited extent, work in industrial sociology also reflects a neoclassical point of view.[16]

It would be useful to look briefly at some of the contributions made to organization theory by the neoclassicists. First to be considered are modifications of the pillars of classical doctrine; second is the informal organization.

## Examples of the Neoclassical Approach to the Pillars of Formal Organization Theory

(1) The *division* of labor has been a long standing subject of comment in the field of human relations. Very early in the history of industrial psychology study was made of industrial fatigue and monotony caused by the specialization of the work.[17] Later, attention shifted to the isolation of the worker, and his feeling of anonymity resulting from insignificant jobs which contributed negligibly to the final product.[18]

Also, specialization influences the work of management. As an organization expands, the need concomitantly arises for managerial motivation and coordination of the activities of others. Both motivation and coordination in turn relate to executive leadership. Thus, in part, stemming from the growth of industrial specialization, the neoclassical school has developed a large body of theory relating to motivation, coordination, and leadership. Much of this theory is derived from the social sciences.

(2) Two aspects of the *scalar and functional* processes which have been treated with some degree of intensity by the neoclassical school are the delegation of authority and responsibility, and gaps in or overlapping of functional jurisdictions. The classical theory assumes something of perfection in the delegation and functionalization processes. The neoclassical

school points out that human problems are caused by imperfections in the way these processes are handled.

For example, too much or insufficient delegation may render an executive incapable of action. The failure to delegate authority and responsibility equally may result in frustration for the delegatee. Overlapping of authorities often causes clashes in personality. Gaps in authority cause failures in getting jobs done, with one party blaming the other for shortcomings in performance.[19]

The neoclassical school says that the scalar and functional processes are theoretically valid, but tend to deteriorate in practice. The ways in which they break down are described, and some of the human causes are pointed out. In addition the neoclassicists make recommendations, suggesting various "human tools" which will facilitate the operation of these processes.

(3) *Structure* provides endless avenues of analysis for the neoclassical theory of organization. The theme is that human behavior disrupts the best laid organizational plans, and thwarts the cleanness of the logical relationships founded in the structure. The neoclassical critique of structure centers on frictions which appear internally among people performing different functions.

Line and staff relations is a problem area, much discussed, in this respect. Many companies seem to have difficulty keeping the line and staff working together harmoniously. Both Dalton[20] and Juran[21] have engaged in research to discover the causes of friction, and to suggest remedies.

Of course, line-staff relations represent only one of the many problems of structural frictions described by the neoclassicists. As often as not, the neoclassicists will offer prescriptions for the elimination of conflict in structure. Among the more important harmony-rendering formulae are participation, junior boards, bottom-up management, joint committees, recognition of human dignity, and "better" communication.

(4) An executive's *span of control* is a function of human determinants, and the reduction of span to a precise, universally applicable ratio is silly, according to the neoclassicists. Some of the determinants of span are individual differences in managerial abilities, the type of people and functions supervised, and the extent of communication effectiveness.

Coupled with the span of control question are the human implications of the type of structure which emerges. That is, is a tall structure with a short span or a flat structure with a wide span more conducive to good human relations and high morale? The answer is situational. Short span results in tight supervision; wide span requires a good deal of delegation with looser controls. Because of individual and organizational differences, sometimes one is better than the other. There is a tendency to favor the looser form of organization, however, for the reason that tall structures breed autocratic leadership, which is often pointed out as a cause of low morale.[22]

### The Neoclassical View of the Informal Organization

Nothing more than the barest mention of the informal organization is given even in the most recent classical treatises on organization theory.[23] Systematic discussion of this form of organization has been left to the neoclassicists. The informal organization refers to people in group associations at work, but these associations are not specified in the "blueprint" of the formal organization. The informal organization means natural groupings of people in the work situation.

In a general way, the informal organization appears in response to the social need—the need of people to associate with others. However, for analytical purposes, this explanation is not particularly satisfying. Research has produced the following, more specific determinants underlying the appearance of informal organizations.

(1) The *location* determinant simply states that in order to form into groups of any lasting nature, people have to have frequent face-to-face contact. Thus, the geography of physical location in a plant or office is an important factor in predicting who will be in what group.[24]

(2) *Occupation* is a key factor determining the rise and composition of informal groups. There is a tendency for people performing similar jobs to group together.[25]

(3) *Interests* are another determinant for informal group formation. Even though people might be in the same location, performing similar jobs, differences of interest among them explain why several small, instead of one large, informal organizations emerge.

(4) *Special issues* often result in the formation of informal groups, but this determinant is set apart from the three previously mentioned. In this case, people who do not necessarily have similar interests, occupations, or locations may join together for a common cause. Once the issue is resolved, then the tendency is to revert to the more "natural" group forms.[26] Thus, special issues give rise to a rather impermanent informal association; groups based on the other three determinants tend to be more lasting.

When informal organizations come into being they assume certain characteristics. Since understanding these characteristics is important for management practice, they are noted below:

(1) Informal organizations act as agencies of *social control*. They generate a culture based on certain norms of conduct which, in turn, demands conformity from group members. These standards may be at odds with

the values set by the formal organization. So an individual may very well find himself in a situation of conflicting demands.

(2) The form of human interrelationships in the informal organization requires *techniques of analysis* different from those used to plot the relationships of people in a formal organization. The method used for determining the structure of the informal group is called sociometric analysis. Sociometry reveals the complex structure of interpersonal relations which is based on premises fundamentally unlike the logic of the formal organization.

(3) Informal organizations have *status and communication* systems peculiar to themselves, not necessarily derived from the formal systems. For example, the grapevine is the subject of much neoclassical study.

(4) Survival of the informal organization requires stable continuing relationships among the people in them. Thus, it has been observed that the informal organization *resists change*.[27] Considerable attention is given by the neoclassicists to overcoming informal resistance to change.

(5) The last aspect of analysis which appears to be central to the neoclassical view of the informal organization is the study of the *informal leader*. Discussion revolves around who the informal leader is, how he assumes this role, what characteristics are peculiar to him, and how he can help the manager accomplish his objectives in the formal organization.[28]

This brief sketch of some of the major facets of informal organization theory has neglected, so far, one important topic treated by the neoclassical school. It is the way in which the formal and informal organizations interact.

A conventional way of looking at the interaction of the two is the "live and let live" point of view. Management should recognize that the informal organization exists, nothing can destroy it, and so the executive might just as well work with it. Working with the informal organization involves not threatening its existence unnecessarily, listening to opinions expressed for the group by the leader, allowing group participation in decision-making situations, and controlling the grapevine by prompt release of accurate information.[29]

While this approach is management centered, it is not unreasonable to expect that informal group standards and norms could make themselves felt on formal organizational policy. An honestly conceived effort by managers to establish a working relationship with the informal organization could result in an association where both formal and informal views would be reciprocally modified. The danger which at all costs should be avoided is that "working with the informal organization" does not degenerate into a shallow disguise for human manipulation.

Some neoclassical writing in organization theory, especially that coming from the management-oriented segment of this school, gives the impression that the formal and informal organizations are distinct, and at times, quite irreconcilable factors in a company. The interaction which takes place between the two is something akin to the interaction between the company and a labor union, or a government agency, or another company.

The concept of the social system is another approach to the interactional climate. While this concept can be properly classified as neoclassical, it borders on the modern theories of organization. The phrase "social system" means that an organization is a complex of mutually interdependent, but variable, factors.

These factors include individuals and their attitudes and motives, jobs, the physical work setting, the formal organization, and the informal organizations. These factors, and many others, are woven into an overall pattern of interdependency. From this point of view, the formal and informal organizations lose their distinctiveness, but find real meaning, in terms of human behavior, in the operation of the system as a whole. Thus, the study of organization turns away from descriptions of its component parts, and is refocused on the system of interrelationships among the parts.

One of the major contributions of the Hawthorne studies was the integration of Pareto's idea of the social system into a meaningful method of analysis for the study of behavior in human organizations.[30] This concept is still vitally important. But unfortunately some work in the field of human relations undertaken by the neoclassicists has overlooked, or perhaps discounted, the significance of this consideration.[31]

The fundamental insight regarding the social system, developed and applied to the industrial scene by the Hawthorne researchers, did not find much extension in subsequent work in the neoclassical vein. Indeed, the neoclassical school after the Hawthorne studies generally seemed content to engage in descriptive generalizations, or particularized empirical research studies which did not have much meaning outside their own context.

The neoclassical school of organization theory has been called bankrupt. Criticisms range from, "human relations is a tool for cynical puppeteering of people," to "human relations is nothing more than a trifling body of empirical and descriptive information." There is a good deal of truth in both criticisms, but another appraisal of the neoclassical school of organization theory is offered here. The neoclassical approach has provided valuable contributions to lore of organization. But, like the classical theory, the neoclassical doctrine suffers from incompleteness, a short-sighted perspective, and lack of integration among the many facets of human behavior studied by it. Modern organization theory has made a move to cover the shortcomings of the current body of theoretical knowledge.

## MODERN ORGANIZATION THEORY

The distinctive qualities of modern organization theory are its conceptual-analytical base, its reliance on empirical research data and, above all, its integrating nature. These qualities are framed in a philosophy which accepts the premise that the only meaningful way to study organization is to study it as a system. As Henderson put it, the study of a system must rely on a method of analysis, ". . . involving the simultaneous variations of mutually dependent variables."[32] Human systems, of course, contain a huge number of dependent variables which defy the most complex simultaneous equations to solve.

Nevertheless, system analysis has its own peculiar point of view which aims to study organization in the way Henderson suggests. It treats organization as a system of mutually dependent variables. As a result, modern organization theory, which accepts system analysis, shifts the conceptual level of organization study above the classical and neoclassical theories. Modern organization theory asks a range of interrelated questions which are not seriously considered by the two other theories.

Key among these questions are: (1) What are the strategic parts of the system? (2) What is the nature of their mutual dependency? (3) What are the main processes in the system which link the parts together, and facilitate their adjustment to each other? (4) What are the goals sought by systems?[33]

Modern organization theory is in no way a unified body of thought. Each writer and researcher has his special emphasis when he considers the system. Perhaps the most evident unifying thread in the study of systems is the effort to look at the organization in its totality. Representative books in this field are March and Simon, *Organizations,*[34] and Haire's anthology, *Modern Organization Theory.*[35]

Instead of attempting a review of different writers' contributions to modern organization theory, it will be more useful to discuss the various ingredients involved in system analysis. They are the parts, the interactions, the processes, and the goals of systems.

### The Parts of the System and Their Interdependency

The first basic part of the system is the *individual,* and the personality structure he brings to the organization. Elementary to an individual's personality are motives and attitudes which condition the range of expectancies he hopes to satisfy by participating in the system.

The second part of the system is the formal arrangement of functions, usually called the *formal organization.* The formal organization is the interrelated pattern of jobs which make up the structure of a system. Certain writers, like Argyris, see a fundamental conflict resulting from the demands made by the system, and the structure of the mature, normal personality. In any event, the individual has expectancies regarding the job he is to perform; and, conversely, the job makes demands on, or has expectancies relating to, the performance of the individual. Considerable attention has been given by writers in modern organization theory to incongruencies resulting from the interaction of organizational and individual demands.[36]

The third part in the organization system is the *informal organization*. Enough has been said already about the nature of this organization. But it must be noted that an interactional pattern exists between the individual and the informal group. This interactional arrangement can be conveniently discussed as the mutual modification of expectancies. The informal organization has demands which it makes on members in terms of anticipated forms of behavior, and the individual has expectancies of satisfaction he hopes to derive from association with people on the job. Both these sets of expectancies interact, resulting in the individual modifying his behavior to accord with the demands of the group, and the group, perhaps, modifying what it expects from an individual because of the impact of his personality on group norms.[37]

Much of what has been said about the various expectancy systems in an organization can also be treated using status and role concepts. Part of modern organization theory rests on research findings in social psychology relative to reciprocal patterns of behavior stemming from role demands generated by both the formal and informal organizations, and role perceptions peculiar to the individual. Bakke's *fusion process* is largely concerned with the modification of role expectancies. The fusion process is a force, according to Bakke, which acts to weld divergent elements together for the preservation of organizational integrity.[38]

The fifth part of system analysis is the *physical setting* in which the job is performed. Although this element of the system may be implicit in what has been said already about the formal organization and its functions, it is well to separate it. In the physical surroundings of work, interactions are present in complex man-machine systems. The "human engineer" cannot approach the problems posed by such interrelationships in a purely technical, engineering fashion. As Haire says, these problems lie in the domain of the social theorist.[39] Attention must be centered on responses demanded from a logically ordered production function, often with the view of minimizing the error in the system. From this standpoint, work cannot be effectively organized unless the psychological, social, and physiological characteristics of people participating in the work environment are considered. Machines and processes should be designed to fit certain generally observed psychological and physiological properties of men, rather than hiring men to fit machines.

In summary, the parts of the system which appear to be of strategic importance are the individual, the formal structure, the informal organization, status and role patterns, and the physical environment of work. Again, these parts are woven into a configuration called the organizational system. The processes which link the parts are taken up next.

## The Linking Processes

One can say, with a good deal of glibness, that all the parts mentioned above are interrelated. Although this observation is quite correct, it does not mean too much in terms of system theory unless some attempt is made to analyze the processes by which the interaction is achieved. Role theory is devoted to certain types of interactional processes. In addition, modern organization theorists point to three other linking activities which appear to be universal to human systems of organized behavior. These processes are communication, balance, and decision making.

(1) Communication is mentioned often in neoclassical theory, but the emphasis is on description of forms of communication activity, i.e., formal-informal, vertical-horizontal, line-staff. Communication, as a mechanism which links the segments of the system together, is overlooked by way of much considered analysis.

One aspect of modern organization theory is study of the communication network in the system. Communication is viewed as the method by which action is evoked from the parts of the system. Communication acts not only as stimuli resulting in action, but also as a control and coordination mechanism linking the decision centers in the system into a synchronized pattern. Deutsch points out that organizations are composed of parts which communicate with each other, receive messages from the outside world, and store information. Taken together, these communication functions of the parts comprise a configuration representing the total system.[40] More is to be said about communication later in the discussion of the cybernetic model.

(2) The concept of *balance* as a linking process involves a series of some rather complex ideas. Balance refers to an equilibrating mechanism whereby the various parts of the system are maintained in a harmoniously structured relationship to each other.

The necessity for the balance concept logically flows from the nature of systems themselves. It is impossible to conceive of an ordered relationship among the parts of a system without also introducing the idea of a stabilizing or an adapting mechanism.

Balance appears in two varieties—quasi-automatic and innovative.

Both forms of balance act to insure system integrity in face of changing conditions, either internal or external to the system. The first form of balance, quasi-automatic, refers to what some think are "homeostatic" properties of systems. That is, systems seem to exhibit built-in propensities to maintain steady states.

If human organizations are open, self-maintaining systems, then control and regulatory processes are necessary. The issue hinges on the degree to which stabilizing processes in systems, when adapting to change, are automatic. March and Simon have an interesting answer to this problem, which in part is based on the type of change and the adjustment necessary to adapt to the change. Systems have programs of action which are put into effect when a change is perceived. If the change is relatively minor, and if the change comes within the purview of established programs of action, then it might be fairly confidently predicted that the adaptation made by the system will be quasi-automatic.[41]

The role of innovative, creative balancing efforts now needs to be examined. The need for innovation arises when adaptation to a change is outside the scope of existing programs designed for the purpose of keeping the system in balance. New programs have to be evolved in order for the system to maintain internal harmony.

New programs are created by trial and error search for feasible action alternatives to cope with a given change. But innovation is subject to the limitations and possibilities inherent in the quantity and variety of information present in a system at a particular time. New combinations of alternatives for innovative purposes depend on:

(a) the possible range of output of the system, or the capacity of the system to supply information.

(b) the range of available information in the memory of the system.

(c) the operating rules (program) governing the analysis and flow of information within the system.

(d) the ability of the system to "forget" previously learned solutions to change problems.[42] A system with too good a memory might narrow its behavioral choices to such an extent as to stifle innovation. In simpler language, old learned programs might be used to adapt to change, when newly innovated programs are necessary.[43]

Much of what has been said about communication and balance brings to mind a cybernetic model in which both these processes have vital roles. Cybernetics has to do with feedback and control in all kinds of systems. Its purpose is to maintain system stability in the face of change. Cybernetics cannot be studied without considering communication networks, information flow, and some kind of balancing process aimed at preserving the integrity of the system.

Cybernetics directs attention to key questions regarding the system.

These questions are: How are communication centers connected, and how are they maintained? Corollary to this question: what is the structure of the feedback system? Next, what information is stored in the organization, and at what points? And as a corollary: how accessible is this information to decision-making centers? Third, how conscious is the organization of the operation of its own parts? That is, to what extent do the policy centers receive control information with sufficient frequency and relevancy to create a real awareness of the operation of the segments of the system? Finally, what are the learning (innovating) capabilities of the system?[44]

Answers to the questions posed by cybernetics are crucial to understanding both the balancing and communication processes in systems.[45] Although cybernetics has been applied largely to technical-engineering problems of automation, the model of feedback, control, and regulation in all systems has a good deal of generality. Cybernetics is a fruitful area which can be used to synthesize the processes of communication and balance.

(3) A wide spectrum of topics dealing with types of decisions in human systems makes up the core of analysis of another important process in organizations. Decision analysis is one of the major contributions of March and Simon in their book *Organizations*. The two major classes of decisions they discuss are decisions to produce and decisions to participate in the system.[46]

Decisions to produce are largely a result of an interaction between individual attitudes and the demands of organization. Motivation analysis becomes central to studying the nature and results of the interaction. Individual decisions to participate in the organization reflect on such issues as the relationship between organizational rewards versus the demands made by the organization. Participation decisions also focus attention on the reasons why individuals remain in or leave organizations.

March and Simon treat decisions as internal variables in an organization which depend on jobs, individual expectations and motivations, and organizational structure. Marschak[47] looks on the decision process as an independent variable upon which the survival of the organization is based. In this case, the organization is viewed as having, inherent in its structure, the ability to maximize survival requisites through its established decision processes.

## The Goals of Organization

Organization has three goals which may be either intermeshed or independent ends in themselves. They are growth, stability, and interaction. The last goal refers to organizations which exist primarily to provide a medium for association of its members with others. Interestingly enough these goals seem to apply to different forms of organization at varying levels of complexity, ranging from simple clockwork mechanisms to social systems.

These similarities in organizational purposes have been observed by a number of people, and a field of thought and research called general system theory has developed, dedicated to the task of discovering organizationed universals. The dream of general system theory is to create a science of organizational universals, or if you will, a universal science using common organizational elements found in all systems as a starting point.

Modern organization theory is on the periphery of general system theory. Both general system theory and modern organization theory study:

(1) the parts (individuals) in aggregates, and the movement of individuals into and out of the system.

(2) the interaction of individuals with the environment found in the system.

(3) the interactions among individuals in the system.

(4) general growth and stability problems of systems.[48]

Modern organization theory and general system theory are similar in that they look at organization as an integrated whole. They differ, however, in terms of their generality. General system theory is concerned with every level of system, whereas modern organizational theory focuses primarily on human organization.

The question might be asked, what can the science of administration gain by the study of system levels other than human? Before attempting an answer, note should be made of what these other levels are. Boulding presents a convenient method of classification:

(1) The static structure—a level of framework, the anatomy of a system; for example, the structure of the universe.

(2) The simple dynamic system—the level of clockworks, predetermined necessary motions.

(3) The cybernetic system—the level of the thermostat, the system moves to maintain a given equilibrium through a process of self-regulation.

(4) The open system—level of self-maintaining systems, moves toward and includes living organisms.

(5) The genetic-societal system—level of cell society, characterized by a division of labor among cells.

(6) Animal systems—level of mobility, evidence of goal-directed behavior.

(7) Human systems—level of symbol interpretation and idea communication.

(8) Social system—level of human organization.

(9) Transcendental systems—level of ultimates and absolutes which exhibit systematic structure but are unknowable in essence.[49]

This approach to the study of systems by finding universals common at all levels of organization offers intriguing possibilities for administrative organization theory. A good deal of light could be thrown on social systems if structurally analogous elements could be found in the simpler types of systems. For example, cybernetic systems have characteristics which seem to be similar to feedback, regulation, and control phenomena in human organizations. Thus, certain facets of cybernetic models could be generalized to human organization. Considerable danger, however, lies in poorly founded analogies. Superficial similarities between simpler system forms and social systems are apparent everywhere. Instinctually based ant societies, for example, do not yield particularly instructive lessons for understanding rationally conceived human organizations. Thus, care should be taken that analogies used to bridge system levels are not mere devices for literary enrichment. For analogies to have usefulness and validity, they must exhibit inherent structural similarities or implicitly identical operational principles.[50]

Modern organization theory leads, as it has been shown, almost inevitably into a discussion of general system theory. A science of organization universals has some strong advocates, particularly among biologists.[51] Organization theorists in administrative science cannot afford to overlook the contributions of general system theory. Indeed, modern organization concepts could offer a great deal to those working with general system theory. But the ideas dealt with in the general theory are exceedingly elusive.

Speaking of the concept of equilibrium as a unifying element in all systems, Easton says, "It (equilibrium) leaves the impression that we have a useful general theory when in fact, lacking measurability, it is a mere pretense for knowledge."[52] The inability to quantify and measure universal organization elements undermines the success of pragmatic tests to which general system theory might be put.

## Organization Theory: Quo Vadis?

Most sciences have a vision of the universe to which they are applied, and administrative science is not an exception. This universe is composed of parts. One purpose of science is to synthesize the parts into an organized conception of its field of study. As a science matures, its theorems about the configuration of its universe change. The direction of change in three sciences, physics, economics, and sociology, are noted briefly for comparison with the development of an administrative view of human organization.

The first comprehensive and empirically verifiable outlook of the physical universe was presented by Newton in his *Principia*. Classical physics, founded on Newton's work, constitutes a grand scheme in which a wide range of physical phenomena could be organized and predicted. Newtonian physics may rightfully be regarded as "macro" in nature, because its system of organization was concerned largely with gross events of which the movement of celestial bodies, waves, energy forms, and strain are examples. For years, classical physics was supreme, being applied continuously to smaller and smaller classes of phenomena in the physical universe. Physicists at one time adopted the view that everything in their realm could be discovered by simply subdividing problems. Physics thus moved into the "micro" order.

But in the nineteenth century a revolution took place motivated largely because events were being noted which could not be explained adequately by the conceptual framework supplied by the classical school. The consequences of this revolution are brilliantly described by Eddington:

> From the point of view of philosophy of science the conception associated with entrophy must I think be ranked as the great contribution of the nineteenth century to scientific thought. It marked a reaction from the view that everything to which science need pay attention is discovered by microscopic dissection of objects. It provided an alternative standpoint in which the centre of interest is shifted from the entities reached by the customary analysis (atoms, electric potentials, etc.) to qualities possessed by the system as a whole, which cannot be split up and located—a little bit here, and a little bit there. . . .
>
> We often think that when we have completed our study of *one* we know all about *two,* because "two" is "one and one." We forget that we have still to make a study of "and." Secondary physics is the study of "and"—that is to say of organization.[53]

Although modern physics often deals in minute quantities and oscillations, the conception of the physicist is on the "macro" scale. He is concerned with the "and," or the organization of the world in which the events occur. These developments did not invalidate classical physics as to its usefulness for explaining a certain range of phenomena. But classical physics is no longer the undisputed law of the universe. It is a special case.

Early economic theory, and Adam Smith's *Wealth of Nations* comes to mind, examined economic problems in the macro order. The *Wealth of Nations* is mainly concerned with matters of national income and welfare. Later, the economics of the firm, micro-economics, dominated the theoretical scene in this science. And, finally, with Keynes' *The General Theory of Employment Interest and Money,* a systematic approach to the economic universe was re-introduced on the macro level.

The first era of the developing science of sociology was occupied by the great social "system builders." Comte, the so-called father of sociology, had a macro view of society in that his chief works are devoted to social reorganization. Comte was concerned with the interrelationships among social, political, religious, and educational institutions. As sociology progressed, the science of society compressed. Emphasis shifted from the macro approach of the pioneers to detailed, empirical study of small social units. The compression of sociological analysis was accompanied by study of social pathology or disorganization.

In general, physics, economics, and sociology appear to have two things in common. First, they offered a macro point of view as their initial systematic comprehension of their area of study. Second, as the science developed, attention fragmented into analysis of the parts of the organization, rather than attending to the system as a whole. This is the micro phase.

In physics and economics, discontent was evidenced by some scientists at the continual atomization of the universe. The reaction to the micro approach was a new theory or theories dealing with the total system, on the macro level again. This third phase of scientific development seems to be more evident in physics and economics than in sociology.

The reason for the "macro-micro-macro" order of scientific progress lies, perhaps, in the hypothesis that usually the things which strike man first are of great magnitude. The scientist attempts to discover order in the vastness. But after macro laws or models of systems are postulated, variations appear which demand analysis, not so much in terms of the entire system, but more in terms of the specific parts which make it up. Then, intense study of microcosm may result in new general laws, replacing the old models of organization. Or, the old and the new models may stand together, each explaining a different class of phenomenon. Or, the old and the new concepts of organization may be welded to produce a single creative synthesis.

Now, what does all this have to do with the problem of organization in administrative science? Organization concepts seem to have gone through the same order of development in this field as in the three just mentioned. It is evident that the classical theory of organization, particularly as in the work of Mooney and Reiley, is concerned with principles common to all organizations. It is a macro-organizational view. The classical approach to organization, however, dealt with the gross anatomical parts and processes of the formal organization. Like classical physics, the classical theory of organization is a special case. Neither are especially well equipped to account for variation from their established framework.

Many variations in the classical administrative model result from human behavior. The only way these variations could be understood was by a microscopic examination of particularized, situational aspects of human behavior. The mission of the neoclassical school thus is "micro-analysis."

It was observed earlier, that somewhere along the line the concept of the social system, which is the key to understanding the Hawthorne studies, faded into the background. Maybe the idea is so obvious that it was lost to the view of researchers and writers in human relations. In any event, the press of research in the micro-cosmic universes of the informal organization, morale and productivity, leadership, participation, and the like forced the notion of the social system into limbo. Now, with the advent of modern organization theory, the social system has been resurrected.

Modern organization theory appears to be concerned with Eddington's "and." This school claims that its operational hypothesis is based on a macro point of view; that is, the study of organization as a whole. This nobility of purpose should not obscure, however, certain difficulties faced by this field as it is presently constituted. Modern organization theory raises two questions which should be explored further. First, would it not be more accurate to speak of modern organization theor*ies*? Second, just how much of modern organization theory is modern?

The first question can be answered with a quick affirmative. Aside from the notion of the system, there are few, if any, other ideas of a unifying nature. Except for several important exceptions,[54] modern organization theorists tend to pursue their pet points of view,[55] suggesting they are part of system theory, but not troubling to show by what mystical means they arrive at this conclusion.

The irony of it all is that a field dealing with systems has, indeed, little system. Modern organization theory needs a framework, and it needs an integration of issues into a common conception of organization. Admittedly, this is a large order. But it is curious not to find serious analytical treatment of subjects like cybernetics or general system theory in Haire's *Modern Organizational Theory,* which claims to be a representative example of work in this field. Beer has ample evidence in his book *Cybernetics and Management* that cybernetics, if imaginatively approached, provides a valuable conceptual base for the study of systems.

The second question suggests an ambiguous answer. Modern organization theory is in part a product of the past; system analysis is not a new idea. Further, modern organization theory relies for supporting data on microcosmic research studies, generally drawn from the journals of the last ten years. The newness of modern organization theory, perhaps, is its effort to synthesize recent research contributions of many fields into a system theory characterized by a reoriented conception of organization.

One might ask, but what is the modern theorist reorienting? A clue is found in the almost snobbish disdain assumed by some authors of the neo-classical human relations school, and particularly, the classical school. Re-evaluation of the classical school of organization is overdue. However, this does not mean that its contributions to organization theory are irrelevant and should be overlooked in the rush to get on the "behavioral science bandwagon."

Haire announces that the papers appearing in *Modern Organization Theory* constitute, "the ragged leading edge of a wave of theoretical development."[56] Ragged, yes; but leading no! The papers appearing in this book do not represent a theoretical breakthrough in the concept of organization. Haire's collection is an interesting potpourri with several contributions of considerable significance. But readers should beware that they will not find vastly new insights into organizational behavior in this book if they have kept up with the literature of the social sciences, and have dabbled to some extent in the esoterica of biological theories of growth, information theory, and mathematical model building. For those who have not maintained the pace, *Modern Organization Theory* serves the admirable purpose of bringing them up-to-date on a rather diversified number of subjects.

Some work in modern organization theory is pioneering, making its appraisal difficult and future uncertain. While the direction of this endeavor is unclear, one thing is patently true. Human behavior in organizations, and indeed, organization itself, cannot be adequately understood within the ground rules of classical and neo-classical doctrines. Appreciation of human organization requires a *creative* synthesis of massive amounts of empirical data, a high order of deductive reasoning, imaginative research studies, and a taste for individual and social values. Accomplishment of all these objectives, and the inclusion of them into a framework of the concept of the system, appears to be the goal of modern organization theory. The vitality of administrative science rests on the advances modern theorists make along this line.

Modern organization theory, 1960 style, is an amorphous aggregation of synthesizers and restaters, with a few extending leadership on the frontier. For the sake of these few, it is well to admonish that pouring old wine into new bottles may make the spirits cloudy. Unfortunately, modern organization theory has almost succeeded in achieving the status of a fad. Popularization and exploitation contributed to the disrepute into which human relations has fallen. It would be a great waste if modern organization theory yields to the same fate, particularly since both modern organization theory and human relations draw from the same promising source of inspiration—system analysis.

Modern organization theory needs tools of analysis and a conceptual framework uniquely its own, but it must also allow for the incorporation of relevant contributions of many fields. It may be that the framework will come from general system theory. New areas of research such as decision theory, information theory, and cybernetics also offer reasonable expectations of analytical and conceptual tools. Modern organization theory represents a frontier of research which has great significance for management. The potential is great, because it offers the opportunity for uniting what is valuable in classical theory with the social and natural sciences into a systematic and integrated concept of human organization.

## REFERENCE LIST

1. Roderick Seidenberg, *Post Historic Man* (Boston: Beacon Press, 1951), p. 1.

2. Robert V. Presthus, "Toward a Theory of Organizational Behavior," *Administrative Science Quarterly,* June, 1958, p. 50.

3. Regulation and predictability of human behavior are matters of degree varying with different organizations on something of a continuum. At one extreme are bureaucratic type organizations with tight bonds of regulation. At the other extreme are voluntary associations, and informal organizations with relatively loose bonds of regulation.

This point has an interesting sidelight. A bureaucracy with tight controls and a high degree of predictability of human action appears to be unable to distinguish between destructive and creative deviations from established values. Thus the only thing which is safeguarded is the *status quo.*

4. The monolithic institutions of the miliary and government are other cases of organizational preoccupation.

5. James D. Mooney and Alan C. Reiley, *Onward Industry* (New York: Harper and Brothers, 1931). Later published by James D. Mooney under the title *Principles of Organization.*

6. E. F. L. Brech, *Organization* (London: Longmans, Green and Company, 1957).

7. Louis A. Allen, *Management and Organization* (New York: McGraw-Hill Book Company, 1958).

8. Usually the division of labor is treated under a topical heading of departmentation, see for example: Harold Koontz and Cyril O'Donnell, *Principles of Management* (New York: McGraw-Hill Book Company, 1959), Chapter 7.

9. These processes are discussed at length in Ralph Currier Davis, *The Fundamentals of Top Management* (New York: Harper and Brothers, 1951), Chapter 7.

10. For a discussion of structure see: William H. Newman, *Administrative Action* (Englewood Cliffs: Prentice-Hall, Incorporated, 1951), Chapter 16.

11. V. A. Graicunas, "Relationships in Organization," *Papers on the Science of Administration* (New York: Columbia University, 1937).

12. Brech, *op. cit.*, p. 78.

13. See: F. J. Roethlisberger and William J. Dickson, *Management and the Worker* (Cambridge: Harvard University Press, 1939).

14. Burleigh B. Gardner and David G. Moore, *Human Relations in Industry* (Homewood: Richard D. Irwin, 1955).

15. Keith Davis, *Human Relations in Business* (New York: McGraw-Hill Book Company, 1957).

16. For example see: Delbert C. Miller and William H. Form, *Industrial Sociology* (New York: Harper and Brothers, 1951).

17. See: Hugo Munsterberg, *Psychology and Industrial Efficiency* (Boston: Houghton Mifflin Company, 1913).

18. Probably the classic work is: Elton Mayo, *The Human Problems of an Industrial Civilization* (Cambridge: Harvard University, 1946, first printed 1933).

19. For further discussion of the human relations implications of the scalar and functional processes see: Keith Davis, *op. cit.*, pp. 60–66.

20. Melville Dalton, "Conflicts between Staff and Line Managerial Officers," *American Sociological Review*, June, 1950, pp. 342–351.

21. J. M. Juran, "Improving the Relationship between Staff and Line," *Personnel*, May, 1956, pp. 515–524.

22. Gardner and Moore, *op. cit.*, pp. 237–243.

23. For example: Brech, *op. cit.*, pp. 27–29; and Allen, *op. cit.*, pp. 61–62.

24. See: Leon Festinger, Stanley Schachter, and Kurt Back, *Social Pressures in Informal Groups* (New York: Harper and Brothers, 1950), pp. 153–163.

25. For example see: W. Fred Cottrell, *The Railroader* (Palo Alto: The Stanford University Press, 1940), Chapter 3.

26. Except in cases where the existence of an organization is necessary for the continued maintenance of employee interest. Under these conditions the previously informal association may emerge as a formal group, such as a union.

27. Probably the classic study of resistance to change is: Lester Coch and John R. P. French, Jr., "Overcoming Resistance to Change," in Schuyler Dean

Hoslett (editor), *Human Factors in Management* (New York: Harper and Brothers, 1951), pp. 242–268.

28. For example see: Robert Saltonstall, *Human Relations in Administration* (New York: McGraw-Hill Book Company, 1959), pp. 330–331; and Keith Davis, *op. cit.*, pp. 99–101.

29. For an example of this approach see: John T. Doutt, "Mangement Must Manage the Informal Group, Too," *Advanced Management*, May 1959, pp. 26–28.

30. See: Roethlisberger and Dickson, *op. cit.*, Chapter 24.

31. A check of management human relations texts, the organization and human relations chapters of principles of management texts, and texts on conventional organization theory for management courses reveals little or no treatment of the concept of the social system.

32. Lawrence J. Henderson, *Pareto's General Sociology* (Cambridge: Harvard University Press, 1935), p. 13.

33. There is another question which cannot be treated in the scope of this paper. It asks, what research tools should be used for the study of the system?

34. James G. March and Herbert A. Simon, *Organization* (New York: John Wiley and Sons, 1958).

35. Mason Haire (editor), *Modern Organization Theory* (New York: John Wiley and Sons, 1959).

36. See Chris Argyris, *Personality and Organization* (New York: Harper and Brothers, 1957), esp. Chapters 2, 3, 7.

37. For a larger treatment of this subject see: George C. Homans, *The Human Group* (New York: Harcourt, Brace and Company, 1950), Chapter 5.

38. E. Wight Bakke, "Concept of the Social Organization," in *Modern Organization Theory, op. cit.*, pp. 60–61.

39. Mason Haire, "Psychology and the Study of Business: Joint Behavioral Sciences," in *Social Science Research on Business: Product and Potential* (New York: Columbia University Press, 1959), pp. 53–59.

40. Karl W. Deutsch, "On Communication Models in the Social Sciences," *Public Opinion Quarterly*, 16 (1952), pp. 356–380.

41. March and Simon, *op. cit.*, pp. 139–140.

42. Mervyn L. Cadwallader, "The Cybernetic Analysis of Change in Complex Social Organization," *The American Journal of Sociology*, September, 1959, p. 156.

43. It is conceivable for innovative behavior to be programmed into the system.

44. These are questions adapted from Deutsch, *op. cit.*, pp. 368–370.

45. Answers to these questions would require a comprehensive volume. One of the best approaches currently available is Stafford Beer, *Cybernetics and Management* (New York: John Wiley and Sons, 1959).

46. March and Simon, *op. cit.*, Chapters 3 and 4.

47. Jacob Marschak, "Efficient and Viable Organizational Forms" in *Modern Organization Theory,* Mason Haire, editor (New York: John Wiley and Sons, 1959), pp. 307–320.

48. Kenneth E. Boulding, "General System Theory—The Skeleton of a Science," *Management Science,* April, 1956, pp. 200–202.

49. *Ibid.*, pp. 202–205.

50. Seidenberg, *op. cit.*, p. 136. The fruitful use of the type of analogies spoken of by Seidenberg is evident in the application of thermodynamic principles, particularly the entropy concept, to communication theory. See: Claude E. Shannon and Warren Weaver, *The Mathematical Theory of Communication* (Urbana: The University of Illinois Press, 1949). Further, the existence of a complete analogy between the operational behavior of thermodynamic systems, electrical communication systems, and biological systems has been noted by: Y. S. Touloukian, *The Concept of Entropy in Communication, Living Organisms, and Thermodynamics,* Research Bulletin 130, Purdue Engineering Experiment Station.

51. For example see: Ludwig von Bertalanffy, *Problem of Life* (London: Watts and Company, 1952).

52. David Easton, "Limits of the Equilibrium Model in Social Research," in *Profits and Problems of Homeostatic Models in the Behavioral Sciences,* Publication 1, Chicago Behavioral Sciences, 1953, p. 39.

53. Sir Arthur Eddington, *The Nature of the Physical World* (Ann Arbor: The University of Michigan Press, 1958), pp. 103–104.

54. For example, E. Wight Bakke, *op. cit.*, pp. 18–75.

55. There is a large selection including decision theory, individual-organization interaction, motivation, vitality, stability, growth, and graph theory, to mention a few.

56. Mason Haire, *"General Issues,"* in Mason Haire (editor), *Modern Organization Theory, op. cit.*, p. 2.

*Hall H. Logan*

# *LINE AND STAFF: AN OBSOLETE CONCEPT?*

The concept that all functions or departments of a business enterprise are either "line" or "staff" is now so firmly entrenched in management theory that any attempt to dislodge it may well seem doomed to failure. Yet it is certainly pertinent to ask, how applicable to business today is this seemingly immutable principle of organization? Does it really serve any practical purpose—other than to add further confusion to the already complex system of interlocking relationships through which any company of any size actually achieves its goals?

Under the line-staff concept, as we all know, line departments are those directly engaged in producing or selling the goods or services the enterprise exists to provide. All other activities are staff—a definition that inevitably relegates staff people to positions of secondary or ancillary importance in the organization. This either-or theory may have some relevance for a company in its earliest stage of development, when there is usually little difficulty in distinguishing the people who are really bringing home the bacon from those whose activities clearly fall into the category of overhead. But as the enterprise grows and its operations become more and more complex, the demarcation between line and staff functions be-

---

Used by permission of the publisher. *Personnel,* vol. 43, no. 1, pp. 26–33, January-February, 1966. 

comes progressively fuzzier until, in the typical large corporation, it is no longer possible to state unequivocally just who is directly engaged in furthering its objectives and who is not.

To take a simple example, who sells more beer—the market research and advertising people or the driver salesman on the beer truck? There can be little dispute as to who is closer to the final product; but a concept of organization that revolves around this matter of direct involvement in the fabrication or sale of the product overlooks the vast amount of work that has to be done before any sales are consummated, as, for example, in the consumer industries. Nor does it recognize the skill and precision that go into the evolution of a product long before it reaches the production stage.

## WHAT KIND OF LABEL?

As an example of the latter, let's consider the case of a company operating under a prime or major secondary contract with the Department of Defense. In such companies, the responsibility for developing design concepts is usually assigned to the Advanced Design department. Once a concept has been sold, responsibility for designing the hardware then passes to the Product Design department. Next, it is up to the Tooling department to establish a manufacturing plan—determining the component breakdown, line stations, major fixtures, etc. This planning phase completed, Tooling then has the responsibility for designing and manufacturing all tools and fixtures.

### What Kind of Departments Are These?

The orthodox would call them "staff," because they never get their hands on the salable article. The more liberal element would say, "Well, if the company's objectives say 'design, manufacture, and sell,' Product Design is a 'line' department. But Advanced Design? Now that's research—or is it? Well, probably they will have to be 'staff.' "

Such answers are attempts to explain organizational relationships on the basis of the type of work performed by each unit of the enterprise. But organizational relationships—the relationships that management establishes between departments, groups, and individuals, and the degree of responsibility and authority it assigns to these various organizational units to meet the needs of the situation—are not determined by type of work per se. While some functions do rather consistently possess a certain kind of authority, modern practice has tended to spread authority more widely, particularly among the skilled functions. The attempt to establish authority by type of function is totally at variance with the relationships that actually exist in the modern corporation.

Later, I shall give some examples of the wide variations that can exist in organizational relationships. At this point, though, I should like to outline a concept of formal organization that portrays what really goes on in business these days.

The aim of formal organization is to insure singleness of purpose. A company's success in attaining its goals depends upon the skill with which management functions and authority are divided and, probably more important, how the divisions are integrated into unified action. In practice, this boils down to first assigning responsibilities and then trying to insure, as far as possible, authority co-equal with these responsibilities.

## AUTHORITY SPELLED OUT

Particularly at the lower echelons of the organizational structure, authority relationships must be well established and thoroughly understood because of the heavy travel over these paths. There must be a clear understanding of who is responsible for what, as well as the degree of this responsibility. Relationships at the top echelons, between corporate staffs and multiplant managers, generally require less explanation, and are expressed in broader terms.

Organizational relationships take three basic forms: line, functional, and staff. Each type achieves its purpose through the exercise of its own kind of authority. Let's take a closer look at these different forms of authority. Here, though, a preliminary definition is called for:

*Authority is the right or power to issue commands and to discipline for violation; an accepted source of information.* This definition must be firmly grasped if the three basic types of organizational relationships are to be clearly understood.

*Line Authority* This inheres in the relationship between superior and subordinate level. It is administrative authority, having the right and power to issue commands, to exact accountability, and to discipline for violations. Rarely, however, does it exist in a pure form. Over and above his line authority, a supervisor invariably has some degree of functional authority also. Line authority never crosses departmental lines horizontally, but is the scalar chain that, regardless of the type of work or function performed, links the lowest unskilled worker through successive echelons of supervision to the president.

*Functional Authority* This is the authority delegated by formal action of management to an "accepted source of information" or a specialist. Functional authority is the right and power of one department to issue orders or instructions to one, several, or all other departments in an enterprise, also with the right of accountability from the addressee. Functional authority is as binding as line authority, but it *does not carry the right to discipline for violation* (or even to threaten) in order to enforce compliance.

This authority to issue orders pertains to a single function, or to a limited number of functions in which the subject department is authorized to act. Functional authority should be formally established by agreement among the departments affected, preferably in written procedures that are approved by middle management and finally by the president, or at least by the manager who supervises all the departments concerned.

Functional authority also implies co-equality of responsibility. The department issuing the orders is responsible for the results of its directives, and thus shares in the total responsibility for other departmental tasks.

Functional authority is usually impersonal in nature. In larger companies, it takes the form of written orders, schedules, inspection reports, and the like. If, however, the individual exercising functional authority cannot, as I said, threaten, or take reprisals outside of his own department, where are the teeth? The prior agreement is the basis for the working relationship. Furthermore, the functional department usually issues periodic reports, or on an emergency basis if necessary, which go both to the supervisor directly concerned and to the next level of supervision above. This feedback permits each supervisor to evaluate the effectiveness of his performance in achieving prescribed targets or goals, and to take corrective action as required.

If management promotes a teamwork philosophy and the use of functional and staff organizations, employees will readily accept orders from authorized sources outside the linear chain of command. A supervisor will no more readily question or reject a functional order than he would one from his immediate superior. But if he honestly believes that he cannot carry out a particular order, he can and does question it, regardless of its origin.

## A KEY DIFFERENCE

It is the right to reprimand that differentiates line from functional relationships and distinguishes today's organizational practices from Taylor's pure functional foremanship. Through functional authority, the benefits of functional specialization are attained while retaining unity of command—for each man, one person-to-person boss relationship.

*Staff Authority* This actually is a misnomer, for the person or department operating in a staff relationship has no authority to issue orders to other departments and no right to demand accountability. "Pure staff" personnel carry out their work through influence. Such relationships exist where the function is variable or intermittent in nature. For example, the industrial engineer may have the responsibility to develop better methods throughout the enterprise. It is usually deemed best to let the I.E. sell individual departments on the value of his proposals. However, in companies where centralized authority is a policy, the I.E. may have the authority to direct each department in how best to perform its work. In the latter situation, the I.E. would have functional authority. Here is one example of how different managements can establish different organizational relationships for what on their respective organizational charts might appear to be the same.

What should we call departments having line relationships, functional authority relationships, or staff relationships? In practice, because of their ambiguous meanings, the terms "line" and "staff" are rarely used to designate a department's exact relationship with other segments of the enterprise. In fact, as subsequent examples will show, departments do not operate with the same authority relationships in all phases of their work.

In their practical, day-to-day work, people are concerned only with how to carry out a particular job and who is involved in the process. In explaining the job to a new worker, the foreman does not say, "You are a line operator; I am a line man; the Production Control people are staff, and so are the Inspection and Process Control people." Most likely his remarks will go something like this: "You are responsible for making a good product, but to be certain that we have uniform quality and that all specifications are met, all parts must be approved by the inspector—that guy over there with the red vest. Orders and schedules come to us from Production Control. You have to make the exact quantity specified on the order and work according to the schedule. The required materials, tools, and engineering drawings are specified on the production order. You get these from the Production Control crib over there.

"And if the order calls for process instruction No. so-and-so, you'll find these instructions in this drawer, filed by number. They are prepared by the Process Control department and are like a part of the engineering design. You must follow them carefully. Now, if the tools won't produce a good part, come to me and we may have to call in the Tool Liaison man. Don't try to rework the tool yourself. That's Tooling's responsibility. . . ."

## FUSING OF OPERATIONS

From the examples I have already cited, it should be clear that, in the modern corporation, the departments operating only through line relationships are by no means confined to the classic sales and production functions. Moreover, there are many functional departments whose activities cannot be reconciled with the proposition that production and sales are the only segments of the organization directly concerned with furthering its prime objectives. Let's consider some further examples bearing out these contentions.

We might begin by reconsidering the question I cited at the outset—the status of the Advanced Design department of a large defense contractor. Under the line-staff concept, this would be a staff department. Actually, in discharging its basic responsibility it will operate through line relationships, though its members might be called upon for advice on certain projects from time to time.

Inspection provides an interesting example of how a particular function's authority relationships can change with the changing demands of the situation. In some companies, Inspection may not even exist as a separate function, each foreman being directly responsible for the quality of the work he supervises. As operations expand, management may, however, permit the foreman to add one or more inspectors and an assistant foreman to relieve him of routine inspection duties. While this group would approve or reject all items produced, it would report to the foreman and thus serve, in the formal sense, as a staff unit.

Later on, quality control may be so crucial to the continued success of the company's over-all operations that it becomes advisable to make it an independent operation. To insure the desired level of quality, Inspection, or Quality Control as it might henceforth be termed, will then have to have functional authority. It will be directly accountable to the vice-president of Manufacturing, or may even be independent of Manufacturing.

Accounting operates through all three types of authority. Usually, the accounting department has functional authority to prescribe the kind of input data it needs and to insure its timely collection or submission. But the ultimate purpose of both internal and external accounting reports is to inform the several levels of management, stockholders, and other interested parties of the results of the company's operations. This is an advisory function carried out through a staff relationship.

## WEARING TWO HATS

Payroll and Accounts Payable perform a basic function of the business through line relationships only, insofar as their output is concerned. Nevertheless, these units exercise functional authority in the collection of time cards, invoices, receiving reports, and other supporting data needed to carry out their responsibility.

Depending on general management policy, Purchasing can operate through line or staff relationships. Thus, if Purchasing is completely subordinate to Production—a purely clerical operation that makes no independent decisions—it will have a staff relationship with the production departments. However, these days, Purchasing is mostly centralized, particularly in larger companies. Though a good purchasing agent will work with the technical departments in selecting suppliers, the actual contractual negotiations, placing of purchase orders, and follow-up are his responsibilities, and are carried out through normal line relationships.

As I earlier pointed out, Industrial Engineering can operate through staff or functional relationships, again depending upon general management policy. Occasionally, Industrial Engineering will be told to "take over and get the job done," after it has sold a proposal to another department. Some experts hold that this is assuming line authority, but it is not the case because, in such a situation, the I.E. does not have full authority of reprimand; he cannot fire or suspend an employee. He will discuss any serious disciplinary problem with the worker's regular supervisor, but leave it to him to take the necessary action. In short, I.E. has temporary functional authority.

Production Control is another function that can operate through staff or functional relationships. Thus, shop orders and schedules may be prepared by a production control group that reports to a superintendent. If all their work is subject to his formal approval, the clerks will have only staff authority even though most of their orders bypass the superintendent because of their routine nature. But a production control department that has clearly defined responsibilities, and reports to the works manager or the vice-president of Manufacturing, will issue orders and schedules directly to first-line supervision. This is a functional authority at this lower level.

In most mass production industries, Tooling carries out its authority through line relationships. It does not advise the shop, nor does it exercise functional direction or authority over it. In fact, since the advent of the numerical control process, responsibility for the accuracy and quality of the final product rests essentially in the tooling function.

The tape instructions are prepared by the tooling programmer. Theoretically, in any event, this reduces the shop operation to pushing a button on the console. If the man who pushes the button can be said to be "advancing the product," who, it must be asked, is more directly concerned with furthering the prime objective of the business?

From the foregoing examples it is clear that the production and direct sales departments are not the only ones with line authority. There are a number of other departments that neither advise nor functionally direct other units, but operate solely through line relationships to discharge their responsibilities. Some of these are in the mainstream of the business—others are less so.

Then there are many other departments that exercise functional authority in their relations with other groups, thus diluting and sharing in the responsibility for the total activities and end products of the latter units.

On the other hand, "pure staff" personnel are relatively few and staff-type departments relatively fewer still.

This presents an entirely different pattern and proportional mix of authority relationships from that of the line-staff concept, about which, incidentally, studies have indicated that 50 percent of the total workforce in sample industries is engaged in staff work. (With present-day competition, can any enterprise afford the luxury of 50 percent "planners" and 50 percent "doers"?)

Regardless of what the theorists may say, in practice, as I have tried to show, working relationships are designed—or evolve—to meet the demands of the situation. In practice, also, the members of the enterprise pay little attention to "line" and "staff" labels. They are concerned only with the responsibility and authority of the persons with whom they associate in carrying out their jobs. As the situation was aptly summed up by one vice-president, "We aren't aware of many staff people around here. Everybody has a job to do and does it, no matter what you call him."

## DISCUSSION QUESTIONS

1. Describe the four key pillars of classical organization theory according to William G. Scott. How do neoclassical and modern writers alter their interpretations of these four pillars?
2. What are the "parts" of modern or systems organization theory according to Professor Scott?
3. How are the "parts" of a modern organization interrelated or linked together?
4. What is the key difference between line and staff positions?
5. What is meant by the concept of functional authority?
6. Give some examples of typical modern organizational positions which combine traditional line and staff functions.

# Part II. Traditional Processes

# Chapter 3. Planning

*Stewart Thompson*

# *WHAT PLANNING INVOLVES*

The contribution of the business planner is this: Despite the impossibility of accurately forecasting the future, he identifies a range of possibilities and prepares for them. Once this is understood, the difference between planning and forecasting becomes clearer. "Forecasting" is the attempt to find the most probable course of events or a range of probabilities. "Planning" is deciding what one will do about them.

Specialists in market research and economic forecasting can be useful in gathering information on which plans for the business can be based. But decisions on what is to be achieved, and why, are business decisions, to be made by top management. This view was generally supported by the managers who participated in this research project. Most of those interviewed in firms which have staff planning departments emphasized that the work of these departments is not that of making business decisions. Instead, they declared, these departments help top management by gathering information, by identifying problems, by recommending procedures to be followed in formulating and reviewing plans. It is top management that decides the kinds of work to be performed, the kinds of material to

---

be used, and the needs of specific customers to be satisfied. Top management decides the risks the company is willing to take and states whether the future of the firm is to be staked on one or more products, on one or more markets. Top management decides what things the company will do as a side line and what things it will do as a life-or-death commitment.

## CHARACTERISTICS OF A BUSINESS PLAN

Even though the future is largely unknown, work in the present takes on added significance when it is performed in contemplation of future results. A business plan states what results are to be achieved and states things that people actually can and should do to achieve them. It also provides for the evaluation and measurement of results.

Underlying the use of planning in business is the insight that management is not only "feel" or experience, but also choice of a rational course of action. The decisions and actions of business men are based on certain ideas regarding the kind of business they manage, the market and economy in which they operate, the resources at their disposal, and the effect of their actions upon the business and upon persons outside the business.

Objectives, assumptions, and risks are always present in the thoughts, decisions, and acts of a manager. Even though these elements may not be always clear to him, he must act on the basis of some ideas about the character of his business: its environment, its resources, its potential. No matter how important intuition and experience may be, business decisions and actions can be rational. A major purpose and contribution of a business plan is to bring out and sharpen this rationality.

A business plan is a preparation for action. It involves making decisions and scheduling results.

Scheduling takes into account the magnitude of the problems in bringing about a result. Scheduling tests the feasibility of a plan. For example, it may show that results needed "immediately" would, in fact, require three years of preparation. Thoughtful scheduling extends the possibility of making business decisions effective. Without schedules, business plans may be only unrealistic dreams. Scheduling has to do with such questions as these: "What must I have completed on what date?" "What stages can be accelerated?" "What stages can be got under way concurrently with other stages?" Scheduling starts with the knowledge of what is desired and works backward.

By tying business decisions to specific times and results, a plan for management can be formulated which, when used imaginatively, can aid in maintaining and augmenting the value of a business to the society of which it is a part.

## THREE KINDS OF BUSINESS PLANNING

In different ways, the experience of managers reported here shows three kinds of business plans: (1) plans for doing current business, (2) plans for continuing in business, and (3) plans for business development and growth. The major emphasis of this study is on business plans of the kinds listed as (2) and (3).

Plans for doing current business are related to creating today's business and to scheduling today's work in accordance with time and quality standards. These are the operating plans of the manager and the supervisor and the worker, piece by piece, order by order. Since they concern customer service and operating efficiency in an immediate way, effective planning and scheduling of today's business are essential to future survival and growth. The importance of this point has been emphasized by David Packard, President of Hewlett-Packard Company, in these words:

> The keystone of our entire program at Hewlett-Packard Company can be summarized in the statement that we believe tomorrow's success is based on today's performance. In our opinion, this is so obvious a statement as hardly to require repetition, but we often see other firms which are so busy worrying about tomorrow that they never quite seem to do otherwise, and the first order of business is almost always to make sure that current operations are on a sound and profitable basis. It is true that this approach is fairly conservative and that our rate of progress has probably been somewhat limited by our desire to avoid overcommitments to the future, but on the other hand we find that, when we have our current situation under firm control, all our key people seem to have a little more time to look constructively toward the future.[1]

Plans for continuing in business are those that deal with the changing character of the customer's business, with the changing habits and expectations of workers and society at large. These plans do not deal specifically with only one order or one customer. Rather, they are plans reasoned from the manager's assumptions on long-term trends and the changes in those trends. These are plans to build the changing values of the customer into the products and services of the business.

In addition to—or instead of—plans made to perpetuate a business in the markets it already serves, the chief executive may see opportunities his business could logically exploit in other areas. Plans made by the top management of Harris-Intertype Corporation to move into electronics are of this kind, in part at least. Plans for business development and growth sometimes involve preparation to open markets different from those traditionally served by the business, with products different from those the business itself makes. Or, the plans may be to serve essentially the same customers with different or more expanded products and services.

For many companies, business planning is the act of making decisions in one or more of these areas. By thinking of plans to meet needs in each of these three areas, a manager can identify the areas in his own company in which planning ought to be accelerated.

## PLANNING AS PRACTICED BY MOST COMPANIES

An analysis of the remarks of the business men who participated in this study shows that their business planning usually involves the following steps:

*a*) Gathering information on both the external environment and the company internally, in order to see the major problems facing the business.

*b*) Identifying and studying the factors which may limit the company's efficiency and growth in the future.

*c*) Formulating basic assumptions (such as, for example, "No major war within the next five years," or "A continuation of the present economic trends for the planning period"). It may also involve determination of several plans for the future, based on a set of markedly different assumptions.

*d*) Laying down the objectives or the goals of the business, based on information gathered, assumptions, predictions, and a study of major problems.

*e*) Determining the actions which must be taken to achieve the objectives.

*f*) Setting up a timetable for these actions. . . .

## THE CONCEPT OF THE BUSINESS BOUNDARY

Through planning, a manager creates a strategy for the survival and growth of his business. What must he do to assure the health of his firm as a growing enterprise? His answer commits money, knowledge, and skills to specific tasks in order to accomplish specific results. These results change the circumstances of the business, change its problems and its opportunities, and may create the need for changes in its character and its plans for the future.

The manager plans his business by defining a particular relationship of work-product-customer to highlight those factors that are of greatest importance to his business. In effect, the manager defines boundaries within which his business will operate. The effectiveness of a business plan depends largely upon the ability of the manager to select appropriate boundaries. A clear statement of business boundaries has the value of concentrating thought on the problems that are vital to the business.

Mason Smith, Vice President and Treasurer of Whirlpool Corporation, emphasized this point when he spoke of the manager's need for a frame of reference for his business:

> A frame of reference is essential for long-range planning—and by "frame of reference" I mean, specifically, the definition and statement of the company's broad objectives and policies in such a way that they are understood clearly by all personnel. I am convinced that any attempt to initiate and maintain a long-range planning program without some general, company-wide understanding of the kind of business that the management is attempting to build will yield very few tangible benefits. In addition to a cold, clear acknowledgment of the company's financial limitations, these objectives and policies should provide some indication of whether the company will intensify within one industry or diversify; whether or not it will integrate; whether it will attempt only to maintain the Number One position in its industry or try to balance size with other considerations; whether it will assume a posture of statesmanship in its industry or operate under short-run principles. Decisions regarding such matters are, of course, subject to review and revision by the board and by management at any time. When they are revised, however, management should be sure that the long-range planning program is following whatever new statement of policy is laid down.[2]

In solving operating problems, the manager reasons from agreed-on boundaries to implications for the particular problem. If seemingly promising lines of action conflict with accepted boundaries, there are two solutions: change the boundaries or drop the action. So it may be said that business planning covers (1) exploration and improvement within boundaries that have been laid down, and (2) the questioning, evaluation, and restructuring of the boundaries themselves.

This testing and correcting of the boundaries is a vital part of business planning. "Who are our customers?" "Why?" "Under what circumstances does a customer become a non-customer?" "To our customers Jackson, Jones, and Johnson, what is the function and value of our product?" "What consulting services does our special competence enable us to provide that our competitors cannot provide?" "Is our main strength in making the product, or in our methods of selling it, or in our company image, or in our knowledge supplied to the customer on how to use, store, and maintain the product?" These are some of the questions that the participants in this study have answered or tried to answer.

## THE NEED FOR BOUNDARIES

According to a statement by one of its executives, the top management of one company which took part in this research had no clear idea of the boundaries of the business. Eventually, a situation arose that sharply pointed up the need for well-defined boundaries. Although some aspects of the situation have been altered in the telling, in order to comply with this film's desire for anonymity, the problem was essentially as reported here.

A researcher came up with a device to aid surgeons by measuring the oxygen content of blood continuously while surgery was in progress. When a vice president discovered that almost $100,000 had been spent on the instrument he ordered the work to be discontinued. Recalled an official of the firm:

> We stopped work on that project, but we did not know why. Nobody, not even the president or the officer who issued the order, seemed to know why. I raised the question: "O.K.," I said, "let's stop work on the project, but let's be sure we know why. Do we not want to do medical research? Do we not have the money to finish the project? Do we want to make only radio and TV sets?" Nobody was prepared to get down to some careful thinking on the issue. We just stopped. The researcher left us, taking his ideas with him. In time, the failure to examine the possibilities the researcher was opening up for us may prove to be one of the greatest fumbles we ever made. As I see it, the fumble was not so much the decision to stop the project, unfortunate as that may have been, but the larger issue of failing to thoroughly consider the areas in which the competence of those in the firm can best be applied. We still lack a central concept about our business. It is badly needed here.

## THE SYSTEM BOUNDARY

There are two concepts of business boundaries. The one just discussed involves the choice of objectives and behavior for the firm. In this case the boundary marks off the area of business purpose and conduct selected by the top management for present or future operations of the company.

The other concept relates to changes in the dynamic structure or climate within which the managerial decisions and plans must be made. This dynamic structure, or "system," consists of the variables affecting and affected by the business. The system includes the interaction of individuals within the firm, the interaction of the firm with its customers and with other businesses, and influences within the society of which the firm is a part. In this context the boundary—more specifically, the system boundary—is the moment of significant change in the variables of the system.

Let us assume that at some point in the operation of a particular business one of its essential variables (for example, its most important customer) does not continue as before. This discontinuity can be described as a system boundary. The business might have to dissolve, or at least its managers would be faced with a grave problem. The business could perhaps establish a new relationship with another type of customer in order to survive. If this were done, a new climate or business system would operate and new variables would govern the company. There would be new factors (or a re-weighting of old factors) to be considered in the new business plan. Business planning seeks to identify such points of major change and to enable the manager to make preparations in case of need. In some cases, proper response may require very significant changes in company concepts, with such results as adding new products, hiring a new president, or selling a division of the company.

## A COMPANY EXPERIENCE

The following case illustrates an evolution of a business and a change in the boundaries within which it operated. The firm's experience points out that changes in the way the firm did business created a new business system. These changes were subtle, not easy to recognize, not easy to define precisely. The president did not call them "boundaries," but he did recognize that at different points in time an isolated change created new stages in his firm's growth and gave rise to new kinds of opportunities and problems and a need for new plans. The firm made storage racks, hand trucks, and other equipment used in handling and storing materials.

> The owners of the firm hired a new president to help achieve higher profits. As the president examined sales records and visited customers, he found that his competitors gained considerable business from the use of attractively prepared and well-illustrated catalogues. It seemed to him highly desirable to have such catalogues, but he felt that his company could not afford them.
>
> The president proceeded to expand his product line to some extent and redesigned much of it to approximate closely the products of one of his principal competitors, a much larger company. In the course of soliciting business, particularly from those firms he knew well, he used his competitor's catalogue, sometimes offering lower prices and usually providing earlier delivery. In addition, he studied the utilization of his equipment in the customer's plants. As his profits increased, he later brought out his own descriptive catalogue, added some especially de-

signed devices, and concentrated on the technical training of his firm's salesmen. His sales proceeded to match and then outstrip the business of even his largest competitors. Salesmen of the competitor sold from the catalogue in a routine way ("Order by number, please"), but this president had his salesmen bring special problem-solving skills to his customers' operations. Incidentally, for many of his salesmen this change in the character of their work launched them on a new career in the firm.

Recognizing an opportunity to depart still further from the traditional marketing methods of "the industry" and to publicize the unique character of his company, the president offered his own help and that of his salesmen to aid customers to solve problems of layout and utilization in their plants. Some of the customers began to request his aid in training members of their own staffs in his techniques of analysis. These requests came with such frequency that for a time he seriously considered setting up another business to deal with the consultations. However, he decided against this idea.

Hearing of his success in his own line, manufacturers of other related products sought to have his firm distribute all or some of their lines. The directors of the firm, well pleased with operations under their president, recommended diversification into other businesses.

A major problem became that of planning and controlling the growth of the business in order to utilize effectively the evolving skills and growing reputation of the firm while avoiding, as far as possible, an uncontrolled dissipation of energy.

## COMPANY CHARACTER

Business decisions that clarify the boundaries within which the business will operate, and a timetable of results, imply as well as a plan a particular conception of "management." The way in which this conception is defined by the individual manager gives "planned character" to his firm. The president's concept of the firm he is managing, for example, largely defines the kind of planning he will do.

There is a difference between financial manipulation and business management. There is a difference between a corporation and its individual components. Sometimes confusion exists as to what kind of planning the managers should do, because the kind of business the chief executive is managing or creating is not clear.

Some managers believe their company operates as a federalized enterprise with a central office and various decentralized divisions, when in actual fact the characteristics of the company are more those of a financial trust. As a financial trust, the primary concern of the central management is the investment of shareholders' capital in various businesses. These investments may be, for the most part, in minority interests. Buying and selling of interests in various firms is done for appreciation of capital rather than for building an enterprise with a logic of its own. Planning in a financial trust type of operation requires different knowledge and skills and addresses itself to kinds of problems which are different from those in a decentralized company.

A "federalized company," as the term is used here, is a firm which has a headquarters office for two or more enterprises, each of which has its unique products, processes, and markets and complements the others. In an enterprise of this type, planning within the divisions applies to the exploration of markets and improved efficiency, within the boundaries laid down. Plans would also include means for clarifying the boundaries of the divisions and of the total enterprise in the light of new problems and opportunities. Problems relating to new product ideas and new markets that do not fall clearly within the scope of one or more of the divisions would have to be resolved. Headquarters as well as divisional management may have parts to play in planning for action to be taken by two or more divisions that may form together a single unit in order to achieve a specific purpose. Business planning at headquarters may involve the raising of capital and the strengthening of management competence in the subsidiary and affiliated businesses, as well as provision for assuring that continuous development of managerial competence is energized within the divisions by themselves. The orientation of management at headquarters may aim to do less and less in the way of managing the divisions, so that top management can concentrate on identifying and planning for those events that most affect the whole firm.

Another form of business that has special planning needs of its own is the holding company. Such firms own either a substantial minority interest or a controlling interest in various enterprises, no single one of which may relate to the markets, products, or processes of the others. The central concern of management of a holding company often is to acquire capital at the most favorable terms. The capital is utilized by the subsidiary enterprises for their growth and expansion and may represent funds which the subsidiaries could not have acquired had they not had affiliation with the holding company. Planning at headquarters may emphasize the appropriation of acquired capital (and regular profits) among the affiliated businesses. Very often, management at headquarters is skilled in dealing with the financial problems of the business but incompetent to deal with the more specialized plans of individual affiliated businesses. To distinguish the areas of competence of headquarters management and to define the kinds of contributions headquarters can make to the profit-producing end of the enterprise (the divisions) is a matter for careful planning and of large consequence.

In addition to the federalized corporation and the holding company, there is the business that does not have a relationship to a central headquarters. This is the one-plant, one-management business. It may or may not be owned by its managers. It may or may not be a large corporation. With regard to planning for this kind of business—as for the others—difference in size is not in itself so major a consideration as is the difference in the kind of problems with which top management must deal. Even a small company, like its larger counterparts, may have many circles of affiliation with other businesses, and these should be recognized in the business plan. There are many forms of affiliation that are becoming increasingly common.[3]

It is most unlikely that any enterprise will fit neatly into such arbitrary classifications as those given here. Nonetheless, managers of individual companies must continually think of their businesses according to some structure of ideas in order to know what they are really doing and whether they are doing the essential things. A manager—of whatever business—cannot do everything. He needs some rational framework for determining which kinds of decisions he will leave for others and which ones he is to decide for himself. In clarifying the definition of this framework, top managers must carefully examine the nature of their relationship to the operating executives. The classification just listed, while oversimplified, may enable managers to question their assumptions regarding the main issues they habitually retain—perhaps without conscious examination—for their own attention.

## INADEQUACIES OF PLANNING

The objective of this report is to describe the kinds of business planning done, and the methods followed, in a selected group of companies. This implies differences in personal preference, from one company to another (or even within the same company), on how planning ought to be done. It implies as well that examples of both good and not-so-good planning are to be found in this report.

Some companies, for example, are currently enamored of change, accelerating change, and innovations and new developments. The intoxicating enthusiasm for change and "new frontiers" sometimes leads to neglect of the stable elements which do not change. Anticipation of and planning for change is fruitless unless it is coupled with anticipation of and planning for factors which will be stable. It is probably a matter of individual emphasis, but the examples in this study weigh heavily on the side of managements' concern for change. They do not express equal awareness of the stable elements of the businesses.

Along the same line is the emphasis on new developments and acquisitions, as contrasted with improved efficiency within existing markets. Commented an official of one firm, "Farming the same farm more efficiently usually has a better chance, I'll wager, than new products or other expansion." He was right in going on to suggest that many companies do not seem to study the possibility of becoming more efficient within the current boundaries of the business with the same thoroughness that characterizes plans for diversification into other fields—which often prove later to be beyond their competence.

Clarifying boundaries and areas of competence is a pressing need in many companies, including some of those represented in this study. . . . [One company's] "Ten-Year Forward-planning Program" . . . does not meet the definition of a plan as proposed in the text. It is a rather vague declaration of intention. A plan stipulates courses of action to produce measurable results. This document does not. A plan must be operational in the sense that it describes actions in terms of things people actually can do. This document does not. The document does speak of improved results. But it will be a plan only when the desired improvement is stated as a recognized standard. A plan states that certain results must be obtained (for example, reduced costs) and states specifically what those results are and what will be done to achieve them.

This is not to say that a document of intention is of no value; such a document may be the precursor of specific and realistic plans. It is sometimes essential to think through, in broad terms, what one intends to do. Good intentions can lead to sound and effective action. (In fact, all action ought to be based on "good intentions.") Still, the manager ought to distinguish a business plan from a statement limited to the expression of good intentions.

In other situations, top management participation in business planning is entirely lacking. Plans are called for from various division and department heads and "coordinated" (a word which is often used but seldom defines clearly the work performed) at the top. A clear view of what the division and department heads must contribute is often lacking. Asking department heads or even senior officers in a firm what it is they would like to do in the coming year or in ten years may be one way to attempt to capture their interest. But it is not business planning. To limit the formulation of a business plan to this kind of procedure is to do little more than make an opportunity for people to do what they want to do, undisciplined by clear purposes and concrete objectives vital to the whole. In such a case, planning is in the nature of recreation or play, where people plan to do the things they enjoy. It is the task of top management to provide the purpose and to set the boundaries, using as directly as possible the best brains in the business (and outside it, too) to do so. But it is correct to view the interests and skills of its people as the company's special strengths. A business plan should include thinking on the numbers and levels of skills required and how they can best be related to each other in order to get the vital work of the business done. Presidents and managers interviewed spoke also of a number of other problems and inadequacies associated with making plans for a business—for example, the following:

*a*) The manager may confine his thinking to largely obsolete or contemporary ideas.

*b*) The manager may be unwilling or unable to see that this plan was either ill-conceived or well-conceived but, in any case, not feasible. He won't believe he is headed for failure until his business is liquidated.

*c*) There is danger of "throwing good money after bad." One may be inclined to invest another $100,000 to try to save a $50,000 investment that is not producing. More thought might bring to mind a more profitable avenue in which to direct the $100,000.

*d*) It is often difficult to stop work on a planned project, even when instructions to do so have been given. In one company a project had been officially stopped because the results planned were not being realized. But it took an additional (and unplanned) $250,000 to bring the works finally to a halt.

*e*) To plan to make something out of a company, if it cannot possibly be made, can be extremely costly if the plan is followed.

*f*) A business plan in itself is no guarantee that desired results will be realized. While deliberate planning is one aspect of good management, it is not a substitute for it.

## HOW FAR INTO THE FUTURE?

Certain characteristics of every business must be identified in order to determine what needs to be planned and for what period of time. The reader will find that many companies that participated in this research study state they plan five years into the future and make annual or half-yearly reviews of accomplishments, with an eye to altering the plan if necessary. Thus each year (or each six months) an entirely new five-year plan may be devised. Other firms establish a five-year plan but make no changes in it except as changes of great magnitude may require, such as unforeseen opportunities and drastic changes in the nation's economy.

A public utility which plans as far as 25 years in advance in order to provide future sites for its system may be exercising no more foresight than another firm, manufacturing consumer products, which plans six months in advance. Both companies have needs to be met in the future which must be prepared for in the present. The wisdom of a lumber business in providing now for wood to be available 100 years hence does not mean that its managers are gifted with some special talent; the fact that they embark on a reforestation program to assure (insofar as possible) that there will be trees does not prove that they are clairvoyant. To be sure, in such cases, the managers would be exercising good judgment. At the same time, it would not be good judgment to lay elaborate plans for an advertising or sales-training program 100 years in advance.

A few managers in this study mention plans for the next ten years. A number of firms have very long-range plans in addition to their basic five- or ten-year plans, but these are more often in the nature of statements of ultimate objectives than of detailed plans.

Insofar as a norm could be discerned among all the company statements, five years seems to be the planning period for many of the participating firms. This does not mean that plans for all aspects of the business are made for a five-year period. Rather, it means that when certain managers spoke of their "long-range plan" they had in mind marketing and product plans (sometimes, other kinds of plans as well) that looked to certain results in five years or intermediate periods. This does not indicate that every business should have a five-year plan. Two of the reasons why some managers think of planning in terms of five years may be that (1) this period is as far in the future as they can or need to anticipate; and (2) constant repetition of the phrase "five-year plan" by commentators speaking and writing about the U.S.S.R. and certain other countries may have had its influence.

Deciding on a range of time for planning is associated with the problems of evaluating the success of a manager. If one evaluates a man's work today, the result may be different than the result of an evaluation in five, ten, or 25 years. In formulating objectives, the manager must visualize the results as he expects them to be in the future. The range of time to be considered is a decision of large consequence in formulating a plan. Planning has to do with identifying what Peter Drucker calls "the futurity of today's decisions." There are some guides to be followed in deciding the "length of futurity" appropriate for the plans of a particular business or special unit within a business.

There are certain characteristics of the operations of each firm that lead to the selection of a particular span of time for planning. Long-range planning for a manufacturer of women's wear may be practically yesterday for the capital goods producer or the large public utility. Factors which lead to a selection of the proper planning time span are the following:

1. Lead time. This is the length of time it takes from the realization that major new products are needed to the completion of their design, production, and distribution, plus a major period of utilization before the product is obsoleted.

2. The length of time required to recover the capital funds invested in plant and equipment and in training skilled personnel. A plan should provide for recovery of the capital funds invested in the actual physical construction of the plant and equipment and in hiring and training managers and skilled personnel. For example, a firm with a heavy investment in manufacturing and other facilities would have to base some of its plans on a period of time during which the machines would remain useful. Often this time span would be well in excess of the time required to manufacture one line of products.
3. The expected future availability of customers. For manufacturers of machinery and equipment used by other manufacturers, this is the time period up to the expected obsolescence of the customers' products.
4. The expected future availability of raw materials and components. If it takes 99 years to grow a forest to replace the trees the company uses in its manufacture of wood products, someone has to think about planting seedlings now. In this area, the planning span would be 99 years. Research may possibly shorten such long planning spans by providing entirely new raw materials.

As previously stated, one useful concept in determining the planning span is lead time. If one is driving a car, for example, and decides to turn a corner, there is either enough time to do it or there is not. If a firm is supplying a foreign market by sea, the manager must make the decision to ship the goods well before the material is at dockside and ready to be loaded.

Lead time should be defined in relation to the kind of action one is willing to take. In situations where the process of production or transportation is familiar, lead time is readily determined. If a ship takes five days to cross the Atlantic and five days are needed to load and unload, the lead time is ten days. This can be shortened, if necessary, by using air express. As another example, a driver can stop an automobile by exerting ordinary pressure on the brakes, or he can come to an emergency stop. Normally, when driving one does not want to make a series of emergency stops; he allows for routine stops. "Lead time," therefore, may be best defined as the period between decision and arrival at the final results. If routine methods are used, the period or range of time would be considered normal lead time.

With respect to planning, the appropriate ranges of time may also be described in terms of lead time. If, for instance, the building of facilities is being considered, one could thus express the relevant lead time required to decide what to build and where to build, plus the time needed to complete the construction.

In planning within the basic direction and limits of company growth, however, a lead time of even 20 to 30 years for facilities construction is not long enough. There is the additional time which represents the useful life of the building or facility. A firm does not normally plan to put up a building and scrap it shortly thereafter. The planning span might well be the total time the facilities are expected to be of use to the firm.

In some cases the time span of the business plan may end with the discontinuation of the business as it is presently conceived. A plan should provide for discontinuing work and jobs that do not need to be done, just as it should provide for discontinuing products and divisions that fail to advance the firm toward its goals. A business plan may have to include an estimate of the date on which the design of products, method of production, and kind of customer to be served will be altered to such a degree that the manager will need to reconceive his aims in terms of being in a new business.

It is evident, then, that the study of lead-time requirements can help in determining the planning span. But a carefully laid plan with a lengthy lead time may become a short-term expedient—if not altogether useless—if the actions of competitors (or of customers or others) create new situations not provided for in the plan. One manufacturer of tacks and nails suddenly found large segments of his market vanishing because of new kinds of adhesives being produced by firms he had never before thought of as competitors. An economic recession may cause the managers of a business to restudy their business plan and the span of time it covers. Vital decisions need to be made: Should the managers cut back on growth plans, thereby keeping outgo commensurate with income? Should they go ahead, with faith in the company, pursuing long-range goals established at a time of abundance? These are questions to be answered by business men who have large areas of responsibility for shaping the future of their businesses and of society as a whole.

## REFERENCE LIST

1. David Packard, "Assuring the Company's Future," American Management Association, General Management Series, no. 175, New York, 1955, p. 27.

2. Mason Smith, "How to Initiate Effective Long-range Planning," *The Dynamics of Management,* American Management Association, Management Report, no. 14, New York, 1958, p. 70.

3. In this regard the following articles are worthy of note: Robert Hershey, "No Job Is Too Big . . . The Multiple Organization: Management's Answer to Complexity," *The Management Review,* February, 1959, p. 9; John J. Corson, "Government and Business: Partners in the Space Age," *The Management Review,* September, 1959, p. 9; and Robert G. Sproul, Jr., "Developing Profitable Partnerships in Overseas Operations," *The Management Review,* October, 1960, p. 4.

*William F. Pounds*

# *THE PROCESS OF PROBLEM FINDING*

## INTRODUCTION

As a result of research efforts over the past twenty years, a number of extremely effective analytical techniques are currently available for the solution of management problems. Linear programming is used routinely in the specification of optimum cattle feeds and fertilizers. Decision rules based on inventory models form the basis for production and inventory control systems in a wide variety of manufacturing companies. Simulation is evolving from a means for doing research on complex managerial problems to a process which can provide useful information to managers on a real-time basis.

Like other technological changes, these methods raise a number of social and organizational issues within the organizations which use them, but their net contribution is no longer seriously in doubt. As a result, in most large organizations and in many smaller ones, operating managers either are aware of these methods or have ready access to help and advice in their application.

---

Used by permission of the publisher. *Industrial Management Review,* vol. 11, no. 1, pp. 1–19, Fall, 1969. 

But the manager's job is not only to solve well-defined problems. He must also identify the problems to be solved. He must somehow assess the cost of analysis and its potential return. He must allocate resources to questions before he knows their answers. To many managers and students of management, the availability of formal problem solving procedures serves only to highlight those parts of the manager's job with which these procedures do *not* deal: problem identification, the assignment of problem priority, and the allocation of scarce resources to problems. These tasks, which must be performed without the benefit of a well-defined body of theory, may be among the most critical of the manager's decision making responsibilities.

This paper is concerned primarily with the first of these tasks—problem identification. It reviews some research relevant to understanding decisions of this type, presents a theoretical structure, and reports some results of an empirical study of the process by which managers in a successful industrial organization define their problems. Because this research was stimulated in part by an interest in the relationship between the so-called new techniques of management and what might be called traditional managerial behavior, similarities between these two modes of management which are suggested both by the theory and the empirical evidence are briefly noted.

## BACKGROUND

Prior to 1945, our understanding of most cognitive tasks within industrial organizations was not much better than our understanding of the process of problem finding is today. Inventory levels were maintained, production schedules were determined, and distribution systems were designed by individuals who, through years of experience, had learned ways to get these jobs done. With few exceptions these individuals were not explicit about how they performed these tasks and, as a result, training for these jobs was a slow process and the development and testing of new procedures was difficult indeed.

So it is with the process of problem finding today. All managers have discovered ways to maintain a list of problems that can occupy their working hours—and other hours as well. They frequently find it difficult, however, to be explicit about the process by which their problems are selected. Consequently, the development of improved problem finding procedures is difficult.

Since 1945, however, some progress has been made in understanding certain cognitive tasks in the areas of production and inventory control.

Decisions rules have been derived from mathematical models of particular tasks, and in a number of cases these rules have performed as well as or better than the complex intuitive process they have replaced. The significant fact about these developments for this discussion is not, however, the economic impact of such rules, although it has been significant. Rather, it is the implication that the essential processes by which important decisions are made may be carried out satisfactorily by simple explicit decision rules which are easy to teach and execute and easy to improve through analysis, simulation, or experimentation.

Of course it is possible to discount these accomplishments by saying that inventory decisions were always rather simple ones to make. The validity of such arguments, however, seems suspiciously dependent on knowledge of what has been accomplished and on a lack of knowledge of inventory systems.

It is true, however, that mathematical analysis has been able only to suggest decision rules for a wide variety of managerial tasks. These tasks, including the definition of problems, seem to require symbols and analytical procedures not readily represented by standard mathematical forms. Some other means for discovering the decision rules by which such tasks are performed is clearly required.

Some progress in this direction has already been made. Encouraged both by the success of the analytical approach to decision problems, and by the availability of large digital computers, Newell, Simon, and others have been studying human decision behavior since the early 1950's. They have focused their attention primarily on tasks which would facilitate the development of a methodology for approaching decision situations not readily describable in mathematical terms. They have considered the decision processes involved in proving theorems in symbolic logic[1] and plane geometry.[2] They have considered decision processes involved in playing games like chess[3] and checkers.[4] They have worked on the assembly line balancing problem[5] and on trust investment.[6] The relevance of this research to problem finding can perhaps best be illustrated by considering the work on chess.

## Research on Chess

Chess is a game with rules simple enough for almost anyone to learn and yet complex enough that even the largest computer cannot play it by working out the consequences of all possible moves. Chess is a game of strategy in which individual moves can not always be evaluated without considering future moves. Chess moves are inconvenient to describe in mathematical terms and few people can be explicit about how they play chess. For these reasons and several others, chess was an attractive medium in which to attempt to unravel human decision processes that could not be modeled mathematically.

Three aspects of the work on chess playing behavior are relevant to this discussion. First, simple explicit decision rules were discovered which make for very good chess play. This result has been tested by programming computers with such rules and observing the quality of play which resulted in response to the play of human experts. Second, the decision rules for chess playing were derived from observations, interviews, and the writings of chess masters. Thus, it is not necessary that simple, explicit decision rules be derived from mathematical or theoretical considerations. They can be abstracted from humans who have themselves never systematically considered the process of their own decision making. And, third, the decision rules by which humans play chess appear to be separable into three rather distinct classes: rules for defining alternative moves, rules for evaluating moves, and rules for choosing a move from among evaluated alternatives. H. A. Simon has called these three classes of behavior intelligence, design, and choice, respectively,[7] and on the basis of his work both on chess and other decision making situations has concluded that the process of intelligence or alternative definition is the key to effective behavior.

The work on chess and other complex tasks does not directly suggest how managers go about finding and defining the problems to which they devote their time. It does suggest, however, that tasks of this same order of complexity may be understood through careful observation of and abstraction from the behavior of human experts. It further suggests that, if useful insights into managerial problem finding can be gained, they may contribute significantly to managerial effectiveness.

## AN EMPIRICAL STUDY OF MANAGERIAL PROBLEM FINDING

Since it was possible to gain useful insights into the process by which humans play chess by observing experts, it seemed likely that insights into the process of managerial problem finding might be derived from careful observation of successful managers. Arrangements were made therefore to interview, observe, and interrogate about 50 executives in a decentralized operating division of a large technically based corporation, which will be referred to as the Southern Company.

The study consisted of four relatively distinct activities. First, interviews were conducted during which executives were asked to describe the problems they faced and the processes by which they had become aware of these problems. Second, observations were made of meetings during which problems were identified, discussed, and sometimes solved. Third, investigations were made of the source and disposition of several specific problems. And, fourth, a questionnaire was devised and administered to each executive who participated in the study.

As data began to accumulate from each of these activities, it became clear that a major objective of the study would be to discover some level of abstraction which would preserve what seemed to be essential details of the managerial situations being observed and at the same time provide a structure which would convert isolated anecdotes into data from which some generalizations might be drawn. This structure will be described in the following pages together with some of the observations it explains. Observations made outside this particular study will also be reported.

## Theoretical Structure

Like any number of other industrial tasks, the process of management can be viewed as the sequential execution of elementary activities. In describing their own work, executives find it easy to think and talk in terms of elementary activities like making out the production schedule, reading the quality control report, visiting a customer, etc. The attractive feature of this view of managerial work is that elementary tasks can be defined at almost any level of detail. Clearly the task of preparing a production schedule is itself made up of more elementary tasks like collecting data on orders and labor availability, which are themselves made up of even more elementary activities. On the other hand, one can aggregate elements like production scheduling into larger units of analysis like managing production.

A choice of some level of abstraction cannot be avoided. For purposes of this study, the level chosen was that which the managers themselves used in describing their activities. Thus, even at the theoretical level, advantage was taken of the fact that the managers' language had evolved as a useful means for processing information about their jobs.

Elements of managerial activity will be referred to as *operators*. An operator transforms a set of input variables into a set of output variables according to some predetermined plan. For example, the operator "lay out a production schedule" takes machine capacities, labor productivities, product requirements, and other input variables and yields man, product, machine, and time associations covering some appropriate period of time. Since the action of an operator produces an effect which is more or less predictable, operators are frequently named for their effect on the environment. The operator "lay out production schedule" changes the production organization from one with no schedule to one with a schedule. The operator "hire qualified lathe operator" changes the size of the work force.[8]

The word "problem" is associated with the difference between some existing situation and some desired situation. The problem of reducing material cost, for example, indicates a difference between the existing material cost and some desired level of material cost. The problems of hiring qualified engineers and of reducing finished goods inventories similarly define differences to be reduced. Because problems are defined by differences and operators can be executed to reduce differences, strong associations are formed between problems and operators. The problem of devising a production schedule can ordinarily be "solved" by applying the operator "lay out production schedule." The problem of "increasing sales volume" can sometimes be "solved" by applying the operator "revise advertising budget." Since operator selection is triggered by the difference to be reduced, the process of problem finding is the process of defining differences. Problem solving, on the other hand, is the process of selecting operators which will reduce differences.

The manager defines differences by comparing what he perceives to be the output of a *model* which predicts the same variables. A difference might be defined by comparing an idle machine to a production schedule which implies high machine utilization. In this case, the production schedule is the model used to define a difference. A difference might be defined by comparing a 10 percent reject rate in a department to a budgeted rate of 2 percent. In this case, the budget is the model. A difference might be defined by comparing available data to those required for a special report. The problem of understanding problem finding is therefore eventually reduced to the problem of understanding the models which managers use to define differences.

It should be noted that the theoretical framework proposed here has drawn on ideas discussed by Miller, Galanter, and Pribram,[9] who in turn refer to some basic work by Newell, Shaw, and Simon.[10] Figure 1 presents a flow chart of the process described in this section and, for comparison, the structures proposed by others.

## MANAGERIAL MODELS FOR PROBLEM FINDING

### Historical Models

On the assumption that recent past experience is the best estimate of the short term future, managers maintain a wide variety of models based on the continuity of historical relationships: April sales exceed March sales

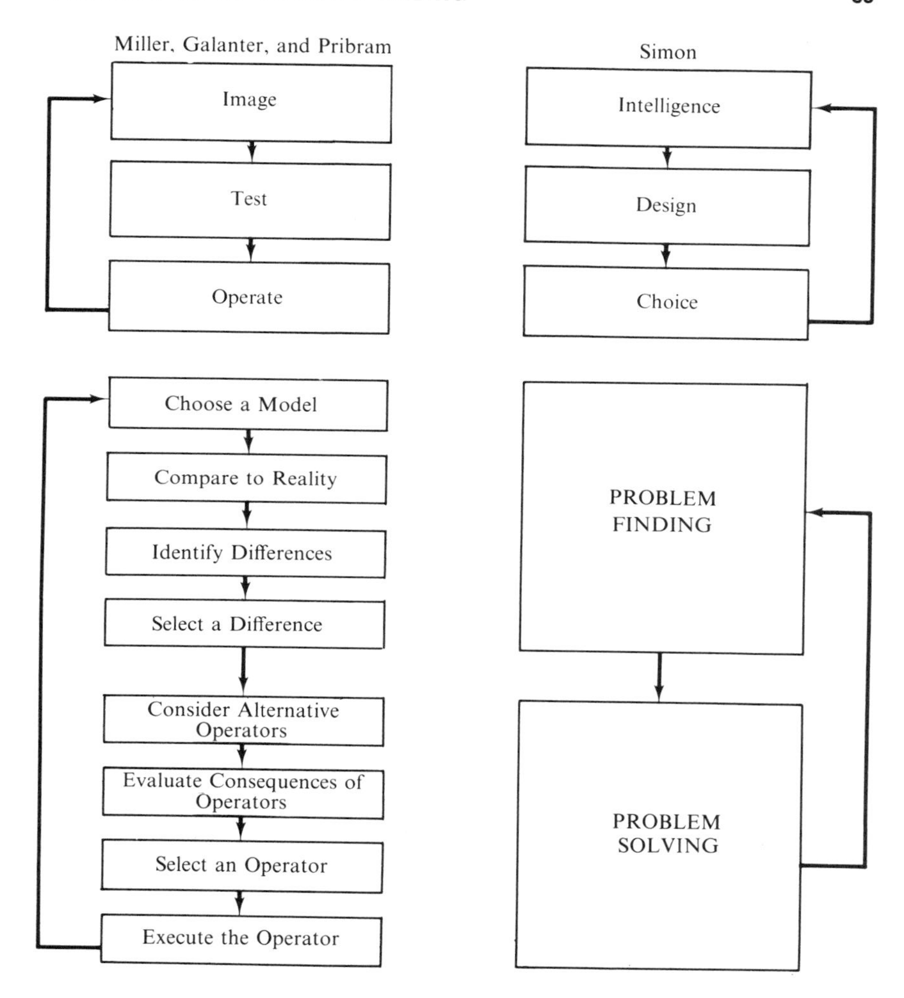


*FIGURE 1* Flow Chart of Managerial Behavior

by 10 percent; Department X runs 5 percent defective product; the cost of making item Y is $10.50 per thousand; the lead time on that raw material is three weeks, etc. Because the manager's world is complex and these models tend to be simple, discrepancies frequently arise between the models' predictions and what actually takes place. Such discrepancies are a major source of problems to which managers devote their time. Why is our inventory account drifting out of line? Why is our reject rate so high this week? What has happened to make so many deliveries late? What can be done to reverse this trend in absenteeism? Why is our safety record suddenly so good? All these problems and a host of others like them are triggered by discrepancies from historical models and can keep a manager and his organization busy all day every day.

For the most part these models are non-explicit. The manager "carries them in his head" or "just knows." In a number of cases, however, these models are strongly supported by routine reports. Pieces of paper on which are printed monthly P & L statements, weekly reports of sales totals, daily reports of orders behind schedule, semi-annual inventories, and many other items of interest flow across the manager's desk in a steady stream and, except in its historical context, each one has little meaning to the manager or anyone else.[11]

Recognizing this fact, most management reports in the Southern Company were prepared in such a way that current figures and recent reports of the same variables appeared side by side. Trends or sharp variations in any variable could be easily noted. The confidence placed in such analysis was clearly indicated by the fact that a large number of variables were added to routine reports following an unanticipated fluctuation in corporate profits. After several months, managers could review their history of "Return on Sales," "Return on Investment," and many other variables in addition to those previously reported.

The importance of routine reports as well as the use of an historical model to identify a problem were both illustrated when the rejection rate of one department moved past an historic high and thereby attracted attention to the Quality Assurance organization. A number of other examples could be cited. Out of 52 managers, 42 agreed with the statement that "most improvements come from correcting unsatisfactory situations," and, for the most part, unsatisfactory situations were defined by departures from historically established models of performance.

Departures of performance in a favorable direction—lower than historical cost or higher than historical sales, for example—were used to modify the historical model, not to define a problem *per se*. Several managers reported that better-than-average performance was frequently used as evidence of what could be accomplished when reduced cost allowances or increased profit expectations were being discussed. At the time of this study, the Southern Company was doing very well relative to its own past performance and a number of managers shared the sentiments of the one who reported, "This year is going too well." They were clearly concerned about their ability to continue to meet what would become a new historical standard. Several were already working on that problem-to-be.

Besides serving as triggers for corrective and innovative problem solving, historical models are used extensively in the process of devising plans for future operations. These plans are in turn converted into budget objectives, and the budget objectives can sometimes serve as models which trigger managerial problem solving. Because of the complex process by which they are devised, managerial planning models will be discussed separately from the more straightforward historical ones.

### Planning Models

Managers in the Southern Company devoted substantial amounts of time to planning future operations. Detailed projections of operating variables for the coming year and less detailed projections for the coming five years were presented annually to corporate officers by each product department manager. When approved, perhaps after some modifications, these projections were used periodically to evaluate managerial performance, and for other purposes as well.

In view of the importance attributed to planning by the Southern Company, it might be expected that planning models would constitute an important part of the problem finding process. In fact they did not. Historical models were more influential on managerial behavior than planning models. To understand why, it is necessary to examine both the function of planning models and the process by which they were devised.

Among other things, plans are organizationally defined limits of managerial independence. So long as the manager is able to perform at least as well as his plan requires, he expects, and is normally granted, the right to define his problems as he sees fit. That is to say, as long as meeting his plan does not itself constitute a problem, the manager can use other criteria for defining his problems. If, however, he is unable to perfom as well as he planned, he can expect to attract the attention of higher levels of management and to receive substantial assistance in problem identification. In other words, he will lose, perhaps only temporarily, the right to manage. One product manager put the matter this way: "The best way to remain in charge is to be successful." Other managers strongly supported this position. Success was defined relative to the predictions of the planning model.

In view of the fact that unfavorable deviations in performance were far more undesirable to managers than favorable deviations, it is not surprising that planning models were not simple descriptions of what the managers expected would happen. On the contrary, planning models represented the minimum performance the manager could reasonably expect if several of his plans failed or were based on the minimum organizational expectations of managerial performance, whichever was higher. Planning models were in general very conservatively biased historical models. For the most part these biases in plans were not injected surreptitiously. After approving a manager's plan, upper level managers always inquired about how he would deal with various contingencies. At this point the manager would reveal some but usually not all of his "hedges" against uncertainty.

If he could report a number of conservative estimates and contingent plans to back up the plan being proposed, this was viewed as highly desirable.

In aggregating departmental plans, further "adjustments" were made which led the plan to depart from expectations. In some cases, these adjustments shifted expected profits from one department to another to "make the package look OK." In other cases, already conservative departmental estimates were "rounded down" to cover contingencies further. Some of these adjustments were made explicit at higher levels.

Even with all its conservative biases, the Division's plan still exceeded the Corporation's minimum profit and volume expectations. It is not surprising, therefore, that the planning model was a far less important source of management problems that historical models. Extrapolations of past performance simply implied much higher levels of performance than the planning model called for. Only in those cases (not observed) where the corporate expectations required improvements over historical trends would one expect planning models to be important in the process of problem finding.

## Other People's Models

Some models which define problems for the manager are maintained by other people. A customer whose model of product quality is violated by the product he receives may notify the manager of the producing organization of this fact and thereby define a problem for him. A higher level manager may lack information to complete an analysis and this discrepancy can define a problem for a lower level manager. An employee may need a decision on vacation policy and his request will define a problem for his supervisor. A basic function of an organization structure is to channel problems which are identified by its various members to individuals especially qualified to solve them. Managers as well as other members of the organization do not always work on problems defined by their own models.

In the Southern Company, invitations to attend meetings, requests to prepare reports, and requests for projects of various kinds whether made by superiors, subordinates, or peers were rarely questioned by managers as appropriate ways to spend their time. While it was sometimes easy to get vehement testimony as to the uselessness of many of these activities, the behavior of managers clearly indicated the strong influence of other people's models. One reason for the influence of these models may be the cost to the manager of doubting them. Any attempt to validate each request made on him could easily imply a heavier workload on the manager than the simple execution of the work requested. In addition, by providing "good service" the manager builds (or at least many managers believe they build) a store of goodwill among other managers toward his own requests.

During the course of the company study, several clear examples of the influence of these models were observed. In a series of interviews, managers were asked to specify the problems currently faced by them and their organizations. Most of them mentioned from five to eight problems. Later in the same interview, each manager was asked to describe in broad terms his own activities for the previous week. In reviewing the data from these interviews as they were collected, it was noted that no manager had reported any activity which could be directly associated with the problems he had described.

In order to be sure that this result was not due to some semantic problem, this point was discussed with several managers—in some cases during the first interview with them and in other cases as a follow-up question. One manager found the point both accurate and amusing. He smiled as he replied, "That's right. I don't have time to work on *my* problems—I'm too busy." Another manager took a different tack in agreeing with the general conclusion. He replied rather confidentially, "I don't really make decisions. I just work here." In further discussion with a number of managers, the power of other people's models was repeatedly indicated. The influence of these models was also noted in the case of a rather involved project which was observed in some detail.

The Plant Engineering Department, using a quite different model, decided to look at the desirability of revising the management of the company's 21 fork trucks. Besides scheduling and other operating questions which were investigated by people within the Engineering Department, studies of the contract under which the trucks were leased and an economic evaluation of leasing versus buying trucks were also felt to be required. The Manager of Plant Engineering called representatives of the Comptroller's organization and the Legal Department to a meeting in which the project was discussed in some detail. This discussion clearly indicated that the project was risky both from the point of view of economic payoff and political considerations. The representatives accepted their tasks, however, and in due course their studies were completed. In neither case did the studies take much time, but the assumption that it was the job of the Accounting Department and the Legal Department to serve the Plant Engineering Department was clear. A problem found by someone in the organization carries with it substantial influence over the problems on which other parts of the organization will work.

Even clearer evidence of the power of other people's models was the time devoted by all the managers in the Southern Company to the preparation of reports "required" by higher management. These reports ranged in their demands on managerial time from a few minutes in the case of a request for routine information to several man months of work on the preparation of a plan for the coming year's operations. In reply to the question, "If you were responsible for the whole company's operations would you require more, the same, or less planning?" four managers responded that they would require more planning, 32 said the same amount of planning, and 16 replied less. For many managers the expectations of the organization were consistent with their own ideas of the time required for effective planning. For a number of others, however, the influence of other people was clear.

In discussing these models as a source of problems, it is difficult to avoid a negative connotation due to the widely held ethic which values individual problem definition. Two points are worth emphasizing. First, the study was conducted to find out how managers do define their problems—not how they should do so—although that, of course, may be a long-term objective of this work. Second, both the organization and the individuals described here would, by almost any standards, be judged to be highly successful and this fact should be included in any attempt to evaluate their behavior.

Because historical, planning, and other people's models require almost no generalization to make them relevant to particular events of interest to the manager, and because these three types of models can easily generate more problems than the manager can reasonably hope to deal with, it is not surprising, perhaps, that models requiring somewhat more generalization are less important elements of the process of problem finding. It is true, however, that on occasion managers draw on experiences other than their own to define problems for themselves and their organizations.

## EXTRA-ORGANIZATIONAL MODELS

Trade journals which report new practices and their effects in other organizations can sometimes define useful areas for managerial analysis. Customers frequently serve the same function by reporting the accomplishments of competitors in the area of price, service, and/or product quality. General Motors is known for its practice of ranking the performance measures of a number of plants producing the same or similar products and making this information available to the managers of these facilities. The implication is strong in these comparisons that problems exist in plants where performance is poor relative to other plants.

In using all such extra-organizational models to define intra-organizational problems, the manager must resolve the difficult question of model validity. "Is the fact that our West Coast plant has lower maintenance costs relevant to our operations? After all, they have newer equipment." "Is the fact that our competitor is lowering its price relevant to our pricing policy? After all, our quality is better." There are enough attributes in any industrial situation to make it unlikely indeed that any extra-organizational model will fit the manager's situation perfectly. Judgments on the question of model validity must frequently be made by operating managers.

In the Southern Company one clear case was observed where two extra-organizational models were employed in an attempt to define a problem. A member of the Plant Engineering Department attended a meeting of an engineering society at which a technique called "work sampling" was discussed in the context of several successful applications in other plants. This model of a current engineering practice, which had not been employed by his department, led this man to consider the problem of finding an application for work sampling in the Southern Company. Clearly if this technique could be successfully applied, it would reduce the difference between his department and his extra-organizational model. A few days later this engineer noticed an idle, unattended fork truck in one of the manufacturing shops and he immediately thought that an analysis of fork truck operations might be the application he was looking for. He discussed this idea with his supervisors and they agreed that the project should be undertaken.

Because of the lack of direct responsibility for fork trucks, Plant Engineering was aware from the beginning of the project that its primary task would be to convince the product departments that their fork trucks indeed constituted a problem. To provide the department managers with evidence on this point, in addition to the internal work sampling study, a survey of fork truck operations was made in six nearby plants engaged in similar manufacturing operations. The explicit purpose of the survey was to define a basis (an extra-organizational model) on which internal fork truck operations could be evaluated.

The six company survey yielded in part the following results:

1. The number of trucks operated ranged from six to 50, with an average of 21—same as Southern Company;

2. Utilization ranged from 50 percent to 71 percent, with an average of 63 percent—18.5 percent higher than Southern Company;

3. Responsibility for trucks was centralized in all six companies—contrary to Southern Company;

4. Trucks were controlled through dispatching or scheduling in five of the six companies (some used radio control)—contrary to Southern Company;

5. All companies owned rather than leased their trucks—contrary to Southern Company;

6. All companies performed their own maintenance of their trucks—contrary to Southern Company;

7. Three companies licensed their drivers, and assigned them full time to driving—contrary to Southern Company.

The fact that the surveyed companies on the average operated the same number of trucks as the Southern Company was clearly cited as evidence supporting the validity of this extra-organizational model.

Because the six company survey and the work sampling study had defined the problem in aggregate terms, the analysis and recommendations proceeded at this level. The Plant Engineering Department decided to make their recommendation on the basis of an overall utilization of 60 percent (the average utilization found in the six company survey) which implied a reduction of five trucks. They then looked at their work sampling data and re-allocated trucks among departments to bring individual truck utilization figures as close to 60 percent as possible. The recommended re-allocation in fact supplied a saving of five trucks. The recommendation went on to suggest that Product Departments "compensate [for this reduction in trucks] by establishing sharing arrangements between departments."

The recommendation also proposed "permanent [full time] licensed drivers" instead of production workers operating the trucks on an *ad hoc* basis as part of their regular duties. As a result of a study which had indicated that leasing was preferable to buying the fork trucks, no change in ownership or maintenance was proposed. The annual savings anticipated from the recommended changes amounted to $7,250.

It is interesting to note that the recommendations themselves constituted problems for the Product Department Managers. The task of "establishing sharing arrangements among departments" had not been resolved by the study and remained a thorny problem. The task of transferring qualified production workers to full-time truck driving duties involved not only complex problems of morale and labor relations but also economic tradeoffs not evaluated by the study. The task of redefining departmental work procedures to relate to centrally controlled truck services was similarly unresolved. In return for these problems, the seven product department managers could expect to share in an annual saving of $7,250. Their response to the recommendation was less than enthusiastic. They agreed, after some bargaining, to return one truck to the leasing company but were not willing to pursue the matter any further.

Despite this rather negative conclusion, it is interesting to note that most managers considered the fork truck study a success. The validity of using the extra-organizational model derived from the survey as a means of defining the problem was never questioned and an evaluation of the existing policy on this basis was considered well-justified.

A more complicated use of extra-organizational models occurred in the case of several managers who had had personal experience in other organizations. In several situations they used this experience to define intra-organizational problems by emphasizing the personal element of this experience as evidence of its validity and by de-emphasizing (or not mentioning) where this experience was gained.

Extra-organizational models have a natural disadvantage as sources of problems because of the question of model validity which can always be raised against them. When extra-organizational experience agrees with local experience (historical model), it is seen as valid, but since it agrees with the local experience, it defines no problem. When extra-organizational experience disagrees with local experience and might therefore define a problem, the discrepancy itself raises the question of model validity. This attribute of extra-organizational models may serve to explain the fact that they were a relatively weak source of management problems in the Southern Company. Out of 52 managers, 47 agreed with the statement: "Most of our new ideas are generated within the company."

In the case of new organizations, of course, historical models are not available and extra-organizational models become more influential. One such situation was observed in the Southern Company. A promising new product was moving from the latter stages of development into the early stages of production and sales. A new product department was formed on an informal basis and the standard procedures of accounting data collection and reporting were instituted. No one expected the new department to be profitable immediately but after some months an executive at the product group level used a model not based on the history of the new department but one based on the performance of other departments to define a problem. He described the process this way:

> The numbers [on the monthly reports] were horrifying. I asked for a report and I got fuzzy answers that I didn't believe so I said, "Fellows, I'm taking over the right to ask questions."
>
> In asking questions I found I could pick holes in their analysis of the situation. Everything was loose.
>
> I analyzed their orders and found that with their overhead they couldn't make money.
>
> The department was reorganized.

In new organizations, extra-organizational models can be powerful sources of management problems.

## SOME NORMATIVE QUESTIONS

The principal objective of this study was to find a relatively simple theoretical structure to explain the process of problem finding used by the managers at the Southern Company, and the set of four models just described represents that structure. These models, which range from ones maintained by other members of the organization, through simple historical and planning models, to those which apply the experience of other organizations to local situations, have been tested against the rather massive sample of data collected at the Southern Company and have been found sufficient to explain all these observations. That is to say, it is possible to trace all the observed behavior back to differences defined by one of these four classes of models. To this extent the study was successful.

But observations like these, even after abstraction into a theoretical structure, are only observations. They do not suggest the consequences of using other kinds of models or using these same models with different frequencies. They do not suggest how managers might behave more effectively than they do. Isolated observations cannot define differences. Observations must be compared to a model before normative questions can be answered.

One way to generate such comparisons would be to conduct comparative studies within and among a number of organizations. One could then answer such questions as: "Are these same models used by unsuccessful managers? If so, how can the difference in performance be explained? If not, what models are used? Do managers in other organizations use these models with different frequencies or under different circumstances? Are there systematic differences in the use of these models at different levels of the organization?" All such questions could be answered by careful study of several organizations or several levels of the same organization and these extra-organizational models might serve to suggest management improvements. Until such studies are completed, however, the only models which can be used to evaluate the behavior observed in the Southern Company are some which were not used there.

## Scientific Models

When compared to models used in the physical and social sciences for quite similar purposes, the models used by the managers in the Southern Company (and elsewhere) are almost startling in their naivete. In the same company, electrical engineers explicitly used quite complex theoretical models to help them define problems associated with the design of a relatively simple electronic control system. Similarly, mechanical engineers employed a variety of quite general theories in the design of new high speed production equipment. In neither of these cases did the engineers base their predictions on their own experience except in a very general sense. They quite confidently applied theories derived from the observations of others and the equipment which resulted from their work required relatively little redesign after construction. Managers, on the other hand, based their expectations on relatively small samples of their own experience. Their rather simple theories, as has already been noted, yielded rather poor predictions, and managers therefore spent a substantial amount of time solving either their own problems or those defined by others.

The behavior of scientists (an extra-organizational model) suggests that there is an alternative to this rather frantic approach to a complex world. When discrepancies arise between a model and the environment, one can undertake to improve the model rather than change the environment. In fact, a scientist might even go so far as to suggest that, until one has a fairly reliable model of the environment, it is not only foolish but perhaps even dangerous to take action when its effect cannot be predicted.

If carried to an extreme, of course, the scientist's tendency to search for better models of the world as it is would leave no time for taking action to change it, and it seems unlikely that this allocation of time and talent would be an appropriate one for the operating manager. In the Southern Company, it must be remembered, those managers who based their actions on very simple models which took very little time to construct were judged to be quite successful by their organization.

On the other hand, the increasing use by managers of more sophisticated modeling techniques like those mentioned earlier in this paper may suggest that the balance between model building and action taking is shifting. A number of companies now base changes in distribution systems, production and inventory control systems, quality control systems, advertising allocation systems, etc., on the predictions of relatively complex models which are based on substantial bodies of theory and empirical evidence. To the extent that these models fail to describe events which take place, they, like the simpler models they replace, can serve to define problems. To the extent that these more complete models take into account events which the manager cannot, or prefers not to, control, these models can serve to protect the manager from problems on which he might otherwise waste his energy.

While it may be true that these more explicit scientific models will gradually replace simple intuitive models, several reasons suggest that the change will take some time. First, many operating managers today find the language of the new techniques foreign, despite increasing attempts to change this situation through training. Second, the new techniques often involve even more generalization than extra-organizational models, and honest questions of model validity will tend to delay their widespread use. And third, the process of problem finding currently used will perpetuate itself simply by keeping managers so busy that they will find little time to learn about and try these new methods of problem finding.

More important than any of these reasons, however, may be one which, curiously, has been created by the advocates of management science. In most, if not all, of the literature describing them, model building techniques are described as means for solving management problems. In their now classical book on operations research, Churchman, Ackoff, and Arnoff, for example, suggest model building as a step which should follow "formulating the problem."[12] The process by which the problem should be formulated, however, is left totally unspecified—and this is where managers as well as students of management frequently report their greatest difficulty. They can see the process by which these techniques can solve problems but they cannot see how to define the problems.

The theory which has been proposed here suggests that problem definition cannot precede model construction. It is impossible to know, for example, that a cost is too high unless one has some basis (a model) which suggests it might be lower. This basis might be one's own experience, the experience of a competitor, or the output of a scientific model. Similarly, one cannot be sure that his distribution costs will be reduced by linear programming until a model is constructed and solved which suggests that rescheduling will lower costs. The imperfections of an inventory system are revealed only by comparing it to some theoretical model; they cannot be defined until after the model has been built. The logical inconsistency which suggests that problems must be clearly defined in order to justify model construction is very likely an important reason that scientific models will only slowly be recognized by operating managers as important aids in the definition of their problems.

Despite their current disadvantages, the so-called new techniques of model building are, as has already been noted, making significant contributions to management effectiveness. They represent, therefore, not only a means for evaluating current managerial behavior but also a new class of models which can be used by managers to define their problems.

## THE PROBLEM OF MODEL SELECTION

The study of managers in the Southern Company indicates that concepts like image and intelligence which have been proposed to explain the process of problem finding can be made somewhat more operational. A rather small set of model classes has been defined which constitutes sufficient stimuli to trigger a fairly large sample of managerial behavior. This is not to say that future observations may not indicate the need for additional model classes or that future work is not required to make the process of managerial model building even more operational and testable. The study of the Southern Company represents perhaps only an encouraging start at understanding an important and little understood area of management.

Even with these initial insights, however, it is possible to see where major theoretical gaps still exist. Chief among these is the problem of model selection. As has already been noted, the requests of other people are sufficient to define a full time job for many managers. The problem of investigating and taking corrective action on discrepancies from historical trends can keep any manager busy all the time. The construction of extra-organizational and/or scientific models and the actions which they trigger are similarly time-consuming. Even after the manager has constructed the models he will use to define his problems, he must somehow select from among the differences which are simultaneously defined by these models. Personal requests, historical discrepancies, extra-organizational ideas, and the stimuli of scientific models do not in general define differences one at a time. The choice of the discrepancy to attend to next may be as important a process as the construction of the models which define them. It seems clear, however, that we must understand the process by which differences are defined before we can worry seriously about understanding the process of selecting from among them. The study in the Southern Company, therefore, largely ignored the priority problem and concentrated on difference definitions only.

It is impossible, however, to observe managers at work without getting some rough ideas about how they deal with the priority problem. Telephone calls for example are very high priority stimuli. A ringing telephone will interrupt work of virtually every kind. This priority rule is complicated sometimes by an intervening secretary but many managers pride themselves on always answering their own phone. One manager reported that he always worked on problems which would "get worse" before he worked on static problems. Thus, he dealt with a problem involving a conflict between a foreman and a troublesome employee before pressing forward on a cost reduction program.

Perhaps the most explicit priorities in the Southern Company were established by means of deadlines. Most problems defined by other members of the organization carried with them a time at which, or by which, the request should be satisfied. Certain reports were due monthly, a fixed number of working days after the end of the preceding month. Meetings were scheduled at stated times. Annual plans were required on a specified date. While a number of such requests might face a manager simultaneously, they almost never would have the same deadline and by this means the manager could decide which to do when. The fact that most problems triggered by other people's models carried deadlines may explain why these problems seemed to be given so much attention. When asked to indicate "Which problems do you usually get to first, time deadline, big payoff or personal interest?" 43 out of 52 managers indicated time deadline.

From a theoretical point of view, one could consider the flow of problems through an organization as analogous to the flow of jobs through a job shop and perhaps apply some of the theories which have been developed there to understand and perhaps prescribe the process of priority assignment. Managers, for example, must trade off relative lateness of their tasks with the duration of the tasks just as a foreman loading machines in a machine shop. Once the problem of problem definition is well understood it would appear that some theory is already available to structure the process of assigning problem priorities. The array of models used by and available to managers suggests that an understanding of the process by which problems are defined will not constitute a complete theory of problem finding. A process which assigns priorities to a set of simultaneously defined problems remains to be specified.

## REFERENCE LIST

1. A. Newell, J. C. Shaw, and H. A. Simon, "Empirical Explorations of the Logic Theory Machine," *Proceedings of the Western Joint Computer Conference* (February, 1957), pp. 218–30.

2. H. L. Gelernter, "Realization of a Geometry Theorem Proving Machine," *UNESCO Conference on Information Processing Proceedings* (1959).

3. A. Newell, J. C. Shaw, and H. A. Simon, "Chess-Playing Programs and the Problem of Complexity," *IBM Journal of Research and Development* (October, 1958), pp. 320–35.

4. A. L. Samuel, "Some Studies in Machine Learning, Using the Game of Checkers," *IBM Journal of Research and Development,* Vol. 3, no. 3 (July, 1959), pp. 210–30.

5. F. M. Tonge, *A Heuristic Program for Assembly-Line Balancing* (Englewood Cliffs, N.J.: Prentice-Hall, 1962).

6. G. P. Clarkson, *Portfolio Selection: A Simulation of Trust Investment* (Englewood Cliffs, N.J.: Prentice-Hall, 1962).

7. H. A. Simon, *The New Science of Management Decision* (New York: Harper and Brothers, 1960).

8. Because this paper is concerned primarily with problem finding, the process of operator selection and execution will not be discussed. The definitions are included only to complete the description of the theoretical structure.

9. G. A. Miller, E. Galanter, and K. H. Pribram, *Plans and the Structure of Behavior* (New York: Henry Holt & Co., 1960).

10. A. Newell, J. C. Shaw, and H. A. Simon, "Report on a General Problem-Solving Program," *Proceedings of the ICIP* (June, 1960). Reprinted in:

*Computers and Automation* (July, 1960), as "A General Problem-Solving Program for a Computer."

11. Budgets, which can also provide context for such data, are discussed in the next section.

12. C. W. Churchman, R. L. Ackoff, and E. L. Arnoff, *Introduction to Operations Research* (New York: John Wiley & Sons, 1957).

## DISCUSSION QUESTIONS

1. According to Professor Thompson, there are three kinds of business planning. What are they?
2. What is meant by the term organizational "boundary"? How do organizational boundaries affect the managerial planning process?
3. What is the difference between short-range and long-range planning? Where is the planning "breakeven point" beyond which further planning efforts are unwarranted?
4. Why is the process of "problem finding" so important? Which is more difficult, problem finding or problem solving?
5. Discuss and compare some of the various managerial models used in the process of problem finding.
6. What normative questions or qualitative considerations affect the process of problem finding?

# Chapter 4. Organizing

*Andre L. Delbecq*

# HOW INFORMAL ORGANIZATION EVOLVES: INTERPERSONAL CHOICE AND SUBGROUP FORMATION

Every student of management knows that the "official" organization (the hierarchy of positions and tasks) is constantly being modified by individual and group behavior, thus affecting the decision-making process. What is often less clear is the nature of the inexorable forces contained within the formal organizational design which contribute to the development of subgroups. The purpose of this brief article is to examine the relationship between structural properties of formal organizations and the formation of informal groups. It is hoped that this study concerning the manner in which the subgroup "overlay" comes into being can be understood in social psychological terms rather than merely intuitively [1, pp. 16–32].

## FACTORS UNDERLYING INTERPERSONAL CHOICES

Attractions and repulsions occur among individual members of an organization, often under conditions of short-lived acquaintanceship. Moreover, individual sociometrically isolated choice patterns are shown in a number of studies to persist over time, and even to become more apparent [2, p. 139]. Therefore, we can talk of the configuration of such choice patterns

Used by permission of the publisher. *Business Perspectives,* vol. 4, no. 3, pp. 17–21, Spring, 1968.

as an element of informal group structure, and of such group structures as part of the informal-organization overlay which permeates formal organizational decision making [1, p. 19].

However, to understand that such interpersonal choices are a ubiquitous aspect of organizational life and that the choice pattern remains relatively stable is not sufficient. In order to relate interpersonal choice to formal organizational designs, the manager must understand the factors which underlie interpersonal choices.

A number of research studies have been devoted to this question [2, p. 127; 3], in which light the following factors appear particularly salient:

1. Proximity
2. Similarities or attractiveness in terms of
    a. work activities
    b. interest or values shared
    c. complementary personality profiles
    d. individual social characteristics (social class, status, rank, etc.)

While it is perilous to rank-order these variables in terms of importance, certain propositions appear defensible. To begin with, promixity is clearly a necessary precondition for group formation, and, thus, is the primary variable [2, p. 139; 4]. Unless physical distance is overcome in some manner, interaction is impossible; since man mediates his behavior conceptually, it is not conceivable that a truly "human" relationship between individual group members could evolve without symbolic interaction [5]. The feasibility of interaction must be assured by some form of proximity (either actual physical proximity or simulated proximity by means of modern communication methods) in order for other structural group characteristics to evolve.

Variables dealing with similarities or attractiveness manifest the following relevant considerations.

1. Individuals can and do distinguish between two dimensions, alternatively conceptualized as "affectional" choices as opposed to "instrumental" choices, [6] and "private" or person-to-person friendships [7] as opposed to "public" choices (feelings toward a person arising from the group as a whole due to the role of the individual in the group) [8].
2. The degree to which task-instrumental or social-emotional considerations pertain to individual choices differs depending on the degree of achievement desires versus affiliation desires of individuals [9].
3. Individuals (particularly in task-oriented groups) tend to make

fewer choices on the basis of personality or social characteristics than on the basis of work criteria [2, p. 139; 10].

4. Groups formed initially on the basis of personality or social characteristics (friendship) tend to be less stable [2].
5. Regardless of the basis of group formation, the stability of the groups and the continuance of the groups are secure only if shared values of interests are present or evolve [11].

It should be noted that sociologically oriented theory has not integrated clinical psychological orientations to group formation. In clinical psychological theory, it is proposed that group formation can be studied from the standpoint of drive relationships and emotional procedures within each member of a group out of which the basis of group formative processes evolves. In one school of clinical thought, it is proposed that groups often polarize around a central person. Ten different roles which the central person might play are then discussed, including such roles as the patriarchal sovereign, the central person as love object, and the central hero.

Our objective is not to elaborate on the theory underlying the propositions themselves, but rather to relate these propositions to group formation in formal organizations. We will, therefore, move directly to the issue of formalization.

## FORMAL "POSITIONS" AND INTERPERSONAL CHOICE

One does not talk about forming groups in classical management models. Rather, one forms a hierarchy of positions. Indeed, the prescriptive classical maxim is to avoid building organizations around people, and to build around positions.

At the same time "position," as a concept, has largely been taken at face value in management literature. By definition, it has been thought of as an individual occupational role encompassing certain tasks. However, the concept "position" includes technical, sociotechnical, and social dimensions, and therefore, is a relatively complex notion. A more detailed discussion of the "position" concept and its dimensions is warranted.

*Technical dimension of "position."* All the physical artifacts which are part of the work activity (dictating machines, adding machines, etc.) are included in the technical dimension. Also, a cognitive content (conceptual program) is necessary so that ways of thinking are built into the "expertise" required of the positional incumbent. This work requires certain subcultural norms and values arising out of the socialization which takes place in the training and developing of expertise. And finally, a degree of ecological separation according to process or function (departmentation) must exist.

Notice that these technical aspects of the work situation implicit in "position" already encompass several factors out of which subgroup formation is fostered: physical proximity of people engaged in similar work activities; common attitudes and values arising out of technical training; and, perhaps, certain social-class similarities which arise from the entrance and training requirements for acceptance into the position.

*Sociotechnical dimension of "position."* The sociotechnical dimension refers to the fact that the total decision-making process (encompassing both problem solving and implementation) requires interaction between individuals occupying specific positions. This work-related interaction reinforces subgrouping and interpersonal choices.

*Social dimension of "position."* Finally, barring incompatible personalities, social relations grow out of contacts fostered by technical and sociotechnical dimensions of work activity. These social activities again reinforce interpersonal choice and subgroupings within the complex organization.

Perhaps a brief example will make the matter clearer. John Doe joins XYZ Corporation as a personnel management trainee. He is assigned to an office on the sixth floor within the personnel management department (proximity). He finds that most of the staff in personnel have been similarly trained in several nearby graduate schools (common training leading to shared concepts, values, and attitudes). In carrying out his early work assignments, he must converse with colleagues primarily within the department (shared work activities and sociotechnical interaction). After several months, he is asked to play golf with other members of the department, and soon the biweekly golf game is a standard recreational item (social dimension of position).

The interrelated technical, sociotechnical, and social dimensions of John Doe's formal position as a personnel trainee create all the necessary conditions for a viable group structure. This subgroup structure, in turn, results in behavior patterns and normative concepts which may or may not be congruent with organizational objectives and the official decision system. John Doe may, for instance, become over-attached to the personnel "gang," thereby tending to be overdefensive of their policy positions rather than adequately analytical. He may tend to interact too exclusively with the personnel group, thus limiting his exposure to other managers. This limited exposure mitigates the possibility of a promotion to a management position in an area related to, but outside of, the personnel department. He may tend to oversell programs initiated inside the department, and undervalue proposals originating outside the personnel department.

The relevant point here is that the type of subgroup suboptimization which has just been described should be the normal state of affairs rather than an aberration in the typical formal organization, since all the conditions for subgroup formation are present (shared activities, facilitated interactions, and common sentiments). By inserting the "positional" dimensions parenthetically into classical propositions about group formation, we see this more clearly. For example:

> The more people associate with one another under conditions of equality (positional congruency and equal organizational influence bases), the more they come to share values and norms, and the more they come to like one another [12].
>
> Interaction between persons (due to technical work requirements) leads to sentiments of liking (reinforced by shared professional norms arising out of training in a functional specialization) and this leads to new activities (social), and these, in turn, mean further interaction. . . . the more frequently persons interact with one another (ecological proximity and sociotechnical requirements), the stronger their sentiments of friendship for one another are apt to be. . . . the more frequently persons interact with one another, the more alike in some respects both their activities and sentiments become [13].

## IMPLICATIONS FOR DECISION MAKING

Organizational subgroups (cliques and informal decision networks) well-documented in research studies [14] are not, then, to be seen as solely the result of political struggles for power and influence—a Machiavellian tone that permeates much discussion on informal organization. Rather, such cleavage also grows out of seemingly innocuous processes of organizational life such as assignments to work positions and departmentation. This implies that the integration of subgroups into an organizational structure which is cohesive and possessive of congruent norms throughout all subgroups require conscious restructuring of interactions (away from the pattern of the bureaucratic model), in order to overcome fundamental propensities toward organizational cleavage [15].

At the same time, political and affective dimensions are an inextricable aspect of subgroup interaction. Thus, political and affective overtones ultimately color the decision-making processes of complex organizations. Organizations are not, therefore, monocratic structures acting as a "corporate personality" with a simple preference function based solely on econological dimensions of a rationalistic choice situation. Attempts to reify organizations as "individual-choice mechanisms" and to ignore socialization within subgroups create an organizational model reinforcing the game of organizational charades (managers pretend to be totally rational while actually pursuing subgroup goals).

## IMPLICATIONS FOR ORGANIZATIONAL DESIGN

This article's treatment of interpersonal choice points out several propositions which develop logically from, and are congruent with, revised organizational theories.

First, membership in organizational work groups should provide for "overlap" so that interaction between members of work groups from several functional areas and several hierarchical levels is facilitated. One theorist talks about this "overlap" as being developed primarily by the supervisor interacting in several groups [16]. Others argue that overlapping membership should encompass more than one member of a relatively autonomous subgroup in order to provide better representation, both from the group to the organization, and from the organization to the group [17]. The latter proposition seems sound, since representation by the supervisor alone is often dyadic, leading to all the dysfunctions of two-person interaction [18]. In either case, the issue is quite similar. Unless the boundary between the relatively autonomous subgroup is overcome through interactions with personnel from outside the group, the increasing propensity for suboptimization is inevitable. Further, this need for overlapping membership is true of subgroups formed by means other than formal departmentation. For example, if the decision making of a college dean or a corporate vice-president is largely mediated by interaction with the same set of advisers (even though the advisers are taken from several functional groups), soon the advisers will form the much criticized self-contained managerial oligarchy relatively closed to other organizational personnel.

Second, given the increasing complexity of much organizational decision making, no single expert of specialization can adequately claim total competence. Thus, mediation of decision making by specialists from several functional areas becomes necessary. However, if the mediation takes the form of power plays between specialist empires, then decision making is hardly satisfactory. Nonetheless, if specialists are generally self-contained within isolated subgroups and seldom interact outside these subgroups, this pattern of power plays is to be expected. Thus, the overlapping participation, while intermittent, cannot be so infrequent that parochialism remains intact.

Third, recent studies show quite clearly that personnel promotions are largely based on managerial acquaintance arising out of frequent socio-technical interactions, rather than based on a broad search process [19]. However, if acquaintances are largely confined to subgroup "cronies," the possibility of adequate consideration of talented personnel from outside the very proximate subgroup is unlikely.

## CONCLUSION

The organizational design which best provides for overlapping membership and which best facilitates work-relevant interaction between varied organizational positions is the task-force or project-group organizational design. Such an organizational strategy provides for overlapping group memberships of short to intermediate duration, bringing together decision-relevant groupings of specialists and administrators. Further, such groupings can be juxtaposed with departmentation for routine decision implementation. Finally, project management satisfies the need for overlapping group membership without artificially imposing the burden of "linking" groups solely on the departmental supervisors.

There are, of course, other arguments favoring the task-force organizational design [20]. The social psychology of interpersonal choices is, however, one more stream of logic supportive of the reconceptualization of organizational structure in the direction of the more organic model of the task-force or project-management design.

## REFERENCE LIST

1. For a development of the "overlay" concept where individual and group behavior is juxtaposed with formal organization pyramids, see John M. Pfiffner and Frank P. Sherwood, *Administrative Organization,* Englewood Cliffs, N.J.: Prentice-Hall, 1960.

2. A. Paul Hare, *Handbook of Small Group Research,* New York: Free Press, 1962.

3. T. M. Newcomb, "The Prediction of Interpersonal Attraction," *American Psychologist,* vol. 11, 1956, pp. 575–586.

4. Leon Festinger, Stanley Schachter, and Kurt Back, *Social Pressures in Informal Groups,* New York: Harper & Row, 1960, pp. 431–444.

5. Alfred R. Lindesmith and Anslem L. Strauss, *Social Psychology,* New York: Holt, 1956, pp. 159–197.

6. David Moment and Abraham Zaleznik, *Role Development and Interpersonal Competence,* Cambridge, Mass.: Harvard, 1963, pp. 42–45; F. Kroupl Taylor, "Quantitative Evaluation of Psychosocial Phenomena in Small Groups," *Journal of Mental Science,* vol. 97, October 1951, p. 698.

7. F. Kroupl Taylor, "The Therapeutic Factors of Group-Analytical Treatments," *Journal of Mental Science,* vol. 96, October 1950, pp. 967–997.

8. Obviously these alternative classifications are not conceptually equal. The first dimension (affectional-instrumental) refers to role played, and the second (public-private) to group situation or task content. Further, the correlation of all four choices often occurs, since there are some "great men" who have skills both "affectional" and "instrumental," and are seen as desirable members in both private and public groups. One of the methodological weaknesses in sociometric tests is the failure to make such distinctions. See Andre L. Delbecq, "The Social-Psychology of Executive Roles Re-examined," *Business Perspectives,* vol. 2, no. 3, Spring 1966.

9. J. R. P. French, "A Formal Theory of Social Power," *Psychological* Review, vol. 63, 1956, pp. 181–194.

10. C. A. Gibb, "The Sociometry of Leadership in Temporary Groups," *Sociometry,* vol. 13, 1950, pp. 226–243; Helen H. Jennings, "Sociometric Differentiation of the Psycho-group and the Socio-group," *Sociometry,* vol. 10, 1947, pp. 71–79.

11. T. M. Newcomb, "Varieties of Interpersonal Attraction," in Dorwin Cartwright and Alvin Zander, *Group Dynamics; Research and Theory,* Evanston, Ill.: Row, Peterson, 1960. See also Fritz Redl, "Group Emotion and Leadership," *Psychiatry,* vol. 5, 1942, pp. 575–584.

12. Bernard Berelson and Gary A. Steiner, *Human Behavior—An Inventory of Scientific Findings,* New York: Harcourt Brace & World, 1964.

13. George C. Homans, *The Human Group,* New York: Harcourt Brace & World, 1950.

14. See, for example, Melville Dalton, *Men Who Manage,* New York: Wiley, 1959, p. 20; Robert K. Merton, "Bureaucratic Structure and Personality," in Amitai Etzioni, *Complex Organizations,* New York: Holt, 1961, pp. 48–61.

15. Studies dealing with group size provide further evidence supporting the propensity toward organizational cleavage. In brief, such studies indicate that people cannot relate psychologically to more than seven individuals, and in general, prefer to interact with only two or three individuals. See J. James, "A Preliminary Study of the Size Determinant in Small Group Interaction," *American Sociological Review,* vol. 16, 1959, pp. 474–477. Thus, the proposition that cleavage rather than cohesiveness is the typical state of organizational affairs does not rest solely on the "Interpersonal Choice" dimension of group structure for theoretical justification.

16. Rensis Likert, *New Patterns of Management,* New York: McGraw-Hill, 1961, p. 113.

17. Robert L. Kahn, Donald N. Wolfe, Robert P. Quinn, J. Diedrick Snork, and Robert A. Rosenthal, *Organizational Stress: Studies in Role Conflict and Ambiguity,* New York: Wiley, 1964, pp. 388–392.

18. For a discussion of dyads and their dysfunctions for both representation and compromise, write to Andre L. Delbecq for "The World Within the Span of Control: Managerial Behavior in Groups of Varied Size," to be published in article form shortly.

19. Theodore M. Alfred, " 'Checkers of Choice' in Manpower Management," *Harvard Business Review,* vol. 45, no. 1, Jan./Feb. 1957, pp. 157–169.

20. John F. Mee, "Ideational Items: Matrix Organization," *Business Horizons,* Summer 1964, pp. 70–72; Fremont A. Shull, *Matrix Structure and Project Authority for Optimizing Organizational Capacity,* Business Science Monograph 1, Business Research Bureau: Southern Illinois University, Carbondale, Ill.; Warren Bennis, "Beyond Bureaucracy," *Trans-action,* Summer 1965.

*Warren G. Bennis*

# *ORGANIZATIONAL DEVELOPMENTS AND THE FATE OF THE BUREAUCRACY*

Organizations are complex, goal-seeking social units. In addition to the penultimate task of realizing goals, they must undertake two related tasks if they are to survive: (1) they must maintain the internal system and coordinate the "human side," and (2) they must adapt to and shape the external environment.

The means employed for the first task is a complicated system of social processes which somehow or other gets organizations and their participants to accommodate to their respective goals. This process of mutual compliance, where the two parties conform to and accommodate one another is called *reciprocity*. The means for the second task has to do with the way the organization transacts and exchanges with its environment; this is called *adaptability*.

The social arrangement developed to accomplish the tasks of reciprocity and adaptability in contemporary society is called bureaucracy. I use that term descriptively, not as an epithet or as a metaphor *à la Kafka's Castle* which conjures up an image of red tape, faceless masses standing in endless lines, and despair. Bureaucracy, as I use it, is a social invention, per-

---

Used by permission of the publisher. *Industrial Management Review,* vol. 8, no. 3, pp. 41–55, Spring, 1966. 

fected during the Industrial Revolution to organize and direct the activities of the firm and later (at the turn of the century) conceptualized by the great German sociologist, Max Weber.

Ironically, though Weber worked heroically to create a value-free science, the term bureaucracy has taken on such negative connotations that even dictionaries use the term in the vernacular. For example, the *Oxford Dictionary* quotes Carlyle as saying: "The Continental nuisance called 'Bureaucracy'." It also defines a bureaucrat as "One who endeavors to concentrate power in his bureau." However empirically valid these descriptions may be, bureaucracy in a more technical sense, revered in theory by sociologists and in practice by most businessmen, has become the most successful and popular device for achieving the major tasks of organization. To paraphrase Churchill's ironic remark about democracy, we can say of bureaucracy that it is the worst possible theory of organization, apart from all others that have so far been tried.

Now is the time to challenge the conceptual and empirical foundations of bureaucracy. To jump to my conclusion first, I will argue that bureaucracy which has served us so well in the past, both as an "ideal type" and a practical form of organization, will not survive as the *dominant* form of human organization in the future. Social organizations behave like other organisms: they transform themselves through selective adaptation, and new shapes, patterns, models—currently recessive—are emerging which promise basic changes. This argument is based on the assertion that the methods and social processes employed by bureaucracy to cope with its internal environment (reciprocity) and its external (adaptability) are hopelessly out of joint with contemporary realities. So within the next 25 to 50 years we will all witness and participate in the end of bureaucracy.[1]

The remainder of this paper elaborates this viewpoint. First, I shall take up the problem of linkage one: how organizations get men to comply, the problem of reciprocity. In this section I shall discuss how contemporary psychologists and students of organizational behavior attempt to resolve this issue. Then I shall discuss the second crucial linkage: adaptability, and then present current thinking about this. Finally, I shall sketch the conditions and structure for organizations of the future.

## LINKAGE ONE: THE PROBLEM OF RECIPROCITY

The problem of reciprocity, like most human problems, has a long and venerable past. The modern version of this one goes back at least 160 years and was precipitated by an historical paradox: the twin births of modern individualism and modern industrialism. The one brought about a deep concern for the constitutional guarantees of personal rights and a passionate interest in individual emotions and growth. The other brought about increased rationalization and mechanization of organized activity. By coinciding, the growth of technology and enterprise tended to subvert the newly won individual freedoms and to subordinate them to the impersonal dictates of the workplace. De Tocqueville, writing in 1835 about his American experience, managed to sum up an epoch and its controversies in a paragraph:

> When a workman is unceasingly and exclusively engaged in the fabrication of one thing, he ultimately does his work with singular dexterity; but at the same time he loses the general faculty of applying his mind to the direction of the work. He every day becomes more adroit and less industrious: so that it may be said of him that in proportion as the workman improves, the man is degraded. . . . Thus at the very time at which the science of manufacture lowers the class of workmen, it raises the class of masters. . . . The object (of managerial elite) is not to govern that population (of workers), but to use it. . . . it first impoverishes and debases the men who serve it and then abandons them to be supported by the charity of the public.[2]

So as technology and rationalization increase, man's passions and liberties are suppressed: as organization becomes more efficient, man's work becomes more demeaning and depersonalized. Thus, De Tocqueville wrote an indictment of industrialization which has not only stuck to the present times but which provided Marx and other nineteenth-century radicals with their main themes. It is also an issue which has captivated the imagination of many scholars and researchers currently interested in the human organization.

In its crudest form, the controversy is a conflict over priorities of criteria: the individual's needs, motives, goals, and growth *versus* the organization's goals and rights. And no matter how often the *Panglosses* of the right and left attempt to minimize this conflict—the former with a "What's good for General Motors is good for the workers" and the latter with "Satisfied workers are effective workers"—I am convinced that is a truly consequential dilemma.

## Enter Bureaucracy

Bureaucracy is a unique solution in that it links man's needs to organizational goals. It achieves this linkage through an influence structure based on *legal-rational* grounds instead of on the vagaries of personal power. The governed agree to obey through the rights of office and the power of reason: superiors rule because of their role incumbency and their technical (rational) competence. In short, bureaucracy is a machine of social influence which relies exclusively on reason and law. Weber once likened the bureaucratic mechanism to a judge *qua* computer:

> Bureaucracy is like a modern judge who is a vending machine into which the pleadings are inserted together with the fee and which then disgorges the judgment together with its reasons mechanically derived from the code.[3]

The bureaucratic machine model was developed as a reaction against the personal subjugation, nepotism, cruelty, emotional vicissitudes, and subjective judgments which passed for managerial practices in the early days of the Industrial Revolution. For Weber, the true hope for man lay in his ability to rationalize, calculate, to use his head, as well as his hands and heart. Roles, institutionalized and reinforced by legal tradition, rather than personalities; rationality and predictability, rather than irrationality and unanticipated consequences; impersonality, rather than close personal relations; technical competence rather than arbitrary rule or iron whims—these are the main characteristics of bureaucracy.[4]

This is bureaucracy: the pyramidal organization which dominates so much of our thinking and planning related to organizational behavior, and which mediates the organization-individual dilemma through a rational system of role constraints.

## Critiquing Bureaucracy

It does not take a great critical imagination to detect the flaws and problems in the bureaucratic model. We have all *experienced* them: bosses with less technical competence than their underlings; arbitrary and zany rules; an informal organization which subverts or replaces the formal apparatus; confusion and conflict among roles; and cruel treatment of subordinates based not on rational grounds but on quasi-legal, or worse, inhumane grounds. Unanticipated consequences abound and provide a mine of material for those comics, like Chaplin or Tati, who can capture with a smile or a shrug the absurdity of authority systems based on pseudologic and inappropriate rules.

Almost everybody else—certainly many students of organizational behavior—approaches bureaucracy with a chip on his shoulder. It has been attacked for many different reasons: for theoretical confusion and contradictions, for moral and ethical reasons, on practical grounds or for inefficiency, for methodological weaknesses, for containing too many implicit values and for containing too few. I have recently cataloged the criticisms of bureaucracy (omitting those related to its boundary maintenance, which will be taken up in the next section), and they outnumber and probably outdo the 95 theses tacked on the church door at Wittenberg in attacking another bureaucracy.[5] The criticisms can be categorized as the following:

1. Bureaucracy does not adequately allow for the personal growth and the development of mature personalities.
2. It develops conformity and "group-think."
3. It does not take into account the "informal organization" and the emergent and unanticipated problems.
4. Its systems of control and authority are hopelessly outdated.
5. It has no adequate juridical process.
6. It does not possess adequate means for resolving differences and conflicts between ranks, and most particularly, between functional groups.
7. Communication (and innovative ideas) are thwarted or distorted due to hierarchical divisions.
8. The full human resources of bureaucracy are not utilized due to mistrust, fear of reprisals, etc.
9. It cannot assimilate the influx of new technology or scientists entering the organization.
10. It modifies the personality structure such that man becomes and reflects the dull, gray, conditioned "organization man."

Weber himself came around to condemn the apparatus he helped immortalize. While he felt that bureaucracy was inescapable, he also thought it might strangle the spirit of capitalism or the entrepreneurial attitude, a theme which Schumpeter later developed. And in a debate on bureaucracy Weber once said, more in sorrow than in anger:

> It is horrible to think that the world could one day be filled with nothing but those little cogs, little men clinging to little jobs and striving towards bigger ones—a state of affairs which is to be seen once more, as in the Egyptian records, playing an ever increasing part in the spirit of our present administrative system, and especially of its offspring, the students. This passion for bureaucracy . . . is enough to drive one to despair. It is as if in politics . . . we were deliberately to become men who need "order" and nothing but order, who become nervous and cowardly if for one moment this order wavers, and helpless if they are torn away from their total incorporation in it. That the world should know no men but these: it is such an evolution that we are already caught up in, and the great question is therefore not how we can promote and hasten it, but what can we oppose to this machinery in order to keep a portion of mankind free from this parcelling-out of the soul, from this supreme mastery of the bureaucratic way of life.[6]

I think it would be fair to say that a good deal of the work on organizational behavior over the past two decades has been a footnote to the bureaucratic "back-lash" which aroused Weber's passion: saving mankind's soul "from the supreme master of bureaucracy." Very few of us have been indifferent to the fact that the bureaucratic mechanism is a social instrument in the service of repression, that it treats man's ego and social needs as a constant, or as nonexistent or as inert, that these confined and constricted needs insinuate themselves into the social processes of organizations in strange, unintended ways, that those very matters which Weber claimed escaped calculation—love, power, hate—are not only calculable and powerful in their effects, but must be reckoned with.

### Resolutions of Linkage One: The Reciprocity Dilemma

Of the three resolutions to the discrepancy between individual and organizational needs, only the last truly holds our interest now. The first resolution minimizes or denies the problem; it asserts that there is no basic conflict. The second is more interesting than this. It allows for conflict, but resolves it through an absolute capitulation on the side of the organization *or* the individual; one or the other, total victory or unconditional surrender. Essentially it is a way *out* of the conflict; for it seems to exclude ambiguity or conflict or the mutual adaption that provides chronic tension.

It might be useful to say more about the second resolution, for it is far from unpopular. Too often, it is chosen by those who view organization solely as a system of impersonal forces *or* solely as a function of individual personalities. Daniel Levinson[7] calls this split vision the "mirage and sponge" theories of organization. The former view, implied in most psychoanalytic literature and held by most romantics, asserts that all role behaviors are functions of personality or mere by-products of unconscious motivations and fantasy. The "sponge" theorists, seen most commonly in sociological circles, hold that man is infinitely plastic and will yield to or be shaped by role demands. If, for example, you view Eichmann solely as an unwitting instrument of the system, of the German bureaucracy, and see the "*banality* of evil," then the sponge theory seems to dominate. If, on the other hand, you tend to focus exclusively on Eichmann himself as evil, and as the victim of aggressive instincts, then the mirage theory seems to hold.

There are many interesting derivatives of the sponge theory. For example, Coser[8] has recently uncovered evidence which shows that "eunuchism" was characteristic of many upwardly mobile people in the early Chinese and Middle Eastern bureaucracies. Emperors could trust them and depend on their loyalty more than on the average citizen. (Originally, eunuchs were trusted servants in the large harems of the rulers, but later they were retained because of their lack of social and family ties.) And

Khrushchev, when asked if he was worried about the possibility of a Goldwater victory, replied that he wasn't particularly concerned: "High office," he said, "tends to moderate extreme positions." And, of course, the so-called "cult of personality" is an attack by Marxist theory on the mirage point of view.

Mirage theories are equally popular and undoubtedly less dull, partly because they oversimplify and partly because they tend to glamorize events through personalization. It is gossip-column analysis: Cuba went Communist because Fidel's brother Raul was jilted by a capitalistic girl. It is the Homeric prose of *Time* magazine and it tends to reinforce our narcissism more than the eunuchism of the sponge theories.

Resolutions one and two interest us only a little because they tend to conceal the predicament: the first, by pretending it doesn't exist and the second, by camouflaging it through imputing false victories. But the problem cannot be disguised or suppressed, and the "giveaway," it seems to me, is the proliferation of paired-opposite terms mutually antagonistic in nature, which flaunt the basic nature of this duality. I refer to the following: individual-organization, personality-pyramid, democratic-autocratic, participative-hierarchical, rational-natural, formal-informal, mechanic-organic, task-maintenance, rational-illogical, human relations-scientific management, external-internal, hard-soft, achievement-socialization, theory X-theory Y, concern for people-concern for production, etc.

These paired dualities—ancient relics, as it were, from a distant, Manichaean world—reflect the two distinct traditions in the study of organizational behavior: the orderly, rational, predictable, Appolonian world of human strivings. Over the past several decades, a number of students of organizations, mindful of this dilemma, have been proposing a number of interesting, theoretical, and practical resolutions which go a long way in revising, if not transforming, the very nature of the bureaucratic mechanism. Let us now sample some of those resolutions.

## TEN APPROACHES TO THE PROBLEM

By way of introduction, I should say a few words about the ten approaches I will present and how I came to choose them. First of all, they are a diverse lot, with only one trait in common: an explicit recognition of the inescapable tension between individual and organizational goals. Aside from that, they approach the problem in a variety of ways using different value systems, theoretical and research traditions, and assigning divergent priorities to the centrality of the problem. Second of all, I have not—nor could I—include all the possible solutions or suggestions that are available. I have ignored, as well, those ubiquitous and important mechanisms of socialization which operate spontaneously and naturally in human organizations, such as reward systems, identification, etc. Nor have I cited the work of personnel psychology or human engineering, both of which are concerned with reducing the discrepancy between individual and organizational goals. Strictly speaking, I have selected for inclusion a number of recent, moderately well-known ideas, associated with a particular author.

The ten approaches can be grouped under five categories:

*Exchange theories*

1. Barnard-Simon: inducement-contribution exchange
2. H. Levinson: psychological contract

*Group theories*

3. Mayo: the managerial elite
4. Likert: the key role of the primary group and "linking pins" between groups

*Value theories*

5. Argyris: interpersonal competence
6. Blake and Mouton: the managerial grid

*Structural theory*

7. Shepard: organic systems

*Situational theories*

8. McGregor: management by objective
9. Leavitt: management by task
10. Thompson and Tuden: management by decision

## Exchange Theories

1. The Barnard-Simon theory of exchange is an equilibrium model, very similar to an economic transaction, which specifies the conditions under which an organization can induce participation. On the one hand, there are inducements offered to the participants by the organization. These usually are wages, income, services. For each inducement there is a corresponding utility value. On the other hand, there are contribution utilities: these are the payments the participant makes to the organization, usually specified as work.

From this abstract generalization, predictions can be made concerning the participants' services by estimating the inducement-contributions balance. The greater the difference between inducements and contributions, the more satisfied—and the more compliant—the participant. In addition, a zero point on the utility scale can be derived which shows the point at which the individual is indifferent to leaving the organization as well as a point at which the participants' dissatisfactions cause search behavior and withdrawal from the organization.

2. The Levinson[9] model of reciprocity is also an equilibrium model, but the terms of the inducement-contribution ratio are converted into motivational units, usually of an unconscious kind. These units of exchange represent the psychological contract. According to Levinson, reciprocity is established by the participants and the organization through fulfilling the terms of the contract. The employees' contributions to the organization are energy, work, and commitment. The organization, for its part, provides a psychological anchor in times of rapid social change and a hedge against personal losses. In addition, the organization, through transference phenomena, provides the employees with defense mechanisms through social structure, an opportunity for growth and mastery, and a focal point for cathexis.

## Group Theories

3. Elton Mayo challenged the fundamental basis of a society which was organized around archaic, economic hypotheses which grew out of an eighteenth-century, purely competitive model of society. Mayo referred to these as the Rabble Hypothesis: society consists of unorganized individuals, every individual acts in a manner calculated to secure his own self-interest, and man is logical. Mayo believed that management was blinded by the economic facts of life to the importance of association and human affiliation as a motivating force. Mayo and his associates were really among the first to view industrial organization as a social system as well as an economic-technical system.

With this profound (now seemingly mundane) insight, Mayo saw the possibilities in using *cooperation* as an instrument to mediate the reciprocity dilemma. But in order to realize the norm of cooperation, a managerial elite, trained in the facts of social life, must take the responsibility. He wrote:

> The administrator of the future must be able to understand the human-social facts for what they are, unfettered by his own emotions or prejudice. He cannot achieve this ability except by careful training—a training that must include knowledge of relevant technical skills, of the systematic order of operations, and of the organization of cooperation.[10]

Thus, success of the organization was based on the manager's ability to develop the effective organization of sustained cooperation.

4. The Likert[11] theory of management also depends heavily on the importance of the cohesive, primary work group as a motivator: to this extent it resembles the Mayo orientation. Yet, there are important differences at the *strategic* level. For Mayo, a managerial elite was a necessity, while for Likert, cooperation between groups could be maintained through points of articulation which Likert refers to as "linking pins." Furthermore, in Likert's theory, decisions should be made at that point of the organizational social space where they are most relevant and where the data are available. Thus, the Likert solution entails a key role performing the linking pin solution—rather than a managerial elite—and the use of the group to mediate the reciprocity dilemma.

### Value Theories

5. Argyris starts from the position that the value system of bureaucracy itself has to be modified before individual growth and productivity can be attained.[12] He argues that bureaucratic values, which dominate organizational life, are basically impersonal values. These bureaucratic values lead to poor, shallow, and mistrustful relationships between members of the organization, or what Argyris calls, "non-authentic" relationships. These, in turn, reduce interpersonal competence, which leads to mistrust, intergroup conflict, rigidity, lowered problem-solving capacity, and eventually to a decrease in whatever criteria the organization uses to measure overall effectiveness. Managers brought up under this system of values are badly cast to play the intricate human roles now required of them. Their ineptitude and anxieties lead to systems of discord and defense which interfere with the effectiveness of the system.

Argyris' solution is to develop the interpersonal competence of the management group such that they can accept and install new values, values which permit and reinforce the expression of feeling, of experimentalism and the norms of individuality, trust, and concern.

6. Blake and Mouton[13] have developed a solution for the reciprocity dilemma which is referred to as the managerial grid. They conceptualize the organization-individual dilemma by dimensionalizing the problem along two axes. On the basis of this two-fold analytic framework, it is possible to locate eight types of managerial styles. One dimension is "concern for people" and the other dimension is "concern for production." Management, according to Blake and Mouton, has to maximize both of these concerns, rather than one or the other. They call this desired state "team management." To arrive at this state, an elaborate system of *organizational training and development* is developed which encompasses both the linking pin function and development of interpersonal competence.

## Structural Theory

7. Shepard,[14] Burns and Stalker,[15] and others have attempted to replace the mechanical structure of bureaucracy with what they call an "organic" structure. Their structural approach presents a strong reaction against the idea of organizations as *mechanisms* which, they claim, has given rise to false conceptions (such as static equilibria, frictional concepts like "resistance to change," etc.) and worse, false notions of social engineering and change such as "pushing social buttons," thinking of the organization *à la* Weber as a machine, etc. Organic systems are proposed as the natural alternative to mechanical systems. They emerge and adapt spontaneously to the needs of the internal and external systems rather than operate through programmed codes of behavior which are contained in formal role specifications of the mechanical structure. As in the Likert group theory, decisions are made at the point of greatest relevance, and roles and jobs devolve to the "natural" incumbent. Shepard claims that the bureaucratic (or mechanical) systems differ from the organic systems in the ways shown in Table 1.

*TABLE 1*

| *Mechanical systems* | *Organic systems* |
|---|---|
| Individual skills | Relationships between and within groups |
| Authority-obedience relationships | Mutual confidence and trust |
| Delegated and divided responsibility rigidly adhered to | Interdependence and shared responsibility |
| Strict division of labor and hierarchical supervision | Multigroup membership and responsibility |
| Centralized decision making | Wide sharing of control and responsibility |
| Conflict resolution through suppression, arbitration or warfare | Conflict resolution through bargaining or problem solving |

## Situational Theories

A number of resolutions have been worked out which stress situational demands as a mediating factor. Three of the most significant of these are the following.

8. Management by Objective, first noted by Drucker and further developed by McGregor,[16] attempts to link organizational goals to individual needs through the principle of "integration." It is a complicated process which entails a "working through" of the conflicts between individual

objectives and organizational goals (almost in the psychotherapeutic sense) by the manager and his subordinates. The working through depends, to some extent, on the self-control and maturity of the individuals concerned and on a norm of collaboration between superiors and subordinates. Thus, integration can be realized only if attention is kept both on the objectives of management and on the human processes which develop collaborative relationships between ranks.

9. Leavitt[17] stresses the task constraints of the organization and the development of managerial practices which are appropriate to the task. Thus, he views the organization as a differentiated set of subsystems, rather than as a unified whole, which leads to the recognition that the organization must fit the task, rather than the other way around. In this way, he seriously challenges some of the other theories proposed above by asserting that in some parts of the system, highly authoritative (sponge theory) systems of management will have to be employed which understress participative norms and which resolve the organization-individual tension in favor of the system. At the same time, other parts of the system will apparently operate with close to minimum discrepancy between organizational goals and individual needs.

In a provocative article with Whisler,[18] Leavitt suggests, keeping an eye on the computerized organizations of the future, that organizations will resemble not the pyramid, but a football (top management) which represents a ruling group very like Coleridge's idea of clerisy, a scholarly elite (trained in the arts of computers, mathematics, and statistics) balanced on the point of a churchbell. "Within the football," they write, "problems of coordination, individual autonomy, and group decision making, and so should arise more intensely than ever. We expect they will be dealt with quite independently of the bell portion of the company, with distinctly different methods of remuneration, control, and communication."

Thus, management-according-to-task will lead to a number of divergent forms of organization within the overall system. In the football and the churchbell resolution, for example, we can envision an organic head and a mechanical bottom.

10. Thompson and Tuden[19] have developed a typology of organizational processes based on the types of decision issues called for. They derive four types of organizational structures which appear appropriate to a particular decision issue. Along one dimension are beliefs about causation of decision and agreement *versus* nonagreement. Table 2 shows the relationships among the fourfold classification.

From this analytic classification, Thompson and Tuden derive four *strategies:* computation, compromise, judgment, and inspiration: and four organizational *structures* appropriate to the particular strategy. Where

*TABLE 2*

| *Beliefs about causation* | *Preference about possible outcomes* | |
|---|---|---|
| | *Agreement* | *Nonagreement* |
| Agreement | Computation in bureaucratic structure | Bargaining in representative structure |
| Nonagreement | Majority judgment in collegial structure | Inspiration in "anomic" structure |

decisions are clearcut, beliefs about causation and agreement about consequences are present, the bureaucratic structure is appropriate for the strategy of computation. Where there is agreement about outcomes but disagreement about causality, then majority judgment is required. Thompson and Tuden argue that a collegial structure, typical of the university and some voluntary organization, would be appropriate. Where there is agreement about causation but disagreement about causality, then majority judgment is required. Where there is agreement about causation but disagreement about outcomes of decision, then compromise through representative government—typical of government operations—would be appropriate.[20]

### Summary

Table 3 summarizes the major resolutions presented and the strategies implied to resolve the reciprocity issue.

These ten resolutions provide a perspective on revisions to the theory of bureaucracy. Some, like the Barnard-Simon model, are conservative, basically neo-Weberian in tone. Others, like the proposals of Argyris and Shepard, call for radical alterations in the value system or structure of bureaucracy. Still others, more moderate in tone, suggest a flexible arrangement based on situational demands. In all cases, they raise serious questions about the viability and nature of the bureaucratic mechanism.

I would like to make one additional remark about these revisions before going on to the next section. In a way, all of them reflect reactions for or against certain humanistic and democratic values and the authors' desire to optimize—certainly assert—these values. The argument is based on the idea that the effectiveness of bureaucracy should be evaluated on human and economic criteria. To this extent, they represent normative resolutions

*TABLE 3* Ten major approaches to resolving the reciprocity dilemma

| *Author* | *Resolution* | *Strategy* |
| --- | --- | --- |
| 1. Barnard-Simon | Inducement-contribution | Economic incentives |
| 2. Levinson | Psychological contract | Psychological reciprocity |
| 3. Elton Mayo | Organization of cooperation | Managerial elite |
| 4. Likert | Group involvement | Linking pin and group development |
| 5. Argyris | Value change | Interpersonal competence |
| 6. Blake | Team management | Group and organization development |
| 7. Shepard | Organic structures | Group and organization development |
| 8. McGregor | Management by objective | Integration through collaboration and self-control |
| 9. Leavitt | Management by task | Task determines organizational arrangements |
| 10. Thompson and Tuden | Organization by decision | Decision determines organizational arrangements |

in that they aim to supplement a restrictive view of organizational effectiveness criteria by including not only some variant of efficiency (productivity, profit, etc.), but also human gains, such as satisfaction or personal growth. Furthermore, their revisions tend to be "inner-directed," if I can use that term in this context. That is, they tend to concentrate on the internal system and its human components rather than the external relations and problems of the environmental transactions.

The emphasis on the normative side and the accompanying inner-directedness has been off target, I believe, and ironically so. For though it appears on the surface that the case against bureaucracy has to do with its ethical-moral posture and its social fabric, the real *coup de grace* to bureaucracy has come from a totally unexpected direction, from the environment. While various proponents of "good human relations" have been fighting bureaucracy on humanistic grounds and for Christian values, bureaucracy seems most likely to founder on its inability to adapt to rapid changes in the environment.

## LINKAGE TWO: THE PROBLEM OF ADAPTABILITY

The capability of bureaucracy to succeed in its transactions and exchanges with its external environments has, until recently, gone unchallenged. For good reason: it was an ideal weapon to harness and routinize the human and mechanical energy which fueled the Industrial Revolution. It could also function in a highly competitive, fairly undifferentiated and stable environment. The pyramidal structure of bureaucracy, where power was concentrated at the top—perhaps by one person or a group that had the knowledge and resources to control the entire enterprise—seemed perfect to "run a railroad." And undoubtedly for tasks like building railroads, for the routinized tasks of the nineteenth and early twentieth centuries, bureaucracy was and is an eminently suitable social arrangement.

Now three new elements, already visible, promise to give new shape to American society and its organizational environments. They are: (1) the exponential growth of science, (2) the growth of intellectual technology, and (3) the growth of research and development activities.[21] As Barbara Ward has said recently:

> Modern industrial civilization, with its technical evolution and intellectual drive, is, as we know, the most aggressive form of civilization that mankind has even known. Its twin impact of science and industry is one that involves a total transformation of all aspects of life —not only of organization and technique but of fundamental habits of thought and social behavior. . . .[22]

Science and technology have profoundly changed the shape and texture of the organizational environment in the following ways.

*The rate of change is accelerating at an increasing rate.* As Ellis Johnson said:

> . . . in those large and complex organizations the once-reliable constants have now become "galloping variables" because of the impact of increasing complexity, trial and error must give way to an organized search for opportunities to make major shifts in the means of achieving organizational objectives.[23]

*The boundary position of the firm is changing.* As A. T. M. Wilson[24] has pointed out, the number and pattern of relations between the manager and eight areas of relevant social activity have become more active and complicated. The eight areas are: government, distributors and consumers, shareholders, competitors, raw material and power suppliers, sources of employees (particularly managers), trade unions, and groups within the firms. Over the last 25 years, the rate of transactions with these eight social institutions has increased and their importance in conducting the enterprise has grown.

*The causal texture of the environment has become turbulent.* Emery and Trist,[25] in an important paper, have conceptualized the field of forces surrounding the firm as a turbulent environment which contains the following characteristics:

> The environment is a field of forces which contains *causal* mechanisms and pose important choices for the firm.
> The field is dynamic with increasing interdependencies among and between the eight social institutions specified above.
> There is, among the institutions relating to the firm, a deepening interdependence between the economic and other facets of society. This means that economic organizations are increasingly enmeshed in legislation and public regulation.
> There is increasing reliance on research and development to achieve competitive advantage and a concomitant change gradient which is continuously felt in the environmental field.
> Finally, maximizing cooperation rather than competition between firms appears desirable because their fates may become basically positively correlated.

The upshot of all this is that the environmental texture of the firm, shaped by the growth of science and technology, has changed in just those ways which make the bureaucratic mechanism most problematical. Bureaucracy thrives under conditions of competition and certainty, where the environment is stable and above all, predictable. The texture of the environment now holds in its turbulent and emergent field of forces causal mechanisms so rapidly changing and unpredictable that it poses insuperable problems for—and implies the end of—bureaucracy.

My argument so far can be summarized quickly. The first assault on bureaucracy arose from its incapacity to resolve the tension between individual and organizational goals. A number of resolutions emerged to mediate this conflict by supplementing the ethic of productivity with the ethic of personal growth and/or satisfaction. The second and more major shock to bureaucracy is caused by the scientific and technological revolution. It is the requirement of adaptability to the environment which leads to the predicted demise of bureaucracy as we know it.

Now, some students of organization have attempted to resolve this current dilemma, though not nearly in the same number or with the same vigor as they have the reciprocity issue. It is noteworthy that those who have made the attempt, like Burns, Stalker, Shepard, Leavitt, Argyris, and Simon, have been particularly attentive to—and have derived many of their ideas from—research and development organizations or professional associations, such as hospitals, universities, and the like. For the organizations of the future will undoubtedly resemble these, and will inherit their problems and attributes.

## A FORECAST FOR ORGANIZATIONS OF THE FUTURE

A forecast falls somewhere between a prediction and a prophecy. It lacks the divine guidance of the latter and the empirical foundation of the former. But somewhere between inspiration and scientific certainty is a vision of the future of organizational life, which can be pieced together by detecting certain trends of the past and certain changes in the present that are on top of us. On this thin empirical ice, I want to set forth some of the conditions of organizational life in the next 25 to 50 years.

*The environment.* As I mentioned before the environment will be shifting and hold relative uncertainty due to the increase of research and development activities. The external environment will become increasingly differentiated, interdependent, and more salient to the firm. There will be greater interpenetration of the legal policy and economic factors, leading more and more to imperfect competition and other features of an oligopolistic and government-business controlled economy. (Telstar and similar operations, partnerships between industry and government, will become typical.) And because of the immensity and expense of the projects, there will be fewer identical units competing for the same buyers or sellers. In short, three main features of the environment will be: interdependence rather than competition, turbulent rather than steady competition, and large rather than small enterprises.

*Aggregate population characteristics.* We are living in what Peter Drucker calls the "educated society," and I think this feature is the most distinctive characteristic of our times. Within 15 years, two-thirds of our population (living in metropolitan areas) will attend college. Adult education programs, not the least of which are the management development courses of such universities as M.I.T., Harvard, and Stanford, are expanding and adding intellectual breadth. All this, of course, is not just "nice" but necessary. For Secretary of Labor Wirtz recently pointed out that computers can do the work of most high school graduates—more cheaply and effectively. Fifty years ago education used to be called non-work and intellectuals on the payroll (and many staff) were considered "overhead." Today, the survival of the firm depends, more than ever before, on the proper exploitation of brain power.

One other characteristic of the population which will aid our understanding of organizations of the future is increasing job mobility. The lowered expense and ease of transportation, coupled with the very real needs of a dynamic environment, will change drastically the idea of "owning" a job—or "roots," for that matter. Participants will be shifted and will change from job to job and employer to employer with much less fuss than we are accustomed to.

*Work-relevant values.* The increased level of education and rate of mobility will bring about certain changes in the values the population will hold regarding work. People will tend to: (1) be more rational, be intellectually committed, and rely more heavily on forms of social influence which correspond to their value system; (2) be more "other-directed," and will rely on their temporary neighbors and workmates for companionships; and (3) require more involvement, participation, and autonomy in their pattern of work.

The first value stems from the effects of education and professionalization. The second is the best empirical guess I can make based on Riesman's ideas[26] and McClelland's data[27] that as industrialization increases, other-directedness increases. My own experience also leads me to think that "having relatives" and "having relationships" are negatively correlated. So we will tend to rely more heavily than we do now on temporary social arrangements, on our immediate and constantly changing colleagues. The third prediction is based on the idea that jobs of the future will require more responsibility and discretion, and that education and need-for-autonomy are positively correlated.

*Tasks and goals of the firm.* The tasks of the firm will be more technical, complicated, and unprogrammed. They will rely far more on intellectual power and the higher cognitive processes than on muscle power. They will be far too complicated for one man to comprehend, not to say control; they will call for the collaboration of professionals in a project organization.

Similarly, goals will become more differentiated and complicated, and over-simplified clichés, like "increasing profits," and "raising productivity" will be heard less than goals having to do with adaptive-innovative-creative capabilities. For one thing (as is true in universities and laboratories today), productivity cannot easily be quantified with the number of budgets produced, articles published, or number of patents. And hospitals have long ago given up the idea of using the number of patients discharged as an index of efficiency. For another thing, meta-goals will have to be articulated and developed: that is, supra-goals which shape and provide the foundation for the goal structure. For example, one meta-goal might be the system for detecting new and changing goals of the firm, or methods for deciding priorities among goals.

Finally, there will be an increase in goal conflict, more and more divergency and contradictoriness between and among effectiveness criteria. Just as in hospitals or universities today, there is conflict between the goal of teaching and the goal of research, so there will be increased conflict among goals in organizations of the future. Part of the reason for this is implied in the fact that there will be more professionals in the organization. Professionals tend to identify as much with their professional organizations as with their employers. In fact, if universities can be used as a case in point, more and more of their income stems from outside professional sources, such as private or public foundations. Professionals tend not to make good "company men" and are divided in their loyalty between professional values and organizational demands.[28] This role conflict and ambiguity are both cause and consequence of the goal conflict.

*Organizational structure.* Given the task structure, population characteristics, and features of environmental turbulence, the social structure in organizations of the future will take on some unique characteristics. First of all, the key word will be temporary: Organizations will become adaptive, rapidly changing *temporary systems.*[29] Second, they will be organized around *problems-to-be-solved.* Third, these problems will be solved by relative groups of *strangers* who represent a diverse set of professional skills. Fourth, given the requirements of coordinating the various projects, *articulating points* or "linking pin" personnel will be necessary who can speak the diverse languages of research and who can relay and mediate between various project groups. Fifth, the groups will be conducted on *organic* rather than on mechanical lines; they will emerge and adapt to the problems, and leadership and influence will fall to those who seem most able to solve the problems rather than to programmed role expectations. People will be differentiated, not according to rank or roles, but according to skills and training.

Adaptive, temporary systems of diverse specialists solving problems, coordinating organically *via* articulating points will gradually replace the theory and practice of bureaucracy. Though no catchy phrase comes to mind, it might be called an *organic-adaptive* structure.

(An as aside: what will happen to the rest of society, to the manual laborers, to the poorly educated, to those who desire to work in conditions of dependency, and so forth? Many such jobs will disappear; automatic jobs will be automated. However, there will be a corresponding growth in the service-type of occupation, such as organizations like the Peace Corps and AID. There will also be jobs, now being seeded, to aid in the enormous challenge of coordinating activities between groups and organizations. For certainly, consortia of various kinds are growing in number and scope and they will require careful attention. In times of change, where there is a wide discrepancy between cultures and generations, an increase in industrialization, and especially urbanization, society becomes the client for skills in human resources. Let us hypothesize that approximately 40 percent of the population would be involved in jobs of this nature, 40 percent in technological jobs, making an organic-adaptive majority with, say, a 20 percent bureaucratic minority.)

*Motivation in organic-adaptive structures.* The way organizations tie people into their systems so that they become effective units is the motivational basis of organizational behavior and its most pressing problem.[30] In fact, the first part of this paper on reciprocity explains how the theory and practice of bureaucracy fail to solve this problem. In the organic-adaptive structure, the reciprocity problem will be eased somewhat because individual and organizational goals should coincide more. This is made possible because organizations will provide more meaningful and satisfactory tasks. In short, the motivational problem will rely heavily on the satisfaction intrinsic to the task and to the participants' identification with his profession.

Of course, professional identification and high task-involvement bring in a cargo of problems just as they ameliorate the reciprocity issue. Professionals are notoriously "disloyal" and tend to split their loyalty between professional values and organizational demands. For example, during the Oppenheimer hearings, Boris Pash of the F.B.I. reported:

> . . . It is believed that the only undivided loyalty that he (Oppenheimer) can give is to science and it is strongly felt that if in his position the Soviet government could offer more for the advancement of scientific cause, he would select that government as the one to which he would express his loyalty.[31]

There is another consequence which I find inescapable but which many will deplore. There will be a reduced commitment to work groups. These groups, as I have already mentioned, will be transient and changing. While skills in human interaction will become more important due to the necessity of collaboration in complex tasks, there will be a concomitant reduction in group cohesiveness. I would predict that in the organic-adaptive system people will have to learn to develop quick and intense relationships on the job, and learn how to endure their loss.

In general, I do not agree with the Kerr *et al.*[32] emphasis on the "New Bohemianism" whereby leisure—not work—becomes the emotional-creative sphere of life, or with Leavitt and Whisler[33] who hold similar views. They assume a technological slowdown and levelling off, and a stabilizing of social mobility. This may be the society of the future, but long before then we will have the challenge of creating that push-button society and a corresponding need for service-type organizations of the organic-adaptive structure.

Jobs in the next century should become *more,* rather than less, involving; man is a problem-solving animal and the tasks of the future guarantee a full agenda of problems. In addition, the adaptive process itself may become captivating to many.

At the same time, I think the future I describe is far from a Utopian or necessarily a "happy" one. Coping with rapid change, living in temporary systems, setting up (in quick-step time) meaningful relations—then breaking them all augur strains and tensions. Learning how to live with ambiguity and to be self-directing will be the task of education and the goal of maturity.

## STRUCTURES OF FREEDOM

I should mention now one last consequence of the new adaptive-organic structure which has a profound interaction with the reciprocity issue which concerned us earlier. In these new organizations, participants will be called on to utilize their minds and imaginations more than any society previously has allowed. New standards will be sought for the development of creative and imaginative cognitive processes. In other words, fantasy and imagination will be legitimized in ways that today seem strange. And if we think of our social structures as instruments of repression with the necessity of repression and suffering derived from it, as Marcuse[34] says, varying with the maturity of the civilization, then perhaps we are approaching an age where organizations can sanction the play and freedom which imagination and thought involve. The need for instinctual renunciation decreases as man achieves rational mastery over nature. In short, organizations of the future will require fewer restrictions and repressive techniques because of the legitimization of play and fantasy, accelerated through the rise of science and intellectual achievements.

Not only will the problem of adaptability be overcome through the organic-adaptive structure, but the problem we started with, reciprocity, will be resolved. Bureaucracy, with its "surplus repression," was a monumental discovery for harnessing muscle power *via* guilt and instinctual renunciation. In today's world, it is a prosthetic device, no longer useful. For we now require organic-adaptive systems as structures of freedom to permit the expression of play and imagination and to exploit the new pleasure of work.

## NOTES

1. The number of years necessary for this transition, of course, is an estimate based on forecasts for the prospects of industrialization. Sociological evolutionists are substantially agreed that within a 25 to 75 year period, most of the people in the world will be living in industrialized societies. But generally speaking, I am talking about the so-called advanced, not the under-, semi-, or partially advanced countries.

2. [6] (Numbers correspond to the reference list which follows.) chapters 17–18.

3. [5], p. 421.

4. For the sake of brevity, I simplify Weber's thinking more than I should. Within the year, a commemorative Weberian conference was held at his former university, Heidelberg. According to most reports, the conference ended in a mood of controversy and chaos caused by a disagreement in intrepreting Weber's thoughts. Certainly many students of bureaucracy (Blau, Gouldner, Etzioni, and Bendix—see References) have been attempting to clarify, order, and reconceptualize Weber's ideas. Weber, for example, never distinguished between the two types of authority he implied, the authority of office and the authority of reason. He was also easy to misinterpret. For example, his theory of bureaucracy could be viewed in a variety of ways: as an ethical system, as a series of hypotheses, as a conceptual framework, and as an anti-Utopian model: various scholars have seen his theory in at least those ways. Most contemporary students of organizations would argue that bureaucracy must be viewed as a condition which can be dimensionalized and which can be found to vary empirically from firm to firm. The six dimensions most frequently cited are: (a) A division of labor based on functional specialization; (b) A well-defined hierarchy of authority; (c) A system of rules covering the rights and duties of the incumbents; (d) Impersonality of interpersonal relations; (e) A system of procedures for dealing with work situations; and (f) Promotion and selection based on technical competence (Hall, 1963).

5. See [7].

6. [5], pp. 455–56.

7. [23].

8. [11].

9. [24].

10. [28], p. 122.

11. [25].

12. [1], [2], [3].

13. [8].

14. [33].

15. [10].

16. [30].

17. [21].

18. [22].

19. [35].

20. For analytic and empirical reasons, namely, its nonexistence in organized activities, the "anomic" structure will not be discussed here.

21. [4], p. 44.

22. [20], p. 266.

23. [17].

24. [36].

25. [12].

26. [32].

27. [29].

28. See [13].

29. See [31].

30. [19].

31. [18], p. 147.

32. [20].

33. [22].

34. [27].

## REFERENCE LIST

1. C. Argyris, *Integrating the Individual and the Organization,* New York: Wiley, 1964.

2. C. Argyris, *Interpersonal Competence and Organizational Effectiveness,* Homewood, Ill.: Irwin-Dorsey, 1962.

3. C. Argyris, *Personality and Organization,* New York: Harper, 1957.

4. D. Bell, "The Post-Industrial Society," *Technology and Social Change,* E. Ginzberg, ed., New York: Columbia, 1964.

5. R. Bendix, *Max Weber: An Intellectual Portrait,* New York: Doubleday, 1960.

6. R. Bendix, *Work and Authority in Industry,* New York: Wiley, 1956.

7. W. G. Bennis, "Theory and Method in Applying Behavioral Science to Planned Organizational Change." Paper presented at the International Operations Research Conference, Cambridge University, England, September 14, 1964.

8. R. R. Blake and J. S. Mouton, *The Managerial Grid,* Houston: Gulf, 1964.

9. P. M. Blau, "Critical Remarks on Weber's Theory of Authority," *The American Political Science Review,* vol. 40, 1963, pp. 305–316.

10. T. Burns and G. M. Stalker, *The Management of Innovation,* Chicago: Quadrangle, 1961.

11. L. Coser, "The Political Functions of Eunuchism," Waltham, Mass.: Brandeis, 1964.

12. F. E. Emery and E. L. Trist, "The Causal Texture of Organizational Environments." Paper read at the International Congress of Psychology, Washington, D.C., September 1963.

12a. A. Etzioni, *A Comparative Analysis of Complex Organizations,* Glencoe, Ill.: Free Press, 1961.

13. A. W. Gouldner, "Cosmopolitans and Locals: Toward an Analysis of Latent Social Roles, I," *Administrative Science Quarterly,* vol. 2, 1957, pp. 281–306.

14. A. W. Gouldner, "Organizational Analysis," *Sociology Today,* R. K. Merton, Leonard Broom, and Leonard S. Cottrell, Jr., eds., New York: Basic Books, 1959, pp. 400–428.

15. A. W. Gouldner, *Patterns of Industrial Bureaucracy,* Glencoe, Ill.: Free Press, 1954.

16. R. H. Hall, "The Concept of Bureaucracy: An Empirical Assessment," *The American Journal of Sociology,* vol. 49, 1963, p. 33.

17. E. A. Johnson, "Introduction," *Operations Research for Management,* McClosky and Trefethen, eds., p. xii. Baltimore: Johns Hopkins, 1954.

18. R. Jungk, *Brighter Than a Thousand Suns,* New York: Grove, 1958, p. 147.

19. D. Katz, "The Motivational Basis of Organizational Behavior," *Behavioral Science,* vol. 9, 1964, 131–146.

20. C. Kerr, J. T. Dunlop, F. Harbison, and C. Myers, *Industrialism and Industrial Man,* Cambridge, Mass.: Harvard, 1960.

21. H. J. Leavitt, "Unhuman Organizations," *Readings in Managerial Psychology,* H. J. Leavitt and L. Pondy, eds., Chicago: University of Chicago, 1964.

22. H. J. Leavitt and T. L. Whisler, "Management in the 1980s," in [21].

23. D. Levinson, "Role, Personality, and Social Structure in the Organizational Setting," *The Journal of Abnormal and Social Psychology,* vol. 43, 1959, 170–180.

24. H. Levinson, "Reciprocation: The Relationship Between Man and Organization." Invited address at the Division of Industrial and Business Psychology, American Psychological Association, September 3, 1963.

25. R. Likert, *New Patterns of Management,* New York: McGraw-Hill, 1961.

26. J. G. March and H. A. Simon, *Organizations,* New York: Wiley, 1958.

27. H. Marcuse, *Eros and Civilization,* Boston: Beacon, 1955.

28. E. Mayo, *The Social Problems of an Industrial Civilization,* Cambridge, Mass., Harvard, 1945.

29. D. McClelland, *The Achieving Society,* Princeton, N.J.: Van Nostrand, 1961.

30. D. McGregor, *The Human Side of Enterprise,* New York: McGraw-Hill, 1960.

31. M. B. Miles, "On Temporary Systems." *Innovation in Education,* M. B. Miles, ed., New York: Bureau of Publications, Teachers College, Columbia University, 1964, 437–490.

32. D. Riesman with N. Glazer and R. Denny, *The Lonely Crowd,* New Haven, Conn.: Yale University Press, 1950.

33. H. A. Shepard, "Changing Interpersonal and Intergroup Relationships in Organizations," *Handbook of Organization,* J. March, ed., New York: Rand McNally (in press).

34. H. A. Simon, "The Corporation: Will It Be Managed by Machines?" in [21].

35. J. D. Thompson and A. Tuden, "Strategies and Processes of Organizational Decision," *Comparative Studies in Administration,* J. D. Thompson, P. B. Hammond, R. W. Hawkes, B. H. Junker, and A. Tuden, eds., Pittsburgh: University of Pittsburgh Press, 1959, 195–216.

36. A. T. M. Wilson, "The Manager and His World," *Industrial Management Review,* Fall 1961.

## DISCUSSION QUESTIONS

1. The informal organization evolves due to interpersonal subgroup choices. What factors affect interpersonal choices within subgroups?
2. Discuss some of the "dimensions" of a formal organizational "position."
3. Explain the organizational design and decision-making implications of subgroup formation and interpersonal choice.
4. How does Bennis use the concepts of "reciprocity" and "adaptability" to analyze the concept of bureaucracy?
5. Explain some of the disadvantages of a bureaucratic organization structure.
6. Describe what Bennis says will be the new organization of the future. Do you agree or disagree with this Bennis viewpoint?

# Chapter 5. Controlling

*John Leslie Livingstone*

# *MANAGEMENT CONTROLS AND ORGANIZATIONAL PERFORMANCE*

Inevitably there are conflicts between the motives of individuals and the demands of the organization. Organization implies some subordination of individual objectives to those of the group. Processes tending to constrain idiosyncratic behavior and to promote conformity with organizational norms are "controls." This usage is very broad, as it includes *incentives* under the classification of controls. However, incentives are often linked with controls—for instance, rewards for exceeding budgeted sales quotas. Therefore, we have explicitly recognized this interdependence by regarding controls broadly as reward-punishment processes aimed at ensuring that members of the organization do work toward its goals.

Individuals in their work are likely to seek ways of fulfilling their personal needs, very possibly at the expense of formal objectives. This tendency is countered, among other things, by budgets, standards, quotas, internal audit, etc. Generically these instruments are usually referred to as "management controls." In this paper I shall examine the impact of management controls on organizational performance.

---

Used by permission of the publisher. *Personnel Administration,* vol. 28, no. 1, pp. 37–43, January-February, 1965.

## HOW DO MANAGEMENT CONTROLS CONTROL?

Management controls, in the form of standards or budgets, are simply quantified statements of management's goals. As Stedry observes, "The setting of the standard is not sufficient of itself to assure or even invite compliance. The problem of directing activity toward a goal is one of 'motivation' . . . a goal, even if externally imposed, must receive . . . internal recognition . . . to be at all effective."[1] This statement has important implications.

The setting of standards requires measurements to be made. In the environment of the organization, however, measurement takes on special characteristics. Using Drucker's example:[2] when we measure the rate of fall of a stone, we are outside the event itself. By measuring we do not change the event, and it does not change us. Therefore measuring is *neutral*. Furthermore, measurements are not likely to vary significantly with different observers—because accurate physical measuring instruments may be used and because there is little probability that different observers would have different perceptions of the event. Therefore measuring is *objective*.

Unlike physical measurement, the measurement of organizational performance is not independent of the events, the persons being evaluated and the observers. It is not neutral. It is subjective and necessarily biased. Management controls are ". . . goal-setting and value-setting . . . They endow events not only with meaning, but with value."[3]

Therefore, in asking how management controls control, we have to consider not only organizational goals and individual goals, but also the interactions between these sets of goals and the values perceived in the management control system itself. Haire gives an example of this interaction:

> Bank managers often complain that their tellers lack zeal in building customers' good will. When a customer approaches, the teller has an air of regretfully interrupting his important work to serve the customer. The customer may even be kept waiting while the teller continues to add his column of figures, concerned that the customer will throw his figures out of balance by making a transaction.[4]

Why should this sort of thing happen? Perhaps management has trained tellers to act just this way. The teller may have been rewarded in the past only for the conscientious balancing of his books, and been punished only for failing to balance. Probably he has never had reward or punishment for his handling of customers.

Because control is such an important feature of banking, bank management may have slid involuntarily into a policy they would not deliberately adopt: balancing the books is all that matters. They never decided to train tellers this way. But the silent emphasis on control has had the effect of a training policy.

The management control process has frequently been identified with servomechanisms,[5] feedback circuits,[6] feedback,[7] and feedback response.[8] This analogy is useful in stressing the importance and worth of feedback. But it is easy, with only a little stretch of the imagination, to assume that the management control system is an *efficient* servomechanism for keeping key variables "in control."

Servomechanisms, however, are sophisticated engineering systems with programmed response patterns. Due to the complex human dynamics of organizational behavior and to the ". . . deficiencies in the available methods of (financial) measurement"[9] this is not true of management control systems—as the example quoted from Haire illustrated.

## MANAGEMENT CONTROLS AND EMPLOYEES

Argyris contends that management controls tend to take away from workers their planning of the work and participation in important decisions affecting them. This loss of control tends to cause employees to feel psychological failure. People experiencing failure may reduce their aspirations much below their capability, leading to increased failure.[10]

> The data suggest that the supervisors dislike budgets of all types because (1) they tend to report only results, not reasons; (2) they emphasize the past and not the present; (3) they are rigid; (4) they apply pressure for an ever-changing goal; (5) they tend to create failure for the supervisor. . . .
>
> As a result of the pressure, tension, and general mistrust of management controls, employees tend to unite *against* management, Psychological research shows that people can stand only a certain amount of pressure and tension. . . . In short, new cohesive groups developed to *combat* management pressure.[11]
>
> . . . management diagnoses the employees to be at fault for high turnover; high absence rates; low productivity, apathy, disinterest. . . . They conclude that stronger dynamic leadership, management controls, and 'human relations' are the answers. Our analysis suggests that instead of ameliorating the basic causes, these three practices tend to reinforce the problems caused by the organization, thus increasing the very behavior these practices were supposed to decrease.[12]

Argyris has been criticized for assuming that man must be in conflict with the organization.[13] Yet most of his critics do not deny the widespread existence of this conflict—rather they ascribe much of it to social attitudes and beliefs. It would, therefore, be dangerous to conclude that management's use of controls is necessarily as deleterious to employee needs as Argyris concludes. It would, however, be no less dangerous to dismiss his conclusions lightly, for many agree with him—Robert K. Merton and C. Wright Mills, to name but two.[14]

## MANAGEMENT CONTROLS AND MANAGERS

The evaluation and compensation of managers is frequently based on production oriented accounting measurements. Successful performance, so measured, usually leads to transfers and promotion. Therefore many managers recognize that

> . . . they can get increased performance and earnings by direct, threatening pressure on their subordinates and their organization . . . such pressure is apt to lead to undesirable turnover . . . and to other forms of organizational deterioration . . . If (a manager's) experience shows that the odds are against his staying in his present job for more than two or three years, he is apt to appreciate that he will probably not be adversely affected by any of the resentments, hostilities, and turnover he creates through hierarchical pressure. . . . Ironically, these managers often achieve a reputation with their top management of being outstandingly able . . . and . . . are not only permitted to dissipate company assets but are rewarded for doing so.[15]

Likert suggests that the remedy is to make periodic approximations of employee attitudes and other human variables. Argyris, however, is very skeptical of the validity of such criteria for organizational well being. What may really be happening, despite the sanguine indices of attitudes, is that employees have simply grown apathetic, devitalized and alienated. Their aspirations fall so low that they accept mediocre performance and resist change.[16]

## INDIVIDUAL ADJUSTMENT TO MANAGEMENT CONTROLS

Research has sought to discover individual predispositions to varying patterns of control. Findings suggests that individual reactions to control patterns tend to differ according to personality. Tannenbaum reviews several studies.[17] Two of these dealt with individual employees' reactions towards a shift to less authoritarian, more participative work organization. Most employees reacted favorably. A few, however, did not—largely those whose personalities were not suited to the new type of authority relations introduced. They preferred to be submissive, dependent and directed. Workers who judged their supervisors to employ participative methods were generally higher in productivity than the remaining workers *providing* subordinates had low scores on measures of authoritarianism.

Despite the existence of different individual preferences for types of authority relations, employees generally felt they had too little control, rather than too much, in their work. They felt they did not, as a group, have as much control as they should, although they did not believe that workers should exercise more control than management. In reply to the same questions, supervisory groups unanimously agreed that workers should not exercise more control than they presently did.

Tannenbaum notes that, whatever the reasons, power is desired. Power can urge the individual toward a greater and greater share of the work load of the organization. Added dimensions of his personality came into play, increasing his effort. He gives more of himself to his work, and is probably more identified, more loyal and more active on behalf of the organization.[18]

However, greater work satisfaction may also be accompanied by greater personal frustration. The responsibility for making big decisions creates strong personal identification with the success or otherwise of the results. This intense personal involvement may be gratifying, perhaps elating, but can also be extremely anxiety-producing. Tannenbaum quotes studies where clerks given increased responsibility, felt greater work satisfaction but less sense of accomplishment; and workers in a newly automated plant, with heightened responsibility and control due to automation, felt generally improved morale but found that their new work made them feel "jumpy" and tense (despite slightly reduced accident danger in the new plant). Some evidence suggests that individuals in positions of control and responsibility also tend to have an above-average incidence of psychosomatic illnesses.[19]

## CONTROL AS A ZERO-SUM GAME

If the total amount of control exercised in an organization were fixed in quantity, increments in the influence of certain individuals and groups would lead to decrements in the power of others. There is, however, strong reason for believing that the "influence pie" need not have constant dimensions. A *laissez faire* leader, exercising little control, may be indifferent to his subordinates' wishes. There is not much influence either way, and the total amount of control is relatively small.

> . . . as seen by them and as seen by the men, the managers in the high-producing departments have much more influence than do the managers in the low-producing departments. The 'influence pie' is seen

as being bigger in the high-performing departments than in the low. . . . Evidently, the manager's leadership methods and skills, including the extent to which he builds his men into a well-knit loyal group with efficient communication, as well as the capacity to *exert influence upward,* affect the amount of authority the manager really has. . . . this better management system, while giving the men more influence, also gives the high-producing managers more influence. The high-producing managers have actually increased the size of the "influence pie" by means of the leadership processes which they use.[20] (Italics added).

In Likert's terms, a more substantial "interaction-influence" system increases the total amount of control, with benefit to all members of the organization. These findings are not isolated. They are corroborated by similar studies in several different types of organization.[21] However, Likert is careful to point out that the research findings do *not* suggest that *every* organization in which there are high degrees of confidence and trust and favorable attitudes will be highly efficient. High performance goals as well as favorable attitudes are needed if an organization is to achieve high productivity.[22] Also, of course, supervisors' attitudes are critical. Unless supervisors are genuinely interested in subordinates' ideas and prepared to act on them, any pretended use of participative devices is likely to be futile.

## MANAGEMENT CONTROLS AND MANAGERS' ASPIRATIONS

Stedry has investigated interactions between self-performance aspirations, budget administration and actual achievement. His experiments showed that where subjects know that goal attainment will be rewarded and non-attainment penalized, performance is significantly affected by the way in which task aspiration levels are determined and the demand of the budget ("high," "medium," "low" or "implicit," i.e., no budget imposed).

An "implicit" budget produced the best performance, followed respectively by "medium," "high" and "low" budgets. However, there was strong interaction between budgets and aspiration levels. The "high" budget group, who received their budgets prior to setting their aspiration levels, outperformed *any* other group. The "high" budget group, who set aspirations before receiving the budget, were outperformed by *all groups.*[23] Stedry admits[24] that only a short span of time was covered by the experiment, and he suggests that further research over an extended period is desirable.

Therefore, his findings are somewhat tentative in their relation to business organizations, especially as it is unlikely that situations will frequently be encountered where the setting of aspiration levels can be delayed until budgets have been received. In a continuing organization one would expect aspiration levels to be perpetually projected out over time, with budgets being introduced at regular intervals. This assumption limits speculation to groups forming aspirations before receiving budgets. In this category, "high" budgets result in lowest performance, "medium" and "implicit" budgets together come extremely close in achieving the best performance and "low" budgets produced performance approximately midway between best and worst. Stedry points out that the group which determines its aspiration level first, in the experimental situation, is closest to the solution proposed by McGregor,[25] who suggests that the department head should plan the budget and then take it to his supervisor who will give him his budget based on his estimate.[26] This is in close accord with the suggestions of Argyris.[27]

## MANAGEMENT CONTROLS AND CONFLICT

If any theme has consistently underlain our discussion, it is that of inevitability of *conflict*—conflict between the accuracy and the imprecision of control instruments; between short-run manager rewards and long-run organizational health; between individual needs and management pressure; between workers' and supervisors' perceptions of the amount of control respectively they should have; between work satisfaction from participation and the frustrations that accompany responsibility; between managers' performance aspirations and the unilateral issue of "high" budgets by their superiors.

Are management controls inexorably linked with conflict? Argyris would have it so. He believes that conflict may be lessened by the ". . . use of job and role enlargement, employee-centered and reality-centered leadership." But:

> Much more research needs to be done . . . the behavioral scientists have little to say on this subject and even less on how one may try to create a formal organization . . . which does not rely for part of its health on a basically antagonistic sub-system.[28]

Likert, too, stresses the ubiquity of conflict. He refers to the increased use of performance measurements and budgets, with the decisions on budgets often highly centralized, and believes that these developments are accompanied by feelings of increased hierarchical pressure and growing resentment against it.[29]

Against this background of greater imposition of controls, suggestions for more employee-centered, participative management may well be perceived by some managers as appeals for anarchy. Is management to abandon its prerogatives? Are decisions to be turned over to the workers?

This does injustice to participative management.

> Democratic leadership is not an absence of leadership . . . We know from experiments and field research that *laissez-faire* leadership creates more tension and anxiety than does *either* democratic or autocratic. Subordinates are frustrated from lack of leadership which in turn frustrates their need for clarity, sense of direction and accomplishment . . .
>
> Nor are we suggesting that democratic leadership is the answer. . . . 'democratic' leadership fulfils primarily the individual's needs. But this is not all of the organization. What is also needed is leadership that tries to fulfill the demands of the organization.[30]

If there are no pat answers to the perplexing problems of control and conflict, let us see what constructive part-answers may exist.

## THE MERITS OF MEASUREMENT

Likert comments that research findings show that the relationships observed between productivity on the one hand and management principles and practices on the other hand, grow sharper as more accurate measurements of productivity are made. Productivity ratings appear to be least accurate when based only on the judgments of the superior, because the superior tends to base his judgment largely on his perception of how the supervisor manages his unit, rather than on actual output. "Superiors tend to rate favorably those supervisors whose pattern of supervision corresponds to the pattern which the superior feels should be used to obtain the best production. Thus, if a superior feels that job-centered supervision yields the best results, he will rate highest those supervisors who use this kind of supervision."[31]

Therefore, measurement plays a powerful part in reducing this perceptual miasma. Accuracy in measurement potentially leads to better decisions, based on better information, and greater motivation to implement these decisions. Likert quotes Mary Parker Follett, "My solution is to depersonalize the giving of orders, to unite all concerned in a study of the situation, to discover the *law of the situation* and obey that . . . One *person* should not give orders to another *person,* both should agree to take their orders from the situation . . . Of course we should exercise authority, but always the authority of the situation."[32] However blunt and imprecise the available measuring instruments may be, they are less personally biased than purely subjective opinions.

Under formal organization theory, all planning and central information is sent from the top of the organization downwards. Performance measurements travel upwards for evaluation. This is known as "feed-back."[33] Under the law of the situation, this flow is inadequate. Each work group should receive the measurements needed for it to see how well it is performing and to make intelligent decisions.

But however free and efficient the dissemination of information, this alone cannot result in depersonalizing its use. Controls may still be perceived as threatening if there are punitive managerial pressures for desired results. There are incentives, then, for the distortion of data that are notorious—withholding of output, spending of over-generous budget allowances for fear of future cuts, fudging favorable performance results to prevent tighter budgets in subsequent periods, and so on.

## CERTAINTY AND UNCERTAINTY

Budgets and standards tend to be deterministic. They express unequivocal performance criteria with aura of exactitude and rectitude. There is no attempt to measure the standard error of the measurements themselves. This is in sharp contrast with the risk and uncertainty characteristic of the business environment. On the other hand, it fits strikingly well with certain authoritarian personality traits:

> Tends to think in rigid dichotomies. He thinks in 'black or white' terms.
>
> Tends to be more concrete in his thinking. Ambiguity threatens him. He sticks close to the everyday details of life.[34]

Accounting estimates are commonly referred to as "measurements." It is true that these "measurements" are often the best available information. But strictly they are not measurements at all, because they do not measure their own error. For instance, it is one thing to say that there is 90% confidence that output will be between 95 and 105 units a day. It is quite another to say that there is 30% confidence that output will be between 50 and 150 units a day. In both cases the accounting "measurement" is likely to be the mean of 100 units a day—but nothing is said about the reliability of the "measurement" itself, despite the significant difference in precision between the two cases.

It is also true, of course, that expected values and dispersion cannot be measured under uncertainty. Also, few managers would expect performance to be exactly equal to the budget or standard in practice. But the spurious air of precision in performance "measurement," and its appeal for the authoritarian mind, may readily cause management controls to be perceived by subordinates as directive, pressure-oriented and subjectively arbitrary. This is remote from the "law of the situation."

## SUPPORTIVE ATMOSPHERE

If managers, in using measurements, are sensitive to the randomness of performance measurement data and, therefore, expect deviations to occur through chance as well as performance variations, perhaps their reactions to information may be less likely to lead to unilateral exercise of authority. Individuals could feel that information is used to help them, not harm them. Errors, instead of being simply *tolerated,* would be *expected.* The emphasis would be placed not so much on avoiding errors, but on quick recognition and correction. Managers willing to develop this leadership pattern should be able to do so. Whether basically authoritarian managers could—or should—be influenced in this direction is doubtful.

Measurements should be regarded as primarily for self guidance, for enabling workers to keep the processes for which they are responsible "in control"—in the statistical sense. The users of measurements should have a say in deciding what measurements should be used so that decisions can be made and implemented ". . . with cooperative motivation . . . the men are able through group processes to exercise influence on the decisions. Both managers and man, as a consequence, have more influence on what goes on, and there is greater coordinated effort and better performance."[35]

In short, the supportive and cooperative use of measurements and controls is simply an inseparable part of Likert's general "linking-pin," "interaction influence" system of organization.[36]

There are research findings sufficient to hypothesize on the nature of highly effective groups and to advance the suggestions we have made above. But, in going from theory to practice, the way is riddled with pitfalls. Some, such as different individual reactions to authority relations and the error of confusing democratic with *laissez-faire* leadership, we have mentioned. There are many others.

Also, it is not suggested that there is any "frictionless" or near-perfect organizational state. Conflicts will probably always be a *sine qua non* of organizations. Discontent is essential to progress. "Is growth and self-fulfillment possible . . . without pain and grief. . . ? If grief and pain are sometimes necessary for growth of the person, then we must learn not to protect people from them automatically as if they were always bad."[37]

The question, then, is not how to suppress conflict but rather how to use it constructively.

> Effective organizations have extraordinary capacity to handle conflict. Their success is due to three very important characteristics:

1. . . . They have an organizational structure which facilitates constructive interaction between individuals and work groups.
2. The personnel of the organization is skilled in the processes of effective interaction and mutual influence. . . .
3. There is a high confidence and trust among the members of the organization in each other, high loyalty to the work group and to the organization, and high motivation to achieve the organization's objectives. . . .[38]

These characteristics are not easily developed in an organization, although sometimes they may be present without full realization of the significance and unified philosophy they connote. Depersonalized performance measurements create forces to move toward development of these characteristics. Therefore, we conclude that the instruments of "management controls" are invaluable. But the emotional connotation and authoritarian flavor of "management controls" make the term—and the concepts it denotes—incongruent with democratic leadership.

## REFERENCE LIST

1. A. C. Stedry, *Budget Control and Cost Behavior* (Englewood Cliffs, N. J.: Prentice-Hall, 1960), p. 12.

2. P. F. Drucker, "Controls, Control and Management" (Papers from Seminar on Basic Research in Management Controls, Graduate School of Business, Stanford University, February 20, 21, and 22, 1963), p. 3.

3. *Ibid.*, p. 4.

4. M. Haire, *Psychology in Management* (New York: McGraw-Hill, 1956), pp. 16–17.

5. C. J. Haberstroh, "Goals, Programs and the Training Function" (Papers from Seminar on Basic Research in Management Controls, Graduate School of Business, Stanford University, February 20, 21 and 22, 1963).

6. L. Petrullo and B. M. Bass (editors), *Leadership and Inter-Personal Behavior* (New York: Holt, Rinehart & Winston, 1961), p. 14.

7. W. T. Jerome, *Executive Control—The Catalyst* (New York: John Wiley & Sons, 1961), p. 26.

8. G. Shillinglaw, "Division Performance Review: An Extension of Budgetary Control" (Papers from Seminar on Basic Research in Management Controls, Graduate School of Business, Stanford University, February 20, 21 and 22, 1963), p. 4.

9. *Ibid.*, p. 6.

10. C. Argyris, *Personality and Organization* (New York: Harper and Brothers, 1957), pp. 132–34.

11. *Ibid.*, p. 137.

12. *Ibid.*, p. 162.

13. J. M. Pfiffner and F. P. Sherwood, *Administrative Organization* (Englewood Cliffs, N. J.; Prentice-Hall, 1960), pp. 434–35.

14. *Ibid.*, p. 433.

15. R. Likert, *New Patterns of Management* (New York: McGraw-Hill, 1961), pp. 75–76.

16. Pfiffner and Sherwood, *op. cit.*, pp. 420–21.

17. A. S. Tannenbaum, "Control in Organizations: Individual Adjustment and Organizational Performance" (Papers from Seminar on Basic Research in Management Controls, Graduate School of Business, Stanford University, February 20, 21 and 22), pp. 6n.

18. *Ibid.*, p. 9.

19. *Ibid.*, p. 12.

20. Likert, *op. cit.*, p. 58.

21. Tannenbaum, *op. cit.*, p. 17.

22. Likert, *op. cit.*, p. 59.

23. Stedry, *op. cit.*, pp. 80–90.

24. *Ibid.*, p. 154.

25. D. McGregor, "An Uneasy Look at Performance Appraisal," *Harvard Business Review*, May-June, 1957.

26. Stedry, *op. cit.*, p. 9.

27. C. Argyris, *The Impact of Budgets on People* (New York: Controllership Foundation, Inc., 1952), p. 28.

28. Argyris, *Personality and Organization*, p. 232.

29. Likert, *op. cit.*, p. 84.

30. Argyris, *Personality and Organization*, pp. 192–93.

31. Likert, *op. cit.*, p. 13.

32. H. C. Metcalf and L. Urwick, *Dynamic Administration, The Collected Papers of Mary Parker Follett* (New York: Harper, 1940), pp. 58–59.

33. See Shillinglaw, *op. cit.*

34. Argyris, *Personality and Organization*, p. 217.

35. Likert, *op. cit.,* p. 180.

36. *Ibid.,* Chapters 8, 11, and 12.

37. A. H. Maslow, *Toward a Psychology of Being* (Princeton, N.J.: Van Nostrand, 1962), p. 8.

38. Likert, *op. cit.,* p. 117.

*William C. Pyle*

# *MONITORING HUMAN RESOURCES— "ON LINE"*

The importance of human resources to the success of an enterprise is widely acclaimed in corporate pronouncements; however, these expressions do not find substance in their accounting systems. Every year industry spends billions of dollars acquiring and developing long term human capabilities. However, accountants treat all such outlays as operating expenses which assumes their benefits are confined to the short term. Because of this practice, the management of human resources is impeded in the following ways:

1. Human resources are not reflected in the firm's capital budget. In contrast to physical plant and equipment, it is therefore more difficult for the manager to justify funds for building human assets since these expenditures are currently charged against revenue in one year. When an organization is, in effect, investing more heavily in creating new human capabilities than they are being consumed, conventional accounting practice actually *overstates* operating expenses and *understates* profitability.

---

Used by permission of the publisher. *Michigan Business Review,* vol. 22, no. 4, pp. 19–32, July, 1970.

*About the Author*—William C. Pyle is Director of Human Resource Accounting Research at the University of Michigan. This project is sponsored jointly by the Institute for Social Research's Center for Research on Utilization of Scientific Knowl-

2. The degree to which human capabilities are being maintained cannot be assessed in financial terms. First, since investments in human resources have not been recognized, and amortization schedules have not been determined, it is difficult to plan for the orderly replacement of these unmeasured assets. Furthermore, improper maintenance of human capabilities before the projected replacement date may not be detected. If a machine becomes obsolete, this loss will increase expenses, thereby reducing profits and earnings per share in the current year. However, if unmeasured human assets expire prematurely, write offs are not recorded. In reality, when human capabilities are being liquidated more rapidly than they are being created, conventional accounting practice understates operating expenses and *overstates* net income.
3. It is also difficult to determine how well human assets are being utilized in various projects. One of the most commonly employed measures of overall efficiency is the return generated on invested capital (ROI). However, investments in human resources are not included in ROI calculations for evaluating current or future projects.

The objective of human resource accounting is to remedy these informational deficiencies by developing and integrating financially oriented measurement techniques to facilitate the management of an organization's people resources. Are sufficient human capabilities being acquired to achieve the objectives of the enterprise? Are they being developed adequately? To what degree are they being maintained? Are these assets being properly utilized by the organization?

Before proceeding with the development of human resource accounting, two points need to be considered. First, it should be established that human resources are important enough to the success of a business that insufficient information about them will make a difference. Secondly, it should be determined whether or not managerial judgment or artisanship can be expected to satisfactorily compensate for current informational deficiencies.

---

edge and the Graduate School of Business Administration. Pyle is responsible for originating and directing development of the first human resource accounting system in industry in conjunction with the R. G. Barry Corporation of Columbus, Ohio. For its joint research with the University of Michigan, the R. G. Barry Corporation received the 1968 research award of the American Society for Personnel Administration. Pyle has authored numerous journal articles and has lectured extensively in the area of human resource accounting.

This article is based, in part, upon papers Pyle delivered to a National Industrial Conference Board Program on "Managing Change" in New York City on January 20, 1970 and the Public Relations World Congress held in Tel Aviv, Israel on June 4, 1970.

## THE IMPORTANCE OF HUMAN RESOURCES

The importance of human resources is reflected by the fact that substantial gaps usually exist between the "book value" of the firm's measured assets and other valuations. The market prices of corporate securities and the amounts for which businesses are bought and sold reflect the value of unmeasured intangible assets including human resources. In a recent study of 169 acquisitions by 26 firms listed on the New York Stock Exchange, the ratio of total unrecorded goodwill ($1,604,993,000) to the total book value of the acquired firms ($652,956,000) was 2.45.[1] Furthermore, evidence suggests that the replacement costs of human resources are substantial. Over a period of years, Rensis Likert has asked managers of many large and successful firms what it would cost them if they had to replace their entire work forces. The typical reply was that the amount would be at least twice their annual payrolls or $700 million dollars based upon the average payroll of $350 million.[2] These estimates are magnified further by the fact that since the turn of the century trends in labor force data indicate that those occupational groupings requiring the highest skills (and largest investments in human resources) have exhibited much greater relative growth than the less skilled, low investment occupations.[3] It seems reasonable to conclude, therefore, that human capabilities are sufficiently important to a firm that current informational deficiencies will significantly affect managerial effectiveness unless they are overcome. To some extent, managerial artisanship may compensate for these limitations.

## MANAGERIAL ARTISANSHIP

As long as organizations have existed, executives have been "accounting," at least subjectively, for those resources in reaching decisions as to which people should be hired, developed, promoted, transferred, or terminated. For example, during a downturn in the economy, managers usually weigh the option of reducing payrolls to improve current indicators of profitability. Even if accountants do not formally recognize investments in human resources, executives surely give some consideration to the write-offs of human assets involved and the new expenditures which will be required to expand employment when economic conditions again improve.

The major question, however, is the *degree* to which managerial artisanship may be expected to overcome current informational deficiencies. Several impediments are likely to be encountered. In the first place, the magnitude of investments in human resources is obscured by the many "hidden" time costs involved in developing human capabilities. For example, the process of starting up a new work force requires a considerable amount of on-the-job training and familiarization. The time required to break in even one high level manager may consume the better part of his first year with the firm. The significance of such investments is clouded not only because the costs are lumped in with salary expenses, but also because their effects are not highly visible. A shiny new machine can be easily observed in contrast to improvements in human capabilities which do not alter physical appearance.

There is also reason to suspect that managerial artisanship will not satisfactorily overcome the problems involved in properly maintaining and utilizing human assets. Since the conventional accounting system does not record investments in human capabilities, the premature liquidation of these investments cannot be formally recognized. In fact, conventional measurements may even create an incentive for managers to improve current profitability indicators at the expense of human assets. Certainly, most managers become painfully aware of the premature loss of good employees; however, these losses are not usually considered within a financial framework. Departmental turnover rates may increase a few points, but these changes are not converted into associated dollar losses. In fact, conventional financial indicators may even show a favorable variance as a result of employee separations. Although additional recruiting and training costs are incurred as a result, these may be more than offset by reductions in salary expenses while the positions are vacant.

Behavioral science research provides additional insight into this question. Rensis Likert contends that liquidations of human resources may be obscured for other reasons. First, two or three years may intervene between some managerial actions which improve profit indicators in the short term, but which are more damaging to the firm in the long run. For example, a severe cost reduction program will generally have an immediately favorable impact upon current profits. However, these data are not adjusted for reductions in future income which may result from the early loss of good people and the reduced efficiency of the remaining organization. Likert believes it is unlikely that managers under pressure for early results will properly associate such causes with their effects—partly because deteriorating attitudes resulting from unreasonable pressure are not normally measured. Furthermore, the situation may be further clouded by the fact that productivity gains based upon normal technological improvements may well mask deteriorations in human performance. Finally, Likert observes that the frequently encountered practice of transferring managers every two or three years may actually result in executives being promoted for "profitability" obtained at the expense of liquidated human assets.[4] Taken together, all of these factors suggest that human resource management stands to be improved through the development and application of new financial information for executives.

## DEVELOPMENT OF HUMAN RESOURCE ACCOUNTING

How should the development of human resource accounting proceed? First, the subject of managing human resources cannot be separated from management in general. Human capabilities are a resource to be managed in their own right; however, they also control or at least influence the other factors of production. Thus, the success an executive enjoys in the management of human capabilities may be expected to have a multiplicative impact on the overall effectiveness of the enterprise.

Secondly, it should be emphasized that managerial and informational systems are highly interrelated. An otherwise effective managerial system will not likely succeed unless it is supported by an adequate informational system. Similarly, an otherwise useful informational system will be of little use if it is linked to a basically unsound managerial system. However, if one system should take precedence over the other, it seems reasonable to suggest that the informational system should be specifically tailored to support the managerial system. If executives are to employ accounting data usefully, they must be able to relate them to their own informational needs which, in turn, are rooted in the managerial system which assigns particular roles and responsibilities to them. For this reason, the development of human resource accounting should be based upon a consideration of the general subject of management. After a brief examination of managerial functions the adequacy of currently available financial information will be assessed in relation to those functions. This will, in turn, lay the ground work for proposing additional information to assist the executive.

## AN OVERVIEW OF THE MANAGER'S JOB

An overview of the executive's job is proposed in Figure 1. Although there is often substantial controversy over what *organizational objectives* should be, whose interests they should reflect, how they should be established, and in what manner they should be realized, practically all students of management ranging from practitioners to behavioral scientists acknowledge the importance of established objectives. To realize these objectives, managers perform two basic tasks, namely managing *current business operations* and the *long term productive capabilities* which sustain these operations.

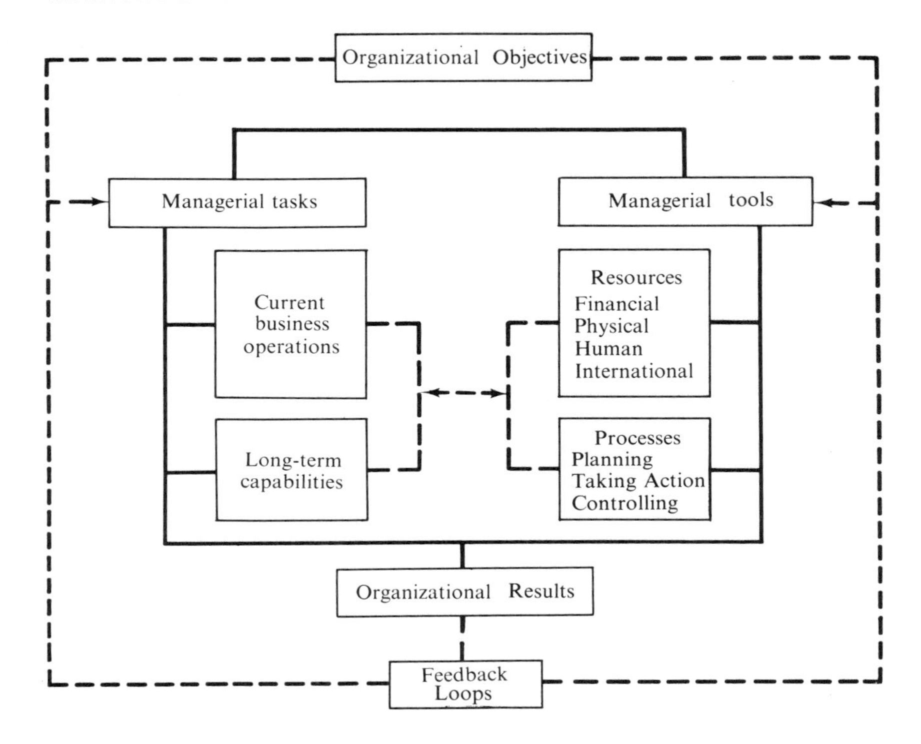


*FIGURE 1*

All managers are responsible for guiding *business operations.* For example, production managers requisition various materials and labor resources which become a part of or are directly consumed in the process of producing a product. Similarly, the personnel executive is also a manager of a business operation. For instance, he receives requisitions which initiate the process of acquiring new employees for the operating departments. Tasks such as these are usually performed over relatively short time cycles, say, less than one year.

In addition to business operations, all executives have responsibilities for managing the long term *productive capabilities* which sustain these operations. A partial listing of these capabilities is seen in Figure 2. Financial capabilities include, for example, liquidity and solvency. Physical capabilities exist in the form of the productive capacity and expansion potential of plant and equipment. Human capabilities are present both in the aptitudes, skills, and experience of individual employees and the leadership skills, team skills and cooperativeness found in the organization. Informational capabilities include the accounting, financial, and

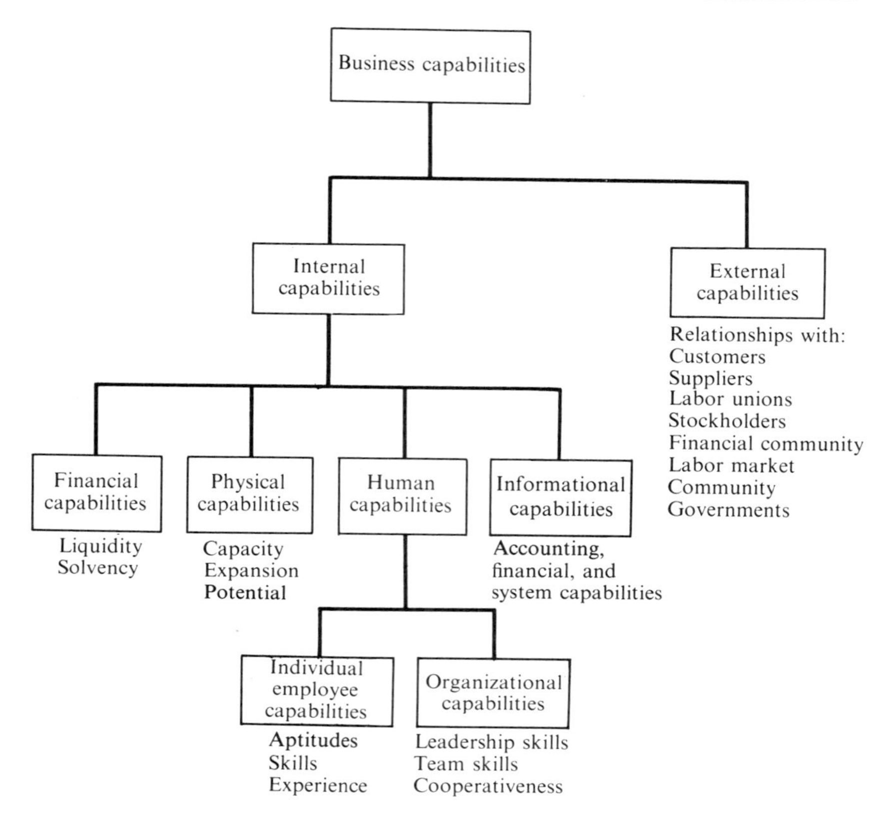


*FIGURE 2*

systems capabilities which managers rely upon to guide their work. Executives also have varying degrees of responsibility for the external capabilities suggested in Figure 2.

Business capabilities do not become a part of the firm's final product nor should they be unduly consumed in its production. For this reason, the management of these capabilities normally takes a much longer time perspective than the management of current operations.

In managing operations and capabilities, executives employ both *resources* and *processes*. The resources may be financial, physical, human, and informational. Some of these inputs are consumed in the course of operations, while others are employed to create long term capabilities. Managerial processes such as planning, taking action, and controlling are also common to managing both operations and capabilities. The integrated performance of these two basic tasks leads to *organizational results* which are assessed against established objectives. As suggested in Figure 1, the degree to which the desired results are achieved provides feedback which leads to modification of objectives and the various managerial activities.

Employing resources and engaging in processes such as planning, action, and control cannot take place in a vacuum. They take substance in the basic tasks of managing operations and long term capabilities. Financial information which is currently available to assist the executive in performance of these functions will now be surveyed.

## CURRENTLY AVAILABLE INFORMATION

What financial information does the manager receive to assess the effectiveness of business operations? The most widely used measure of overall organizational efficiency matches revenue from the sale of the firm's product or service with the costs incurred to produce that revenue. In oversimplified terms, the difference between revenue and expenses is the profit or loss associated with a particular business operation.

Accountants exercise particular care to insure that revenue is properly matched with associated expenses to determine net income. Otherwise, distortions in profit measurements will result. For example, capital expenditures for plant and equipment items are not charged off against revenue in one year. Rather, these costs are matched against revenue generated over the expected lives of the assets. However, costs incurred for building long term human capabilities are all treated as expenses which understate revenue in the short term. Accordingly, measures of the efficiency of business operations are distorted. Corresponding informational deficiencies are also present in financial data used to evaluate the management of certain long term business capabilities.

Unfortunately, short term measures of operational efficiency do not insure that long term business capabilities are properly managed. For example, it is well known that indicators of profitability may be improved if physical resources such as plant and equipment are improperly maintained or are used too intensively. For this reason, the writer advocates that managerial and informational systems be designed to give specialized attention to both business operations and capabilities.

The accounting profession has not been unmindful of the fact that measures of the efficiency of operations are inadequate to the task of insuring that productive capabilities are properly managed. For certain capabilities at least, accountants currently provide the manager with additional information indicating how well they are being acquired, developed, maintained, and utilized. For physical resources, accountants recognize costs incurred in acquiring plant and equipment as long term investments, which appear on the firm's balance sheet as assets. These expenditures, unlike expenses, are not matched against short term revenue in measuring profitability. These investments are written down or amortized over the period of expected benefit. However, if such capabilities expire prematurely due to improper management or otherwise, the investment is written down more rapidly than planned under the original amortization schedule. Such a premature write-off or loss becomes an expense item which is then matched against revenue during the current year. Accordingly, reported profitability is reduced and the responsible manager is held to account. Unfortunately, the protection given to physical assets has not been extended to their human counterparts. One major objective of human resource accounting is to remedy this informational deficiency.

## NEW INFORMATION FOR MANAGERS

Two interrelated approaches to human resource accounting are being pursued in a University of Michigan project sponsored jointly by the Institute for Social Research's Center for Research on Utilization of Scientific Knowledge and the Graduate School of Business Administration. The first approach relies upon extending to human resources, accounting concepts and procedures that are currently employed in the management of physical and financial resources. Dollar investments in human capabilities are now being recognized. Once incurred, such investments are amortized over their expected useful lives. If they expire prematurely due to early employee separations or skill obsolescence, losses or write-offs are reported to management.

Monitoring human resource costs is only a partial answer to the informational needs of the manager. In themselves, these data do not adequately reflect the *value* of human resources. How can return on investments in human resources be determined? How can the worth of different leadership styles, team skills, and cooperativeness be measured? The second approach to human resource accounting focuses on the development of alternative means for assessing the productive capability of human resources and how this may be changing through time.

Although some insight into this question may be gained through extension of conventional financial analyses to human resources, much greater reliance is being placed upon the use of social psychological measurement techniques such as those developed by Rensis Likert and his colleagues at the Institute for Social Research. This approach to human resource accounting will be discussed after the investment measurement approach is examined.

## RESEARCH AT THE R. G. BARRY CORPORATION

The "cost approach" to human resource accounting has been developed in collaboration with the management of the R. G. Barry Corporation of Columbus, Ohio. The firm's 1,700 employees are engaged in the manufacture of a wide variety of personal comfort items including foam-cushioned slippers, sandals, robes, pillows, and other leisure wear which are marketed nationally in leading department stores and other outlets under brand names such as Angel Treads, Dearform, and Bernardo. The corporate headquarters and four production facilities are located in Columbus, Ohio. Several other plants, warehouses, and sales offices are located across the country. The firm has expanded from a sales volume of about $5½ million in 1962 to over $25 million in 1969.

It had become increasingly apparent to the firm's president, Gordon Zacks, and Personnel Vice President Robert L. Woodruff, Jr., that success in the business was crucially linked to the firm's human resources. Physical capital requirements were relatively low and entry into the industry was not seriously impeded on that count. Rather, success was more closely related to excellence achieved in acquiring, developing, maintaining, and utilizing their human and customer loyalty assets. However, in accepting this conclusion, the corporation faced the problem that their conventional accounting system maintained detailed surveillance over the relatively less important physical assets, but failed to recognize the more important human and customer loyalty assets of the business. This dissatisfaction led Mr. Zacks and Mr. Woodruff to discuss the problem with the University of Michigan's Institute for Social Research.

When the research effort began, the writer had only proposed rather general concepts for measuring dollar investments in human resources.[5] As a result, in late 1966, a joint university-industry team was formed to consider the problem in more detail. This continuing group is composed of the author, and a team of R. G. Barry managers which, in addition to the President and Personnel Vice President, include Edward Stan, Treasurer, and Richard Burrell, Controller. During the first half of 1967, the team members met regularly to develop a set of theoretical constructs for categorizing and measuring the ways in which a firm invests in its human organization.[6] The remainder of the year was devoted to translating these concepts into detailed procedures for recognizing investments in human resources as well as expirations which might occur in these assets.[7] In January, 1968 an investment accounting system was established for the firm's managers. In June, 1969 this system was extended to cover factory and clerical employees in two plants. In July, 1970, two additional plants will be included in the system. At the end of the first quarter of 1970, the R. G. Barry Corporation reported a "book value" figure of $1,765,100 based upon 147 managers and 425 factory and clerical personnel. On an individual basis, the firm invests approximately $3,000 in a first line supervisor, $15,000 in a middle manager and upwards of $30,000 in hiring, familiarizing, and developing a top level executive.

## CAPITAL BUDGETING FOR HUMAN RESOURCES

It was noted earlier that conventional accounting practice impedes the acquisition and development of human capabilities by treating all such expenditures as business expenses to be charged against revenue in one year. For internal management purposes, the Barry Corporation has changed this practice. In the latter part of 1969, the firm prepared what is believed to be industry's first capital budget for human resources. Expenditures undertaken with the objective of building long term capabilities are charged against revenue over the period of expected benefit.

Based upon the plans they have submitted, managers receive quarterly human resource reports indicating the "book value" of investments in their subordinates at the beginning and end of the quarter. Increases and decreases occurring during the period are also highlighted. The report form presented in Figure 3 indicates the type of information which R. G. Barry's executives are now using to guide the management of human resources. The firm's Vice President of Personnel, Robert L. Woodruff, Jr., describes how this new information is being used:

> Capital budgeting for human resources, together with reporting actual performance against the plan, gives the manager an additional perspective on the total effectiveness of his unit. Investments made in additional personnel, replacement personnel, training and development as well as write-offs incurred through turnover and obsolescence of prior investments are reported against the manager's plan. The transfer of human assets from one department to another is also planned. For the corporation as a whole "transfers in" must equal "transfers out."
>
> This quarterly report informs the manager whether planned developmental investments are in fact being made as planned, and whether write-offs of investments due to separations are exceeding his original expectations. For each profit center, the net of new investment less write-offs is applied as an adjustment to the conventional profit figure which reflects either a positive or a negative impact on the important bottom line number.

Human resource accounting techniques are employed not only to evaluate the performance of current operations, but are also used in analysis

*FIGURE 3* Human Resource Capital Budget 1970

Location: Corporate total
Supervisor: President
Quarter ending: June 30, 1970

Beginning balance $1,325,000

| Actual # of People | Dollars Plan | Dollars Actual | | Year-to-date Dollars Plan | Year-to-date Dollars Actual | 12 month Plan |
|---|---|---|---|---|---|---|
| | | | New Investments | | | |
| | | | Management Personnel | | | |
| 3 | $ 25,000 | $ 19,500 | Additions | $40,000 | $ 30,000 | $110,000 |
| 7 | 42,000 | 51,000 | Replacement | 84,000 | 90,000 | 168,000 |
| 18 | 11,500 | 10,000 | Development | 20,000 | 17,800 | 60,000 |
| 3 | 21,000 | 14,000 | Transfer In | 42,000 | 35,000 | 84,000 |
| 121 | 120,000 | 130,000 | Hourly Personnel | 250,000 | 264,500 | 510,000 |
| | $219,500 | $225,100 | Total | $436,000 | $437,300 | $932,000 |
| | | | Write-Offs | | | |
| | | | Management Personnel | | | |
| | $ 17,250 | $ 19,100 | Amortization | $ 34,500 | $ 36,000 | $138,000 |
| | | | Turnover Losses | | | |
| 3 | 10,000 | 11,000 | Voluntary | 20,000 | 24,000 | 80,000 |
| 1 | 7,500 | 4,800 | Involuntary | 15,000 | 11,400 | 60,000 |
| — | 17,000 | 800 | Obsolescence | 2,500 | 1,100 | 5,000 |
| 3 | 21,000 | 14,000 | Transfer Out | 42,000 | 35,000 | 84,000 |
| 111 | 120,000 | 117,400 | Hourly Personnel | 230,000 | 251,600 | 480,000 |
| | $192,750 | $167,100 | Total | $344,000 | $359,100 | $847,000 |

Ending Balance $1,383,000
Net Change $58,000

and selection of new business opportunities. The firm's President, Gordon Zacks, describes this application:

> We use human resource accounting information in strategic decision-making. The information is employed in evaluating alternative investment opportunities. We have rejected the conventional return-on-assets approach because it does not recognize human investments. In evaluating a project, we take the physical assets into account as everyone else does, but we also add to that the investment to be made in the human resources required to support the opportunity. And when we develop relationships to profit, it is the relationship of all of those resources, tangible and human, to a particular profit opportunity.

In this regard, the firm's controller, Richard Burrell, adds, "Human resource accounting data provide still another tool to evaluate the allocation of resources among profit opportunities to maximize the return on all corporate resources." The report format seen in Figure 3 may also be used as a device to evaluate new business opportunities. The required capital expenditures for human resources (and write-offs of prior investments) may be projected and included along with similar information for the physical resources associated with each option under consideration. When a particular opportunity is selected, these data then serve as the plan against which actual experience is reported. In addition to special purpose analyses such as these, human resource data are also being integrated with the firm's conventional financial statements for internal management purposes.

## NEW FINANCIAL STATEMENTS

Although reported on a pro forma basis, the R. G. Barry Corporation's 1969 Annual Report contains industry's first published financial statements to include human resource data. This information is contrasted with their conventional financial statements in a special section of the report dealing with human resources. As seen in Figure 4, net investments in managerial personnel of approximately one million dollars are recognized. The liabilities and stockholders' equity side of the balance sheet indicates approximately $500,000 for "Deferred Federal Income Taxes as a Result of Appropriation for Human Resources" and an equal amount for an "Appropriation for Human Resources" under retained earnings.

Turning to the income statement, a net change of $173,569 in human resource investments during 1969 is applied as a positive adjustment to income before taxes. After taxes, this change results in an upward adjustment of about $87,000 to conventionally determined net income of about $700,000. This adjustment reflects the fact that during 1969, new invest-

*FIGURE 4* Financial Statements Reflecting Human Resources at the R. G. Barry Corporation "THE TOTAL CONCEPT" R. G. Barry Corporation and Subsidiaries Pro forma (Financial and Human Resource Accounting)

| Balance sheet | 1969 Financial and human resource | 1969 Financial only |
|---|---|---|
| Assets | | |
| Total Current Assets .................. | $10,003,628 | $10,003,628 |
| Net Property, Plant and Equipment ....... | 1,770,717 | 1,770,717 |
| Excess of Purchase Price of Subsidiaries over Net Assets Acquired ................ | 1,188,704 | 1,188,704 |
| Net Investments in Human Resources ..... | 986,094 | — |
| Other Assets ........................ | 106,783 | 106,783 |
| | $14,055,926 | $13,069,832 |
| Liabilities and Stockholders' Equity | | |
| Total Current Liabilities ................ | $ 5,715,708 | $ 7,715,708 |
| Long Term Debt, Excluding Current Installments ........................ | 1,935,500 | 1,935,500 |
| Deferred Compensation ............... | 62,380 | 62,380 |
| Deferred Federal Income Taxes as a Result of Appropriation for Human Resources .... | 493,047 | — |
| Stockholders' Equity: | | |
| Capital Stock ...................... | 879,116 | 879,116 |
| Additional Capital in Excess of Par Value . | 1,736,253 | 1,736,253 |
| Retained Earnings: | | |
| Financial ...................... | 2,740,875 | 2,740,875 |
| Appropriation for Human Resources .. | 493,047 | — |
| Total Stockholders' Equity ........ | 5,849,291 | 5,356,244 |
| | $14,055,296 | $13,069,832 |

| Statement of income | 1969 Financial and human resource | 1969 Financial only |
|---|---|---|
| Net Sales ........................... | $25,310,588 | $25,310,588 |
| Cost of sales ......................... | 16,275,876 | 16,275,876 |
| Gross profit ..................... | 9,034,712 | 9,034,712 |
| Selling, general and administrative expenses . | 6,737,313 | 6,737,313 |
| Operating income ................ | 2,297,399 | 2,297,399 |
| Other deductions, net ................. | 953,177 | 953,177 |
| Income before Federal income taxes ... | 1,344,222 | 1,344,222 |
| Human Resource expenses applicable to future periods ..................... | 173,569 | — |
| Adjusted income before Federal income taxes | 1,517,791 | 1,344,222 |
| Federal income taxes .................. | 730,785 | 644,000 |
| Net income ..................... | $ 787,006 | $ 700,222 |

Source: 1969 R. G. Barry Corporation Annual Report, p. 14.

ments in human resources were undertaken more rapidly than they were written down.

Considerable attention could be given to the rationale behind the particular accounting entries which appear in these new financial statements. For example, the treatment of federal income taxes could be argued several ways. However, a detailed examination of such questions is beyond the scope of this paper. Topics such as these are also the subject of continuing discussion in conventional accounting practice. According to the R. G. Barry Corporation's Treasurer, Edward Stan, the important thing to emphasize at this point is that human resource data are now being reported to management on a basis which will be followed consistently from year to year.

The primary purpose for developing human resource accounting at the R. G. Barry Corporation is to improve internal management. However, Mr. Stan also believes such data will eventually be employed by parties outside the business:

> Although a milestone has been reached by incorporating human resource accounting data into a published balance sheet and profit and loss statement, the true significance will not be apparent until comparative years are available. In order for these data to become useful for outside financial analysts, a credibility must be established and an activity-results pattern set up. Once this has been accomplished, the analyst, whether he is an investor or lender, will have an important additional tool for his decision making.

Evidence suggests that influential segments of the accounting fraternity would also welcome such a development. For example, a committee of the American Accounting Association has proposed that procedures be developed for allocating expenditures for personnel recruitment and training to asset and expense categories.[8] Sidney Davidson of the Accounting Principles Board of the American Institute of Certified Public Accountants also recommends that costs incurred for such purposes be carried as assets and amortized against future earnings.[9]

Although human resource cost data provide the manager with new information to assist him in the acquisition, development and maintenance of human capabilities, these data only have limited significance for assessing the value of human resources and how it may be changing through time.

## THE VALUE OF HUMAN RESOURCES

In a most general sense the real worth of human resources may be defined as the present discounted value of their future contributions less the costs of acquiring, developing, maintaining, and utilizing those resources in the organization. Because of the difficulties involved in predicting future contributions and costs, value information will always remain indeterminate to a large degree. It is for this reason, among others, that accountants have based their valuations of physical assets upon more easily measured historical costs less depreciation.[10] Despite the limitations of such information, managers are nonetheless required to make value judgments about human resources every time they hire, train, assign, develop, transfer, and replace personnel. Human resource accounting may help the manager gain insight into the value of human assets in several ways.

### (1) Measuring Return on Assets Employed

As noted earlier, one of the most commonly used measures of value is the return generated on assets employed in a business undertaking. However, capital outlays for human resources are not included in ROI calculations used to evaluate current or future projects. The addition of human resource data will improve these measures, especially where the ratios of human to other assets vary significantly across profit centers or projects being compared. Thus, conventional measures of value may be made more reflective of the human contribution. However, these calculations do not usually identify that portion of the return associated with the human component alone.

### (2) Measuring Return on Investments in Human Resources

If a profit center is highly human resource intensive, an ROI measure will indicate what is essentially a return on human capital. However, in most instances, ROI calculations reflect the product of a "resource mix"; in such cases it is difficult, if not impossible, to link a certain portion of the return to human resources. However, where adequate performance criteria and relatively stable environmental conditions exist, insight into this question may be gained through controlled experiments. Human resource investments may be varied while other factors are held constant to the degree possible. For example, one type of recruiting practice may be followed for experimental groups while another may be pursued for control groups.

In the absence of reliable performance criteria or where dynamic environmental factors preclude controlled experiments, ROI trends may be estimated through indices based upon social-psychological measurement techniques. For example, members of work groups can be asked the degree to which they believe prior investment in recruiting or development have been effective. For example, if such data show that employees perceive a lowering in the quality of new hires, this information will at least alert the manager to the fact that return on investments in recruiting may be falling off, even if it cannot be quantified in monetary terms. Data such as these are being collected annually at the R. G. Barry Corporation.[11]

### (3) Adjusted Costs

Conventional asset valuations are based upon historical costs less depreciation. A similar treatment has now been extended to human resources. When an organization invests in a new employee, it does so with the obvious expectation that returns will exceed the costs involved even though this value cannot usually be quantified. Otherwise, the person would not be hired. Thus, it is reasonable to suggest that historical costs *at least* represent a minimum statement of the average position holder's value which can be easily identified. Despite the inherent limitations of cost information alone, it is possible to make these data more reflective of the value of human resources. For example, historical costs may be adjusted upward or downward based upon changes in (a) the replacement cost of personnel, (b) the expected tenure of employees, and (c) the performance and/or potential of personnel.

*(a) Replacement Cost Adjustments.* Like their physical resource counterparts, historical investments in human resources are "sunk costs." Although these data may be usefully employed as a basis for evaluating prior investments, the cost of replacing human capabilities provides the manager with a closer approximation of an individual's value to the organization. If a particular position should become vacant, it would not be rational to hire a new employee unless it was expected that he will contribute something in excess of the replacement costs involved. This type of information is especially useful in long range manpower planning. Cost standards developed at the R. G. Barry Corporation are periodically updated for such purposes.

Although replacement cost data are a closer approximation of value than historical costs, they are not necessarily reflective of a particular individual's value to the organization. The worth of an employee is a function of two interrelated variables: (1) his expected tenure and (2) the quality of his contributions over that period of time. Further adjustments based upon these factors will now be considered.

*(b) Expected Tenure Adjustments.* In principle, conventionally measured assets are written down over their expected economic life at a rate which is proportional to the timing of their anticipated contributions. Similar procedures are now being used for amortizing investments in human resources. Cost-less-depreciation information (or "book value") reflects the fact that—other things equal—the employee with more ex-

pected tenure is of greater value to the organization than the individual with a lesser amount of remaining service. However, this type of information for human resources might well appear to be no more reflective of value than similar information currently reported for plant and equipment items. This would be true if the same amortization procedures were applied to both types of assets.

Physical assets are normally written down over a fixed period of time which is not subject to adjustment.[12] However, different procedures have been adopted for human resources because of the fact that employees, unlike capital equipment, can, in large measure, vary their own length of service. For this reason, the expected tenure of personnel is periodically reassessed based upon changes in those factors which influence length of service. For example, the "book value" of an employee may actually be greater *after* he has spent one year on the job because the probability of his staying longer with the organization is greater at that time.[13] Some of the other major variables which affect tenure include a person's age, organizational level, and degree of job satisfaction. A crucial component of human resource accounting research focuses upon identification of relationships between changes in such factors and variations in expected working life.

Human resource "book values" are revised periodically, based upon the following formula:

$$\text{Human Resource ("Book Value")} = \frac{\text{Expected Remaining Tenure}}{\text{Present Tenure} + \text{Expected Remaining Tenure}} \times \text{Current Replacement Cost}$$

It should be emphasized that *changes* in "book value" are more important than the absolute figures. The direction of trends in such data are accurate indicators of changes in the value of employees whose performance remains relatively constant. This condition tends to prevail in many operative jobs where performance is determined largely by physical technology or in more highly skilled positions if performance is uniformly high. However, such uniformity frequently does not prevail and further adjustments may be required to make human resource cost data more reflective of changes in value.

(*c*) *Performance and Potential Adjustments.* Human resource costs may be adjusted still further to reflect changes in an individual's performance and/or potential. For example, "book values" can be adjusted positively or negatively in relation to changes in various employee ratings.

In such cases, valuations may well exceed current replacement costs. The range of these adjustments can be based upon dollar estimates of the degree to which an individual may benefit (or harm) the organization. Very little research has been conducted in this area, and judgments as to the potential usefulness of such information must be deferred at this point.

Most of the research undertaken in human resource accounting has dealt with measurement of investments in individual employees. Alternative approaches for gaining insight into the value of these assets have also been discussed. However, it is well known that human resource value exists not only in capabilities of individuals, but it is also dependent upon the effective interaction of employees. To be complete, human resource accounting must also assess the productive capability of various organizational groupings and how this may be changing through time.

### (4) Social-Psychological Measurements

For over two decades, the Institute for Social Research, under the leadership of Rensis Likert, has been developing concepts and techniques for measuring the social-psychological properties of organizations and how they change through time. "Causal variables," such as organizational structure and patterns of management behavior have been shown to affect "intervening variables" such as employee loyalties, attitudes, perceptions, and motivations, which in turn have been linked to changes in conventionally measured "end-result variables" such as productivity and earnings.[14] These measures reflect changes in the productive capabilities or *value* of an organization's human resources which cannot be adequately measured through costs alone. However, both measurement concepts need to be considered as it is through variation of costs that managers exert a major influence on the value or future productive capabilities of both the human and physical resources of the business.[15]

## CONCLUSIONS

The development, implementation, and application of human resource accounting has been described, first by relating the importance of human resources to the overall process of management and the general informational needs of executives. Conventional accounting systems do fairly well in informing managers how well they are managing business operations. They also provide useful data which indicate how successfully the physical and financial capabilities of the business are being managed. For example, investments in these capabilities are recognized and written down over their expected useful lives. If they expire prematurely due to improper management or otherwise, dollar losses are reported. However, the executive does not receive similar information which indicates the degree to which human capabilities are being acquired, developed, maintained, and utilized. Human resource accounting seeks to remedy this informational deficiency through two interrelated approaches: (1) development of investment measurement capabilities for human resources, such as those now in use at the R. G. Barry Corporation, and (2) development of measures of the value or productive capabilities of a firm's human organization through both conventional and social psychological measurement techniques, such as those developed by Rensis Likert and his colleagues at the Institute for Social Research.

What is the outlook for development of human resource accounting in industry? The measurement of investments in human resources employs concepts and procedures which are generally familiar to financial analysts. Many measurement problems remain here, but these are no more troublesome than those typically encountered in accounting for physical assets. However, the measurement tools of the social scientist do not have their counterparts in accounting for physical resources. This at once presents a new measurement opportunity, but it also poses the problem of acclimating financial people to basically new measurement techniques unique to human resources. However, the concepts and procedures for measuring human resource costs are more familiar and may help bridge this methodological gap.

## REFERENCE LIST

1. Copeland, Ronald and Wojdak, Joseph, "Valuations of Unrecorded Goodwill in Merger-Minded Firms," *Financial Analysts Journal,* September-October, 1969.

2. Likert, Rensis, *The Human Organization, Its Management and Value,* New York: McGraw-Hill, 1967, p. 103.

3. United States Bureau of the Census, *Historical Statistics of the United States,* Colonial Times to 1957, Washington, D.C.: U.S. Government Printing Office, 1961, pp. 74–75; 202–14.

4. Likert, Rensis, *loc. cit.*

5. Pyle, William C., "Accounting for Investments in Human Capital," Research proposal, Institute for Social Research, The University of Michigan, September, 1966.

6. Pyle, William C., "Accounting System for Human Resources," *Innovation,* Number 10, 1970, pp. 46–54, and Woodruff, Robert L., "What Price People," *The Personnel Administrator,* January-February, 1969.

7. In the latter part of 1967, the author invited his colleague R. Lee Brummet, a well known accountant and C.P.A., to join in developmental work on the project. This collaborative work led to a number of significant developments and permitted the research to progress more rapidly. Eric Flamholtz also assisted the developmental team at this time. Lee Brummet is continuing to serve as a consultant to the Institute for Social Research on the overall human resource accounting project.

8. American Accounting Association, *A Statement of Basic Accounting Theory,* 1966, pp. 35–36.

9. Based upon an interview with Sidney Davidson reported in *Forbes,* April 1, 1970, p. 40.

10. The standard of verifiability is especially important to accountants in reporting to external parties such as stockholders, creditors, and governmental agencies. However, it may well be acceptable to report more relevant but less verifiable information to an organization's management for internal use.

11. This phase of the research is being conducted by Ramon Henson of the Institute for Social Research.

12. Exceptions to this generalization, of course, do occur. When an item is written off prematurely, the amortization period is, in effect, shortened.

13. Unlike physical asset valuations which only move in a downward direction, human resource book values may move either upward or downward. This treatment makes the data more reflective of underlying changes in the value of human resources. Holding performance constant, if more people are inclined to stay with the firm a longer period of time, "book values" will increase because of this change. However, if the opposite occurs, human asset valuations will decline since book values are recalculated, based upon shorter amortization periods.

14. This approach to human resource accounting is described in more detail by Likert in "How to Increase a Firm's Lead Time in Recognizing and Dealing with Problems of Managing Its Human Organization," *Michigan Business Review,* January, 1969; *The Human Organization, Its Management and Value,* New York: McGraw-Hill, 1967 and *New Patterns of Management,* New York: McGraw-Hill, 1961.

15. The interrelationships between these two approaches to human resource accounting are discussed in more detail in Brummet, R. Lee, Pyle, William C., and Flamholtz, Eric G., in "Accounting for Human Resources," *Michigan Business Review,* March, 1968.

## DISCUSSION QUESTIONS

1. What roles do "servomechanisms" and "feedback" play in the overall control process?

2. Is control best described as a "fixed" or "variable" sum? Defend your answer.
3. What is the impact of formal controls on conflict and creativity in an organization?
4. What is the meaning of the concept of "human resource accounting"?
5. How can the value of human organizational assets be reflected in a company's financial statements?
6. What are the advantages of having a human resource accounting system? What if any disadvantages are there with such an accounting system?

# Part III. Behavioral Processes

# Chapter 6. Leading

*Robert C. Albrook*

# *PARTICIPATIVE MANAGEMENT: TIME FOR A SECOND LOOK*

The management of change has become a central preoccupation of U.S. business. When the directors have approved the record capital budget and congratulated themselves on "progress," when the banquet speaker has used his last superlative to describe the "world of tomorrow," the talk turns, inevitably, to the question: "Who will make it all work?" Some people resist change. Some hold the keys to it. Some admit the need for new ways but don't know how to begin. The question becomes what kind of management can ease the inevitable pains, unlock the talent, energy, and knowledge where they're needed, help valuable men to contribute to and shape change rather than be flattened by it.

The recipe is elusive, and increasingly business has turned to the academic world for help, particularly to the behavioral scientists—the psychologists, sociologists, and anthropologists whose studies have now become the showpieces of the better business schools. A number of major corporations, such as General Electric, Texas Instruments, and Standard Oil (N.J.), have brought social scientists onto their staffs. Some companies collaborate closely with university-based scholars and are contributing importantly to advanced theoretical work, just as industry's

Used by permission of the publisher. *Fortune,* vol. 75, no. 5, pp. 166–170 and 197–200, May, 1967.

physicists, chemists, and engineers have become significant contributors of new knowledge in their respective realms. Hundreds of companies, large and small, have tried one or another formulation of basic behavioral theory, such as the many schemes for sharing cost savings with employees and actively soliciting their ideas for improved efficiency.

For forty years the quantity and quality of academic expertise in this field have been steadily improving, and there has lately been a new burst of ideas which suggest that the researchers in the business schools and other centers of learning are really getting down to cases. The newest concepts already represent a considerable spinoff from the appealingly simple notions on which the behavioral pioneers first concentrated. The essential message these outriders had for business was this: recognize the social needs of employees in their work, as well as their need for money; they will respond with a deeper commitment and better performance, help to shape the organization's changing goals and make them their own. For blue-collar workers this meant such steps as organizing work around tasks large enough to have meaning and inviting workers' ideas; for middle and upper management it meant more participation in decision making, wider sharing of authority and responsibility, more open and more candid communication, up, down, and sideways.

The new work suggests that neither the basic philosophy nor all of the early prescriptions of this management style were scientifically sound or universally workable. The word from the behavioral scientists is becoming more specific and "scientific," less simple and moralistic. At Harvard, M.I.T., the University of Michigan, Chicago, U.C.L.A., Stanford, and elsewhere, they are mounting bigger, longer, and more rigorous studies of the human factors in management than ever before undertaken.

One conclusion is that the "participative" or "group" approach doesn't seem to work with all people and in all situations. Research has shown that satisfied, happy workers are sometimes more productive—and sometimes merely happy. Some managers and workers are able to take only limited responsibility, however much the company tries to give them. Some people will recognize the need to delegate but "can't let go." In a profit squeeze the only way to get costs under control fast enough often seems to be with centralized, "get tough" management.

Few, if any, behaviorists espouse a general return to authoritarian management. Instead, they are seeking a more thorough, systematic way to apply participative principles on a sustained schedule that will give the theory a better chance to work. Others are insisting that management must be tailor-made, suited to the work or the people, rather than packaged in a standard mixture. Some people aren't and never will be suited for "democracy" on the job, according to one viewpoint, while others insist that new kinds of psychological training can fit most executives for the rugged give-and-take of successful group management.

As more variables are brought into their concepts, and as they look increasingly at the specifics of a management situation, the behaviorists are also being drawn toward collaboration with the systems designers and the theorists of data processing. Born in reaction to the cold scientism of the earlier "scientific management" experts with their stopwatches and measuring tapes, the "human relations" or behavioral school of today may be getting ready at last to bury that hatchet in a joint search for a broadly useful "general theory" of management.

## WHY EXECUTIVES DON'T PRACTICE WHAT THEY PREACH

Before any general theory can be evolved, a great deal more has to be known about the difficulty of putting theory into practice—i.e., of transforming a simple managerial attitude into an effective managerial style. "There are plenty of executives," observes Stanley Seashore, a social psychologist at the University of Michigan's Institute for Social Research, "who'll decide one morning they're going to be more participative and by the afternoon have concluded it doesn't work."

What's often lacking is an understanding of how deeply and specifically management style affects corporate operations. The executive who seeks a more effective approach needs a map of the whole terrain of management activity. Rensis Likert, director of the Michigan institute, has developed a chart [Figure 1] to assist managers in gaining a deeper understanding of the way they operate. By answering the questions in the left-hand column of the chart (e.g., "Are subordinates' ideas sought and used?"), an executive sketches a profile of the way his company is run and whether it leans to the "authoritative" or the "participative." Hundreds of businessmen have used the chart, under Likert's direction, and many have discovered a good deal they didn't realize about the way they were handling people.

Likert leads his subjects in deliberate steps to a conclusion that most of them do not practice what they say they believe. First, the executive is asked to think of the most successful company (or division of a company) he knows intimately. He then checks off on the chart his answers as they apply to that company. When the executive has finished this exercise, he has nearly always traced the profile of a strongly "participative" management system, well to the right on Likert's chart. He is next asked to repeat the procedure for the least successful company (or division) he knows well. Again, the profiles are nearly always the same, but this time

*FIGURE 1*

| | | System 1 Exploitive Authoritative | System 2 Benevolent Authoritative | System 3 Consultative | System 4 Participative Group |
|---|---|---|---|---|---|
| Leadership | How much confidence is shown in subordinates? | None | Condescending | Substantial | Complete |
| | How free do they feel to talk to superiors about job? | Not at all | Not very | Rather free | Fully free |
| | Are subordinates' ideas sought and used, if worthy? | Seldom | Sometimes | Usually | Always |
| Motivation | Is predominant use made of 1 fear, 2 threats, 3 punishment, 4 rewards, 5 involvement? | 1,2,3, occasionally 4 | 4, some 3 | 4, some 3 and 5 | 5,4, based on group set goals |
| | Where is responsibility felt for achieving organization's goals? | Mostly at top | Top and middle | Fairly general | At all levels |
| Communication | How much communication is aimed at achieving organization's objectives? | Very little | Little | Quite a bit | A great deal |
| | What is the direction of information flow? | Downward | Mostly downward | Down and up | Down up and sideways |
| | How is downward communication accepted? | With suspicion | Possibly with suspicion | With caution | With an open mind |
| | How accurate is upward communication? | Often wrong | Censored for the boss | Limited accuracy | Accurate |
| | How well do superiors know problems faced by subordinates? | Know little | Some knowledge | Quite well | Very well |

| | | | | | |
|---|---|---|---|---|---|
| Decisions | At what level are decisions formally made? | Mostly at top | Policy at top, some delegation | Broad policy at top, more delegation | Throughout but well integrated |
| | What is the origin of technical and professional knowledge used in decision making? | Top management | Upper and middle | To a certain extent, throughout | To a great extent, throughout |
| | Are subordinates involved in decisions related to their work? | Not at all | Occasionally consulted | Generally consulted | Fully involved |
| | What does decision-making process contribute to motivation? | Nothing, often weakens it | Relatively little | Some contribution | Substantial contribution |
| Goals | How are organizational goals established? | Orders issued | Orders, some comment invited | After discussion, by orders | By group action (except in crisis) |
| | How much covert resistance to goals is present? | Strong resistance | Moderate resistance | Some resistance at times | Little or none |
| Control | How concentrated are review and control functions? | Highly at top | Relatively highly at top | Moderate delegation to lower levels | Quite widely shared |
| | Is there an informal organization resisting the formal one? | Yes | Usually | Sometimes | No-same goals as formal |
| | What are cost, productivity, and other control data used for? | Policing, punishment | Reward and punishment | Reward, some self-guidance | Self-guidance, problem solving |

**Adapted, with permission, from** ***The Human Organization: Its Management and Value,*** by Rensis Likert, published in April, 1967, by McGraw-Hill.

they portray a strongly "authoritative" system, far to the left on the chart.

Then comes the point of the exercise. The executive is asked to describe his own company or division. Almost always, the resulting profile is that of a company somewhere in the middle, a blend of the "benevolent authoritative" and the "consultative"—well to the left of what the executive had previously identified as the most successful style. To check out the reliability of this self-analysis, Likert sometimes asks employees in the same company or division to draw its profile, too. They tend to rate it as slightly more "authoritative" than the boss does.

Likert believes that the predominant management style in U.S. industry today falls about in the middle of his chart, even though most managers seem to know from personal observation of other organizations that a more participative approach works better. What accounts for their consistent failure to emulate what they consider successful? Reaching for a general explanation, Likert asks his subjects one final question: "In your experience, what happens when the senior officer becomes concerned about earnings and takes steps to cut costs, increase productivity, and improve profits?" Most reply that the company's management profile shifts left, toward the authoritarian style. General orders to economize—and promptly—often result in quick, across-the-board budget cuts. Some programs with high potential are sacrified along with obvious losers. Carefully laid, logical plans go down the drain. Some people are laid off—usually the least essential ones. But the best people in the organization sooner or later rebel at arbitrary decisions, and many of them leave.

At the outset, the arbitrary cost cutting produces a fairly prompt improvement in earnings, of course. But there is an unrecognized trade-off in the subsequent loss of human capital, which shows up still later in loss of business. In due course, management has to "swing right" again, rebuilding its human assets at great expense in order to restore good performance. Yet the manager who puts his firm through this dreary cycle, Likert observes, is often rewarded with a bonus at the outset, when things still look good. Indeed, he may be sent off to work his magic in another division!

Likert acknowledges that there are emergencies when sharp and sudden belt-tightening is inescapable. The trouble, he says, is that it is frequently at the expense of human assets and relationships that have taken years to build. Often it would make more sense to sell off inventory or dispose of a plant. But such possibilities are overlooked because human assets do not show up in the traditional balance sheet the way physical assets do. A company can of course, lose $100,000 worth of talent and look better on its statement than if it sells off $10,000 worth of inventory at half price.

A dollars-and-cents way of listing the value of a good engineering staff, an experienced shop crew, or an executive group with effective, established working relations might indeed steady the hand of a hard-pressed president whose banker is on the phone. Likert believes he is now on the trail of a way to assign such values—values that should be at least as realistic as the often arbitrary and outdated figures given for real estate and plant. It will take some doing to get the notion accepted by bankers and accountants, however sophisticated his method turns out to be. But today's executives are hardly unaware that their long payrolls of expensive scientific and managerial talent represent an asset as well as an expense. Indeed, it is an asset that is often bankable. A merely more regular, explicit recognition of human assets in cost-cutting decisions would help to ensure that human assets get at least an even break with plant and inventory in time of trouble.

Likert and his institute colleagues are negotiating with several corporations to enlist them in a systematic five-year study, in effect a controlled experiment, that should put a firmer footing under tentative conclusions and hypotheses. This study will test Likert's belief that across-the-board participative management, carefully developed, sustained through thick and thin, and supported by a balance sheet that somehow reckons the human factor, will show better long-run results than the cyclical swing between authoritarian and participative styles reflected in the typical middle-ground profile on his chart.

## CONVERSION IN A PAJAMA FACTORY

Already there's enough evidence in industry experience to suggest that participative management gets in trouble when it is adopted too fast. In some cases, an authoritarian management has abruptly ordered junior executives or employees to start taking on more responsibility, not recognizing that the directive itself reasserted the fact of continuing centralized control. Sometimes, of course, a hard shove may be necessary, as in the recent experience of Harwood Manufacturing Corp. of Marion, Virginia, which has employed participative practices widely for many years. When it acquired a rival pajama maker, Weldon Manufacturing Co., the latter's long-held authoritarian traditions were hard to crack. With patient but firm prodding by outside consultants, who acknowledge an initial element of "coercion," the switch in style was finally accomplished.

Ideally, in the view of Likert and others, a move of this kind should begin with the patient education of top executives, followed by the development of the needed skills in internal communication, group leadership, and the other requisites of the new system. Given time, this will produce better employee attitudes and begin to harness personal motivation to corporate goals. Still later, there will be improved productivity, less waste, lower turnover and absence rates, fewer grievances and slowdowns, improved product quality, and, finally, better customer relations.

The transformation may take several years. A checkup too early in the game might prove that participative management, even when thoroughly understood and embraced at the top, doesn't produce better results. By the same token, a management that is retreating from the new style in a typical cost squeeze may still be nominally participative, yet may already have thrown away the fruits of the system. Some research findings do indicate that participation isn't producing the hoped-for results. In Likert's view, these were spot checks, made without regard to which way the company was tending and where it was in the cycle of change.

A growing number of behaviorists, however, have begun to question whether the participative style is an ideal toward which all management should strive. If they once believed it was, more as a matter of faith in their long struggle against the "scientific" manager's machine-like view of man than as a finding from any new science of their own, they now are ready to take a second look at the proposition.

It seems plain enough that a research scientist generally benefits from a good deal of freedom and autonomy, and that top executives, confronted every day by new problems that no routine can anticipate, operate better with maximum consultation and uninhibited contributions from every member of the team. If the vice-president for finance can't talk candidly with the vice-president for production about financing the new plant, a lot of time can be wasted. In sales, group effort—instead of the usual competition—can be highly productive. But in the accounting department, things must go by the book. "Creative accounting" sounds more like a formula for jail than for the old behaviorists' dream of personal self-fulfillment on the job. And so with quality control in the chemical plant. An inspired adjustment here and there isn't welcome, thank you; just follow the specifications.

In the production department, automation has washed out a lot of the old problem of man as a prisoner of the assembly line, the kind of problem that first brought the "human relations" experts into the factories in the 1920's and 1930's. If a shop is full of computer-controlled machine tools busily reproducing themselves, the boy with the broom who sweeps away the shavings may be the only one who can put a personal flourish into his work. The creativity is all upstairs in the engineering and programming departments. But then, so are most of the people.

"Look what's happened in the last twenty years," says Harold J. Leavitt, a social psychologist who recently moved to Stanford after some years at Carnegie Tech. "Originally the concern of the human-relations people was with the blue-collar worker. Then the focus began to shift to foremen and to middle management. Now its concentrated in special areas like research and development and in top management. Why? Because the 'group' style works best where nobody knows exactly and all the time what they're supposed to be doing, where there's a continuous need to change and adapt."

## DEMOCRACY WORKS BETTER IN PLASTICS

One conclusion that has been drawn from this is that management style has to be custom-designed to fit the particular characteristics of each industry. The participative approach will work best in those industries that are in the vanguard of change. A Harvard Business School study has compared high-performance companies in three related, but subtly different, fields: plastics, packaging food, and standard containers. The plastics company faced the greatest uncertainties and change in research, new products, and market developments. The food company's business was somewhat more stable, while the container company encountered little or no requirement for innovation. The three achieved good results using markedly different management styles. The plastics firm provided for wide dispersal of responsibility for major decisions, the food company for moderate decentalization of authority, and the container company operated with fairly centralized control.

Less successful enterprises in each of the three industries were also examined, and their managements were compared with those of the high-performance companies. From this part of the study, Harvard researchers Paul Lawrence and Jay Lorsch drew another conclusion: not only may each industry have its own appropriate management style, but so may the individual operations within the same company. The companies that do best are those which allow for variations among their departments and know how to take these variations into account in coordinating the whole corporate effort.

Both the sales and the research departments in a fast-moving plastics company, for example, may adopt a style that encourages employees to participate actively in departmental decision making. But in special ways the two operations still need to differ. The research worker, for example, thinks in long-range terms, focusing on results expected in two or three years. The sales executive has his sights set on results next week or next month. This different sense of time may make it hard for the two departments to understand each other. But if top management recognizes the reasons and the need for such differences, each department will do its own job better, and they can be better coordinated. On the other hand, if top management ignores the differences and insists, for example, on rigidly uniform budgeting and planning timetables, there will be a loss of effectiveness.

It seems an obvious point that sales must be allowed to operate like sales, accounting like accounting, and production like production. But as Lawrence comments, "The mark of a good idea in this field is that as soon as it is articulated, it does seem obvious. People forget that, five minutes before, it wasn't. One curse of the behavioral scientist is that anything he comes up with is going to seem that way, because anything that's good *is* obvious."

## PEOPLE, TOO, HAVE THEIR STYLES

Other behavioral scientists take the view that management style should be determined not so much by the nature of the particular business operation involved, but by the personality traits of the people themselves. There may be some tendency for certain kinds of jobs to attract certain kinds of people. But in nearly any shop or office a wide range of personality types may be observed. There is, for example, the outgoing, socially oriented scientist as well as the supposedly more typical introverted recluse. There are mature, confident managers, and there are those who somehow fill the job despite nagging self-doubt and a consuming need for reassurance.

For a long time, personality tests seemed to offer a way to steer people into the psychologically right kind of work. Whether such testing for placement is worth while is now a matter of some dispute. In any case, the whole question of individual differences is often reduced to little more than an office guessing game. Will Sue cooperate with Jane? Can Dorothy stand working for Jim? Will Harry take suggestions?

The participative approach to management may be based upon a greatly oversimplified notion about people, in the view of psychologist Clare Graves of Union College in Schenectady, New York. On the basis of limited samplings, he tentatively concludes that as many as half the people in the northeastern U.S., and a larger proportion nationwide, are not and many never will be the eager-beaver workers on whom the late Douglas McGregor of M.I.T. based his "Theory Y." Only some variation of old-style authoritarian management will meet their psychological needs, Graves contends.

Graves believes he has identified seven fairly distinct personality types, although he acknowledges that many people are not "purebreds" who would fit his abstractions perfectly and that new and higher personality forms may still be evolving. At the bottom of his well-ordered hierarchy he places the childlike "autistic" personality, which requires "close care and nurturing." Next up the scale are the "animistic" type, which must be dealt with by sheer force or enticement; the "ordered" personality that responds best to a moralistic management; and the "materialistic" individual who calls for pragmatic, hard bargaining. None of these are suited for the participative kind of management.

At the top of Grave's personality ladder are the "sociocentric," the "cognitive," and the "apprehending" types of people. They are motivated, respectively, by a need for "belonging," for "information," and for an "understanding" of the total situation in which they are involved. For each of these levels some form of participative management will work. However, those at the very top, the unemotional "apprehending" individuals, must be allowed pretty much to set their own terms for work. Management can trust such people to contribute usefully only according to their own cool perception of what is needed. They will seldom take the trouble to fight authority when they disagree with it, but merely withdraw, do a passable but not excellent job, and wait for management to see things their way. In that sense, these highest-level people are probably not ideal participators.

Graves believes most adults are stuck at one level throughout their lifetimes or move up a single notch, at best. He finds, incidentally, that there can be bright or dull, mature or immature behavior at nearly all levels. The stages simply represent psychological growth toward a larger and larger awareness of the individual's relationships to society.

If a company has a mixture of personality types, as most do, it must somehow sort them out. One way would be to place participative-type managers in charge of some groups, and authoritarian managers in charge of others. Employees would then be encouraged to transfer into sections where the management style best suits them. This would hardly simplify corporate life. But companies pushing the group approach might at least avoid substituting harmful new rigidities—"participate, or else!"—for the old ones.

## THE ANTHROPOLOGICAL VIEW

Behaviorists who have been studying management problems from an anthropological viewpoint naturally stress cultural rather than individual differences. Manning Nash, of the University of Chicago's business school, for example, observes that the American emphasis on egalitarianism and performance has always tempered management style in the U.S. "No matter what your role is, if you don't perform, no one in this country will defer to you," he says. "Americans won't act unless they respect you. You couldn't have an American Charge of the Light Brigade." But try to export that attitude to a country with a more autocratic social tradition, and, in the words of Stanley Davis of Harvard, "it won't be bought and may not be workable."

Within the U.S. there are many cultural differences that might provide guides to managerial style if they could be successfully analyzed. Recent research by Lawrence and Arthur N. Turner at the Harvard Business School hints at important differences between blue-collar workers in cities and those in smaller towns, although religious and other factors fog the results. Town workers seem to seek "a relatively large amount of variety, autonomy, interaction, skill and responsibility" in their work, whereas city workers "find more simple tasks less stress-producing and more satisfying."

In managerial areas where democratic techniques *are* likely to work, the problem is how to give managers skill and practice in participation. The National Education Association's National Training Laboratories twenty years ago pioneered a way of doing this called "sensitivity training" (see "Two Weeks in a T-Group," *Fortune,* August, 1961). Small groups of men, commonly drawn from the executive ranks, sit down with a professional trainer but without agenda or rule book and "see what happens." The "vacuum" draws out first one and then another participant, in a way that tends to expose in fairly short order how he comes across to others .

The technique has had many critics, few more vocal than William Gomberg of the University of Pennsylvania's Wharton School. Renewing his assault recently, he called the "training" groups "titillating therapy, management development's most fashionable fad." When people from the same company are in the group, he argues, the whole exercise is an invasion of privacy, an abuse of the therapeutic technique to help the company, not the individual. For top executives in such groups, Gomberg and others contend, the technique offers mainly a catharsis for their loneliness or insecurity.

## "PSYCHING OUT THE BOSS"

Undoubtedly the T-group can be abused, intentionally or otherwise. But today's sensitivity trainers are trying to make sure the experience leads to useful results for both the individual and his firm. They realize that early groups, made up of total strangers gathered at some remote "cultural island," often gave the executive little notion of how to apply his new knowledge back on the job. To bring more realism to the exercise, the National Training Laboratories began ten years ago to make up groups of executives and managers from the same company, but not men who had working relationships with one another. These "cousin labs" have led, in turn, to some training of actual management "families," a boss and his subordinates. At the West Coast headquarters of the T-group movement, the business school at U.C.L.A., some now call such training "task-group therapy."

Many businessmen insist T-groups have helped them. Forty-three presidents and chairmen and hundreds of lesser executives are National Training Laboratories alumni. U.C.L.A. is besieged by applicants, and many are turned away.

Sensitivity training is supposed to help most in business situations where there is a great deal of uncertainty, as there is in the training sessions themselves. In such situations in the corporate setting there is sometimes a tendency for executives to withdraw, to defer action, to play a kind of game with other people in the organization to see who will climb out on a limb first. A chief ploy is "psyching out the boss," which means trying to anticipate the way the winds of ultimate decision will blow and to set course accordingly.

The aim of sensitivity training is to stop all this, to get the executive's nerve up so that he faces facts, or, in the words of U.C.L.A.'s James V. Clark, to "lay bare the stress and strain faster and get a resolution of the problem." In that limited sense, such therapy could well serve any style of management. In Clark's view, this kind of training, early in the game, might save many a company a costly detour on the road to company-wide "democracy." He cites the experience of Non-Linear Systems, Inc., of Del Mar, California, a manufacturer of such electronic gear as digital voltmeters and data-logging equipment and an important supplier to aerospace contractors. The company is headed by Andrew Kay, a leading champion of the participative style. At the lower levels, Kay's application of participative concepts worked well. He gave workers responsibility for "the whole black box," instead of for pieces of his complex finished products. Because it was still a box, with some definite boundaries, the workers seized the new opportunity without fear or hesitation. The psychological magic of meaningful work, as opposed to the hopelessly specialized chore, took hold. Productivity rose.

## VICE-PRESIDENTS IN MIDAIR

But at the executive level, Kay moved too quickly, failing to prepare his executives for broad and undefined responsibilities—or failing to choose men better suited for the challenge. One vice-president was put in charge of "innovation." Suspended in midair, without the support of departments or functional groups and lacking even so much as a job description, most of the V.P.'s became passive and incapable of making decisions. "They lost touch with reality—including the reality of the market," recalls Clark. When the industry suffered a general slump and new competition entered the field, Non-Linear wasn't ready. Sales dropped 16 percent, according to Kay. In time he realized he was surrounded with dependent men, untrained to participate in the fashion he had peremptorily commanded. He trimmed his executive group and expects to set a new sales record this year.

Sheldon Davis of TRW Systems in Redondo Beach, California, blames the behavioral scientists themselves for breakdowns like Non-Linear's. Too often, he argues, "their messages come out sounding soft and easy, as if what we are trying to do is build happy teams of employees who feel 'good' about things, rather than saying we're trying to build effective organizations with groups that function well and that can zero in quickly on their problems and deal with them rationally."

To Davis, participation should mean "tough, open exchange," focused on the problem, not the organizational chart. Old-style managers who simply dictate a solution are wrong, he argues, and so are those new-style managers who think the idea is simply to go along with a subordinate's proposals if they're earnestly offered. Neither approach taps the full potential of the executive group. When problems are faced squarely, Davis believes, the boss—who should remain boss—gets the best solution because all relevant factors are thoroughly considered. And because everyone has contributed to the solution and feels responsible for it, it is also the solution most likely to be carried out.

One of the most useful new developments in the behavioral study of management is a fresh emphasis on collaboration with technology. In the early days of the human-relations movement in industry, technology was often regarded as "the enemy," the source of the personal and social problems that the psychologists were trying to treat. But from the beginning, some social scientists wanted to move right in and help fashion machines and industrial processes so as to reduce or eliminate their supposedly anti-human effects. Today this concept is more than mere talk. The idea is to develop socalled "socio-technical" systems that permit man and technology *together* to produce the best performance.

Some early experimentation in the British coal mines, by London's Tavistock Institute, as well as scattered work in this country and in Scandinavia, have already demonstrated practical results from such a collaboration. Tavistock found that an attempt to apply specialized factory-style technology to coal mining had isolated the miners from one another. They missed the sense of group support and self-direction that had helped them cope with uncertainty and danger deep in the coal faces. Productivity suffered. In this case, Tavistock's solution was to redesign the new system so that man could still work in groups.

In the United States a manufacturer of small household appliances installed some highly sophisticated new technical processes that put the company well in the front of its field. But the engineers had broken down the jobs to such an extent that workers were getting no satisfaction out of their performance and productivity declined. Costs went up and, in the end, some of the new machinery had to be scrapped.

Some technologists seem more than ready to welcome a partnership with the human-relations expert. Louis Davis, a professor of engineering, has joined the U.C.L.A. business-school faculty to lead a six-man socio-technical research group that includes several behaviorists. Among them is Eric Trist, a highly respected psychologist from the Tavistock Institute. Davis hopes today's collaboration will lead in time to a new breed of experts knowledgeable in both the engineering and the social disciplines.

## "IT'S TIME WE STOPPED BUILDING RIVAL DICTIONARIES"

The importance of time, the nature of the task, the differences within a large organization, the nature of the people, the cultural setting, the psychological preparation of management, the relationship to technology —all these and other variables are making the search for effective managerial style more and more complex. But the growing recognition of these complexities has drained the human-relations movement of much of its antagonism toward the "super-rationalism" of management science. Humanists must be more systematic and rational if they are to make some useful sense of the scattered and half-tested concepts they have thus far developed, and put their new theories to a real test.

A number of behaviorists believe it is well past time to bury the hatchet and collaborate in earnest with the mathematicians and economists. Some business schools and commercial consulting groups are already realigning their staffs to encourage such work. It won't be easy. Most "systems" thinkers are preoccupied with bringing all the relevant knowledge to bear on a management problem in a systematic way, seeking the theoretically "best" solution. Most behaviorists have tended to assume that the solution which is *most likely to be carried out* is the best one, hence their focus on involving lots of people in the decision making so that they will follow through. Where the "experts" who shape decisions are also in charge of getting the job done, the two approaches sometimes blend, in practice. But in many organizations, it is a long, long road from a creative and imaginative decision to actual performance. A general theory of management must show how to build systematic expertise into a style that is also well suited to people.

The reapproachment among management theorists has a distinguished herald, Fritz J. Roethlisberger of Harvard Business School, one of the human-relations pioneers who first disclosed the potential of the "small group" in industrial experiments forty years ago. He laughs quickly at any suggestion that a unified approach will come easily. "But after all, we are all looking at the same thing," he says. "It's time we stopped building rival dictionaries and learned to make some sentences that really say something."

*W. J. Reddin*

# *THE 3-D MANAGEMENT STYLE THEORY: A TYPOLOGY BASED ON TASK AND RELATIONSHIPS ORIENTATIONS*

Trainers are currently showing great interest in the classification of the typical behavior of managers. This has also occupied the attention of political and administrative scientists, sociologists and psychologists for some years. It is widely recognized that such classifications may enable organizational, group, or even personal life to be better understood and changed.

Trainers, though, have special needs. They must have a classification or a cognitive map, that is as close to reality as possible. If they use one that is not, it will be seen as too gimmicky, unreal, too academic, too soft-nosed, or simply useless.

Figure 1 shows six managerial typologies, used to varying degrees, together with their apparent basis of classification.

## THE TWO UNDERLYING VARIABLES

Speaking very generally, the underlying theoretical components of four of these six psychological typologies are two fundamental personality variables which might be called Task Orientation and Relationships Orientation. These two variables go under the names shown in Figure 2.

Used by permission of the publisher. *Training and Development Journal*, vol. 21, no. 4, pp. 8–18, April, 1967.

*FIGURE 1* Psychological Managerial Typologies

| Author | Basis of classification | Types |
|---|---|---|
| Lewin-Lippitt-White[12] | Initiation<br>Guidance | Democratic, Laissez-Faire, Autocratic |
| McGregor[14] | Assumptions About the Nature of Man | Theory "X," Theory "Y" |
| Jennings[11] | Power Impulse, Hierarchical Orientation, Order Impulse, et al. | Abdicrat, Bureaucrat, Autocrat, Democrat, Neurocrat, Executive |
| Blake-Mouton[3] | Concern for Production<br>Concern for People | 1,1; 1,9; 9,1; 5,5; 9,9 |
| Raskin[18] | Factor Analysis | Leadership Skills, Hostile Self Seeking, Dependent-Exploited, Interpersonal Orderly |
| Carron[4] | Consideration Scores<br>Structure Scores | Laissez-Faire, Democratic, Autocratic, Paternalistic |

The importance of these two underlying variables is well grounded in empirical findings, in particular the Ohio State Leadership Studies, the Michigan Leadership Studies, and the work of Bales[2] at Harvard.

*FIGURE 2* Two Underlying Variables

| Author | Task orientation | Relationships orientation |
|---|---|---|
| Blake-Mouton | Concern for Production | Concern for People |
| McGregor | Theory "X" | Theory "Y" |
| Carron | Structure | Consideration |
| Lewin-Lippitt-White | Initiation | Guidance |

## OHIO STATE LEADERSHIP STUDIES

The Ohio State Leadership Studies isolated two independent factors to describe management behavior. One is initiating structure and the other is consideration. As they are independent, a score on one factor may be combined with any score on the other. It appears that a high score on both tends to correlate best with effectiveness, but that some studies show that low scores on both may lead to effectiveness. In any case, a certain minimum amount of consideration appears to be critical.

A factor analytic study by Halpin and Winer,[10] part of the Ohio State Leadership Studies, suggests that most of the individual differences in leadership performance can be explained by positing these two variables. In their study of air-crew commanders they found that these two factors together accounted for 83 percent of the differences in leader behavior.

## MICHIGAN LEADERSHIP STUDIES

The Michigan Leadership Studies, based on extensive interview work, produced a continuum with production-centered at one end and employee-

*FIGURE 3* Research Support for Two Underlying Variables

| | Task orientation | Relationships orientation |
|---|---|---|
| Ohio State | Structure | Consideration |
| Michigan | Production Centered | Employee Centered |
| Bales | Task Leadership | Socio-Emotional Leadership |
| Zelditch | Task Specialist | Maintenance Specialist |

centered at the other. This continuum grew, in part, out of boys' club studies. On some dimensions, democratically-conducted boys' clubs did better than clubs led in an autocratic or laissez-faire manner. While there is a great deal of evidence that the employee-centered leadership is often effective, it is clear also that production-centered leadership is sometimes just as effective.

## BALES' STUDIES

The studies of small groups at Harvard have derived two leadership types; the Task Leader and the Social-Emotional Leader. These appear to be independent leadership types. To be high on one does not correlate with being high on the other.

This task and relationship dichotomy is a widespread social phenomenon. Zelditch[21] studied role differentiation in the basic family unit in fifty-six societies. He found that, within the family, there was a characteristic differentiation into the task specialist and maintenance specialist roles.

The male adult was typically the task specialist; the female adult, the maintenance specialist.

It seems then that many studies refer to similar underlying dimensions. While each study defines the dimension in its own way, and not all posit independence, they might reasonably be presented by the terms, Task Orientation and Relationships Orientation which appear to capture the common thread of meaning.

That task and relationships orientation are fundamental and independent measures of managerial performance has high face validity. What is there that cannot be said to be part of either the manager's job or the people who inhabit the manager's environment? Many studies such as Raskin[18] support these two measures as fundamental and independent.

Definitions which appear to be broad enough to incorporate the findings, orientations, and definitions, of the studies cited are:

*Task Orientation* is defined as the extent to which a manager is likely to direct his own and his subordinates' efforts toward goal attainment. Those with high task orientation tend to direct more than others through planning, communicating, informing, scheduling and introducing new ideas.

*Relationships Orientation* is defined as the extent to which a manager is likely to have highly personal job relationships characterized by mutual trust, respect for subordinates' ideas and consideration of their feelings. Those with high relationships or orientation have good rapport with others and good two-way communication.

These definitions relate closely to Structures (S) and Consideration (C) of the "Leadership Opinion Questionnaire" (Fleishman, 1951, 1953, 1957, 1960).[5,6,7,8]

The two dimensions of the "Leadership Opinion Questionnaire" are independent ($r = -.01$) when several studies are considered together, although higher correlations ($r = -.47$) have been reported on individual studies.

## THE NON-NORMATIVE STYLES

If these variables are treated as independent and continuous, the four type typology of Latent Non-Normative styles is obtained.

No claims can be made that any one of these four styles is more effective than the other. Attempts to consider "the manager" as a single, internally undifferentiated job function have proven consistently fruitless. It is now clear that management jobs vary widely in the behavior required for successful performance. Thus, while task and relationships orientation may be powerful personality factors, any particular combination is not, in itself, effective or otherwise. Some jobs, to be performed effectively, demand a high relationships orientation and low task orientation. Some require the opposite.

In the mid 1920's, E. K. Strong, Jr.[20] attempted to develop an "executive" scale for his vocational interest blank. The scale he attempted to develop did not meet the validity standards for the Strong Vocational Interest Blank and was not used in it. Instead he successfully developed scales for production managers, sales managers, personnel managers and others. This supports the view that the positing of an ideal manager type may be less useful than positing the existence of several possible ideal types.

*FIGURE 4* Latent Styles

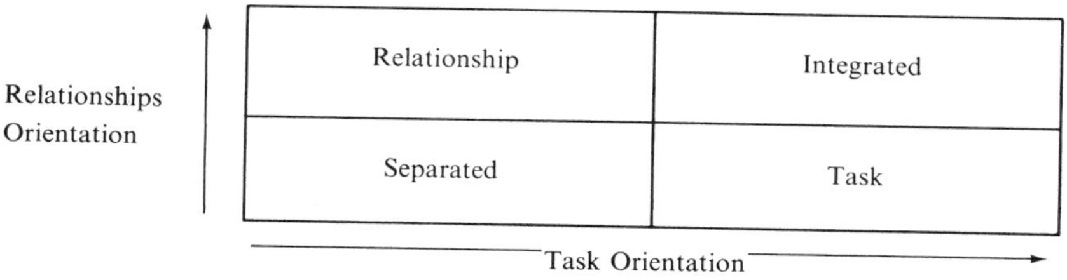

| Relationships Orientation ↑ | | |
|---|---|---|
| | Relationship | Integrated |
| | Separated | Task |
| | Task Orientation → | |

That management jobs are significantly different from one another is further supported by the finding that different jobs appear to demand or create different values in effective managers. Nash[17] points out that the economic scale of the Allport-Vernon Study of Values correlates with criteria of management effectiveness positively in a large mail order house to distinctly negatively related for public administrators (Mandell),[15] (Mandell & Adkins).[16]

An important finding (Fleishman & Peters)[9] was that the consideration and structure scores of managers in a manufacturing organization they investigated were not correlated with the effectiveness scores given by top management. Thus effectiveness, in this one organization at least, appears as an independent variable.

Anderson[1] reviewed forty-nine studies in which authoritarian and democratic leadership have been experimentally compared. He concluded that the evidence available demonstrates that neither authoritarian nor democratic leadership is consistently associated with better performance and that therefore the authoritarian-democratic construct provides an inadequate conception of leadership behavior.

All this does appear to be rather strong evidence that when speaking of managers, in general, it is inappropriate to consider that any one combination of task and relationships orientation is more likely to lead to effectiveness than another. It seems best then to treat as non-normative the four styles, created by dichotomizing the task and relationships variables.

## NORMATIVE STYLE TYPOLOGIES

Several typologies however do posit a single normatively good type. For example theory "Y" of McGregor and the 9,9 style of Blake. They each express a particular management philosophy. This arises in part because these and some other typologies are culture bound. Most of them, all North American, give some positive value to the permissive, democratic, human-relations approach. McGregor uses two types which might be simply labeled normatively as "Good" and "Bad." All this is nothing new. As Liu[13] points out, this "Good" and "Bad" classification was used in China in the 11th century and before. There were the Chun-Tzu (Virtuous Man) and Hsiao-Jen (Unworthy Person). The Confucian political philosophy used this dichotomy to classify bureaucrats:

> The virtuous ones are those loyal to the state or the sovereign, steadfast in their moral and political principles, cordial toward their colleagues, kind toward the common people, and dedicated to the Confucian ideal of government, which is to improve both the material welfare and moral well-being of society.

Liu points out that in the Chinese cultural environment, a moralistic basis was more important than a rational-legal basis for classification. This Chinese model, so obviously culture bound, leads us to look at current typologies to see to what extent they suffer from this. Obviously, most of them do.

The arguments for having a single normatively good type are many, though the notion itself is theoretically unsound. Many management style typologies are directed toward managers who appear to want to be told how to act; some of the typologies are used as identification models in the design of management development courses where having one type may facilitate the course design but not necessarily a manager's personal growth.

When the typologist bases his theoretical constructs on a particular work situation, he might be expected to posit an effective type that fits that situation. Unfortunately, however, there has been a tendency to call the particular typologies general typologies. Blake, from his work with top management in an industrial situation, has developed an effective type with a high task and relationships orientation. This may be correct for the top management in an industry in the U.S.A. but it may also be limited to it. Similarly, McGregor, in the context of his work in university administration, has produced a "Y" type with a very strong coaching supportive role. For teachers or university administrators who need not meet a payroll this type probably is the best one. It may not always be suited to industry.

The style of an effective manager in the army, the church, the civil service, and industry, may all be different. A style typology must recognize these differences if it is to be most useful. Positing a single effective style is inappropriate. A useful typology must allow that a variety of styles may be effective or ineffective depending on the situation.

## RESOLVING THE NORMATIVE ISSUE

If any style may be less-effective or more-effective, depending on circumstances, then each Non-Normative or Latent Style will have two behavioral counterparts, one less-effective and the other more-effective. Thus the four-style typology produced by dichotomizing the two underlying variables of task and relationships orientation, is expanded to a twelve-style typology of four less-effective types, four latent types and four more-effective types.[19]

Here is a capsule description of the eight types:

### Deserter

One who often displays his lack of interest in both task and relationships. He is ineffective not only because of his lack of interest but also because of his effect on morale. He may not only desert but may also hinder the performance of others through intervention or by withholding information.

*FIGURE 5* The Twelve 3-D Styles

| | No orientation | Relationships orientation | Task orientation | Task and relationships orientation |
|---|---|---|---|---|
| Ineffective | Deserter | Missionary | Autocrat | Compromiser |
| Latent | Separated | Relationships | Task | Integrated |
| Effective | Bureaucrat | Developer | Benevolent Autocrat | Executive |

### Missionary

One who puts harmony and relationships above other considerations. He is ineffective because his desire to see himself and be seen as a "good person" prevents him from risking a disruption of relationships in order to get production.

### Autocrat

One who puts the immediate task before all other considerations. He is ineffective in that he makes it obvious that he has no concern for relationships and has little confidence in others. While many may fear him they also dislike him and are thus motivated to work only when he applies direct pressure.

### Compromiser

One who recognizes the advantages of being oriented to both task and relationships but who is incapable or unwilling to make sound decisions. Ambivalence and compromise are his stock-in-trade. The strongest influence in his decision making is the most recent or heaviest pressure. He tries to minimize immediate problems rather than maximize long term production. He attempts to keep those people who can influence his career as happy as possible.

### Bureaucrat

One who is not really interested in either task or relationships but who, by simply following the rules, does not make this too obvious and thus does not let it affect morale. He is effective in that he follows the rules and maintains a mask of interest.

### Developer

One who places implicit trust in people. He sees his job as primarily concerned with developing the talents of others and of providing a work atmosphere conducive to maximizing individual satisfaction and motivation. He is effective in that the work environment he creates is conducive to his subordinates developing commitment to both himself and the job. While successful in obtaining high production, his high relationships orientation would on occasion lead him to put the personal development of others before short or long run production, even though this personal development may be unrelated to the job and the development of successors to his position.

### Benevolent Autocrat

One who places implicit trust in himself and is concerned with both the immediate and long run task. He is effective in that he has a skill in

*FIGURE 6* 3-D Theory

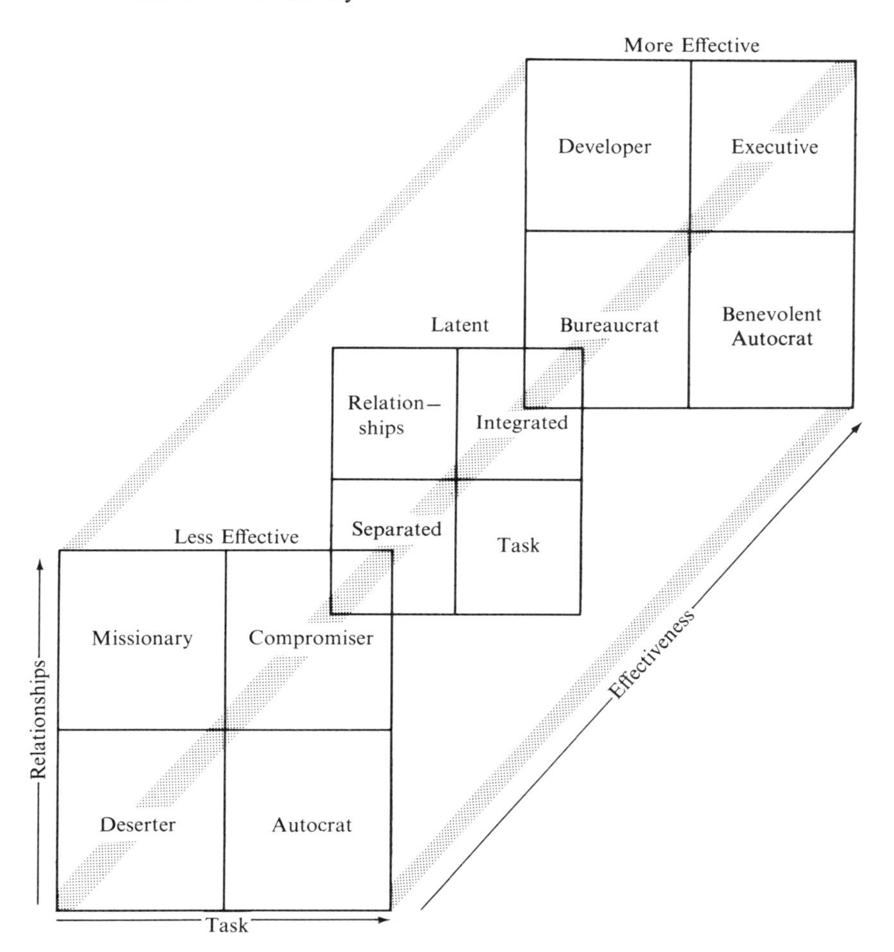


inducing others to do what he wants them to do without creating enough resentment so that production might drop. He creates, with some skill, an environment which minimizes aggression toward him and which maximizes obedience to his commands.

## Executive

One who sees his job as effectively maximizing the effort of others in relationship to the short and long run task. He sets high standards for production and performance and recognizes that because of individual differences and expectations that he will have to treat everyone differently. He is effective in that his commitment to both task and relationships is evident to all. This acts as a powerful motivator. His effectiveness in obtaining results with both of these dimensions also leads naturally to optimum production.

## EFFECTIVENESS

The essential difference between less-effective types and more-effective types is often expressed in terms of the qualities a manager possesses. When a single effective type is posited, this amounts to a return to the trait theory of leadership. A better explanation of effectiveness would appear to lay in the extent to which a manager's style, his combination of task and relationships orientation, fits the style demands of the situation he is in. Five elements compose the style demands. Two pairs of elements are related.

**Style Demands of Situation:**

1. The style demands of the job.
2. The style demands of the superior:
   A. The corporate philosophy
   B. The style of the superior
3. The style demand of subordinates:
   A. The expectations of subordinates
   B. The styles of subordinates

The third dimension is thus an output variable that is a function of the appropriateness of the underlying style to the demands of the job. A separated underlying style, for instance, might prove more-effective in a job where an orientation to routine was demanded; thus, the Bureaucrat style. The same underlying style in an aggressive sales organization would probably produce Deserter-style tendencies.

Management style theories such as these have more than simply entertainment value. Once a realistic set of types of managers has been established and agreed on, industry can use it many ways, and has done so. Management appraisal is made much more effective, as is management counselling. Several tests using the 3-D theory have been developed which may be used in appraisal or counselling. The appraisal tests compare a manager's leanings to each of the eight types with that of other managers. The counselling tests allow a manager to say what he thinks is the best style behavior under various conditions; his answers are then discussed with him.

A recently-developed use is that of training and organizational change. Style models are used as the central theme of training courses. They provide a concrete framework by which behavior on such courses may be discussed. Organizational change is also facilitated as organizations too have styles which may be diagnosed, held up for inspection, and parts modified as necessary. The 3-D typology has been used in all of these ways.

## IN SUMMARY

**3-D Theory Distinctiveness:**

- Not normative, culture-bound, or tied to single sterotype ideal national or industrial style.
- Four potentially more-effective styles.
- Effectiveness is function of match of style to situation.
- Key managerial qualities leading to effectiveness not task and relationships orientation but diagnostic skill and style flexibility.
- The five situational elements identified.
- Several observable styles included which previously have received little attention.
- Effectiveness is emphasized.
- Clear theoretical framework.

## REFERENCE LIST

1. Anderson, Richard C. "Learning In Discussions, A Resume Of The Authoritarian-Democratic Studies." *Harvard Education Review*, 29 (1959), 201–215.

2. Bales, R. F. "The Equilibrium Problem in Small Groups," 111–161. In T. Parson, R. F. Bales, and E. A. Shils (eds.), *"Working Papers in the Theory of Action."* Glencoe, Ill.: Free Press, 1953.

3. Blake, R. R., J. S. Mouton. *"The Managerial Grid."* Houston: Gulf Publishing, 1964.

4. Carron, T. J. "Human Relations Training and Attitude Change: A Vector Analysis." *Personnel Psychology,* 17, 4, Winter 1964.

5. Fleishman, E. A. *Leadership Climate and Supervisory Behavior.* Columbus, Ohio: Personnel Research Board, Ohio State University, 1951.

6. Fleishman, E. A. "The Measurement of Leadership Attitudes In Industry." *Journal of Applied Psychology,* XXXVII (1953), 153–158.

7. Fleishman, E. A. "The Leadership Opinion Questionnaire." In Stogdill, R. M. and Coons, A. E. (eds.), *Leader Behavior, Its Description and Measurement.* Columbus, Ohio: Bureau of Business Research, Ohio State University, 1957.

8. Fleishman, E. A. "Manual for Administering The Leadership Opinion Questionnaire." Chicago: Science Research Associates, 1960.

9. Fleishman, E. A. and D. R. Peters. "International Values, Leadership Attitudes, and Managerial 'Success'." *Personnel Psychology,* 15, 2 (1962), 127–143.

10. Halpin, A. W. and B. J. Winer, "A Factorial Study of the Leader Behavior Descriptions." In R. M. Stogdill and A. E. Coons (eds.), *Leader Behavior: Its Description and Measurement.* Columbus, Ohio: Bureau of Business Research Monograph 88, Ohio State University, 1957.

11. Jennings, E. E. *The Executive.* New York: Harper & Row, 1962.

12. Lewin, K., R. Lippitt, and R. K. White. "Patterns of Aggressive Behavior in Experimentally Created 'Social Climates'." *Journal of Social Psychology,* 10 (1939), 271–279.

13. Liu, James T. C. "Eleventh-Century Chinese Bureaucrats: Some Historical Classifications and Behavioral Types." *Administrative Science Quarterly,* 4, 2 (1959), 207–226.

14. McGregor, D. *The Human Side of Enterprise,* New York: McGraw-Hill, 1960.

15. Mandell, M. M. "The Selection of Executives." In Dooher, M. J. and E. Marting (eds.), *The Selection of Management Personnel,* I and II. New York: American Management Association, 1957.

16. Mandell, M. M. and D. C. Adkins, "The Validity of Written Tests for The Selection of Administrative Personnel." *Educational and Psychological Measurement,* VI (1946), 293–312.

17. Nash, A. N. "Vocational Interests of Effective Managers: A Review of the Literature." *Personnel Psychology,* 18, 1 (1965), 21–37.

18. Raskin, A. J., K. Boruchow, and R. Golob. "The Concept of Task Versus Person Orientation in Nursing." *Journal of Applied Psychology,* 49, 3 (1965), 182–187.

19. Reddin, W. J. "The Tri-Dimensional Grid." *Training Directors Journal,* 18, 7 (July 1964), 9–18 (an early formulation).

20. Strong, E. K., Jr., "Vocational Guidance of Executive." *Journal of Applied Psychology,* XI (1927), 311–347.

21. Zelditch, M. "Role Differentiation in the Nuclear Family: A Comparative Study." In T. Parsons, R. E. Bales *et al.* (eds.), "Family Socialization, and Interaction Process." Glencoe, Ill.: Free Press, 1955.

## DISCUSSION QUESTIONS

1. Do current research studies support or refute the idea of participative management? Defend your answer.
2. Identify and distinguish differences among the four management leadership styles as viewed by Professor Likert.
3. Is participative management always the best leadership style? If not, when would a participative style be inappropriate?
4. What two fundamental personality variables account for theoretical differences within most psychological managerial typologies?
5. Identify and explain the third dimension contained within Reddin's 3-D theory of management styles.
6. Compare and contrast "normative" and "non-normative" managerial-style typologies.

# Chapter 7. Staffing

*Winston Oberg*

# MAKE PERFORMANCE APPRAISAL RELEVANT

These frequently voiced goals of performance appraisal programs underscore the importance of such programs to any ongoing business organization:

- Help or prod supervisors to observe their subordinates more closely and to do a better coaching job.
- Motivate employees by providing feedback on how they are doing.
- Provide back-up data for management decisions concerning merit increases, transfers, dismissals, and so on.
- Improve organization development by identifying people with promotion potential and pinpointing development needs.
- Establish a research and reference base for personnel decisions.

It has been estimated that over three fourths of U.S. companies now have performance appraisal programs.[1]

In actual practice, however, formal performance appraisal programs have often yielded unsatisfactory and disappointing results, as the growing body of critical literature attests.[2] Some critics even suggest that we

---

Used by permission of the publisher. *Harvard Business Review,* vol. 50, no. 1, pp. 61–67, January-February, 1972. 

abandon performance appraisal as a lost hope, and they point to scores of problems and pitfalls as evidence.

But considering the potential of appraisal programs, the issue should not be whether to scrap them; rather, it should be how to make them better. I have found that one reason for failures is that companies often select indiscriminately from the wide battery of available performance appraisal techniques without really thinking about which particular technique is best suited to a particular appraisal objective.

For example, the most commonly used appraisal techniques include:

1. Essay appraisal.
2. Graphic rating scale.
3. Field review.
4. Forced-choice rating.
5. Critical incident appraisal.
6. Management-by-objectives approach.
7. Work-standards approach.
8. Ranking methods.
9. Assessment centers.

Each of these has its own combination of strengths and weaknesses, and none is able to achieve all of the purposes for which management institutes performance appraisal systems. Nor is any one technique able to evade all of the pitfalls. The best anyone can hope to do is to match an appropriate appraisal method to a particular performance appraisal goal.

In this article, I shall attempt to lay the groundwork for such a matching effort. First, I shall review some familiar pitfalls in appraisal programs; then, against this background, I shall assess the strengths and weaknesses of the nine commonly used appraisal techniques. In the last section, I shall match the organizational objectives listed at the outset of this article with the techniques best suited to achieving them.

## SOME COMMON PITFALLS

Obstacles to the success of formal performance appraisal programs should be familiar to most managers, either from painful personal experience or from the growing body of critical literature. Here are the most troublesome and frequently cited drawbacks:

- Performance appraisal programs demand too much from supervisors. Formal performance appraisals obviously require at least periodic supervisor observation of subordinates' performance. However, the typical first-line supervisor can hardly know, in a very adequate way, just what each of 20, 30, or more subordinates is doing.

• Standards and ratings tend to vary widely and, often, unfairly. Some raters are tough, others are lenient. Some departments have highly competent people; others have less competent people. Consequently, employees subject to less competition or lenient ratings can receive higher appraisals than equally competent or superior associates.

• Personal values and bias can replace organizational standards. An appraiser may not lack standards, but the standards he uses are sometimes the wrong ones. For example, unfairly low ratings may be given to valued subordinates so they will not be promoted out of the rater's department. More often, however, outright bias dictates favored treatment for some employees.

• Because of lack of communication, employees may not know how they are rated. The standards by which employees think they are being judged are sometimes different from those their superiors actually use. No performance appraisal system can be very effective for management decisions, organization development, or any other purpose until the people being appraised know what is expected of them and by what criteria they are being judged.

• Appraisal techniques tend to be used as performance panaceas. If a worker lacks the basic ability or has not been given the necessary training for his job, it is neither reasonable to try to stimulate adequate performance through performance appraisals, nor fair to base salary, dismissal, or other negative decisions on such an appraisal. No appraisal program can substitute for sound selection, placement, and training programs. Poor performance represents someone else's failure.

• In many cases, the validity of ratings is reduced by supervisory resistance to making the ratings. Rather than confront their less effective subordinates with negative ratings, negative feedback in appraisal interviews, and below-average salary increases, supervisors often take the more comfortable way out and give average or above-average ratings to inferior performers.

• Performance appraisal ratings can boomerang when communicated to employees. Negative feedback (i.e., criticism) not only fails to motivate the typical employee, but also can cause him to perform worse.[3] Only those employees who have a high degree of self-esteem appear to be stimulated by criticism to improve their performance.

• Performance appraisals interfere with the more constructive coaching relationship that should exist between a superior and his subordinates. Performance appraisal interviews tend to emphasize the superior position of the supervisor by placing him in the role of judge, thus countering his equally important role of teacher and coach. This is particularly damaging in organizations that are attempting to maintain a more participative organizational climate.

## A LOOK AT METHODS

The foregoing list of major program pitfalls represents a formidable challenge, even considering the available battery of appraisal techniques. But attempting to avoid these pitfalls by doing away with appraisals themselves is like trying to solve the problems of life by committing suicide. The more logical task is to identify those appraisal practices that are (a) most likely to achieve a particular objective and (b) least vulnerable to the obstacles already discussed.

Before relating the specific techniques to the goals of performance appraisal stated at the outset of the article, I shall briefly review each, taking them more or less in an order of increasing complexity. The best-known techniques will be treated most briefly.

### *1. Essay appraisal*

In its simplest form, this technique asks the rater to write a paragraph or more covering an individual's strengths, weaknesses, potential, and so on. In most selection situations, particularly those involving professional, sales, or managerial positions, essay appraisals from former employers, teachers, or associates carry significant weight. The assumption seems to be that an honest and informed statement—either by word of mouth or in writing—from someone who knows a man well, is fully as valid as more formal and more complicated methods.

The biggest drawbacks to essay appraisals is their variability in length and content. Moreover, since different essays touch on different aspects of a man's performance or personal qualifications, essay ratings are difficult to combine or compare. For comparability, some type of more formal method, like the graphic rating scale, is desirable.

### *2. Graphic rating scale*

This technique may not yield the depth of an essay appraisal, but it is more consistent and reliable. Typically, a graphic scale assesses a person on the quality and quantity of his work (is he outstanding, above average, average, or unsatisfactory?) and on a variety of other factors that vary with the job but usually include personal traits like reliability and cooperation. It may also include specific performance items like oral and written communication.

The graphic scale has come under frequent attack, but remains the most widely used rating method. In a classic comparison between the "old-fashioned" graphic scale and the much more sophisticated forced-choice technique, the former proved to be fully as valid as the best of the forced-choice forms, and better than most of them.[4] It is also cheaper to develop and more acceptable to raters than the forced-choice form. For many purposes there is no need to use anything more complicated than a graphic scale supplemented by a few essay questions.

### *3. Field review*

When there is reason to suspect rater bias, when some raters appear to be using higher standards than others, or when comparability of ratings is essential, essay or graphic ratings are often combined with a systematic review process. The field review is one of several techniques for doing this. A member of the personnel or central administrative staff meets with small groups of raters from each supervisory unit and goes over each employee's rating with them to (a) identify areas of inter-rater disagreement, (b) help the group arrive at a consensus, and (c) determine that each rater conceives the standards similarly.

This group-judgment technique tends to be more fair and more valid than individual ratings and permits the central staff to develop an awareness of the varying degrees of leniency or severity—as well as bias—exhibited by raters in different departments. On the negative side, the process is very time consuming.

### *4. Forced-choice rating*

Like the field review, this technique was developed to reduce bias and establish objective standards of comparison between individuals, but it does not involve the intervention of a third party. Although there are many variations of this method, the most common one asks raters to choose from among groups of statements those which *best* fit the individual being rated and those which *least* fit him. The statements are then weighted or scored, very much the way a psychological test is scored. People with high scores are, by definition, the better employees; those with low scores are the poorer ones. Since the rater does not know what the scoring weights for each statement are, in theory at least, he cannot play favorites. He simply describes his people, and someone in the personnel department applies the scoring weights to determine who gets the best rating.

The rationale behind this technique is difficult to fault. It is the same rationale used in developing selection test batteries. In practice, however, the forced-choice method tends to irritate raters who feel they are not being trusted. They want to say openly how they rate someone and not be second-guessed or tricked into making "honest" appraisals.

A few clever raters have even found ways to beat the system. When they want to give average employee Harry Smith a high rating, they simply describe the best employee they know. If the best employee is Elliott Jones, they describe Jones on Smith's forced-choice form. Thus, Smith gets a good rating and hopefully a raise.

An additional drawback is the difficulty and cost of developing forms. Consequently, the technique is usually limited to middle- and lower-management levels where the jobs are sufficiently similar to make standard or common forms feasible.

Finally, forced-choice forms tend to be of little value—and probably have a negative effect—when used in performance appraisal interviews.

*5. Critical incident appraisal*

The discussion of ratings with employees has, in many companies, proved to be a traumatic experience for supervisors. Some have learned from bitter experience what General Electric later documented; people who receive honest but negative feedback are typically not motivated to do better —and often do worse—after the appraisal interview.[5] Consequently, supervisors tend to avoid such interviews, or if forced to hold them, avoid giving negative ratings when the ratings have to be shown to the employee.

One stumbling block has no doubt been the unsatisfactory rating form used. Typically, these are graphic scales that often include rather vague traits like initiative, cooperativeness, reliability, and even personality. Discussing these with an employee can be difficult.

The critical incident technique looks like a natural to some people for performance review interviews, because it gives a supervisor actual, factual incidents to discuss with an employee. Supervisors are asked to keep a record, a "little black book," on each employee and to record actual incidents of positive or negative behavior. For example:

Bob Mitchell, who has been rated as somewhat unreliable, fails to meet several deadlines during the appraisal period. His supervisor makes a note of these incidents and is now prepared with hard, factual data:

"Bob, I rated you down on reliability because, on three different occasions over the last two months, you told me you would do something and you didn't do it. You remember six weeks ago when I. . . ."

Instead of arguing over traits, the discussion now deals with actual behavior. Possibly, Bob has misunderstood the supervisor or has good reasons for his apparent "unreliability." If so, he now has an opportunity to respond. His performance, not his personality, is being criticized. He knows specifically how to perform differently if he wants to be rated higher the next time. Of course, Bob might feel the supervisor was using unfairly high standards in evaluating his performance. But at least he would know just what those standards are.

There are, however, several drawbacks to this approach. It requires that supervisors jot down incidents on a daily or, at the very least, a weekly basis. This can become a chore. Furthermore, the critical incident rating technique need not, but may, cause a supervisor to delay feedback to employees. And it is hardly desirable to wait six months or a year to confront an employee with a misdeed or mistake.

Finally, the supervisor sets the standards. If they seem unfair to a subordinate, might he not be more motivated if he at least has some say in setting, or at least agreeing to, the standards against which he is judged?

### 6. *Management by objectives*

To avoid, or to deal with, the feeling that they are being judged by unfairly high standards, employees in some organizations are being asked to set—or help set—their own performance goals. Within the past five or six years, MBO has become something of a fad and is so familiar to most managers that I will not dwell on it here.

It should be noted, however, that when MBO is applied at lower organizational levels, employees do not always want to be involved in their own goal setting. As Arthur N. Turner and Paul R. Lawrence discovered, many do not want self-direction or autonomy.[6] As a result, more coercive variations of MBO are becoming increasingly common, and some critics see MBO drifting into a kind of manipulative form of management in which pseudo-participation substitutes for the real thing. Employees are consulted, but management ends up imposing its standards and its objectives.[7]

Some organizations, therefore, are introducing a work-standards approach to goal setting in which the goals are openly set by management. In fact, there appears to be something of a vogue in the setting of such work standards in white-collar and service areas.

### 7. *Work-standards approach*

Instead of asking employees to set their own performance goals, many organizations set measured daily work standards. In short, the work-standards technique establishes work and staffing targets aimed at improving productivity. When realistically used, it can make possible an objective and accurate appraisal of the work of employees and supervisors.

To be effective, the standards must be visible and fair. Hence a good deal of time is spent observing employees on the job, simplifying and improving the job where possible, and attempting to arrive at realistic output standards.

It is not clear, in every case, that work standards have been integrated with an organization's performance appraisal program. However, since the work-standards program provides each employee with a more or less complete set of his job duties, it would seem only natural that supervisors will eventually relate performance appraisal and interview comments to these duties. I would expect this to happen increasingly where work standards exist. The use of work standards should make performance interviews less threatening than the use of personal, more subjective standards alone.

The most serious drawback appears to be the problem of comparability. If people are evaluated on different standards, how can the ratings be brought together for comparison purposes when decisions have to be made on promotions or on salary increases? For these purposes some form of ranking is necessary.

### *8. Ranking methods*

For comparative purposes, particularly when it is necessary to compare people who work for different supervisors, individual statements, ratings, or appraisal forms are not particularly useful. Instead, it is necessary to recognize that comparisons involve an overall subjective judgment to which a host of additional facts and impressions must somehow be added. There is no single form or way to do this.

Comparing people in different units for the purpose of, say, choosing a service supervisor or determining the relative size of salary increases for different supervisors, requires subjective judgment, not statistics. The best approach appears to be a ranking technique involving pooled judgment. The two most effective methods are alternation ranking and paired comparison ranking.

*Alternation ranking:* In this method, the names of employees are listed on the left-hand side of a sheet of paper—preferably in random order. If the rankings are for salary purposes, a supervisor is asked to choose the "most valuable" employee on the list, cross his name off, and put it at the top of the column on the right-hand side of the sheet. Next, he selects the "least valuable" employee on the list, crosses his name off, and puts it at the bottom of the right-hand column. The ranker then selects the "most valuable" person from the remaining list, crosses his name off and enters it below the top name on the right-hand list, and so on.

*Paired-comparison ranking:* This technique is probably just as accurate as alternation ranking and might be more so. But with large numbers of employees it becomes extremely time consuming and cumbersome.

To illustrate the method, let us say we have five employees: Mr. Abbott, Mr. Barnes, Mr. Cox, Mr. Drew, and Mr. Eliot. We list their names on the left-hand side of the sheet. We compare Abbott with Barnes on whatever criterion we have chosen, say, present value to the organization. If we feel Abbott is more valuable than Barnes, we put a tally beside Abbott's name. We then compare Abbott with Cox, with Drew, and with Eliot. The process is repeated for each individual. The man with the most tallies is the most valuable person, at least in the eyes of the rater; the man with no tallies at all is regarded as the least valuable person.

Both ranking techniques, particularly when combined with multiple rankings (i.e., when two or more people are asked to make independent rankings of the same work group and their lists are averaged), are among the best available for generating valid order-of-merit rankings for salary administration purposes.

### 9. *Assessment centers*

So far, we have been talking about assessing past performance. What about the assessment of future performance or potential? In any placement decision and even more so in promotion decisions, some prediction of future performance is necessary. How can this kind of prediction be made most validly and most fairly?

One widely used rule of thumb is that "what a man has done is the best predictor of what he will do in the future." But suppose you are picking a man to be a supervisor and this person has never held supervisory responsibility? Or suppose you are selecting a man for a job from among a group of candidates, none of whom has done the job or one like it? In these situations, many organizations use assessment centers to predict future performance more accurately.

Typically, individuals from different departments are brought together to spend two or three days working on individual and group assignments similar to the ones they will be handling if they are promoted. The pooled judgment of observers—sometimes derived by paired comparison or alternation ranking—leads to an order-of-merit ranking for each participant. Less structured, subjective judgments are also made.

There is a good deal of evidence that people chosen by assessment center methods work out better than those not chosen by these methods.[8] The center also makes it possible for people who are working for departments of low status or low visibility in an organization to become visible and, in the competitive situation of an assessment center, show how they stack up against people from more well-known departments. This has the effect of equalizing opportunity, improving morale, and enlarging the pool of possible promotion candidates.

## FITTING PRACTICE TO PURPOSE

In the foregoing analysis, I have tried to show that each performance appraisal technique has its own combination of strengths and weaknesses. The success of any program that makes use of these techniques will largely depend on how they are used relative to the goals of that program.

For example, goal-setting and work-standards methods will be most effective for objective coaching, counseling, and motivational purposes, but some form of critical incident appraisal is better when a supervisor's personal judgment and criticism are necessary.

Comparisons of individuals, especially in win-lose situations when only one person can be promoted or only a limited number can be given large salary increases, necessitate a still different approach. Each person should be rated on the same form, which must be as simple as possible, probably involving essay and graphic responses. Then order-of-merit rankings and final averaging should follow. To be more explicit, here are the appraisal goals listed at the outset of this article and the techniques best suited to them.

*Help or prod supervisors to observe their subordinates more closely and to do a better coaching job.*

The critical incident appraisal appears to be ideal for this purpose, if supervisors can be convinced they should take the time to look for, and record, significant events. Time delays, however, are a major drawback to this technique and should be kept as short as possible. Still, over the longer term, a supervisor will gain a better knowledge of his own performance standards, including his possible biases, as he reviews the incidents he has recorded. He may even decide to change or reweight his own criteria.

Another technique that is useful for coaching purposes is, of course, MBO. Like the critical incident method, it focuses on actual behavior and actual results which can be discussed objectively and constructively, with little or no need for a supervisor to "play God."

*Motivate employees by providing feedback on how they are doing.*

The MBO approach, if it involves real participation, appears to be most likely to lead to an inner commitment to improved performance. However, the work-standards approach can also motivate, although in a more coercive way. If organizations staff to meet their work standards, the work force is reduced and people are compelled to work harder.

The former technique is more "democratic," while the latter technique is more "autocratic." Both can be effective; both make use of specific work goals or targets, and both provide for knowledge of results.

If performance appraisal information is to be communicated to subordinates, either in writing or in an interview, the two most effective techniques are the management-by-objectives approach and the critical incident method. The latter, by communicating not only factual data but also the flavor of a supervisor's own values and biases, can be effective in an area where objective work standards or quantitative goals are not available.

*Provide back-up data for management decisions concerning merit increases, promotions, transfers, dismissals, and so on.*

Most decisions involving employees require a comparison of people doing very different kinds of work. In this respect, the more specifically job-related techniques like management by objectives or work standards are not appropriate, or, if used, must be supplemented by less restricted methods.

For promotion to supervisory positions, the forced-choice rating form, if carefully developed and validated, could prove best. But the difficulty and cost of developing such a form and the resistance of raters to its use render it impractical except in large organizations.

Companies faced with the problem of selecting promotable men from a number of departments or divisions might consider using an assessment center. This minimizes the bias resulting from differences in departmental "visibility" and enlarges the pool of potential promotables.

The best appraisal method for most other management decisions will probably involve a very simple kind of graphic form or a combined graphic and essay form. If this is supplemented by the use of field reviews, it will be measurably strengthened. Following the individual appraisals, groups of supervisors should then be asked to rank the people they have rated, using a technique like alternation ranking or paired comparison. Pooled or averaged rankings will then tend to cancel out the most extreme forms of bias and should yield fair and valid order-of-merit lists.

*Improve organization development by identifying people with promotion potential and pinpointing development needs.*

Comparison of people for promotion purposes has already been discussed. However, identification of training and development needs will probably best—and most simply—come from the essay part of the combined graphic/essay rating form recommended for the previous goal.

*Establish a reference and research base for personnel decisions.*

For this goal, the simplest form is the best form. A graphic/essay combination is adequate for most reference purposes. But order-of-merit salary rankings should be used to develop criterion groups of good and poor performers.

## CONCLUSION

Formal systems for appraising performance are neither worthless nor evil, as some critics have implied. Nor are they panaceas, as many managers might wish. A formal appraisal system is, at the very least, a commendable attempt to make visible, and hence improvable, a set of essential organization activities. Personal judgments about employee performance are inescapable, and subjective values and fallible human perception are always involved. Formal appraisal systems, to the degree that they bring these perceptions and values into the open, make it possible for at least some of the inherent bias and error to be recognized and remedied.

By improving the probability that good performance will be recognized and rewarded and poor performance corrected, a sound appraisal system can contribute both to organizational morale and organizational performance. Moreover, the alternative to a bad appraisal program need not be no appraisal program at all, as some critics have suggested. It can and ought to be a better appraisal program. And the first step in that direction is a thoughtful matching of practice to purpose.

## REFERENCE LIST

1. See W. R. Spriegel and Edwin W. Mumma, *Merit Rating of Supervisors and Executives* (Austin, Bureau of Business Research, University of Texas, 1961); and Richard V. Miller, "Merit Rating in Industry: A Survey of Current Practices and Problems," ILR Research, Fall 1959.

2. See, for example, Douglas McGregor, "An Uneasy Look at Performance Appraisal," HBR May-June 1957, p. 89; Paul H. Thompson and Gene W. Dalton, "Performance Appraisals Managers Beware," HBR January-February 1970, p. 149; and Albert W. Schrader, "Let's Abolish the Annual Performance Review," *Management of Personnel Quarterly,* Fall 1969, p. 293.

3. See Herbert H. Meyer, Emanuel Kay, and John R. P. French, Jr., "Split Roles in Performance Appraisal," HBR January-February 1965, p. 123.

4. James Berkshire and Richard Highland, "Forced-Choice Performance Rating on a Methodological Study," *Personnel Psychology,* Autumn 1953, p. 355.

5. Meyer, Kay, and French, *op. cit.*

6. *Industrial Jobs and the Worker* (Boston, Division of Research, Harvard Business School, 1965).

7. See, for example, Harry Levinson, "Management by Whose Objectives?" HBR July-August 1970, p. 125.

8. See, for example, Robert C. Albrook, "Spot Executives Early," *Fortune,* July 1968, p. 106; and William C. Byham, "Assessment Centers for Spotting Future Managers," HBR July-August 1970, p. 150.

*George S. Odiorne and Edwin L. Miller*

# *SELECTION BY OBJECTIVES: A NEW APPROACH TO MANAGERIAL SELECTION*

> The foreman of a gang of lumberjacks was being solicited for a job by a rather spindly looking little man. The giant gang-boss scoffed: "Why, this work would kill you. Just to show you what I mean, why don't you take this ax and go chop down that giant fir?"
>
> Despite the grins of the regular crew, the little man approached the tree and with a quick flurry of blows had the giant conifer on the ground. The grins turned to whistles of awe, and the foreman's voice took on a tone of respect.
>
> "Holy Mackeral, fella, that's great! Where did you learn to chop down trees like that?"
>
> "I worked on the Sahara forest job."
>
> "Forest? I thought the Sahara was a desert."
>
> "*Now* it is."

This tale might be an illustration of how selection by objectives would look in the lumbering business. No personality tests, no aptitude tests, little concern about degrees held. Just a good record of having achieved good results in the past and an on-the-spot demonstration of some of the key behavior which might be required on the job ahead.

---

Used by permission of the publisher. *Management of Personnel Quarterly,* vol. 5, no. 3, pp. 2–11, Fall, 1966.

The entire matter of employment methods is under serious fire from a number of quarters, and perhaps a new approach to the selection of persons for employment, or for promotion—which is really internal selection—is indicated.

## WHAT'S WRONG WITH PRESENT SELECTION METHODS

The major shortcomings of present day selection methods seem to fall into these major categories:

- *Techniques are mainly for low-level workers.* Since Hugo Munsterberg and others about sixty years ago seriously undertook the study of employment testing, the major emphasis has been upon the selection of workers.[1] The problems of early identification of high talent manpower and the techniques for hiring and promoting managers, engineers and staff persons are different and at this stage very problematical.[2]
- *Psychological testing has come under serious fire.* From within the profession and from outside, numerous attacks have been leveled at psychological tests.[3] They comprise an invasion of privacy, some hold. They have logical improprieties, say others. They breed conformity, say still others. Whatever the merits of these charges, the effect nonetheless has been to cast a cloud over their use in selection. A small fringe of charlatans promising psychological miracles in a manner akin to the snake-oil peddlers of old have not done much to clarify the issues.
- *The civil rights laws have shaken many long-accepted practices.* The civil rights law of 1964 has shaken traditional employment practices seriously.[4] Not only are racial guidelines to hiring barred, but women are protected from discrimination in hiring and promotion because of sex.
- *The mad rush is to college graduates.* Despite a rapidly rising curve of enrollment in the colleges, the rush at the exit door of the institutes of higher learning is greater.[5] Surely one of the most bizarre and absurd fads ever to sweep industry, the clamor to collect degree holders for every white collar position, shows no sign of abatement. There is apparently little inkling of manpower planning to identify which job requires a degree and which one doesn't.

While all of these shortcomings could be expanded at length, and the list itself lengthened, they comprise typical evidence of the illness that presently besets the hiring and promotion process.

This article outlines a *new approach* to the selection process. It makes a quick tour of the four major methods now being used in selection, then turns to a more detailed explanation of a new—or fifth—approach to selection. The purpose isn't to deny the value of the four, but to place them in a new perspective and improve the effectiveness with which they are used.

The paper is based on experiments done in industrial and governmental organizations in applying the system of management by objectives to the selection process. The method described here thus becomes *Selection by Objectives.*

The article presumes that the first step in management is to establish objectives and to obtain commitments in advance to seek them.[6] It also presumes that the person who has achieved objectives consistently in the past is more likely to achieve them in new situations. It is further proposed that these selection criteria have primacy over testing, hunch, behavioral inventories, or background. Thus, the major purpose of selection procedures should be to uncover evidences of achievements against objectives in the past.

Personnel staffing decisions are gambles in much the same way that a decision to bet on a particular horse is a gamble. Both decisions are based on predictions of performance among alternative choices. Predictions of the future are estimates or expectations based upon observations of past and present achievements and the known or assumed relationships between these observations and future wants.[7] For the horseplayer, prediction of the outcome of a race might be based on such variables as ancestry of the horse, performance in previous outings, current times, and physical condition of the horse and the jockey. For the manager involved in personnel staffing decisions, the prediction of a candidate's performance will be based upon observations of variables believed to be associated with or determinative of the desired level of future performance. In either case, the horseplayer or the manager is seeking to identify the winner. Needless to say, there are many poor choices and many disappointed people.

Employment managers and supervisors have always concerned themselves with trying to identify the best man for the job. Typically the supervisor makes his decision based upon his ability to size up a man. In far too many instances, this method has led to failure and unsatisfactory performance. Errors in personnel staffing decisions can be costly mistakes. For the individual poorly placed, his inability to perform his work competently, and the consequent prospect of reprimand or dismissal can lead to his frustration and possible personal bodily harm. For the company, mistakes in personnel staffing decisions frequently lead to increased expense to the business in terms of recruiting, selection, training, and production. Although major stages in the development of a scientific approach to selection are well known, the objectives-result approach—tried experimentally by the authors (and on a tentative and sometimes unconscious basis in many places)—has not to their knowledge been consciously described. Such a description of the Fifth Approach is the purpose of this article.

## THE FOUR APPROACHES TO SELECTION NOW IN USE

The systems of selection used to date have fallen into four major categories, described here in summary form. These selection techniques are based upon the major presumptions of the person applying them.

1. The personal preference method. This is still the most commonly-used method, even when disguised by the apparatus of science; the hunch of the manager, his biases, or his likes and dislikes determine the selection of employees.

2. The occupational characteristics approach. Earliest of the scientifically based methods, this method applied aptitude measurements to applicants, and allowed one to attempt to predict success on the job.

3. The behavioral approach. Another scientific approach to selection of employees was that of identifying behavior patterns out of the past, and predicting that such behavior (as demonstrated in tests or verified through resumé and reference checks) would continue into the future. With these results matched against job requirements, success could be predicted.

4. The background approach. The fourth method is evidenced most strongly in the career pattern studies of Warner and Abblegen, and evidenced by the search for college graduates in campus recruiting. It presumes that successful managers and professionals can best be selected by studying the careers of the already successful, and hiring those who best seem to duplicate them.

### The Fifth Approach

What is suggested here is that a new approach is now possible, synthesizing the useful features of the others plus an important new addition, a new point of origin for selection. Because it proposes to supplant the others, and in fact has proven more successful where applied, a brief review of each of the former four methods is in order.

### The Personal Preference Method

The proprietary rights of an owner to make the decisions about who shall be hired or who shall not be hired to work in his business grows out of the property rights of ownership. If the small merchant or manufacturer decides to hire only members of his own lodge, church, or family, there are few constraints upon his doing so. Title VII of the Civil Rights Act of 1964, if applicable to him, theoretically limits his exercise of this right in the public interest. Clearly he cannot flout the law openly, but his preferences may lead him to the creation of standards which make the law ineffective while serving his preferential biases. The administration of the law in future years may corner him in these subterfuges, although at present the strong voluntary compliance aspects of the law can leave him relatively untouched. Since many of his biases are unconscious—and hotly denied if pointed out—they are difficult to eradicate from outside the firm. Kahn's studies of the employment of Jews,[8] and the open challenging of tests in the Motorola decision on the basis of their "culture biased" aspects illustrate the tacit application of how bias might be used or alleged.

These personal preferences originate in the emotions and sentiments of the employer and extend from hiring alumni to Zulus simply because the employer feels the way he does about the people he wants around.

## The Internal Characteristics Approach

Since psychologists are usually the only professionals qualified to devise and validate tests of psychological characteristics it is not surprising that testing of various kinds has all of the strengths and limitations of psychology itself as a science. In recent years, this approach has come under fire for a variety of reasons. Writers of a moralist type have written with great fervor about the invasion of privacy which attends testing. By selecting questions out of the body of extensive test batteries congressional committees and critical writers have generated righteous wrath. "Did you ever want to kill your father," for example, reads poorly when it becomes a headline in a Washington newspaper. Martin Gross, Vance Packard, and others have attacked the indignities which occur when psychologists pry.[9] Other criticisms have come from within the profession itself. Logical improprieties in testing are often discussed in professional journals. Still other critics have been behavioral scientists who have queried the scientific propriety of some testing methods.[10] As a result, it is now forbidden in government agencies to use personality tests upon job applicants, and this ban has recently been extended to government contractors by letters sent to all such contractors. Not totally banned, the list of limits placed upon their use has been sufficiently complicated that the actual effect will be a falling-off of this kind of testing.

*Two Families of Tests.* The purpose here isn't to outline the varieties of tests and their advantages and disadvantages; the aim is to outline only the objectives of tests which comprise the "inward characteristics" approach to selection. Achievement tests would not fall into this approach, since they measure demonstrable behavior being observed, but two others do: aptitude and personality tests.

*Aptitude Tests.* Because of the magnitude of the wastes and losses in selection there has arisen a more and more insistent demand to reduce errors in staffing decisions. It is this necessity that has given rise to aptitude prediction by means of testing. At the present, various kinds of psychological tests are the chief means for making aptitude prognosis.

Testing in all applied sciences is performed on the basis of samples, and human aptitude testing is not essentially different from the application of tests in other sciences. The thing sampled in aptitude tests is, in most cases, human behavior. Specifically, a psychological test is the measurement of some phase of a carefully chosen sample of an individual's behavior from which extrapolations and inferences are made. Measuring differences among people through the use of psychological tests has made a signal advance to understanding and predicting human behavior.

In its simplest terms, aptitude testing rests on a correlation relationship between a normally distributed predictor variable (which may or may not be related to the skills and abilities required on the job) on the one hand, and another normally distributed measure of satisfactory performance on the other hand.[11] The simple matching task is to eliminate, on the basis of the relatively inexpensive predictor variable, those individuals with little likelihood of success on the job—obviously an easy task in theory but beset by complexities in practice.

The conception of specialized aptitudes and the desirability of having tests of behavior which will indicate in advance latent capacity has its roots in ancient history. Over twenty-three hundred years ago, Plato proposed a series of tests for the guardians of his ideal republic. His proposal was realized in the United States Army mental tests of World War I.

The use of tests to measure aptitudes didn't receive much interest until the late nineteenth century when a number of psychologists became interested in mental testing and the psychology of individual differences.[12] The tests of the early aptitude psychologists were largely individual tests. This approach changed with the advent of World War I. Based on the pioneering work of A. S. Otis, a set of tests which not only could be administered to a large number of subjects at the same time but could be scored by semimechanical means appeared on the scene.[13] Nearly two million army recruits were tested, and aptitude testing on a group basis was born.

Following rapidly upon the heels of the spectacular accomplishment of psychological testing in the army, industry picked up the cue that tests could be effectively used in employment and personnel work. The individual worker came to be considered a conglomerate of traits that could be measured by tests. It did not matter whether these traits were regarded as innate or acquired. What mattered from the employer's viewpoint was that tests could be utilized in the selection and job placement of workers. The result of this hasty and ill-advised exploitation of an approach really useful in its own field was temporary failure and disillusionment. Quite naturally, a distinct reaction against aptitude testing set in.

The road back from almost complete denial of aptitude testing in industry has been paved with both successes and failures. Today, aptitude testing has proven to be helpful in staffing decisions involving clerical personnel, salesmen, and certain other industrial occupations; however, in that area where effective prediction is most desperately needed—in managerial selection—aptitude testing has met with only limited success.[14]

One of the most telling criticisms of aptitude testing is that made by Hull in 1928.[15] He suggested that something in the neighborhood of .50 might be a practical limit for validities of tests. Nothing in the history of selection testing has radically revised this figure after almost 40 years. Nevertheless the quest goes on—to develop tests which can efficiently estimate or forecast aptitudes and success on the job from test scores.

*Personality Tests.* Success on the job is not solely determined by ability; it is also attributable in part to the personality and interest of the worker. Aptitude tests are not tests of motivation and interest; consequently something else is needed to measure these dimensions of the worker. Not only is the supervisor interested in finding out whether the worker *can do* the job, he is also interested in determining whether he *will do* the job. It is to this question that personality and interest inventories in the industrial setting are addressed.

The instruments used to assess the "will do" side in prediction come in all shapes and sizes. Some of these devices are simple inventories, others are based on specific personality or motivational theories. Some seek to measure those aspects of the personality called temperament traits. Still others are projective in design and are intended for "global assessments" of personality.[16]

These instruments are impressive in their diversity and approach. However, notwithstanding their multiplicity of technique and design, the history of personality and interest measurements in industrial selection has been something less than spectacular. Much of the variety in approaches to the measurement of personality stems from the desire to overcome the deficiencies in existing tests and the fact that the relationship between the predictor variable and the criteria are infinitely complex and dynamic.

Many of the tests presently used in assessment, particularly in the selection of managers, are general personality tests which have not been validated for managerial performance but rather for the identification of particular personality traits. The relevance of these traits or characteristics to successful performance on the job frequently comes about because of some intuitive judgment as to the type of man one would like to have. Relatively few attempts have been made to forecast accurately the demands placed on the applicant once he is in the organization. Thus, it seems that we may be playing Russian Roulette with the future of the enterprise by attempting to select managers through screening devices which in effect merely assure us that all those admitted to managerial ranks are alike. Fortunately, this is not the problem for the organization today as it might be in the future. At present, the validities of personality tests are low enough so that the consistent use of any of the personality tests will allow enough people to slip by that the organization will be protected against poor judgment about the qualities it thinks it is selecting.

What is needed by management with regard to its personnel staffing is apparently a heterogeneous supply of human resources from which individuals can be selected to fill a variety of specific but unpredictable needs. Thus the problem with personality tests is much more than that of overcoming distortion due to faking, presenting an idealized concept of oneself rather than a realistic self-appraisal, and a lack of self-insight. The basic issue is ability to predict the future with an extremely high level of probability. This clairvoyance will be a long time in coming.[17]

### The Behavioral or Skills Approach

A third approach to selection has been through tests which are less concerned with inner qualities, or inferences about such qualities. Behavior—activity which can be seen or measured—has been the subject of measurement and observation in this cluster of selection devices. In its simplest form, it was the test applied to the itinerant craftsman who wandered from town to town in the early part of the century. The boss of the machine shop would simply give him a piece of metal and a drawing and tell him to "make this." If he made the piece to precise specifications, did it quickly, with few errors, he was hired. The achievement test of typing skill was to place the applicant in front of a typewriter and have her type. Her work was timed, checked for errors, and if she performed well she was hired.

Such tests—which certainly aren't any more psychological than the height and weight of the applicant are psychological—are still used, and are extremely useful screening devices. There has been an attempt to extend such testing to selection of managerial applicants, or candidates for sales, professional, or technical positions. Perhaps the most comprehensive plan for this approach is that of Robert N. McMurry, whose pattern interview program,[18] coupled with tests and full dress exploration of behavior histories, is widely used by many firms.

Actually a combination of personality, aptitude, and behavior history approaches, McMurry's system hypothesizes that the prediction of what a man will do in future assignments is already written in the record of his past behavior. Determinism is the underlying assumption here. If a man has been a job hopper in the past (has held five jobs in the past five years) he will probably be a job hopper in the future. The goal of the pattern interview then is to probe intensively into the resumé, filling in each gap to uncover "patterns" of behavior. It is presumed that these patterns will persist into the future.

The McMurry system, which has been widely adopted and copied by firms and by a corps of consultants who have developed similar plans, delves into attitudes by eliciting verbal reactions to the conditions of past employment. An applicant who states that most of his past employers have been incompetent, unpleasant, or otherwise deficient may be predicted to adopt similar verbal responses about the new employer after the initial period of adjustment is over. Further, one may predict such things as leadership, creativity, and maturity by asking questions which get at past behavior from which reasonable inferences can be made. Figure 1 shows how such questions might be devised in this behavioral approach to managerial selection.

*FIGURE 1*

**Using verbal responses to obtain predictors of future attitudes or capacities.**

| *Trait* | *Question which will highlight the trait* |
|---|---|
| Creativity | Has the applicant ever created anything? |
| Leadership | Has he ever led anything? |
| Loyalty | Does he speak well for former employers, school, parents, and associates? |
| Maturity | Has he been dependent upon others? Has he destroyed things which were his responsibility? |
| | Has his behavior been excessively oriented toward pleasurable activities? |

The assumptions in this line of questioning are that people's behavior doesn't change, or that it may be costly to change it. Such being true, the time to find the undesirable behavior pattern in applicants is when they are still applicants. One might even hire persons with less than desirable behavior patterns, knowing what the defects are and allowing for them.

Clearly more scientific than some of the more esoteric methods of personality and aptitude testing, McMurry's system nonetheless shares the limitation that it is deterministic, and is more apt to achieve conformity in hiring than any other outcome.

The distinctive feature of this approach is that it presumes that a *pattern of behavior* is the key ingredient in hiring. Reference checks, intensive attention to past behavior, and the reports of past observers about the behavior of individuals, are coupled with the hardest possible probing into every aspect of the applicant's past results in order to create an extensive dossier which gives the interviewer the equivalent of many years of personal acquaintanceship with the applicant. The interview which is vital in this approach may be non-directive when it will manipulate the individual into revealing things he might not otherwise divulge. Telephone checks of former employers are larded with probing questions to strip aside the amenities which former employers customarily drape over people they've fired.

The method's most important shortcoming, although it comes closer than many other approaches, is that it deals mainly with behavior and not with the effects of that behavior in results.

### The Background Approach to Selection

One of the fastest rising in popularity, the background approach has resulted in a dramatic rise in campus recruiting in recent years. In fact, much of the pressure upon the campus recruiting process has grown out of an unstated and sometimes unconscious assumption that a college degree is needed for most managerial and staff positions. There are some interesting assumptions here.

1. It is assumed that the person who has a degree learned something in college. It is further assumed that this learning is something which he will carry to his first and subsequent positions. It is further assumed that the learning will convert into behavior on the job, and the behavior in turn will produce results that could not be produced by the non-college graduate.

2. Much of the drive to garner diploma-holders was caused by studies which show that 75% of the present crop of chief executives of the largest firms are college graduates. The studies of Warner, Abegglen and others it is held, comprise predictors of the promotability of college graduates.[19] To some extent, this has become describable by the favorite cliché of the psychologist—"a self-fulfilling prophecy." Companies which presume that only college graduates can do managerial work enact policies which permit only college graduates to become managers. As a result, over time their ranks become filled with college graduate managers. As example, one utility company for many years recruited at colleges, limiting interviews to those in the upper brackets of their class in grades. Later they found that only high mark students succeeded.[20]

#### Where are the soft spots?

There are many studies which show that the most successful automobile dealers, real estate men, and successful small business operators are not college men.[21]

The two largest firms in the country in sales and profit have diametrically opposed policies with respect to the promotion of college men into managerial positions. In AT&T the college man enjoys a distinct edge. In General Motors, where results are primary guides to internal selection, a vast majority of managers are not college graduates, including at this writing the president. GM *has* an extensive college recruiting program; however, its assumptions are different from some of its corporate counterparts. GM assumes when it hires a college graduate that he will demonstrate what he has learned once he is on the job, and that this learning will be verified by the results he achieves rather than by the degree he acquired before joining the firm. (Ford, number two in manufacturing industries, shares GM's pattern of selecting managers.)

The background approach has the limitations of all the single-cause approaches to selection. It examines a single variable (academic degree) and generalizes this as a predictor. In fact, some combinations of degrees are automatic guarantees of rapid rise in the large corporation. The man with a BS degree from Massachusetts Institute of Technology and an MBA from Harvard, for example, may never have to really work again. His rise to the general management post is assured. Admittedly, he has already, as a youth, gone through several screens that many fail to survive, but his subsequent progress will not be measured by his results-achieved until he reaches a crucial position in the firm. Who would dare to give him a bad appraisal? He might remember it when he gets on top. His salary progress will be swift in order that the jump need not be too great when he arrives at the top.

The suggestion here isn't that background is not useful information, but rather that as a single predictor it has the limitations of all single-cause explanations for multiple-cause outcomes. Meanwhile, this approach to selection gains momentum. The average cost of recruiting an MBA at Michigan in 1966 was $2100. This doesn't include any of the cost of education, merely the cost of moving the inexperienced graduate from classroom to his first office. After he arrived he received an average monthly pay of $750, with a range running up to $2000 for certain rare types in the upper reaches of academic grade achievement.[22] What this is doing to salary administration inside these firms staggers the imagination. The average monthly salary in 1966 was some 30% above that offered three years ago.

## THE FIFTH APPROACH

An objectives-result approach doesn't presume to displace all of the presently-used methods. It merely subsumes them to other criteria and shapes the plan for selection in somewhat different terms.

It starts with statements of job objectives for the job being filled, rather than with job descriptions which have been oriented toward skills, experience, and man-requirements. The method turns secondly to a measurement of the candidates' results on past jobs.

The approach breaks these objectives down into three major categories of objectives, and uses the selection process to uncover predictors in the individual's history which would point up probabilities of his operating at each of the three levels. The presumption in this selection of managers is that routine duties are a *must* requirement and that movement into the higher levels is demonstrated by problem solving results and, most especially, by innovative or change-making abilities. (A special and somewhat temporary kind of objective will be learning-objectives, in which the candidate must complete a learning or training program in order to bring himself up to the minimum (regular) requirements of the position for which he is applying.)

These duties comprise an ascending scale of excellence in management achievement, and the tools of selection should be designed to identify these objectives in the job and to uncover, in the candidate's results on past jobs, predictors of these kinds of results for the future.

*FIGURE 2*

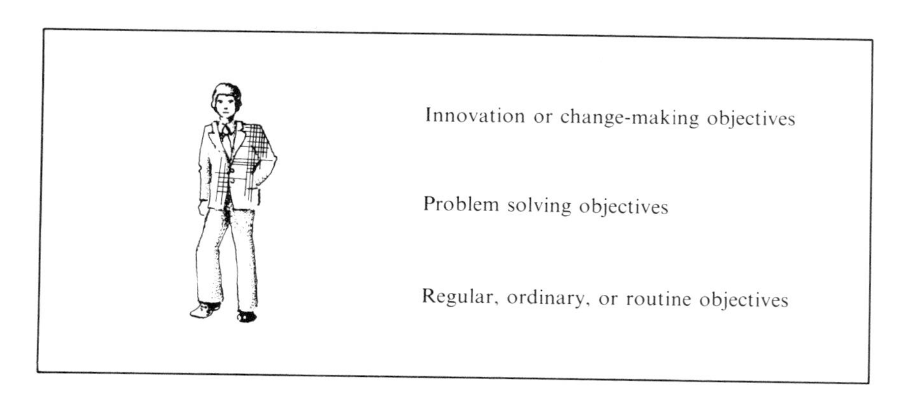


## Defining the Objectives

This fifth approach to selection starts with a clarification of the objectives of regular or routine duties, of the problems to be solved, and of the innovations sought. The first step in the fifth approach calls for a change in the job requisitioning procedures. For a typical position in which a job applicant might be considered, the employment manager or recruiter—or the manager himself if he is to do his own hiring—constructs a roster of job objectives, broken into the major categories. A sample description of the objectives for a general foreman (manufacturing) is shown in Figure 3. From this guide it is seen that this position has more regular duties than

*FIGURE 3*

**Sample Job Objectives for General Foreman—Manufacturing**

| *Objectives* | *Indicative past achievements* |
| --- | --- |
| 1. To aid in selection of foreman for production | Has he ever picked a foreman, or does he have some firm ideas on what a foreman's functions should be? |
| 2. Train foremen on the plant floor | Does he know the foreman's major objectives and functions? Has he ever broken in a new one? How many? Have any of them been subsequently released? Promoted? |
| 3. Production quantity | What departments has he led? What were the output requirements? Did the department meet them? Exceed them? What occurred during his tenure in office in terms of levels of output? What did he do which might have affected output? |
| 4. Quality | What was the reject rate when he started? What direction did it go? How did he get along with the inspectors? Quality manager? What techniques for improvement did he use? |
| 5. Cost control | What cost results did he achieve? How did his prime costs vary? His indirect labor? Indirect materials? Direct materials? Direct labor? Did he use any cost reduction methods such as work simplification? What were the effects? Has he submitted any improvement ideas in cost? |
| 6. Employee relations | What was the turnover rate when he assumed charge? Did it change? Grievance rates? Absenteeism? Any special methods used or introduced? Were any attitude surveys done in his area, and with what effect? |

*FIGURE 4*

**List of Typical Functions and Results Criteria for a Systems Engineer**

| *Function* | *Result criteria* |
| --- | --- |
| 1. Interprets organization objectives when laying out project | Upon receiving tasks, projects, or assignments must develop working plans and approaches to achieve them which requires interpretation of sponsor's objectives. |
| 2. Checking progress for compliance | Must check with superior or customer to determine whether direction and rate of progress are satisfactory. Has few if any complaints that he is checking back too often (being too dependent) or too infrequently, thus getting off the track too far. |
| 3. Making stop-or-proceed decisions | Makes decisions on work whether to proceed a course of study or action or to drop that course and try another. Generally gets concurrence of customer or superior. Should run into occasional blank wall if he is really experimenting. |
| 4. System engineering skill | Applies law and principles of systems to the solution of specific problems in the project. Has well stocked memory for principles, has access to many more, and learns new ones quickly. Manipulates memories into new and original mixes. |
| 5. Visual display of concepts | Devises, plans and executes visual displays (drawings, sketches, working models, breadboards, etc.) of the underlying concepts. |
| 6. Communicating ideas | Clarifies ideas, converts them into the language of the receiver, transmits them effectively, gets feedback to assure understanding: includes report writing and technical manuals. |
| 7. Adherence to policy | Stays customarily within accepted and promulgated guides to technical action in that firm, the industry, the lab unless overriding reasons dictate otherwise. |

Others rated highly important included Self-Development activity, and introduction of new ideas.

it has problem-solving or innovative duties. These could be broken out as selection criteria. Other positions might emphasize the requirements of problem solving.

Figure 4 shows the objectives for a systems engineer. This list of objectives, constructed by a group of 100 managers in systems engineering laboratories, could inspire an entirely different approach to selection from the traditional method. Here is an example of a different approach to selection, based on this set of objectives. Acme System Company is recruiting people for engineering posts to fulfill a long-run contract. It also hopes that out of this group will emerge some managers for the future. Some tangible effects might alter the selection procedure:

1. Despite the common nature of many of the activities, this work will be primarily innovative or problem solving. All job information sought in interview should aim at reaching a conclusion about such results achieved by the candidate in the past.

2. Certain kinds of objectives cannot be expected from new hires directly from college. In the objectives shown in Figure 4, those which could be expected of the beginner are handled apart from those which would be required of the experienced professional who might be expected to start in immediately and achieve most of his objectives.

3. The inquiry about the candidate should aim at uncovering how his past results in each of these areas indicate probable achievements of similar results in the future. Such questions as the following might be used.

| *Objective* | *Line of questioning* |
|---|---|
| To apply laws and principles of systems engineering to specific problems in a project. | • Courses taken?<br>• Grades?<br>• Do they apply here?<br>• Special research done?<br>• List of past projects?<br>• Key issues in technical field?<br>• Does he see any interdisciplinary approaches?<br>• Is he mathematically sound? |
| To interpret objectives for technical projects. | • What projects has he designed experiments for?<br>• How has he decided on working plans and approaches? |

It is apparent that the one conducting the interview and making umpire-like judgments as to past achievements in terms of results must be conversant with the objective of the man's job. The specifics of the question aren't of major concern here, but rather that the interviewer be seeking evidence of results in both kind and amount. The short illustration presented above demonstrates that the end product of selection by objectives comes from a different look at the work the man is expected to do when he is hired.

## When Objectives Are Set for the First Time

Before a company can select by objectives, it must establish what the objectives for the position being filled actually are. The statements of the systems engineer's functions had to be constructed for this study since they did not exist in the firm at the time of the study. The statements of responsibilities were hammered out in small conference groups with the managers of these engineers. Only those statements which over 90% of the managers felt were of above average significance for the jobs of the systems engineers in that lab were included. Others were specifically reflected by the majority. (Community and civic activities, training technicians, and delegation to technicians were rated as of little or no significance.) While one may deplore the standards set by the managers in some areas, it must be realized that this is the climate into which the new engineers are going to be hired.

The same step can be taken elsewhere, partially by asking the present incumbents what they think their objectives are, but more importantly, by asking the manager of the position to clarify the objectives for that position. It is he who will administer salaries, appraise for the annual performance report, coach, and recommend promotions.

## Predicting Success on the Basis of Results

Once job objectives are in hand, all selection methods should focus on uncovering result-getting activity in the history of the applicant. If the accustomed way of thinking about hiring suggests "Why, we're doing that right now," please read on. Most application forms or proposed resumé forms do not demand specific statements of results achieved. Take the case of the government agency which was stymied by its selection problem because it found so many people at the higher levels had resumés including such information as the following:

> 1956–59 Director of Underground Utilization of Overhead Manpower, Department of Midair Coordination and Development. GS-15
>
> Had full responsibility for coordination and implementation of all liaison missions of this service base. Reported directly to the deputy chief of staff-Coordination. Base operated with 6000 military and civilian personnel, and annual budget of $32 million.

Such nonsense implies that the applicant is the sole leader of 6000 men, spending thirty million dollars yearly, and it surrounds him with an aura of responsibility. The agency requires that the resumés be written to include answers to the question:

> What did you actually achieve during that period; give year by year summaries. Who could we talk with to verify these achievements? How many of them were attributable to your efforts, how many were jointly performed with others?

The replies were matched with some intensive looks at the vacant positions to see what the objectives and criteria were for the persons being hired. The result was a drastic change in the way selections were made, and while it is still early to be certain, preliminary reports indicate a sharpening of performance in the newly-placed persons.

Another example occurred in a firm which was seeking a college grad trainee for a marketing management position. One of the prime candidates was labelled as having "leadership" because he was president of the student council in college. At the urging of the writers, the firm probed a little deeper along these lines:

> During your year as president what did the council do? What condition was the treasury in when you took over? When you left? Did you finish any projects which would make a lasting effect on student life? Who could we talk to that would know best what the achievements of the council were under your leadership?

This intensive line of questioning elicited from the young man himself the fact that the year had been marked with constant trouble growing out of his inability to handle the officers and get programs going. He had been selected "on my good looks, I guess, and the coeds make up a big part of the vote." The very king-pin criterion of the selection decision proved to be the weakest link.

Job applicants have increasingly recognized the values of listing accomplishments on their resumés rather than claiming attributes or positions which emit golden glows. Some personnel men have shied away from the use of such information, because "Most people will dress it up, and you can't really tell whether the interviewee was responsible, or just went along for the ride."

The same cautious skepticism is needed in evaluating accomplishments and results as is needed in statements of responsibilities, personality, or background. How can one overcome the tendency of applicants to paint an over-rosy picture?

1. Ask specifically how much of the achievements listed are genuinely attributable to their own efforts and how much were shared with others. For example the following question has produced some candid responses in interviews observed and reported:

> "Your record shows some fine achievements in this past job. Now many of us do things jointly with others. What *percentage* of this achievement would you say is directly attributable to you or your subordinates?"
>
> "Now, you note that these achievements are partially shared with Mr. A, the controller. You estimate that . . . . % of this is rightly attributable to you and your organization. Do you think that Mr. A would agree with your estimate of that percentage?"

The only reason, generally, a candid and honestly-held estimate may be withheld is that the applicant doesn't know, is deluding himself, or is lying. Verification procedures, reference checks and telephone reference chats substantiate the information. Rather than checking such matters as initiative, drive, personality, and the like, the interviewer restates the achievements the applicant has claimed and simply asks the informant, "Would you agree that the achievements he has stated for his performance in your company are accurate? If not, how did they differ?"

## PRIVATE GOOD AND PUBLIC WEAL—A CONCLUSION

Hiring and promotion policy and practice badly need an overhaul. The perpetuation of our firms, and the observance of public interest through equitable selection are at stake. We have learned from all of our past experiences. Selection by objectives won't guarantee success, but may help us improve our averages. It may also stem the onrushing trend toward hiring overqualified people and ease the job opportunities for the present unemployables. It is a method of rewarding excellence rather than conformity or social class of origin.

## NOTES

1. Hugo Munsterberg, *Psychology of Industrial Efficiency,* Boston, Houghton Mifflin, 1913.

2. M. Joseph Dooher and Elizabeth Mauting, *Selection of Management Personnel,* Vol. 1, New York, American Management Association, 1957.
Thomas A. Mahoney, Thomas H. Jerdee, and Allen N. Nash, *The Identification of Management Potential,* Dubuque, Wm. C. Brown Co., 1961.

3. William H. Whyte, Jr., *The Organization Man,* New York, Simon and Schuster, 1956.

4. Howard C. Lockwood, "Critical Problems in Achieving Equal Employment Opportunity," *Personnel Psychology,* XIX, Spring, 1966, pp. 3–10.

A. G. Bayroff, "Test Technology and Equal Employment Opportunity," *Personnel Psychology,* XIX, Spring, 1966, pp. 35–39.

5. John S. Fielden, "The Right Young People for Business," *Harvard Business Review,* XLIV, March-April, 1966, pp. 76–83.

6. George S. Odiorne, *Management by Objectives,* New York, Pitman Publishing Corp., 1965.
Edward C. Schleh, *Management by Results,* New York, McGraw-Hill Book Co., 1961.

7. Marvin D. Dunnette and Wayne K. Kirchner, *Psychology Applied to Industry,* New York, Appleton-Century-Crofts, 1965.

8. Robert Kahn *et al., Discrimination Without Prejudice,* Institute for Social Research, Survey Research Center, University of Michigan, 1964.

9. Vance Packard, *The Pyramid Climbers,* New York, McGraw-Hill Book Co., 1962, pp. 279–285.
Martin Gross, *The Brain Watchers,* New York, Random House, 1962.

10. Harry Levinson, "The Psychologist in Industry," *Harvard Business Review,* XXXVII, September-October, 1959, pp. 93–99.

11. Mason Haire, "Psychological Problems Relevant to Business and Industry," *Psychological Bulletin,* LVI, May, 1959, pp. 174–175.

12. Anne Anastasi, *Psychological Testing,* New York, Macmillan Co., 1954, pp. 8–18.

13. Clark Hill, *Aptitude Testing,* New York, World Book Co., 1928, pp. 16–19.

14. Robert M. Guion, *Personnel Testing,* New York, McGraw-Hill Book Co., 1965, pp. 469–471.

15. Hull, *op. cit.*

16. Five widely used inventories are:
1. California Psychology Inventory
2. Gordon Personal Profile
3. Guilford-Zimmerman Temperament Survey
4. Minnesota Multiphasic Personality Inventory
5. Thurston Temperament Schedule

17. As Guion has commented concerning personality measurement: "The available measures have generally been developed for clinical and counseling purposes rather than for selection, they are too subjective, and the evidence of their value is too weak."

18. Robert N. McMurry, "Validating the Patterned Interview," *Personnel,* XXIII, January, 1947, pp. 263–272.

19. W. Lloyd Warner and James C. Abegglen, *Occupational Mobility in*

*American Business and Industry,* Minneapolis, University of Minnesota Press, 1955, pp. 95–97.

20. Frederick R. Kappel, "From the World of College to the World of Work," *Bell Telephone Magazine,* Spring, 1962.

21. Warner and Abegglen, *loc. cit.*

22. Arthur S. Hann, *Salary Summary of Job Offers and Acceptances to Date, Spring, 1966,* Graduate School of Business Administration, Ann Arbor, University of Michigan, June, 1966.

## DISCUSSION QUESTIONS

1. Identify some of the frequently mentioned goals of performance appraisal programs.
2. What are some of the most commonly used appraisal techniques?
3. What are some of the most common pitfalls or obstacles to the success of formal performance appraisal programs?
4. Comment on some of the major shortcomings of present day selection methods.
5. Briefly describe the five approaches to selection as envisioned by Professors Odiorne and Miller.
6. Summarize the key features of the "selection by objectives" approach to managerial selection.

# Chapter 8. Motivating

*J. G. Hunt and J. W. Hill*

# THE NEW LOOK IN MOTIVATION THEORY FOR ORGANIZATIONAL RESEARCH

During the last few years the treatment of motivation with respect to industrial and other formal organizations has more often than not been in terms of models by Maslow or Herzberg.[1] Where theories are apparently so thoroughly accepted, one naturally assumes a fairly substantial amount of data leading to empirical verification. However, as we shall show, there is relatively little empirical evidence concerning Maslow's theory; and while there are many studies bearing on Herzberg's theory, it remains controversial. After comparing these two approaches and reviewing their present status, we will describe a newer motivation theory developed by Vroom, which is similar to those developed by Atkinson *et al.* and Edwards in experimental psychology, and Peak, Rosenberg and Fishbein in social psychology.[2] It is our contention, on both theoretical and empirical grounds, that Vroom's theory, more than Maslow's or Herzberg's, is in line with the thinking of contemporary psychologists and industrial sociologists and is the best yet developed for organizational use.

---

Used by permission of the publisher. *Human Organization,* vol. 28, no. 2, pp. 100–109, Summer, 1969.

## THE MASLOW MODEL

Maslow's theory hypothesizes five broad classes of needs arranged in hierarchical levels of prepotency so that when one need level is satisfied, the next level is activated. The levels are: (1) physiological needs; (2) security or safety needs; (3) social, belonging, or membership needs; (4) esteem needs further subdivided into esteem of others and self-esteem including autonomy; and (5) self-actualization or self-fulfillment needs.

The original papers present very little empirical evidence in support of the theory and no research at all that tests the model in its entirety. Indeed, Maslow argues that the theory is primarily a framework for future research. He also discusses at length some of the limitations of the model and readily admits that these needs may be unconscious rather than conscious. While Maslow discusses his model and its limitations in detail, a widely publicized paper by McGregor gives the impression that the model can be accepted without question and also that it is fairly easy to apply.[3] In truth, the model is difficult to test, which is probably why there are so few empirical studies to either prove or refute the theory.

Porter provides the most empirical data concerning the model.[4] At the conscious level he measures all except the physiological needs. His samples are based only on managers, but they cover different managerial levels in a wide range of business organizations in the United States and thirteen other countries. Porter's studies have a number of interesting findings, but here we are primarily concerned with two: (1) in the United States and Britain (but not in the other twelve countries) there tends to be a hierarchical satisfaction of needs as Maslow hypothesizes; and (2) regardless of country or managerial level there is a tendency for those needs which managers feel are most important to be least satisfied.

A study by Beer of female clerks provides additional data concerning the model.[5] He examines the relationship between participative and considerate or human relations-oriented supervisory leadership styles and satisfaction of needs. He also goes one step further and argues that need satisfaction, as such, does not necessarily lead to motivation. Rather, motivation results only from need satisfaction which occurs in the process of task-oriented work. He reasons that a participative leadership style should meet this condition since it presumably allows for the satisfaction of the higher order needs (self-actualization, autonomy, and esteem). Beer found that the workers forced to arrange needs in a hierarchy (as required by his ranking method) tend to arrange them as predicted by Maslow. He also found that self-actualization, autonomy and social needs were most important while esteem and security needs were least important, although his method (unlike Porter's) did not allow a consideration of the relationship between importance and need satisfaction. Interestingly enough, there was no significant relationship between need satisfaction and Beer's measure of motivation nor between any of the leadership style dimensions and motivation. There were, however, significant relationships between leadership style dimensions and need satisfaction. Beer concludes that the model has questionable usefulness for a theory of industrial motivation although it may provide a fairly reliable measurement of the *a priori* needs of industrial workers.

We have found only three studies that systematically consider the Maslow theory in terms of performance.[6]

The first of these, by Clark, attempts to fit a number of empirical studies conducted for different purposes into a framework which provides for progressive activation and satisfaction of needs at each of the hierarchical levels. The findings are used to make predictions concerning productivity, absenteeism, and turnover as each need level is activated and then satisfied. While the article does not explicitly test the Maslow model, it is highly suggestive in terms of hypotheses for future research that might relate the theory to work group performance.

A second study, by Lawler and Porter, correlates satisfaction of managers' needs (except physiological) with rankings of their performance by superiors and peers. All correlations are significant but low, ranging from .16 to .30. Lawler and Porter conclude that satisfaction of higher order needs is more closely related to performance than satisfaction of lower order needs. However, the differences are not very great and they are not tested for significance. For example, correlations of superior ratings for the lower order security and social needs are .21 and .23 while for the higher order esteem, autonomy, and self-actualization needs they are .24, .18, and .30. Peer correlations are similar. Thus, unlike Lawler and Porter, we conclude that in this study the correlations for lower order needs are about the same as for higher order needs.

A more recent Porter and Lawler investigation seems to provide additional support for their earlier findings by showing that higher order needs accounted for more relationships significant at the .01 level than lower order needs. However, they do not report correlations between these needs and performance and so we cannot evaluate their conclusion as we did for their earlier study.

## THE HERZBERG MODEL

A second frequently mentioned motivational model is that proposed by Herzberg and his associates in 1959.[7] They used a semi-structured interview technique to get respondents to recall events experienced at work which resulted in a marked improvement or a marked reduction in their job satisfaction. Interviewees were also asked, among other things, how their feelings of satisfaction or dissatisfaction affected their work performance, personal relationships, and well-being. Content analysis of the interviews suggested that certain job characteristics led to job satisfaction, while *different* job characteristics led to job dissatisfaction. For instance, job achievement was related to satisfaction while working conditions were related to dissatisfaction. Poor conditions led to dissatisfaction, but good conditions did not necessarily lead to satisfaction. Thus, satisfaction and dissatisfaction are not simple opposites. Hence a two-factor theory of satisfaction is needed.

The job content characteristics which produced satisfaction were called "motivators" by Herzberg and his associates because they satisfied the individual's need for self-actualization at work. The job environment characteristics which led to dissatisfaction were called "hygienes" because they were work-supporting or contextual rather than task-determined and hence were analogous to the "preventive" or "environmental" factors recognized in medicine. According to this dichotomy, motivators include achievement, recognition, advancement, possibility of growth, responsibility, and work itself. Hygienes, on the other hand, include salary; interpersonal relations with superiors, subordinates, and peers; technical supervision; company policy and administration; personal life; working conditions; status; and job security.

There is considerable empirical evidence for this theory. Herzberg himself, in a summary of research through early 1966, includes ten studies of seventeen populations which used essentially the same method as his original study.[8] In addition, he reviews twenty more studies which used a variety of methodologies to test the two-factor theory. Of the studies included in his review, those using his critical incident method generally confirm the theory. Those using other methods give less clear results, which Herzberg acknowledges but attempts to dismiss for methodological reasons. At least nine other studies, most of which have appeared since Herzberg's 1966 review, raise even more doubts about the theory.[9]

While it is beyond the scope of the present article to consider these studies in detail, they raise serious questions as to whether the factors leading to satisfaction and dissatisfaction are really different from each other. A number of the studies show that certain job dimensions appear to be more important for *both* satisfaction and dissatisfaction. Dunnette, Campbell, and Hakel for example, conclude from these and also from their own studies that Herzberg is shackled to his method and that achievement, recognition, and responsibility seem important for both satisfaction *and* dissatisfaction while such dimensions as security, salary, and working conditions are less important.[10] They also raise by implication an issue concerning Herzberg's methodology which deserves further comment. That is, if data are analyzed in terms of percentage differences between groups, one result is obtained; if they are analyzed in terms of ranks within groups, another result occurs. The first type of analysis is appropriate for identifying factors which account for differences between events (as Herzberg did in his original hypothesis). The second type of analysis is appropriate if we want to know the most important factors within the event categories (which is what Herzberg claims he was doing). Analyzing the findings of Dunnette and his colleagues by the first method, we confirm Herzberg's theory; but if we rank the findings within categories, as Dunnette *et al.* also did, we find no confirmation. If we want to know whether "achievement" is important in job satisfaction we must look at its relative rank among other factors mentioned in the events leading to satisfaction, not whether it is mentioned a greater percentage of the time in satisfying events than in dissatisfying events. This distinction in analytical methods was discussed several years ago by Viteles and even earlier by Kornhauser.[11]

We conclude that any meaningful discussion of Herzberg's theory must recognize recent negative evidence even though the model seems to make a great deal of intuitive sense. Much the same can be said of Maslow's theory.

## FURTHER CONSIDERATIONS IN USING THE MASLOW AND HERZBERG THEORIES

Putting aside for the moment the empirical considerations presented by the two models, it is instructive to compare them at the conceptual level suggested in Figure 1. While the figure shows obvious similarities between the Maslow and Herzberg models, there are important differences as well. Where Maslow assumes that any need can be a motivator if it is relatively unsatisfied, Herzberg argues that only the higher order needs serve as motivators and that a worker can have unsatisfied needs in both the hygiene and motivator areas simultaneously. One might argue that the reason higher order needs are motivators is that lower order needs have essentially been satisfied. However, Herzberg presents some evidence that even in relatively low level blue-collar and service jobs, where presumably lower order needs are less well-satisfied, the higher order needs are still the only ones seen by the workers as motivators.[12]

Another important consideration is the relationship of these models to the accomplishment of organizational objectives. Even if there were unequivocal empirical support for the theories, there is need to translate the findings into usable incentives for promoting such objectives as superior

*FIGURE 1* Maslow's Need-Priority Model Compared with Herzberg's Motivation-Hygiene Model

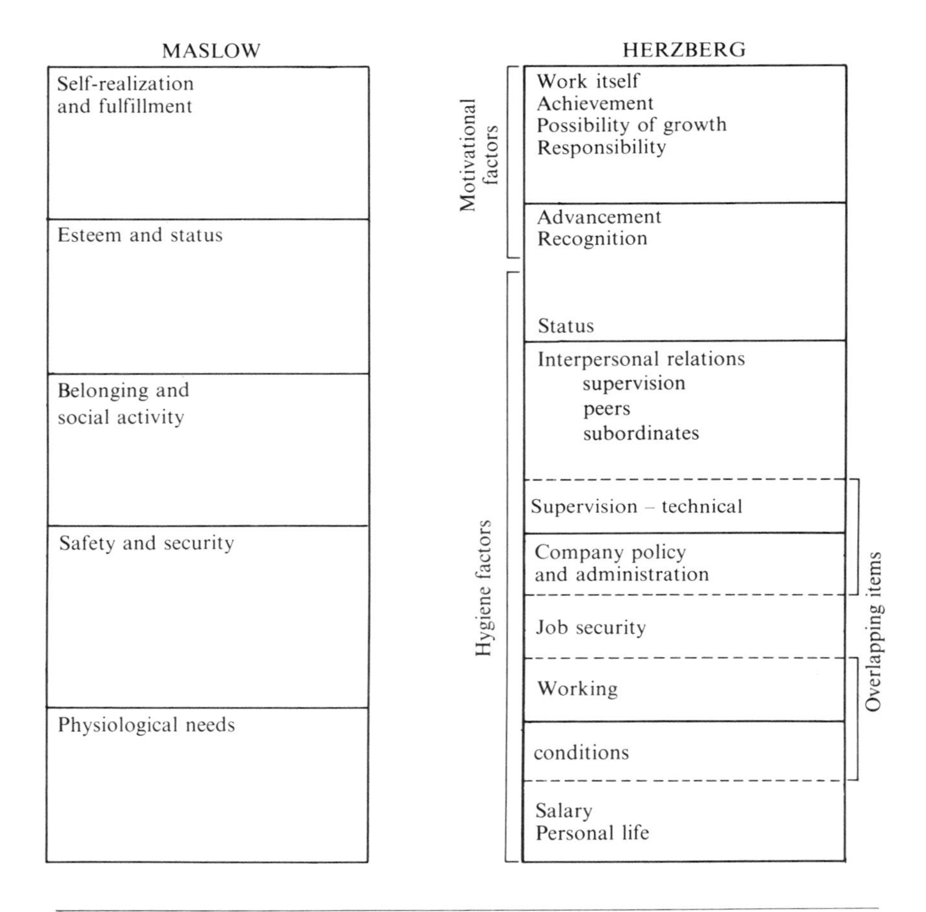


Adapted from K. Davis, *Human Relations at Work,* New York, McGraw-Hill, 1967, p. 37.

performance, lower turnover, lower absenteeism, etc. If not, they are of little use to industrial organizations. As indicated earlier, there is relatively little evidence empirically relating Maslow's model to performance, or even to psychological well-being. Furthermore, the one Lawler and Porter study seems to show that satisfaction of higher and lower order needs are about equally related to performance, although their later investigation suggests that the former are more strongly related to performance than the latter. But we cannot tell for sure because correlations and differences between correlations are not reported.

Similarly, although Herzberg asked his respondents for effects of job events on their performance, he reports only two studies which attempt to measure performance independent of the respondent's estimate. These seem to show the performance is favorably influenced as more "motivators" are provided in the job.[13] However, insufficient data are presented to permit evaluation of the adequacy of the experimental design and performance measures. A study by Friedlander and Walton that considered employee turnover used a modification of Herzberg's technique and found that employees' reasons for staying on the job were different than their reasons for leaving.[14] The reasons for staying would be called "motivators" while those for leaving were "hygiene" factors.

We conclude that Herzberg's two-factor theory *may* be related to turnover and performance; but present studies are subject to serious criticisms. And we could find only two empirical investigations which related Maslow's model to any of these outputs.

In addition, it should be noted that neither model adequately handles the theoretical problem of some kind of linkage by which individual need satisfaction is related to the achievement of organizational objectives. Given the present formulation, it is entirely possible that there can be need satisfaction which is *not necessarily* directed toward the accomplishment of organizational goals. For example, an important organizational objective might be increased production, but workers might conceivably receive more need satisfaction from turning out a higher quality product at a sacrifice in quantity. They might also be meeting their social needs through identification with a work group with strong sanctions against "rate busting."

Finally, neither of these theories as they stand can really handle the problem of individual differences in motivation. Maslow, for example, explains that his model may not hold for persons with particular experiences. His theory is therefore nonpredictive because data that do not support it can be interpreted in terms of individual differences in previous need gratification leading to greater or lesser prepotency of a given need-category.[15] Herzberg, in similar fashion, describes seven types of people differentiated by the extent to which they are motivator or hygiene seekers, or some combination of the two, although he never relates these differences empirically to actual job performance. We turn then to a model which explicitly recognizes these issues and appears to offer great potential for understanding motivation in organizations.

## THE VROOM MODEL

Brayfield and Crockett as long ago as 1955 suggested an explicit theoretical linkage between satisfaction, motivation and the organizational goal of productivity. They said:

> It makes sense to us to assume that individuals are motivated to achieve certain environmental goals and that the achievement of these goals results in satisfaction. Productivity is seldom a goal in itself but is more commonly a means to goal attainment. Therefore, . . . we might expect high satisfaction and high productivity to occur together when productivity is perceived as a path to certain important goals and when these goals are achieved.[16]

Georgopoulas, Mahoney and Jones provide some early empirical support for this notion in their test of the "path goal hypothesis."[17] Essentially, they argue that an individual's motivation to produce at a given level depends upon his particular needs as reflected in the goals toward which he is moving *and* his perception of the relative usefulness of productivity behavior as a path to attainment of these goals. They qualify this, however, by saying that the need must be sufficiently high, no other economical paths must be available to the individual, and there must be a lack of restraining practices.

More recently, Vroom has developed a motivational model which extends the above concepts and is also related to earlier work of experimental and social psychologists.[18] He defines motivation as a "process governing choices, made by persons or lower organisms, among alternative forms of voluntary activity."[19] The concept is incorporated in Figure 2, which depicts Vroom's model graphically. Here, the individual is shown as a role occupant faced with a set of alternative "first-level outcomes." His preference choice among these first-level outcomes is determined by their expected relationship to possible "second-level outcomes."

Two concepts are introduced to explain the precise method of determining preferences for these first-level outcomes. These concepts are *valence* and *instrumentality*. Valence refers to the strength of an individual's desire for a particular outcome. Instrumentally indicates an individual's perception of the relationship between a first-level outcome and a second-level outcome or, in other words, the extent to which a first-level outcome is seen as leading to the accomplishment of a second-level outcome.

Valence is measured by instructing workers to rank important individual goals in order of their desirability, or they may rate goals on Likert-type scales. Instrumentality can be measured by rating scales which involve perceived differences in the direction and strength of relationships between various first- and second-level outcomes. Important goals of industrial workers often cited in the empirical behavioral science literature are promotion, pay, pleasant working conditions and job security. The goals can be ranked by individual workers in terms of their desirability. The resulting scores are measures of valence.

In addition, each individual can be instructed to indicate on an appro-

*FIGURE 2* Vroom's Motivational Model

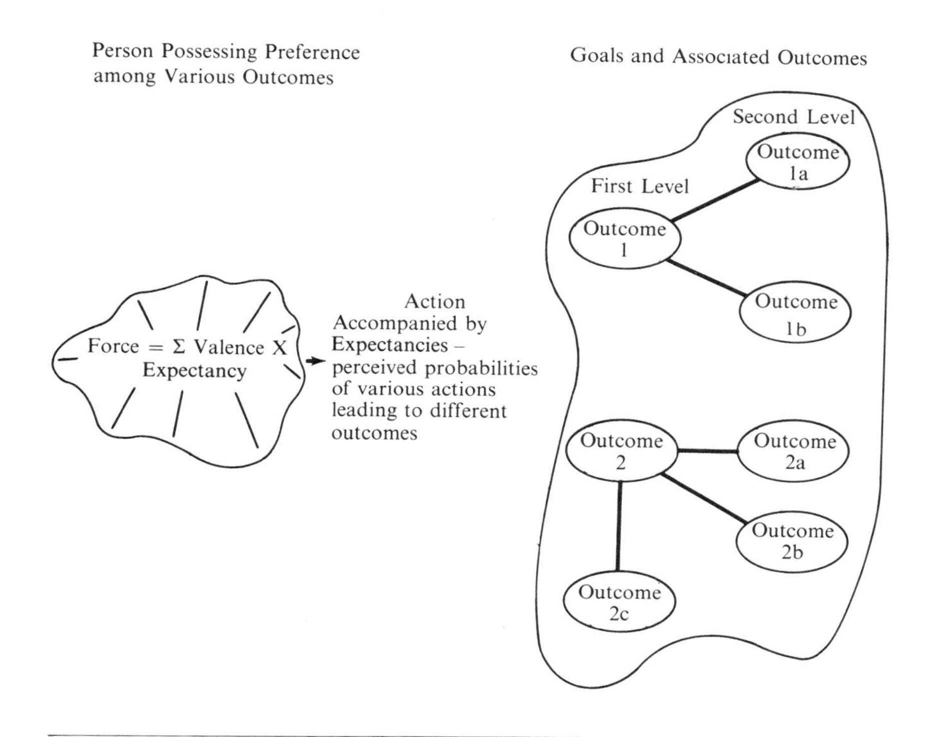


Adapted from M. D. Dunnette, "The Motives of Industrial Managers," *Organizational Behavior and Human Performance,* vol. 2, 1967, p. 178. (Copyright, Academic Press, Inc.)

priate scale the likelihood that a certain job behavior, e.g., high productivity, will lead to each of the four goals described. This score is the instrumental relationship between productivity and a specified goal. Obviously there are alternative methods of measurement available for the concepts; we will leave these for a more detailed discussion later.

Vroom expresses the valence of a first-level outcome to a person "as a monotonically increasing function of an algebraic sum of the products of the valences of all [second-level] outcomes and his conceptions of its instrumentality for the attainment of the [second-level] outcomes."[20]

For example, assume that an individual desires promotion and feels that superior performance is a very strong factor in achieving that goal. His first-level outcomes are then superior, average, or poor performance. His second-level outcome is promotion. The first-level outcome of high performance thus acquires a positive valence by virtue of its expected relationship to the preferred second-level outcome of promotion. Assuming no negative second-level outcomes associated with high performance and no other first-level outcomes that contribute to promotion, we expect motivation toward superior performance because promotion is important and superior performance is seen as instrumental in its accomplishment. Or, to put it in Vroom's terms, performance varies directly with the product of the valence of the reward (promotion) and the perceived instrumentality of performance for the attainment of the reward.

An additional concept in Vroom's theory is *expectancy*. This is a belief concerning the likelihood that a particular action or effort will be followed by a particular first-level outcome and can be expressed as a subjective probability ranging from 0 to 1. Expectancy differs from instrumentality in that it relates *efforts* to first-level outcomes where instrumentality relates first- and second-level outcomes to each other. Vroom ties this concept to his previous one by stating, "the force on a person to perform an [action] is a monotonically increasing function of the algebraic sum of the products of the valences of all [first-level] outcomes and the strength of his expectancies that the [action] will be followed by the attainment of these outcomes."[21] "Force" here is similar to our concept of motivation.

This motivational model, unlike those discussed earlier, emphasizes individual differences in motivation and makes possible the examination of very explicit relationships between motivation and the accomplishment of organizational goals, whatever these goals may be. Thus instead of assuming that satisfaction of a specific need is likely to influence organizational objectives in a certain way, we can find out how important to the employees are the various second-level outcomes (worker goals), the instrumentality of various first-level outcomes (organizational objectives) for their attainment, and the expectancies that are held with respect to the employees' ability to influence the first-level outcomes.

## EMPIRICAL TESTS OF VROOM'S MODEL

Vroom has already shown how his model can integrate many of the empirical findings in the literature on motivation in organizations.[22] However, because it is a relatively recent development, empirical tests of the model itself are just beginning to appear. Here we shall consider four such investigations.

In the first study, Vroom is concerned with predicting the organizational choices of graduating college students on the basis of their instrumentality-goal index scores.[23] These scores reflect the extent to which membership in an organization was perceived by the student as being related to the acquisition of desired goals. According to the theory, the chosen organization should be the one with the highest instrumentality-goal index. Ratings were used to obtain preferences for fifteen different goals and the extent to which these goals could be attained through membership in three different organizations. These two ratings were thus measures of the valences of second-level outcomes and the instrumentality of organized membership for attainment of these outcomes, respectively. The instrumentality-goal index was the correlation between these two measures. But Vroom's theory also involves consideration of expectancy, i.e., how probable is it that the student can become a member of a particular organization. The choice is not his alone but depends upon whether he is acceptable to the organization. A rough measure of expectancy in this study was whether or not the student had received an offer by the organization. If he had received an offer, expectancy would be high; if not, it would be low. The results show that, considering only organizations from which offers of employment were actually received, 76 percent of the students chose the organization with the highest instrumentality-goal index score. The evidence thus strongly supports Vroom's theory.

The next study, by Galbraith and Cummings, utilizes the model to predict the productivity of operative workers.[24] Graphic rating scales were used to measure the instrumentality of performance for five goals—money, fringe benefits, promotion, supervisor's support, and group acceptance. Similar ratings were used for measuring the desirability of each of the goals for the worker. The authors anticipated that a worker's expectation that he could produce at a high level would have a probability of one because the jobs were independent and productivity was a function of the worker's own effort independent of other human or machine pacing. Figure 3 outlines the research design.

Multiple regression analysis showed that productivity was significantly related positively to the instrumentality-goal interactions for supervisor support and money, and there was an almost significant ($p < .10$) relationship with group acceptance. The other factors did not approach significance and the authors explain this lack of significance in terms of the situational context. That is, fringe benefits were dependent not so much on productivity as on a union/management contract, and promotion was based primarily on seniority. Thus the instrumentality of productivity for the attainment of these goals was low and the model would predict no relationship.

The Galbraith and Cummings study thus supports Vroom's contention that motivation is related to productivity in those situations where the acquisition of desired goals is dependent upon the individual's production and not when desired outcomes are contingent on other factors.

A third study is that of Hill relating a model similar to Vroom's to behavior in a utility company.[25] Hill's model is based upon Edward's sub-

*FIGURE 3* Individual Goals and Productivity as Measured by Vroom's Model in One Industrial Plant

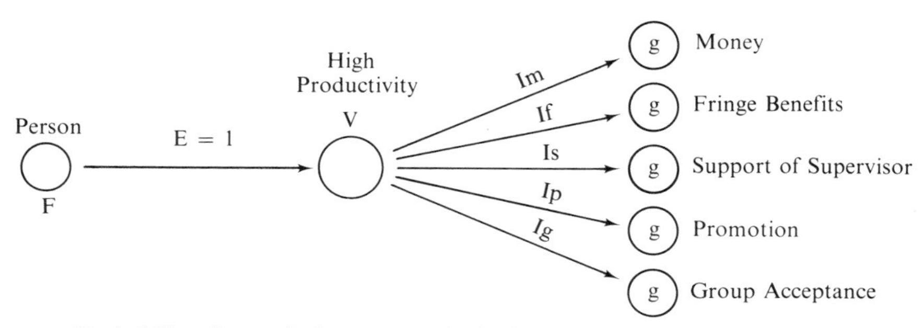


g = Desirability of a particular outcome (rating)
I = Instrumentality of production for particular outcome (rating of relationship)
E = Expectancy (= 1 here because worker sets own pace and is assumed to be capable of high productivity)
V = (Valence) the sum of the cross products of instrumentality and g
F = (Force) expectancy times the valence of productivity
Productivity = Objective measures of amount of production in relation to the production standard

---

Based on data from J. Galbraith and L. L. Cummings. See Reference 23.

jective expected utility maximization theory of decision making.[26] Here one given a choice between alternatives A and/or B will select that alternative which maximizes his subjective expected utility or expected value. If the outcomes associated with action A are more desirable than those associated with B, and their probability of occurrence is greater than or equal to those associated with B, then an individual will choose behavior A over behavior B. The basic concepts are subjective expectation and subjective utility or valence. Expectation and utility are multiplicatively related and can be measured by the same techniques used to test Vroom's theory. Where a relationship is found between Subjective Expected Utility (S.E.U.) and overt behavior, it can be interpreted as support for Vroom.

The behavior considered in Hill's study is that of job bidding. This behavior is encountered in organizations that post descriptions of job openings on employee bulletin boards and encourage qualified employees to "bid" (apply) for them. Here records were kept of the number of bids made over a three-year period by groups of semi-skilled electrical repairmen matched in learning ability, seniority in grade, and age. The men were asked about the consequences of bidding and not bidding on the next higher grade job, and rated the consequence on a seven-point scale of desirability and a similar scale of probability of occurrence. Bidders were those who had bid three or more times during that time.

Fourteen different S.E.U. indices were computed from interview data to determine the relative validity of each in predicting bidding behavior. Typical of these indices were: (1) the sums of the cross products of expectation and utility for the positive consequences of bidding ($\Sigma\ \text{S.}\overset{+}{\text{E}}\text{.U.}$); (2) the same score for the negative consequences of bidding ($\Sigma\ \text{S.}\overset{-}{\text{E}}\text{.U.}$); and (3) the cross products of the *mean* expectation and utility scores for positive and negative consequences $\left(\frac{\Sigma\ \text{S.}\overset{+}{\text{E}}\text{.U.}}{\text{N}}, \frac{\Sigma\ \text{S.}\overset{-}{\text{E}}\text{.U.}}{\text{N}}\right)$. In addition to these S.E.U. indices, two traditional attitudinal and motivational measures were used. Semantic Differential scales measured each subject's respective evaluation of bidding on the next higher grade job and each subject's Need for Achievement was obtained.[27]

It was hypothesized that: (1) there would be a positive correlation between the S.E.U. indices and bidding; and (2) the S.E.U. indices would be more highly related to bidding behavior than the traditional measures.

We do not discuss relationships for all of the indices here but do consider results for one of the more comprehensive indices and those from multiple regression analysis. This index is the algebraic sum of the cross products of the positive and negative consequences of bidding minus the same score for not bidding for each individual. The correlation of this index with bidding was .26, $p < .05$ for a one-tailed test. The correlations between the two Semantic Differential scales and bidding were —.09 and —.25, respectively. Neither of these is significant for a one-tailed test predicting a positive correlation. The correlation between Need for Achievement and bidding was a nonsignificant .17. A multiple regression analysis determined the relative contribution of the S.E.U. indices to the prediction of bidding. A variable was selected for analysis on the basis of its relationship to the criterion and its intercorrelation with the other predictors. The multiple correlation for bidding and seven selected variables was .61, $p < .05$. This correlation included four S.E.U. indices, all of which had higher beta weights than the Semantic Differentials or Need for Achievement. Thus these variables accounted for more variance in the criterion than did the traditional attitudinal and motivational measures. Both hypotheses were therefore confirmed. This study adds support to the usefulness of this type of model in the study of motivation.

Finally, Lawler and Porter report a study that attempts to relate managerial attitudes to job performance rankings by superiors and peers.[28] In it, 154 managers from five different organizations completed questionnaires concerning seven kinds of rewards, and their expectations that different kinds of behavior would lead to these rewards. The expectations and the ratings of the importance of instrumentality and valence, respectively, were combined multiplicatively to yield multiple correlations which were significantly related to supervisor and peer rankings of the manager's effort to perform his job well. The correlations were higher with effort to perform the job than with the rankings of job performance. Lawler and Porter predicted this result because they reasoned that job performance is influenced by variables other than motivation—e.g., by ability and role perceptions. Of course, Vroom's model is not a behavioral theory but one of motivation only. Motivation is not going to improve performance if ability is low or role perceptions are inaccurate. Vroom's model explains how goals influence effort and that is exactly the relationship found by Lawler and Porter.

## CONCLUSION

Taken together, the four studies discussed in the previous section seem to show that Vroom's model holds great promise for predicting behavior in organizations. There still remain some unanswered questions. We do not know all of the goals that have positive valence in a work situation. We do not know how much of a difference in force is necessary before one kind of outcome is chosen over another. Nor do we know what combination of measures yields the best prediction in a given situation. The answers to these and other questions await further research.

One more point should perhaps be made concerning the four studies and their measurement of Vroom's concepts. While it is true that all of them used subjective measures, the model can in fact be tested with more objective devices. Instrumentality can be inferred from organization practices, expectations can be manipulated by instructions, and goals can be inferred from observed approach and avoidance behaviors. Of course, all of these techniques require assumptions concerning their relationship to the worker's subjective perceptions of the situation; but the model is certainly not bound to the methods of measurement used so far. In fact, Vroom specifies in considerable detail the different kinds of techniques that might be used to test his model.[29]

More work must be done before we can make any statements concerning the overall validity of Vroom's model. But the rigor of his formulation, the relative ease of making the concepts operational, and the model's emphasis on individual differences show considerable promise. We are also encouraged by the results of relatively sophisticated studies testing the theory. We believe it is time for those interested in organizational behavior to take a more thoroughly scientific look at this very complex subject of industrial motivation, and Vroom's model seems a big step in that direction.

## NOTES

1. A. H. Maslow, *Motivation and Personality,* Harper and Row, New York, 1954 ; "A Theory of Human Motivation," *Psychological Review,* Vol. 50, 1943, pp. 370–396; and *Eupsychian Management,* Homewood, Illinois, Irwin-Dorsey, 1965; F. Herzberg, B. Mausner, and B. B. Snyderman, *The Motivation to Work,* Wiley, New York, 1959; and F. Herzberg, *Work and the Nature of Man,* World Publishing Co., Cleveland, Ohio, 1966, pp. 130–131. V. H. Vroom, *Work and Motivation,* Wiley, New York, 1964.

2. J. W. Atkinson, J. R. Bastian, R. W. Earl, and G. H. Litwin, "The Achievement Motive, Goal Setting, and Probability Preferences," *Journal of Abnormal and Social Psychology,* Vol. 60, 1960, pp. 27–36; W. Edwards, "Behavioral Decision Theory," *Annual Review of Psychology,* Annual Reviews Inc., Palo Alto, California, 1961, pp. 473–499; H. Peak, "Attitude and Motivation," *Nebraska Symposium on Motivation,* University of Nebraska Press, Lincoln, Nebraska, 1955, pp. 148–184; M. Rosenberg, "Cognitive Structure and Attitudinal Affect," *Journal of Abnormal and Social Psychology,* Vol. 53, 1956, pp. 367–372; M. Fishbein, "An Operational Definition of Belief and Attitude," *Human Relations,* Vol. 15, 1962, pp. 35–43.

3. D. McGregor, "Adventure in Thought and Action," *Proceedings of the Fifth Anniversary Convocation of the School of Industrial Management, Massachusetts Institute of Technology,* Massachusetts Institute of Technology, Cambridge, Massachusetts, 1957, pp. 23–30.

4. L. W. Porter, *Organizational Patterns of Managerial Job Attitudes,* American Foundation for Management Research, New York, 1964. See also M. Haire, E. Ghiselli and L. W. Porter, *Managerial Thinking: An International Study,* Wiley, New York, 1966, especially chapters 4 and 5.

5. M. Beer, *Leadership, Employee Needs, and Motivation,* Bureau of Business Research, Ohio State University, Columbus, Ohio, 1966.

6. J. V. Clark, "Motivation in Work Groups: A Tentative View," *Human Organization,* Vol. 19, 1960, pp. 199–208. E. E. Lawler and L. W. Porter, "The Effect of Performance on Job Satisfaction," *Industrial Relations,* Vol. 7, No. 1, 1967, pp. 20–28. L. W. Porter and E. E. Lawler, *Managerial Attitudes and Performances,* Irwin-Dorsey, Homewood, Illinois, 1968, pp. 148, 150.

7. Herzberg, Mausner and Snyderman, *op. cit.*

8. Herzberg, *op. cit.,* chapters 7, 8. See also K. Davis, *Human Relations at Work* (Third Edition) McGraw-Hill, New York, 1967, pp. 32–36; and R. J. Burke, "Are Herzberg's Motivators and Hygienes Undimensional?" *Journal of Applied Psychology,* Vol. 50, 1966, pp. 217–321.

9. For a review of six of these studies as well as a report on their own similar findings see M. D. Dunnette, J. P. Campbell, and M. D. Hakel, "Factors Contributing to Job Satisfaction and Job Dissatisfaction in Six Occupational Groups," *Organizational Behavior and Human Performance,* Vol. 2, 1967, pp. 143–174. See also C. L. Hulin and P. A. Smith, "An Empirical Investigation of Two Implications of the Two-Factor Theory of Job Satisfaction," *Journal of Applied Psychology,* Vol. 51, 1967, pp. 396–402; C. A. Lindsay, E. Marks, and L. Gorlow, "The Herzberg Theory: A Critique and Reformulation," *Journal of Applied Psychology,* Vol. 51, 1967, pp. 330–339. This latter study and one by J. R. Hinrichs and L. A. Mischkind, "Empirical and Theoretical Limitations of the Two-Factor Hypothesis of Job Satisfaction," *Journal of Applied Psychology,* Vol. 51, 1967, pp. 191–200, are especially useful for suggesting possible reformulations and extensions of the theory which may help overcome some of the objections voiced in the studies mentioned above.

10. Dunnette, Campbell and Hakel, *op. cit.,* pp. 169–173.

11. M. S. Viteles, *Motivation and Morale in Industry,* Norton, New York, 1953, chapter 14: A. Kornhauser, "Psychological Studies of Employee Attitudes," *Journal of Consulting Psychology,* Vol. 8, 1944, pp. 127–143.

12. Herzberg, *op. cit.,* Chapters 7–9.

13. Herzberg, *op. cit.,* Chapter 8.

14. F. Friedlander and E. Walton, "Positive and Negative Motivations Toward Work," *Administrative Science Quarterly,* Vol. 9, 1964, pp. 194–207.

15. It should be noted that the Porter and Lawler research reported above extends the Maslow model by providing an explicit linkage between need satisfaction and performance and also implicitly recognizes individual motivational differences. To do these things, their research makes use of the Vroomian concepts discussed in the next section.

16. A. H. Brayfield and W. H. Crockett, "Employee Attitudes and Employee Performance," *Psychological Bulletin,* Vol. 52, 1955, p. 416.

17. B. S. Georgopoulas, G. M. Mahoney, and N. W. Jones, "A Path-Goal Approach to Productivity," *Journal of Applied Psychology,* Vol. 41, 1957, pp. 345–353.

18. This section is based especially on discussions in Vroom, *op. cit.,* Chapters 2 and 7. See also J. Galbraith and L. L. Cummings, "An Empirical Investigation of the Motivational Determinants of Task Performance: Interactive Effects between Instrumentality-Valence and Motivation-Ability," *Organization Behavior and Human Performance,* Vol. 2, 1967, pp. 237–257.

19. Vroom, *op. cit.*, p. 6.

20. Vroom, *op. cit.*, p. 17.

21. Vroom, *op. cit.*, p. 18.

22. Vroom, *op. cit.*

23. V. H. Vroom, "Organizational Choice: A Study of Pre- and Post-decision Processes," *Organizational Behavior and Human Performance*, Vol. 1, 1966, pp. 212–225.

24. Galbraith and Cummings, *op. cit.*, pp. 237–257.

25. J. W. Hill, "An Application of Decision Theory to Complex Industrial Behavior," unpublished dissertation, Wayne State University, Detroit, Michigan, 1965.

26. Edwards, *op. cit.*, 473–499.

27. For discussions of these measures see C. Osgood, G. Suci, and P. Tannenbaum, *The Measurement of Meaning*, University of Illlinois Press, Urbana, Ill., 1957; A. L. Edwards, *Personal Preference Schedule Manual*, Psychological Corporation, New York, 1959.

28. E. E. Lawler and L. W. Porter, "Antecedent Attitudes of Effective Managerial Performance," *Organizational Behavior and Human Performance*, Vol. 2, 1967, pp. 122–142.

29. Vroom, *Work and Motivation*, *op. cit.*, Chapter 2.

*Melvin Sorcher and Herbert H. Meyer*

# *MOTIVATING FACTORY EMPLOYEES*

In the design of factory jobs, maximum simplification of manual operations is generally the first consideration, presumably because this simplification has at least three advantages.

1. It enables management to hire employees with minimal qualifications at lower rates.
2. It minimizes training costs.
3. It reduces the possibility of errors that result in rejects.

On the other hand, simplification of jobs also has some disadvantages. It has almost eliminated any interest and challenge in the jobs of many factory workers. Surveys show that hourly-paid workers, especially those in assembly-line jobs, frequently report that their work has little or no meaning and just seems to go on endlessly and monotonously. This kind of work not only leads to boredom, apathy, fatigue, and dissatisfaction, but leads to resentment and active resistance, too, which may be reflected in poor workmanship, costly employee turnover, and even work stoppages, slowdowns, and strikes. In the long run, these negative effects of oversimplifying jobs outweigh the cost savings that it is intended to bring about.

In addition, current social trends indicate that the oversimplification of jobs may compound these problems in the future. In the first place, more

---

Used by permission of the publisher. *Personnel,* vol. 45, no. 1, pp. 22–28, January-February, 1968. 

and better education for young people means that members of the workforce will want to have more meaningful and challenging jobs, and surveys have consistently shown that the more education a worker has, the less well satisfied he is with factory work. Second, attitudes toward authority are changing with each generation. People today are less inclined than they were in past years to follow orders blindly; they want to have some say in determining what they do and how they do it and are more inclined to question the directions they get from superiors. Third, with the gradual movement of our society toward the welfare state, there is the possibility that people will be able to choose between working at undesirable jobs and living at the expense of the government.

Because of these developments, employers who take a critical look at the way in which jobs are designed and take steps to reverse the practice of oversimplifying tasks and extracting all meaning from them should have a decided competitive advantage in attracting and holding employees, especially in tight labor markets.

With this in mind, as the first phase of a large-scale research program to examine the problem of job design for factory workers, an exploratory study was conducted at several manufacturing plants of the General Electric Company. The purpose of the study was to identify job-related factors (cycle time, training, repetitiveness, and so forth) that seem to have a significant influence on worker motivation and on quality of work output.

Shop operations and quality control managers of five large plants, each independent of the others, were asked to identify those groups in their plants that consistently showed either very high or very low quality of output. From this number, 25 groups judged to be at the high end of the quality continuum and 25 groups at the low end were selected for study.

The foreman of each of these groups was interviewed for information about job-related factors such as cycle time, group size, and the like, with emphasis on factual data rather than opinions. In addition, a sample of employees from each work group, randomly selected by the researcher, was asked to complete a brief questionnaire designed to measure several dimensions or components of motivation at work, including pride in work, job meaningfulness, sense of accomplishment, monotony, identification with the product and the company, and attitudes toward management. Each of these factors was scored on a favorableness scale, and the sum of the scores on this questionnaire constituted the measure of "productive motivation" for the study.

## HIGH VS. LOW QUALITY

A general finding was the fact that, in almost every case, factors associated with poor-quality workmanship were also associated with a lower level of motivation among the employees in the work groups. Among the factors that seemed to contribute to both low-quality work and poor productive motivation were the following:

### Minimal Job Training

In general, the less training employees had received, the lower was their productive motivation, and employees in the low-quality output groups were also more likely to have received minimal job training. Among the 14 groups in which workers required virtually no technical knowledge or training to perform their jobs, for example, ten were low-quality output groups.

The amount of training given was largely determined by the nature of the jobs. Simple, routine jobs obviously require little training, but in work groups where jobs were similar, if employees had more than minimal training they were consistently in the high-quality output group.

### Lack of Clearly Defined Goals

In 41 of the 50 work groups that were studied, employees could get no idea of the completed product from the work they were doing. Many, particularly in the more repetitive operations, reported that the work just seemed to go on and on endlessly. There were few work groups with whom any attempt had been made by management to capitalize on the use of goals as a motivational technique, but in those few cases where it did, they turned out to be high-quality output groups.

### Lack of Performance Feedback

Most of the groups in which members received regular feedback about past performance were high in productive motivation and output quality. On the other hand, in most of the groups where employees received either no feedback or feedback only when their quality dropped below acceptable standards, the employees were low in both productive motivation and output quality.

### Messy Work Areas

The work areas for each of the 50 work groups were judged on a scale of neatness, evaluated against four criteria: (a) whether or not tote boxes were labeled legibly; (b) the degree to which packages, boxes, and other materials were stacked on the floor; (c) whether or not process sheets were neatly placed, easy to check, and legible; and (d) the extent to which scrap material, tools, wire, and so on, were left on the work surfaces or on the floor when not in use.

Of the 50 work areas studied, 23 were judged to be "very neat and orderly." Of these 23, 20 were occupied by groups that ranked high in quality of workmanship. None of the fourteen areas judged to be "definitely messy" were occupied by high-quality output groups.

### Social Facilitation or Social Distraction

When we looked at the effects of work group arrangement, we found an interesting and seemingly contradictory situation. Quality of workmanship was highest where conversation at work was either very easy, because there was little noise and distance between work stations, or impossible. When conversation opportunities were marginal—that is, possible but difficult because of noise or distance between work stations—quality of workmanship was considerably lower. It was apparent that under these conditions, talking must be distracting.

### Repetitiveness of the Work

Productive motivation and quality of output were lower among (a) groups with very short cycle times, (b) groups in which the number of operations was limited to one or two, and (c) groups where freedom of movement during work was markedly restricted. Thus, it appeared that the oversimplification of jobs actually contributed to quality costs instead of minimizing them.

## IMPROVING PRODUCTIVE MOTIVATION

Based on the findings of this exploratory study, several recommendations can be made to shop managers for improving the productive motivation of employees in routine jobs. In some cases the data were quite conclusive. In others, the data available from the study alone were perhaps insufficient to draw firm conclusions, but the trends uncovered were consistent with the findings of other researchers who have studied the effects of job design for factory workers.

Each of the recommendations listed here should help to improve quality of worker output, as well as the productive morale of workers.

• *Provide for more than minimum required training for assemblyline employees.* If some kind of formal training beyond the required minimum were given factory workers, they would feel greater personal involvement in the job; the job should become more meaningful and thus enhance the employee's self-esteem. For example, several days (or parts of days) spent in "vestibule training," designed not only to develop skills but also to provide an understanding of the function being performed and the importance of the completed product, could make a job seem more significant. Simpler, take-home reading materials on new technological developments and information relevant to the technical aspects of the job in the factory might also contribute to improvement of productive motivation.

Even if these training activities are not required for minimally satisfactory job performance, by making the work content seem more important, they make the employee feel more important. Thus, not only should motivation and work performance be favorably affected, but also employees might identify more strongly with the organization, and this side effect could, in itself, result in cost savings due to fewer work disruptions.

• *Create subgoals to measure accomplishment.* There is considerable experimental evidence indicating that a sense of completion is an important motivational variable. When individuals work toward clearly defined goals, rather than working in what appears to be an endless routine, performance is better, and there is likely to be greater interest in the work. Working toward a specific goal should reduce monotony and its related effects of psychological fatigue.

A good example of the imaginative use of subgoals was observed in one assembly-line operation where employees placed completed subassemblies on an endless belt that transported the completed units to the main assembly line. In one of these groups the manager had provided boxes similar to egg crates, compartments corresponding to the number of subassemblies needed for one complete unit of the product being manufactured. Here, instead of placing completed subassemblies on the moving belt, the worker filled up his crate and then placed the completed crate on the assembly line. Thus, he experienced a sense of accomplishment as each crate was filled and, at the same time, a better understanding of how his work was contributing to the completed product.

• *Provide results feedback on a regular and frequent basis.* A large body of psychological research has demonstrated that people perform best when they receive positive as well as negative feedback about their performance on a regular and frequent basis. In many assembly-line operations, however, the individual employee gets no feedback about the quality of his output, especially where several workers perform the same operation. Rejects are attributed to the group as a whole, so the individual has little incentive to strive for perfection. Research has shown that an individual can improve his performance only if (a) he gets some feedback regarding his past performance; (b) he has the ability or is trained to improve his performance; and (c) he has the incentive to improve.

• *Maintain a neat and orderly work area.* The foreman usually has control over area neatness, so employees may feel that if their foreman is unconcerned with neatness, they need not be concerned about it either. This attitude may also affect the quality of their workmanship.

• *Arrange work stations so that conversation between employees is either easy or impossible.* Many routine jobs can be performed by experienced workers with little or no attention to the task; in these circumstances, conversation while working may reduce the monotony and retard fatigue. Thus, quality losses can probably be minimized if work areas are arranged so that workers can converse easily without distracting themselves from their work. In cases where conversation is not desirable because of the complexity of the jobs, all opportunity to talk while working should probably be removed, but more frequent rest breaks should be given to alleviate fatigue.

• *Increase the number of operations performed by each employee wherever possible.* By increasing cycle time on routine jobs through additional operations, the psychological fatigue effects of repetition on job quality should be reduced significantly. The added responsibility may be an important factor in improving productive motivation, too.

The same results might also be achieved without expanding the activities at a single work station, if that would be impractical for any reason—for example, because of the sizable cost of duplicate tools and equipment. Instead, monotony may sometimes be reduced by job rotation. With a minimum of training, employees can easily learn different repetitive jobs, and moving between stations varies the work. The generally favorable effects of job rotation have been brought out in other studies.

• *Structure jobs so that workers can, at least occasionally, move about the work area.* Besides job rotation, there are other ways to provide for physical movement, such as letting employees get their own parts, prints, or tools, or adding operations that require some moderate physical activity. In the exploratory study it was found that job satisfaction and quality of output were generally low in the groups where a minimum of physical energy was expended in the more sedentary activities. When a good deal of physical energy was used, as in heavier assembly or machine shop activities, this tendency was reversed, and more favorable job-related attitudes and higher quality were more typical.

• *Explore ways to assign greater personal responsibility to the individual.* The advantages to expect are greater self-esteem and greater job meaningfulness. One way to enlarge an individual's responsibility is to let him inspect his own work. Others overlap recommendations made for other purposes: adding operations, letting the worker do his own setups and secure his own process sheets, tools, and equipment. In this study, employees who were responsible for making some decisions (even if minor) reported more interest in and less boredom with their work.

To sum up, the design of jobs in the factory must take into account the human needs of operators as well as the technical requirements of an efficient production system and the economic needs of the business. Attention must be given not only to the tasks that need to be performed, but the aspects of those tasks that will affect the motivation of the operator.

Until our manufacturing operations become completely automated, and this state will probably never be reached, we will also need motivated workers to perform many jobs. The exploratory investigations described here lead to the conclusion that there are a number of easy-to-apply techniques to give routine jobs more meaning and make them more interesting and satisfying, and thus meet some of the human needs of employees without sacrificing the technological needs of the production process.

## DISCUSSION QUESTIONS

1. Compare and contrast Maslow's hierarchy of needs model with Herzberg's motivation-hygiene theory.
2. Explain the Vroom concepts of "valence," "instrumentality," and "expectancy."
3. What conclusions do Professors Hunt and Hill reach in their analyses of current managerial motivation models?
4. What factors seem to contribute to both low quality work and poor productive motivation?
5. What recommendations can be made to shop managers for improving the productive motivation of employees performing routine jobs?
6. Identify some of the advantages and disadvantages of job simplification.

# Part IV. Coordinating Processes

# Chapter 9. Decision Making

*Peer O. Soelberg*

# UNPROGRAMMED DECISION MAKING


## ABSTRACT

The research reported below has implications for management practice if one accepts the following three propositions: (1) information processing and decision making are central functions of modern organizations; (2) in order to improve management decision making it is useful to know how organizations presently make decisions;[1] (3) as long as people remain the chief instrument of corporate policy, a key feature of management decision making will be the choice processes of individual human beings.


This paper is a report on how individuals make important, difficult, and highly judgmental decisions. It has become customary to contrast so-called unprogrammed with more highly programmed types of decisions. The latter are choices or actions that follow routinely from the decision maker's application of explicit decision rules to whatever stimulus or input data face him in his task environment.

The management of most companies' daily operations abounds with highly programmed decisions. Consider merely the routinized rules that

---

Used by permission of the publisher. *Industrial Management Review*, vol. 8, no. 3, pp. 19–29, Spring, 1967. 

normally guide the everyday management of inventories, production schedules, machine and manpower allocations, cost estimation, mark-up pricing, etc. A famous description of highly programmed decision making is G. P. E. Clarkson's portfolio selection study, in which he demonstrated that the investment decisions made by a bank trust officer were so well programmed that his decisions could be predicted by a computer six months after his investment rules had been elicited by an interviewer and described as a computer program.

In contrast, this study focuses on highly unprogrammed decision making, a subject that usually gets relegated to the mystical realm of managerial "judgment."[2] Every day critical decisions are produced for which the decision maker can explicate no identifiable rules or preprogrammed decision procedure. This is not to say that a person may not be following some sort of generalized guidelines when rendering his so-called judgment. But if you asked him directly, he would insist that the unprogrammed problem confronting him had to be solved in its own unique context. Moreover, observing him solve the program, you would find:

1. The decision maker applied few special-purpose rules when arriving at his choice.
2. The decision maker might not even be able to specify, *a priori,* the nature of an ideal solution to his problem.
3. A number of the decision criteria that he wished to apply were not operational before he tackled the problem.
4. Many of his choice alternatives were unknown when he started out.
5. Information about the alternatives' consequences and relative worth was not immediately available from the task environment.

Yet it is precisely this type of unstructured or unprogrammed decision making that forms the basis for allocating billions of dollars worth of resources in our economy every year. Ironically, until we understand the nature of such human decision processes better, our sophisticated computer technology will be of slight aid in making these types of decisions. In other words, the potential payoff to management of a scientific understanding of the economic, psychological, and sociopolitical "laws" of nonprogrammed human judgment is enormous.

## AVAILABLE THEORIES

Traditional economists have long tried to get along with little more than the concepts of "utility" and "probability" for explaining unprogrammed choice among uncertain alternatives. A utility function is an assumed linear preference ordering of all possible combinations of the goods and services that a person values, and as such is felt by economists to be an adequate basis for describing any decision maker's value structure. Likewise, objective (or personal) distributive probability measures are felt to capture the essence of how decision makers think about the "factual" connections which they are believed to perceive between each of the available solution alternatives and the possible, but uncertain, consequences of their choosing a specific alternative. It does not take much observation of decision makers in action to convince oneself that the mathematical elegance of the probability-utility concepts may be a deceptive property that easily can mislead anyone interested in arriving at empirically testable descriptions of decision behavior.

The best known exception to traditional probability-utility theory appears in the work of Herbert Simon. The latter's notion of limited rationality, his "means-ends satisficing" model of information processing and his insistence on attaining a close correspondence between the intermediate outputs of his process simulation models of problem solving, and observable verbal behavior, have significantly reoriented and vitalized social science research on decision making.

Simon characterizes unprogrammed decision making in terms of the following three-phase process model:

> *Intelligence.* Finding occasions for making a decision;
>
> *Design.* Finding, inventing, developing, and analyzing alternative courses of action;
>
> *Choice.* Selecting a particular course of action from those available.

In our research we used the following, slightly expanded phase structure as a framework for analyzing unprogrammed decision processes:

> *Participation.* The decision maker is somehow induced to work in a given task environment, in which he is then motivated to attain one or more non-trivial objectives.
>
> *Recognition and Definition.* The decision maker surveys his task environment, discovers, selects, or is somehow provided with problems, and then defines operationally the particular problem he intends to solve.[3]
>
> *Understanding.* The decision maker investigates his task environment, trying to develop an appropriate set of event classifications (i.e., concepts) in order to formulate and test hypotheses about the apparent cause-effect relationships in the environment. The latter in turn suggest design operators for, or help generate, viable solution alternatives.
>
> *Design and Evaluation.* The decision maker develops or searches for alternative courses of action. Rather than estimating probabilities to attach to a set of mutually exclusive consequences associated with each alternative, the decision maker searches "within" each alternative until

he feels he has enough information about each important goal attribute of that alternative, or until he exhausts his search resources. If the alternative is not rejected, the decision maker assigns some value measure or range of possible values, to each goal attribute, but does not yet compare these values across goal attributes and alternatives.

*Choice Reduction.* The decision maker reduces his set of investigated viable decision alternatives to a single one, i.e., he makes a choice.

*Implementation.* The decision maker introduces and manages his solution in the task environment.[4]

*Feedback and Control.* The decision maker receives and evaluates information from the task environment regarding the effects of his implemented decision, and if required, either changes his problem definition, modifies his goals or strategies, or takes appropriate follow-up action. Thus nonlinear dynamics is introduced into the decision making process.

This framework was our point of departure for re-examining the literature of decision making and problem solving in search of testable hypotheses that would either make operational or be incompatible with our process outline.

## RESEARCH STRATEGY

In order to explore empirically the detail structure of the above generalized decision process, we should obviously have to investigate, at great length, the information processes of a large number of decision makers solving many different types of problems. The specific unprogrammed decision situation we chose to study sought to focus on decision makers who were:

1. Well-trained for problem solving, as well as able and motivated to talk at some length about their information processing while they were actually engaged in producing their decisions;
2. Highly involved with the problem confronting them, it being personally important for each to reach the "right" decision;
3. Quite unfamiliar with the type of problem with which they were faced; they had encountered few such problems before and did not expect to do so again in the near future;
4. Engaged in making the decisions over a long period of time (several weeks) in order to minimize possible observer measurement effects, yet allow a number of observations to be made at different phases of the decision process;
5. Easily and inexpensively accessible to the investigator in reasonable number (in order to minimize our idiosyncratic interpretation of data from individuals, by enabling immediate cross-comparison of the thinking-aloud protocols of a fairly large sample of decision makers).

The above criteria for choice of subjects were designed to help us focus on as pure and "uncontaminated" a set of decision process observations as we thought could be found in industrial practice. MIT Sloan School of Management Master's and doctoral candidates, making postgraduate job decisions, fitted this bill reasonably well. In addition to satisfying our research criteria, these subjects would allow us readily to test whatever rejectable hypotheses might be generated by our initial phase of investigation, on succeeding years' samples of graduating management aspirants.

Initially our goal was to design a longitudinal (i.e. periodic "over time") questionnaire that could chart efficiently and adequately the course of our subjects' job decision processes. For that purpose we put together an elaborate set of questions, which took three or four hours every week to complete. This was clearly too long, trying as it did to cover every possible theoretical contingency. For example, one part of the questionnaire was derived from probabilistic utility theory. In this part the decision maker was asked to identify, weight, and then rate whatever goal dimensions he felt entered into his decision. It turned out that the goal weights which the subjects provided during decision making could not be trusted; the reported weights varied quite unreliably both with respect to the specific alternatives that the decision maker referred to when answering the goal weight questions, and with the temporal phasing of the decision process.

We therefore had to give up the questionnaire as a poor job. It had become obvious that unless our questionnaire was made up largely of items that were closely compatible with the manner in which the decision maker actually stored and manipulated his decision information "internally," during his own thinking about the problem, the answers he provided to our questions would, for explanatory as well as predictive purposes, be spurious at best and entirely misleading at worst.

We therefore resolved to rely, almost exclusively at first, on periodic, open-ended, and highly detailed interviews with the decision makers. These interviews provided our first insight into some rather surprising aspects of unprogrammed decision making. Preliminary analysis of nearly 100 open-ended interviews, each ranging from one-half hour to two and one-half hours in length, with 20 different decision makers over three- to five-month choice periods, provided the basis for our first Generalizable Decision Processing model (for short, GDP-I). The latter was first presented at Carnegie Institute of Technology in June, 1964.

Each interview protocol was thereafter reduced to comparable format by the following three-step method: First, each protocol was transcribed verbatim and its decision phase structure, according to GDP-I, was annotated in the margin. Thereafter the relevant protocol contents were summarized in a synoptic coding language derived directly from the variables and process hypotheses of GDP-I. This provided us with decision process data that were comparable across subjects. Finally the current state of each person's decision making and his active solution alternatives, at that point in time, were entered on a multidimensional, Gantt type process chart. The standardized data produced by the last two steps of the analysis served as our basis for quantifying each protocol. Fitting these data to the hypotheses of our generalizable decision process model provided (*post hoc*) support for a number of GDP-I hypotheses, relating principally to the phases in our above process outline, labeled Design and Evaluation, and Choice Reduction. The more interesting hypotheses that were supported by the data are summarized below:

1. The decision maker defines his career problem by deriving an ideal solution to it, which in turn guides his planning of a set of operational criteria for evaluating specific job alternatives.
2. The decision maker believes *a priori* that he will make his decision by weighting all relevant factors with respect to each alternative, and then "add up numbers" in order to identify the best one. In fact, he does not generally do this; and if he does, it is done *after* he has made an "implicit" selection among alternatives.
3. The decision maker will search in parallel for alternatives, by activating one or more "alternatives generators"—procedures which, once activated, allow him to search passively, by deciding whether or not to follow up investigating particular ones of a stream of alternatives presented by his generators.
4. The decision maker will usually be evaluating more than one alternative at any one point in time, each evaluation consisting of a *series* of investigation and evaluation cycles.
5. Evaluation during the search phase takes the form of screening each alternative along a number of noncompared goal dimensions; no evidence of factor weighting is apparent at this stage.
6. Search will not necessarily halt as soon as the decision maker has identified an acceptable alternative (one that is not rejected by his various screening criteria); conversely, when he ends his search for new alternatives, he will usually have more than a single acceptable alternative in his "active roster."
7. When the subject terminates his search for new alternatives before his search resources run out, he will already have identified a favorite alternative in his roster of acceptable alternatives; this alternative (his choice candidate) can be identified by considering his primary goal attributes (usually one or two) alone.
8. At the point of search termination a person generally will *not* have compared his alternatives with one another, will not possess a transitive rank ordering of alternatives, and will refuse to admit that his implicit choice has been made.
9. Before a decision maker will recognize his choice explicitly, he will engage in a sometimes quite lengthy (two or three months) confirmation processing of his roster of acceptable alternatives; alternatives *will* get compared to each other, factor by factor.

10. During confirmation processing the roster of acceptable alternatives, if greater than two, quickly will be reduced to two alternatives—the choice candidate and a "confirmation candidate." If only one alternative, the choice candidate, is viable at this time, the decision maker will try to obtain another acceptable alternative (confirmation candidate) as soon as possible "in order to have something to compare it with."

11. Confirmation processing aims to resolve the residual uncertainties and problems connected with the choice candidate, and to arrive at a decision rule which shows unequivocally that the choice candidate dominates the confirmation candidate—Pareto dominance being the ideal goal strived for.

12. During confirmation processing a great deal of perceptual and interpretational distortion takes place in favor of the choice candidate, to the detriment of the confirmation candidate; goal attribute "weights" are arrived at, or changed, to fit the perceived data and the desired decision outcome.

13. The decision is "made" when a satisfactorily Pareto dominant decision rule has been constructed, or when the decision maker runs up against an inescapable time deadline during confirmation processing.

## LIMITED GENERALITY OF THE PROBLEM STUDIED

Though our process hypotheses of job decision making have been stated in readily generalizable form, it should be obvious that the GDP-I model, as it stands, is by no means applicable to *any* unprogrammed problem situation. Some of the characteristics limiting the problem situations to which our hypotheses should apply are the following:

The alternatives are well-defined and separately identifiable. Instances of unprogrammed decision alternatives that are not well-defined are common in research and development work, for example. In such a case, the problem solver must laboriously seek out at least one feasible alternative before he can begin to choose among alternatives. His prime objective is not to select a "best" alternative among several acceptable ones, but merely to invent a single solution that works. For GDP-I to be applicable without modification, the task environment must be susceptible to the use of "search generators," procedures that present the decision maker with streams of reasonable alternatives, thus allowing him to search passively for alternatives by screening out undesirable possibilities.

Another limitation of our job choice study as a basis for generalizing about human decision processes may derive from the interactive relationship of the job seeker versus his alternatives. The latter are by no means passive pebbles to be picked at leisure. Whether or not a job possibility is to be a viable alternative for the decision maker depends on the employer's making an offer. Nevertheless, we *could* (to preserve generality) relegate the question of whether or not an alternative is "viable" to being just another goal attribute to be evaluated by the decision maker.

A third limiting characteristic of the class of decisions described above derives from the fact that the choices we studied were individual processes, largely controlled by single persons. The social or interpersonal aspects of organizational decision making are therefore not captured by the GDP-I model. Indeed, studying and providing for the effects of interpersonal group variables represents, in the author's opinion, the single most promising direction in which the GDP-I model should be developed.

A fourth obvious limit of generalizing from any model derived from observations of job decisions derives from the definiteness, or discreteness, with which solutions to the defined problem are arrived at. In contrast, we easily can think of decision problems to which solutions are found only gradually, or for which decisions have to be made repeatedly (in which case we might expect homeostatic decision rules to develop that would help the decision maker *adapt* to a preferred alternative).

## A FOLLOW-UP STUDY

Our initial study provided insight into the information processes of unprogrammed human job decisions and laid the groundwork for the design of a predictively valid questionnaire instrument for testing some of the key hypotheses in the GDP-I model. In contrast to the protocol "curve fitting" exercise reported above, our follow-up investigation was thus truly a "prediction study." All hypotheses, with process-valid measures of their variables, were specified a priori. Moreover, disregarding our personal belief in the GDP-I model, most other decision models yielded small prior likelihoods that the hypotheses we set out to test were in fact true. To most orthodox theorists our predictions would appear to be "shots in the dark."

To keep the study manageable we focused on the Design, Evaluation, and Choice Reduction phases of the decision framework outlined above. We were particularly intrigued with the confirmation process that had been identified in the interview protocols. We wanted to test our ability to identify the onset of confirmation processing, which, if it took the form we were postulating, should enable us to predict the job decisions that people would make far in advance of their admission that they had made up their minds. The following six hypotheses, therefore, are merely consecutive building blocks of one long process hypothesis, derived to establish the existence of the confirmation process. A longitudinal job choice questionnaire was designed with quadruple redundancy checks for each item, to operationalize the variables in the hypotheses. The hypotheses, derived from GDP-I, took the following form:

1. Search for new alternatives ends a significant period of time before the decision maker (referred to as Dm) is willing to admit having made his decision.

2. In observation periods prior to the end of his search for new alternatives, Dm will, more often than not, already have available one or more acceptable choice alternatives.

3. When Dm ends his search for new alternatives, he will report significant uncertainty about which alternative he will select as his choice.

4. Should Dm not have obtained a firm job offer from more than one acceptable alternative at the time of search termination, he will have tried hard, and will usually have obtained, at least one other acceptable offer (according to GDP-I, in order to have something with which to compare his choice candidate) by the time he is ready to announce his decision.

5. When Dm ends his search for new alternatives, his favorite alternative can be identified by asking him a set of simple questions. When Dm's subsequent confirmation processing of alternative ends, i.e. at the time of choice announcement, his decision will be to select that alternative.

6. Effective or perceptive dissonance reduction, in the form of a "spreading apart" of Dm's liking for his accepted versus rejected alternatives, will *not* generally be observed after choice has been announced.

Those familiar with aspiration-level, sequential search choice models may recall that according to this theory the first four hypotheses should not be reasonable. Similarly, according to cognitive dissonance reduction theory, the sixth proposition would be disturbing.

## RESULTS OF THE FOLLOW-UP STUDY

Below we can no more than summarize the findings pertaining to the above six hypotheses, based on data from 256 questionnaire response sets provided by 32 members of the 1965 graduating class of MIT Sloan School of Management Master's and doctoral candidates. Each decision maker in the sample provided answers to eight biweekly questionnaires over the period in which he made his job decision. (For a small number of persons—a different subset with respect to each hypothesis—the path of their decision processes, as recorded by the questionnaires, provided inadequate data with which to test a given hypothesis. Thus each total reported below may add to less than 32.)

*Hypothesis 1.* Twenty-seven of 31 Dms (87 percent) terminated the search for new alternatives 10 days or more before the date on which they reported having made their decision. Fifteen of 31 Dms terminated search three weeks or more before choice was made.

*Hypothesis 2.* Using a highly conservative measure of an alternative's acceptability, 17 of 24 Dms (74 percent) reported having available one or more acceptable alternatives two weeks or more before they terminated search for new alternatives.

*Hypothesis 3.* The average personal probability distribution of 28 Dms reporting, at time of search termination, regarding the likelihood that they would choose either the alternatives that we independently had identified as being their "choice candidate," their second most preferred alternative, and "all other alternatives," was respectively: (.29, .24, .47). In other words, great uncertainty was expressed by Dms at the time of search termination regarding which alternative they were to choose.

*Hypothesis 4.* Thirteen of 16 Dms (81 percent) who did not have, or had not been promised, an offer from more than one alternative at time of search termination, did report having at least one such other offer in hand before they made their decision.

*Hypothesis 5.* Twenty-five and one-half of 29 Dms (87 percent) (one-half since one Dm could reasonably be classified either way) eventually selected as their final decision that alternative which at the time of search termination, one to 12 weeks earlier (median of three weeks), had independently been identified as their favorite alternative, i.e. choice candidate.

*Hypothesis 6. No* Dm reported a consistent dissonance reduction "spreading apart" of his liking for accepted versus rejected alternatives over the periods of observation immediately following decision commitment. However, two Dms exhibited what we might call latent dissonance reduction, i.e. one which took effect two or more weeks *after* Dm had committed himself to the decision. Nine of 26 Dms (35 percent) showed an *initial* "spreading apart" effect of their relative liking for alternatives, a gap which, however, was reduced again in subsequent periods of observation. Ten of 26 Dms (38 percent) exhibited no change whatever in their reporting liking differentials in the observation periods following choice. The remaining five exhibited post-choice dissonance *expansion,* i.e. they narrowed down their liking differential between alternatives after they had made their decision.

In summary, the six decision process hypotheses described above were supported rather convincingly by the data in our longitudinal prediction study.

## CHIEF IMPLICATIONS FOR A THEORY

Below are some of our study's more central implications for decision theory, which may not be obvious from the above, severely summarized report of our findings.

First, scalar utility theory is a poor way of representing the structure of human values. Decision value attributes are usually multi-dimensional; they are not compared or substituted for each other during choice. No stable utility weighting function can be elicited from a decision maker prior to his selection of a preferred alternative, nor do such weights appear to enter into each person's decision processing. His noncomparison of goal attributes during the alternatives screening and selection phases also obviates the decision maker's need for, and the reasonableness of our postulating the existence of, a multidimensional utility indifference map.

Second, probability theory, either in its objective frequency or personal estimate Bayesian form, does not provide adequate representation of how our decision makers perceived and dealt with uncertainty during their unprogrammed decision making. The "probability" indices with which our highly trained decision makers provided us were neither additive nor cardinally scaled. It seems that a decision maker does not normally think of his choice alternatives in terms of multiple consequences, each of which is then seen to depend conditionally on a specific reaction to his decision by the task environment. Instead he thinks of each choice alternative in terms of a set of noncomparable goal attributes. Uncertainty in this context is more appropriately represented in terms of equally likely *ranges* of a specific alternative's rating along its various uncertain goal attributes. In other words decision uncertainty rarely takes the form of a "pure" or probability-risk *consequence* uncertainty. More commonly, uncertainty—a nonadditive quantity—is associated with the decision maker's personal evalution of an alternative's uncertain attributes.

The mathematics of how most decision makers compare such multiple-attribute uncertainty-ranged alternatives is quite simple, but unfortunately would take too much space to illustrate here. By the same token of limited rationality, one might argue that it is the simplicity of Dm's information processing computations that effectively prevents him from operating with the $m$ conditional probability distributions for each alternative which, according to distributive probability theory, the decision maker *should* be associating with each multiconsequence, multivalued alternative.

Third, search for alternatives is a parallel process, i.e. several potentially acceptable alternatives are considered by the decision maker at one time. This contrasts with the hypothesis of sequential search aspiration level models. In addition, a subject's evalution of an alternative is a multi-stage affair; at each step new information is collected and evaluated about a subset of attributes of the given alternative. In other words, search *within* alternatives is as important a process for us to understand formally as the traditionally described search *across* alternatives.

During the search phase the decision maker does not view his evaluation of alternatives as final. Alternatives that fall short on important goal attributes are rejected immediately. But acceptable alternatives are merely put into the decision maker's "active roster," with little or no systematic comparison performed across the different acceptable alternatives, until the person is ready to make his final decision. In other words, the decision maker may well continue to search for new alternatives, even though he has already discovered a perfectly satisfactory one (one that was not rejected by any of his important goal attributes).

Fourth, making the final decision, what we have called decision confirmation, takes place *after* the decision maker has terminated search for new alternatives. This appears to be a highly involved and affectively a most painful process for a person to engage in. This is the period during which the decision maker has to reject alternatives that seem perfectly satisfactory to him, in some ways perhaps better than the one he finally ends up choosing. It is at this point that the decision maker is forced systematically to *compare* patently noncomparable alternatives.

It is a major thesis of this study that persons generally solve this problem in the simplest manner conceivable, by not entering into this difficult period of decision making until one of the alternatives can be identified as an implicit "favorite." In other words, decision making during its confirmation phase is an *exercise in prejudice,* of making sure that one's implicit favorite will indeed be the "right" choice. This proposition gives the key to a surprising degree of predictability in decision making, demonstrated with the data of Hypothesis 5 above, in which we predicted 87 percent of the career jobs taken two to eight weeks before the decision makers would admit that they had reached a decision.

It is not feasible here to go into detail regarding the nature of confirmation processing, yet the following are some of its more outstanding characteristics:

The criteria that the decision maker uses for identifying his favorite alternative are very few; not more than one or two of what we have called *prime* goal attributes account for most of the observed variance.

The decision maker's comparison among alternatives quickly reduces to a pro-con argument between two, and only two alternatives (see Hypothesis 4), the object of the decision maker being to bring his perception of the facts, and his evaluation of goal attributes, into line with his predisposition that the preferred choice candidate dominates his second-best alternative (which we call the confirmation candidate) on all important goal attributes, secondary and primary.

The decision maker finally makes his decision when he has constructed a satisfactory decision rule—a goal weighting function, if you please—that enables him to *explain* the Pareto dominance of his choice candidate (unless, of course, the decision maker is forced by some deadline to make his decision before that time. If so, he will still choose his choice candidate, but with much more expressed uncertainty about the "rightness" of his decision).

Fifth, dissonance reduction, in the sense that it has been described by Leon Festinger, must be viewed as a conditional phenomenon. In a loose sense, confirmation processing might be viewed as part of the decision maker's "dissonance reduction" process. But according to Festinger, the onset of dissonance reduction awaits the decision maker's *commitment* to his choice, which in our data is synonymous with the point of the person's choice announcement. In this study dissonance reduction after that point in time was observed in only 35 percent of the cases; in all of them the effect dissipated during subsequent periods of observations.

We propose as a testable explanation of our observations: Post-choice dissonance reduction will be observed only when the person, at the time of choice commitment, is not satisfied with his confirmation decision rule —i.e. with the intellectual rationale for why he chose the way he did. Thus dissonance reduction constitutes an *affective* compensation on the part of the decision maker for his lack of a socially acceptable, cognitive justification for his behavior.

This hypothesis also explains the observed second-order dissonance reduction effect: With time we expect all men to be able to invent better and better rationales for why they behaved as they did. Correspondingly, we should observe that any initial affective (dissonance reduction) compensation, with which a person first may be protecting his decision, will be dissolved over time as his intellectual argument gets better.

## IMPLICATIONS FOR MANAGEMENT PRACTICE

Let us conclude by considering briefly some lessons of these findings for management. The reader can surely think of some other implications; nevertheless, here are a few obvious ones:

1. Our generalizable decision model (GDP-I) should help a manager to recognize when others have reached an implicit decision, i.e. when they are merely confirming their favorite alternative. Such knowledge should enable managers not to waste time or resources or lose face by remaining party to a choice process that for most purposes has already been closed. This lesson should be particularly useful in situations where a manager or his company has been cast in the role of "confirmation candidate" by the decision maker.

2. The existence of a confirmation process that goes into effect prior to public choice commitment emphasizes the desirability of getting one's alternatives into the decision process early. On bids for government research and development contracts, for example, Edward Roberts has

uncovered evidence that a bidding company needs to get in there well before the official invitation to bid on a contract has left the government agency—that at this time one can predict with disturbing success which firm will get the contract, simply by looking at the order of names on the list of those invited to bid.

3. The confirmation process also suggests a way of manipulating decision deadlines in a manager's favor. If he has evidence that his company happens to be his adversary's favorite alternative, the manager can safely clinch the deal by imposing a stringent deadline on decision making, trust to dissonance reduction to carry the day, and save himself time, needless anxiety, and the risk of that rare alternative arriving on the decision maker's horizon in time to upset the apple cart.

4. The existence of the confirmation process also explains the often observed asymmetry of administrative decision making. Once made, decisions are usually very hard to unmake, or to get remade. A most obvious explanation of this is that a manager balks at having to go through all the pain of changing his tailor-made decision rule to fit a new pair of alternatives. (That *might* sound too much like "rationalizing," and thus go against the grain of men who like to think of themselves as orderly, rational decision makers.) Besides, the decision rule offers ready arguments, in *m* dimensions, why few alternatives can be expected to be as good as the chosen one. And these arguments get themselves strengthened and elaborated as time passes—partly through the self-fullfilling prophecy which will bias all future interactions between a manager and his rejected versus accepted alternatives.

The implication for action is that a manager must "watch" his own subsequent interactions with a rejected alternative, such as a subordinate he has not promoted, in order to avoid setting up self-fulfilling chains of interactions between himself and the rejectee. Similarly, the latter should take the manager's postchoice prejudices somewhat "philosophically," and not see the latter's behaviors as necessarily reflecting a personalized form of beastliness.

5. Our description of the nature of the confirmation process also offers a complementary explanation of the observed difficulty of changing people's cognitive attitudes. As soon as the manager is successful in winning a battle on one secondary point in the decision maker's rule, the latter will quickly mend his breach, either by pooh-poohing that particular goal attribute, or by countering with a compensating argument along some other goal dimension. Only if the manager can zero in on the decision maker's *primary* goal attributes (often carried around in a person's head quite inaccessibly, in the form of some uncommunicable existentialist "feel" for the problem situation), can the manager hope to change a person's decision behavior. Even then, the manager faces the difficult task of demonstrating convincingly to his opponent that this person's old favorite is indeed dominated by the manager's own favorite alternative. (This proposition might, incidentally, help explain why public debates are so ineffective as a means of changing anyone's political allegiance or voting behavior.)

## IMPROVEMENT OF MANAGEMENT DECISION

This study has implications for how management decision making might be improved. Three of these implications are given below:

1. A manager should work on integrating his formal models of rational decision making with his intuitive, judgmental, common sense manner of solving choice problems and seek to adapt the former to fit the latter, rather than submit to a bastardization of his intuition in the name of some modern mathematical technique. Mechanical aids to management decision, like computer-based management information systems, will (and should) be resisted to the extent that their structure is incompatible either with the manner in which a manager codes relevant information for his own use, or the manner in which the manager intuitively feels that information should be reduced for arriving at a decision.

   To be more specific, a formal goal attribute weighting scheme, an imposed set of operating decision rules, or an explicit framework for estimating and operating with personal probabilities, will be circumvented by reasonable managers, we hypothesize, to the extent that the area in which the technique is to be applied has not been carefully chosen to match the structure of the decision maker's intuitive (culturally learned) process of working through multi-valued and uncertain decision alternatives. This is *not* to say, however, that a manager should not try to educate his personal decision-making judgment, although the question of which are the more effective techniques for accomplishing this remains a hotly debated issue in our schools of management. We would recommend that a major part of the manager's initial effort in this regard be directed toward a more explicit understanding of his personal processes of exercising managerial judgment in a variety of decision situations.

2. One way that a manager might start training himself to make decisions would be to become more aware of his personal predispositions and prejudices (i.e. of his prime goals) when operating in different task contexts. Rapid feedback regarding his apparent decision behavior from people whom the manager trusts and respects should be of much aid in that regard. The attempt to avoid forming opinion early about complex sets of alternatives seems from anecdotal evidence to create an uncomfortable state of tension in most people. Perhaps the manager might try devising private "holding" heuristics to allow "sufficient" unbiased information about his available alternatives to be collected, and to prevent him from modifying his decision criteria until he has reached an explicit decision to start doing so. (A counter-argument, which we do not advocate, is that decision making and action taking under time pressure is so difficult to get accomplished under any circumstances, that a manager needs to use all the short-cuts and tension-reducing rules of thumb that he can devise, just to make a decision, even if in some cases such heuristics will lead him to very biased solutions.)

3. Our theory leads us to expect that different managers will exhibit different degrees of the tendency to commit themselves to alternatives early in the decision process. Perhaps such a predisposition could be effectively counteracted simply by pointing out to a manager that this is the way he tends to operate. But perhaps the characteristic is sufficiently difficult or expensive to change that we should consider developing standard laboratory testing problems to help screen out of critical managerial positions those persons who too early, on too meager evidence, jump to conclusions about solutions to complex problems.

## NOTES

1. The second proposition parallels the now familiar argument regarding why engineers ought to know the science underlying their engineering rules of thumb. The less validated the engineering principles are, the more an engineer needs to understand the science on which his practice rests.

2. It is of interest to note that, prior to Clarkson's study, the trust officer also felt that his investment decisions were highly unprogrammed and "judgmental."

3. Problem recognition for the decision maker may arise from: (1) the discovery of a barrier to progress toward an objective, (2) a request from others within the organization, (3) a performance indicator dropping below a target level, (4) perception of a previously "coded problem" pattern. Problem definition for the decision maker may take these forms: (1) a description of differences between status and goal along one or more attributes, (2) a description of strategy associated with a previously encountered problem with a similar stimulus configuration, (3) a prescription of an ideal solution to the encountered problem.

4. This phase of decision making, usually critical for practical purposes, is customarily left out of formal decision models (the consequences of which operations research consultants have had to discover the hard way).

***Rex V. Brown***

# *DO MANAGERS FIND DECISION THEORY USEFUL?*

For thousands of years, businessmen have been making decisions in the face of uncertainty about the future. Such decisions have often served to separate "the men from the boys" in business—and perhaps always will. In recent years, however, the problem executives face has been altered by the introduction of a set of techniques of quantitative analysis which I shall refer to here as Decision Theory Analysis (DTA). These methods are familiar to HBR readers,[1] and they have, in fact, stimulated widespread attention, both critical and laudatory, in the business world.

As might be expected when a radically new approach is used, business executives have often found DTA methods frustrating and unrewarding. Nevertheless, there is a steadily growing conviction in the management community that DTA should and will occupy a very important place in an executive's arsenal of problem-solving techniques. Only time can tell if, as some enthusiasts claim, decision theory will be to the executive of tomorrow what the slide rule is to the engineer of today. But clearly, in my opinion, the *potential* impact of DTA is great.

---

Used by permission of the publisher. *Harvard Business Review,* vol. 48, no. 3, pp. 78–89, May-June, 1970. 

*Author's note:* I wish to acknowledge the assistance of Paul Vatter, Howard Raiffa, Stanley Buchin, and Robert Buzzell in arranging contacts for the survey discussed in this article.

The primary purpose of this article, which is based on a survey of 20 companies made in 1969, is to present some of the experiences of practitioners who have been exploring various applications of DTA techniques to management decision making. These experiences should help would-be users to identify particular situations in their own companies where the new technology might greatly benefit them, and to build on the lessons learned the hard way by earlier users.

Executives and staff specialists in the companies provided the bulk of the material. The companies included three organizations with several years of active experience with DTA (Du Pont, Pillsbury, and General Electric); a sampling of corporations that have taken up DTA in the past two or three years and are now quite active in employing it (e.g., General Mills and Inmont Corporation); one or two organizations whose experience with DTA has been disappointing; a few companies (such as Ford Motor and Time, Inc.) where there is a definite interest in DTA but—at least, as of 1969—little application; and a couple of consulting firms with well-known expertise in the area (notably Arthur D. Little, Inc. and McKinsey & Company).

During the course of the survey, particular attention was focused on such questions as the following, which will be discussed in this article:

What tangible impact does DTA have on how businesses are run and on how individual decisions are made?

What areas of decision making is DTA best suited for?

What practical benefits result?

What trends in usage are apparent?

What obstacles and pitfalls lie in the way of more effective usage?

What organization steps should management take to use DTA more effectively?

What remains to be done in developing and expanding the usefulness of DTA?

## DTA IN REVIEW

Before turning to the findings of the survey, let us review some of the elements of DTA. (The theory does not, by the way, always go under this name. Sometimes it is called "Personalist Decision Theory" or "Bayesian Decision Theory.")

First, what information does DTA demand of the executive? It requires such inputs as executive judgment, experience, and attitudes, along with any "hard data," such as historical records. In particular, the executive is asked to:

1. Stipulate what decision alternatives are to be considered in the analysis of a problem.

2. Make a probabilistic statement of his assessment of critical uncertainties.

3. Quantify some possible consequences of various actions and his attitudes toward these consequences.

The logically preferred decision can then be derived routinely according to the highly developed statistical theory that underlies DTA, using decision trees, computer programs, and/or other computational devices.

The use of DTA is not restricted to investment, marketing, or other types of business decisions. Potential and actual applications are also to be found in the area of medical, military, engineering, and governmental decisions. The most ambitious application of decision theory yet reported apparently was employed in the hypothetical problem of whether to push the nuclear button if the President receives different kinds of ambiguous evidence of an impending Russian attack on the United States.

The analyst does not need to keep in his head all the considerations that are taken into account, and, indeed, all the considerations do not need to be evaluated by the same person (although whoever makes the decision must *accept* the evaluations). For instance:

The company president might determine the company's attitude toward risk in new product planning.

The vice president of marketing might choose the business decisions to be compared.

The director of research might provide information on development times, likely success in solving technical problems, and so on.

The probable costs might come from the controller's office.

The probable sales might come from a sales manager or forecasting specialist.

Contentious elements in the analysis can be lifted out, and revised assessments substituted for them, without the analyst's having to reconsider every issue.

While, in principle, any decision problem *can* be analyzed by DTA methods, this is a very far cry from arguing that it always *should* be. In various instances, traditional decision making may be more economical, practical, and sound than modern methods of quantitative analysis.

(For a simplified illustration of problem solving by DTA, see Figure 1.)

## GROWING USE

Only a few U.S. companies appear to have used DTA in operations for any length of time. Two of these companies are Du Pont, which got started with the approach in the late 1950's, and Pillsbury, which got started in the early 1960's. However, there has been a dramatic increase in DTA

[*text continued on p. 290*]

*FIGURE 1* An Example of Decision Tree Analysis

A. The Problem

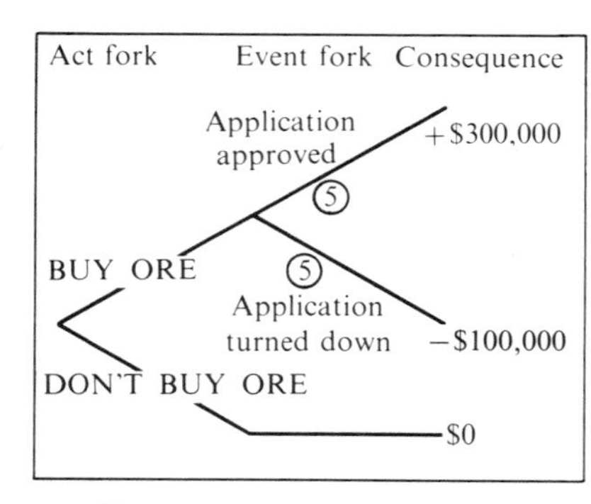


B. The Solution

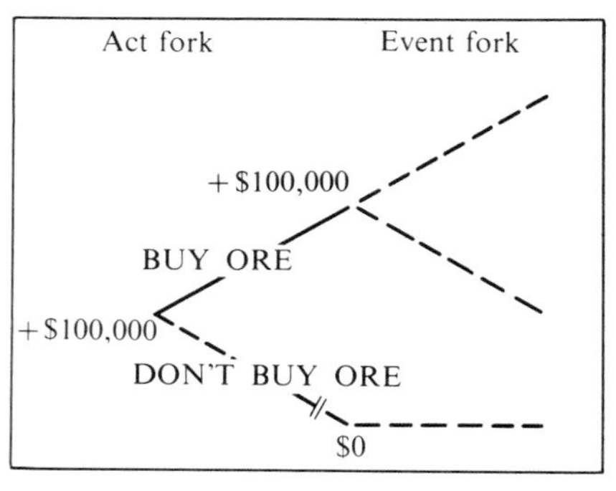


Key: ◯ Probabilities; —//—Rejected acts; $000 Consequences or expected consequences

## *How DTA works*

One version of DTA—the "decision tree" approach—lends itself readily to simple manual computations, and can be used to illustrate the general ideas involved in this subject.

All elements which an executive considers important to a decision, however subjective, can be represented on a decision tree. To show how the process of common-sense decision making can be expressed in the necessary manner, let us take an example involving a hypothetical, but realistic, business decision.

Suppose that a New York metal broker has an option to buy 100,000 tons of iron ore from a Far Eastern government at an advantageous price, of, say, $5 a ton. Other brokers have received the same offer, and so our man in New York feels that an immediate decision must be made. He knows how he can get $8 a ton for this ore, but he believes there is a 50-50 chance that the U.S. government will refuse to grant an import license. In such an event, the contract would be annulled at a penalty of $1 a ton.

A decision tree, representing what I shall call the initial problem, is shown in Part A of Figure 1. Note that both the "act forks" (labeled in capitals) and the "event forks" (lower case) are represented by branches on the decision tree, and that at each fork there are as many branches as there are alternatives.

The choice between alternative acts (in this case, the decision whether or not to buy the ore) is under the control of the decision maker. On the other hand, the occurrence of a particular event (the approval or refusal of the import license) is beyond his control. He estimates a 50-50 chance of approval. The probabilities are noted in parentheses.

The uncertainty about the license makes it impossible to know in advance what the "best" decision would be. Every path through the tree corresponds

FIGURE 1–*Continued*

to a possible sequence of acts and events, each with its own unique consequence. For example, if our broker decides to buy ore, but his license application is rejected, he stands to lose (assuming a penalty of $1 a ton) $100,000.

In order to reach a good decision, the broker clearly has to take into account the probabilities, as he sees them, of each of the two events, approval or refusal of the import license. Intuitively, it is easy to see that if the broker assesses a high probability of approval, he would be wise to go ahead and buy the ore; but since he actually thinks there is only a 50-50 chance of approval, he is faced with a 50% chance of obtaining $300,000 (his best estimate now of the potential profit) against an equal chance of losing $100,000. His estimates of the gains and losses are shown to the right of the decision tree, in Figure 1-A.

Which act should he prefer? His attitude toward possible consequences must be noted. Suppose he has a general policy of "playing the averages" and is not at all averse to taking risks. This can be restated formally as maximizing the "expected" monetary consequences. (By contrast, other people "play it safe" or, conversely, are "gamblers," indicating they like to deviate from the averages.)

Formal analysis begins by computing an "expected" consequence for all event forks at the right-hand edge of the decision tree. This value is treated as if it were the certain consequence of reaching the base of the event fork. Its value is then substituted for the actual event fork and its consequences, as shown in Figure 1-B. In this case, there is only one event fork (approval or rejection of the application) on the tree; it is therefore replaced by $100,000—that is, .5($300,000) + .5(−$100,000). If there were several event forks on the right, each would be replaced by an expected consequence.[a]

Since the event fork is now eliminated, only the act fork is left. The branch which has the highest expected consequence is now selected. That is the "Buy ore" branch with a consequence of $100,000. The analysis of this problem is now complete.

With such a simple problem, it may hardly seem worth going to the trouble of a formal analysis. The real pay-off is likely to occur when the problem has more separable elements than the decision maker can comfortably take account of in his head. Typically, in such cases, there will be more than two "echelons" of forks in a decision tree, and more than one fork at each echelon. By alternating the two methods described for eliminating event and act forks respectively, the origin at the left-hand side of the tree will eventually be reached, and both the optimum strategy and its expected consequence will be determined.

Although the analysis depicted in Figure 1 could be perfectly adequate in representing our New York broker's first thoughts about his problem, a little reflection may lead him to take into account new considerations whose action implications are less easy to think through informally. For instance, it may occur to him that the acts "Buy ore" and "Don't buy ore" are not the only ones immediately available for consideration. As in most business problems,

Figure 1–*Continued*

he may have the option of delaying his decision while he gathers more information. If so, the additional options and the consequences of every set of act-event sequences could be shown on the decision tree, and an optimum strategy determined in essentially the same way. Similarly, he might want to take into account some aversion to risk that he may possess in certain circumstances, the possibility of nonmonetary side effects (like goodwill), or uncertainty about quantities he had previously treated as certain (such as the price he can get for the ore).

These considerations, too, can be handled in the same format and with very little in the way of additional technique.[b] However, more ambitious forms of DTA, such as computer simulations, often prove to be more convenient when there is a technical specialist available.

[a]See the examples discussed by John Magee in "Decision Trees for Decision Making," HBR (July-August, 1964), p. 126, and "How to Use Decision Trees in Capital Investment," HBR (September-October, 1964), p. 123; see also John S. Hammond, III, "Better Decisions with Preference Theory," HBR (November-December, 1967), p. 123.

[b]See Robert D. Buzzell, Donald F. Cox, and Rex V. Brown, *Marketing Research and Information Systems* (New York: McGraw-Hill Book Company, Inc., 1969), Chapters 9 and 10.

---

activity since about 1964. That is when executive interest began to be stimulated, notably by articles in HBR, executive orientation seminars, and reports of successful applications on the part of pioneering companies, and, perhaps most important of all, a steady stream of DTA-trained MBAs who began to enter managerial ranks in substantial numbers. The principal intellectual thrust behind nearly all of these developments was the technical work and teaching of Robert O. Schlaifer and Howard Raiffa at the Harvard Business School.[2]

Stimulated by such developments, executives in a number of companies began to explore the potential applications of DTA to their own operations. For example:

General Electric set up an intensive study of DTA by a high-level committee that led to major changes in plant appropriation methods.

Ford Motor and other companies put literally hundreds of their middle and senior managers through training programs varying in length from a few days to several weeks.

Other companies, including General Mills, began to introduce DTA on a project-by-project basis.

## IMPACT ON DECISION MAKING

Since the companies in the survey were selected on the basis of their actual or imputed use of DTA, no special significance can be attached to the fact that most of them do indeed use the tools. What is significant, in my opinion, is that even these companies, leaders though they are, do not show drastic changes in their general decision-making procedures as a result of DTA. However, *individual* decisions are often profoundly affected. Examples from the experience of the most active companies interviewed—Du Pont, Pillsbury, GE, and Inmont—give some measure of how DTA is being used by managers.

### Application at Du Pont

Substantial DTA activity is going on throughout the Du Pont organization, stimulated by staff groups in the Development Department and elsewhere. Managers in the various departments have shown increasing interest in the staff groups' services (which are supplied for a fee) during the past ten years. Yet, even after all this time, Dr. Sig Andersen, manager of one of the consulting groups and perhaps the most prominent figure in the application of DTA, says he feels that DTA has not yet reached the point where it really has a major impact at the general manager level in Du Pont. J. T. Axon, Manager of the Management Sciences Division, says:

> I think [Andersen and his colleagues] have indeed been pioneers and missionaries on behalf of DTA within Du Pont, and I share with them the conviction that their work has improved the quality of numerous decisions around the company. Their impact has been seriously limited, however, by the absence of appropriate educational efforts aimed at the decision makers. Even at this date, we have in Du Pont, in my judgment, very few key decision makers who are "alive" to the possibilities of DTA and comfortable in its use. It is this lack that has dragged down the Du Pont effort.

At Du Pont, middle and even senior managers increasingly will take action or submit recommendations that include DTA along with more conventional analyses, but the presentation to top management is likely to be supported by more informal reasoning, not DTA. Thus, in the case of a new product which had just reached the prototype stage at Du Pont, the question before management was: On what scale should initial pilot production be carried out? Critical uncertainties involved the reliability of the military demand for which the prototype had been originally designed, and the amount of supplementary commercial business that would be generated.

DTA was performed on a computer to produce "risk profiles" of return on investment for various plant sizes and pricing strategies. The inputs included probability assessments of demand for each possible end-use of the product (based on market research), as well as assessments of cost and timing. The analysis indicated that, on the basis of the assessments used, a certain price was optimal, and a $3-million pilot plant would have the highest expected rate of return.

When this conclusion was transmitted to top management, it was couched in the language of informal reasoning, not of DTA. Management opted for a smaller, $1-million plant, but adopted—unchanged—the pricing recommendation of the study. It appears that top management, without explicitly disagreeing with the assumptions underlying the analysis, possessed an aversion to risk which was not assumed in the analysis.

### Pillsbury's Approach

James R. Petersen, Vice President of The Pillsbury Company and General Manager of the Grocery Products Company, uses decision trees regularly in evaluating major recommendations submitted to him. More than a dozen marketing decisions a year are approved by him on the basis of the findings of detailed DTA. (Many more decisions in his divisions are rendered after first using a skeletal decision tree to clarify the key problem issues.)

Typically, a middle manager in the Grocery Products Company will spend a week or so developing a DTA approach, often with the help of a staff specialist. When the middle manager's recommendation comes to be considered by Petersen, this analysis is the vehicle for discussion. For instance, in one case, the issue before management was whether to switch from a box to a bag as a package for a certain grocery product. Petersen and his sales manager had been disposed to retain the box on the grounds of greater customer appeal. The brand manager, however, favored the bag on cost considerations. He supported his recommendation with a DTA based on his own best assessments of probable economic, marketing, and other consequences. Even when the sales manager's more pessimistic assessments of the market impact of a bag were substituted for the brand manager's, the bag still looked more profitable. Petersen adopted the recommendation, the bag was introduced, and the profits on the product climbed substantially.

During the course of discussions, some Pillsbury executives urged that the bag be test-marketed before management made a firm decision. The original DTA showed, however, only a one-in-ten chance that the bag would prove unprofitable—and if that occurred, it would probably be not too unprofitable. A simple, supplementary DTA showed that the value of making a market test could not remotely approach its cost. Accordingly, no test marketing was undertaken. Management's confidence in the analysis was later confirmed by the bag's success.

## Uses at GE

At General Electric there has recently been a formal head office requirement that all investment requests of more than $500,000 be supported by a probabilistic assessment of rate of return and other key measures. In the wake of this requirement, and largely in the area of plant appropriations, more than 500 instances of computerized DTA have been recorded over the past four years.

Heavy use is made of a library of special DTA programs developed largely by Robert Newman, Manager of Planning Services, who works with managers in other GE operations on a consulting basis. The consulting relationship, no doubt enhanced by Newman's own experience in line management, often has an impact on issues beyond the scope of the originating inquiry, as the following example shows:

One GE division was faced with a shortage of manufacturing capacity for a mature industrial product. Using the information and assessments supplied by the division manager (including a suspicion that the product was obsolescent), Newman spent a few hours on a DTA which suggested that the division should not increase capacity, but raise prices. Both the consultant and the manager felt uneasy about this conclusion.

Further discussion yielded new but confidential information that the division was developing a product which promised to supplant the old one. This intelligence, plus various estimates of the probability of success and related matters, led to a new DTA (which employed GE's prepackaged computer programs). This study pointed to the conclusion that research and development expenditures on the new product should be increased by a factor of 20. The recommendation was adopted, the new product went into production two years later, and it achieved highly profitable sales of some $20 million a year.

## Inmont's Programs

Although Inmont Corporation's usage of DTA is less extensive than that of the three companies just discussed, James T. Hill, President, comments that he often uses computer simulations in evaluating potential acquisition candidates. Preliminary information available on such candidates is programmed into a model by his assistant. This model is part of a prepackaged DTA simulation program which merges Inmont and the acquisition candidate according to the specific purchase strategy that Inmont is contemplating. The computer prints out detailed information as to the cost to Inmont and the return to the individual shareholders of the acquired company, including a pro forma balance sheet and income statement both before and after conversion of convertible securities.

Once the results are reviewed by Hill and his top executives, any alternative financing schemes that have been suggested can be explored in a matter of minutes in order to determine the best financial plan. Computer terminals are available at strategic decision-making locations in the head office, and the program is designed so as to enable any executive's secretary to put in data for different possible modes of acquisition. It is an easy matter, therefore, for alternative strategies to be evaluated quickly at any stage in the decision-making process.

When the most desirable financial approach has been determined, a second program can be utilized to run projected pro forma balance sheets and income statements for any period into the future. This program uses probability theory to arrive at the "best guess" as to the outcome of various operating strategies. It also enables executives to determine the factors most crucial to the future return on investment of a proposed merger. This "sensitivity analysis" thus focuses on the critical questions with which Inmont's management would have to deal if it were to undertake the acquisition.

This is what Hill says about Inmont's use of the procedure:

> The two programs, together, help ensure that the decision as to a potential acquisition is made after a comprehensive analysis of alternatives. It is not necessary to choose only one method of financing or one method of operation, for example. Rather, it is possible to explore, in a very short period of time, numerous strategies to discover that which will maximize the benefits to the merged companies. It is understood that the decision is no better than the reliability of the inputs, including the assigned probabilities.

Various other companies responding to my survey report that they are using DTA on a more-or-less systematic basis for marketing and allied decisions, most frequently in the area of new product selection and development, but also in promotion, pricing, test marketing, and other activities. In fact, about 50 specific applications of DTA to marketing problems are noted—and some of these will be mentioned subsequently in this article.

## OBSTACLES & PITFALLS

Enthusiasm for DTA is very great in many quarters. For example, Robert Newman of General Electric predicts:

> Within 10 years, decision theory, conversational computers, and library programs should occupy the same role for the manager as calculus, slide rules, and mathematical tables do for the engineer today. The engineer of Roman times had none of these, but he could make perfectly good bridges. However, he could not compete today, even in bridge building, let alone astro-engineering. Management is today at the stage of Roman engineering. Needless to say, managers will still use specialists, just as engineers use heat transfer experts.

While Newman's time schedule may be optimistic, my survey findings in no way contradict the substance of his view. However, a number of more or less serious obstacles—many no doubt attributable to inexperience in using DTA—lie in the path of a major revolution such as Newman envisages.

### Personal Competence

It is clear that companies will experience only limited success with a new analytical approach like DTA unless they have executives who are alive to its possibilities and use it effectively. While there is a substantial and rapidly expanding number of DTA-oriented executives in positions to influence management decisions, they represent a tiny fraction of the total managerial pool. The momentum of educational processes will remedy this problem in time—but it will take time.

Much the same can be said about the current scarcity of trained technical specialists needed to carry out or advise managers on DTA. After all, the first comprehensive handbook on applied DTA was published only recently.[3]

However, even if there were no manpower shortage, serious obstacles to successful and expanding use of DTA would still exist. Removing them may require more deliberate initiative and research on management's part than will correcting the lack of line and staff training.

### Uncertainty Over Return

For one thing, no substantial personal or corporate benefits of using the technique may be apparent to the potential user. Many effective managers have a "show me" attitude toward new decision-making techniques, and as yet there is little to show. Indeed, no firm evidence is available to prove that DTA *does* have widespread practical value. The evidence from my survey is encouraging, but far from conclusive; enough disappointments have been reported to sustain the doubts harbored by many businessmen. For example:

A central staff team for an international manufacturer of industrial components carried out a sophisticated and competent DTA designed to help a regional subsidiary choose which of several alternative markets to compete in. When the DTA part of the study was presented to the subsidiary's president, however, he perceived it as having little relevance to him in his decision making. He told me that the market forecast and other input data gathered for the analysis were certainly of substantial value to him, but he could not see that the DTA itself added much that was useful. Indeed, while the market data provided a basis for much of the subsidiary's subsequent strategy, no specific action appeared to be traceable to the DTA part of the study (though some people in the company felt that the analysis had some diffuse influence on several decisions).

The managers of the subsidiary are seeking to adapt the DTA to meet their needs, and the prospects look encouraging. Moreover, the staff team from the head office has since introduced DTA to *other* subsidiaries with, it seems, substantial success.

Note that this experience was the first the company had had with DTA. Almost all of the most successful users of DTA have started out with one or more disappointing experiences. What accounts for such disappointments? Let us take the international manufacturer again as a case example. Its experience is typical of that of several other companies I know about:

1. The logic and language of DTA was unfamiliar to the president and his senior executives, and they could not readily and comfortably incorporate it into their normal mode of thinking. A more gradual introduction of the complex technology would surely have been more digestible.

2. The decision options addressed by the DTA turned out *not* to be the ones the president was concerned about. (For example, he was more interested in deciding *how* to develop a particular market sector than in *whether* to be in it at all.) Fuller and earlier communication between executive and staff analysts helps to counter this very common problem experienced in applying DTA.

3. The DTA was initiated and performed by "head office" people over whom the subsidiary had no direct control, and the subsidiary president may have felt some threat to his autonomy. Having such an analysis performed or commissioned by his own people would have removed the threat.

4. The subsidiary president told me that the way to make money in his business was to get good data and implement decisions effectively. He had little interest in improved ways of *processing* data to make decisions, which is, of course, the special province of DTA.

## Diffused Decision Making

At Ford Motor Company, some 200 senior executives have passed through a brief DTA-oriented program during the past five years; the program has been followed up in some divisions by intensive workshops for junior executives. And yet, according to George H. Brown, former Director of Marketing Research at Ford headquarters, usage of DTA at Ford has been negligible in the marketing area, and the prospects unpromising, at least as of the time of this survey. In his opinion, large organizations with diffused decision-making processes (like Ford) are not well suited to the effective use of DTA as, say, the small or one-man organization is.

John J. Nevin, now Vice President of Marketing for Ford, adds the following observations:

> I am not sure that there is any reason to be discouraged by the fact that, in many companies, DTA may be far more accepted and far more utilized by middle management. Maybe all analytical tools sneak into general usage through the back door. It does not seem to me to be improbable that the middle management people, who are more comfortable with these techniques and are using them on very specific technical problems today, will, as they grow to top management positions, feel as uncomfortable switching to some new decision-making process as many of today's managers feel in switching to a more disciplined analysis.

He also notes that the average executive has difficulty picking up all of the variables in a complex decision-making problem. He attributes this in large part to the executive's inability to discipline himself to use a new technique.

Nevertheless, several Ford divisions are now exploring DTA applications at their most senior executive levels. Since my survey began, early in 1969, there have been some cases of successful implementation. For instance, at Ford Tractor, a product policy decision was recently required. In a regional market suffering from competitive inroads, the main options were to reduce prices or to introduce one of several possible new models; a modest DTA was carried out on these choices. Several runs incorporating assessments and modifications advanced by the marketing manager, the assistant general manager, and the general manager were made. The somewhat controversial conclusion to introduce a certain model was presented in DTA form to the general manager, who adopted it and initiated the necessary engineering studies.

## Organizational Obstacles

If there is one dominant feature that distinguishes the successful from the less successful applications of DTA, judging from the findings of this survey, it is the organizational arrangements for offering DTA. The most successful appears to be the "vest pocket" approach, where the analyst works intimately with the executive and typically reports directly to him (Pillsbury's Grocery Products Company and Inmont Corporation provide excellent examples of this approach).

At the other end of the spectrum is the arms'-length approach, which is characteristic of much operations research. In this approach the analysis is performed by a staff group which is organizationally distant from the executive being served. In such instances, the executive may feel threatened rather than supported by DTA, and critical weaknesses may thus develop in the communication of the problem and its analyses.

## Relation with Consultants

The epitome of the arms'-length arrangement appears in the role of the outside consultant. The survey suggests that consulting firms are doing relatively little DTA work for their clients. (One exception is McKinsey & Company, which reports substantial DTA work in nonmarketing areas.) I find this significant, in view of the facts that potentially, at least, consulting firms are a major resource for companies that want to use DTA, and that leading consultants have done much to explain DTA to businessmen.[4]

It seems that clients often insist on holding some of their cards close to their chests—and effective DTA depends critically on incorporating in the analysis *all* of the elements that the decision maker sees as important. Many clients prefer to limit consultants to performing clearly specified technical or data-gathering tasks with a minimum of two-way communication; executives worry about jeopardizing company security and giving the consultant too much say in their business.

Dr. Harlan Meal, a departmental manager for Arthur D. Little, makes a telling observation concerning the role of consultants and general obstacles to the adoption of DTA:

> Many of the executives who hire consultants or who employ expert technical staff do so in order to reduce the uncertainty in their decision making, rather than to improve their ability to deal with uncertain situations. Many of the clients we have want to buy from us information which will make the outcome of a particular course of action more cer-

tain than it would otherwise have been. If all we can do for them is reduce the chance of making an incorrect decision or improve the expected performance of the decision they do make in the face of uncertainty, they are not very interested.

It is on this point that I think the application of decision theory analysis gets stuck nearly every time. Very few executives think of themselves as gamblers or of making the best kind of decisions in a gambling situation. They want, instead, to think of themselves as individuals whose greater grasp of the available information and whose greater insight remove the uncertainty from the situation.

When the information quality is so poor that the assignment of probabilities to outcomes seems an exercise in futility, decision theory analysis can be most useful. Yet most executives in such a situation say that the only thing which really can be useful is their own experienced intuition. The executive is going to behave as though he has information about the situation, whether he has it or not.

### Technical Questions

A further obstacle to the widespread use of DTA has to do with the logical underpinnings of DTA. Some potential users, especially in staff positions, take the position that where information about an uncertain quantity is weak, there is no point in *attempting* to measure that uncertainty. This amounts to a rejection of a basic tenet of DTA, viz., that subjective judgment, however tenuous, must be taken into account *somehow* by the decision maker, and that a DTA approach may do the job more effectively than unaided intuition.

In addition, increase in the effectiveness of DTA is to some extent dependent on the state of the art. The development and propagation of economical and quick routines utilizing inputs and outputs that can be readily communicated will no doubt be a major factor. Such routines affect the practicality and appeal of DTA in a management setting. However, it seems clear that purely theoretical developments are not holding up further application of DTA; the frontiers of the technology are way ahead of the applications, in most cases.

## REALIZING THE POTENTIALS

How beneficial is a DTA to a company? Does it lead to "better" decisions than other approaches to decision making? Logic alone cannot give us the answer. However, it seems clear that DTA may *not* be the best approach if:

1. The subjective inputs required for the analysis are inaccurately measured and recorded. (Executives, as Meal suggests in the comment quoted

earlier in this article, may not explicitly admit to uncertainty about some critical variable, whereas they may take it into account in their informal reasoning.)

2. The DTA does not incorporate all the considerations which the executive would informally take into account—for example, some non-monetary side effect like goodwill. (Where there is good communication between executive and analyst, the executive often can and does make "eyeball" adjustments for anything that has been left out of the analysis. Sometimes, though, such adjustments are so substantial that they swamp and thereby invalidate the entire DTA.)

Considering all the angles and factors that bear on a good DTA (or any other analysis) is time-consuming and sometimes quite frustrating. Clearly, though, it is one of the prerequisites of making this approach. The following experience should suffice to make the point:

A corporate staff team at General Mills evaluated an acquisition opportunity by means of a DTA computer program that took four months to develop and another two months to run with successively modified inputs corresponding to new assessments and assumptions made by the researchers and executives. In all, 140 computer runs were made before arriving at a recommendation to make the acquisition and to adopt a specific marketing and production strategy. The recommendation was rejected by top management, however, when the company's legal counsel advised against the acquisition on certain legal grounds. The lawyers discovered that a critical consideration had been omitted from the analysis which rendered it unusable for the purpose at hand.

It should be noted that this was the company's first major attempt at applying DTA, and the experience performed a valuable function in exposing line and staff to the scope and pitfalls of DTA. The company's record with DTA since then has been quite successful.

## Cost vs. Benefits

The costs of applying DTA are by no means inconsequential. It is true that the out-of-pocket costs for technicians and computers, even for a large-scale analysis, may be relatively trivial. Moreover, these costs can be expected to decline as DTA technology becomes more streamlined. Other, less obvious costs, however, are not trivial and are unlikely to become so. For example, critical decisions may be unacceptably delayed while an analysis is being completed. (When General Mills does not use DTA for market planning decisions, this is cited as the most common reason.) A busy executive needs to devote some of his valuable time to making sure that all of the relevant judgments he can make have been fed into the analysis.

Even more serious a "cost" is the discomfort an executive feels as he forces his traditional way of thinking into an unfamiliar mold and lays bare to the discretion of a DTA specialist the most delicate considerations that enter into his decision making. These considerations sometimes include confidential information (as in the GE new product example previously noted), admissions of uncertainty (which often run counter to the prevailing managerial culture), and embarrassing motivations. In one instance of an elaborate analysis of possible locations for a European subsidiary, the actual decision was dominated by the fact that key personnel wanted to be near the International School in Geneva. Somehow, that consideration seemed too noneconomic and nonrational to be fed into the analysis.

However, such costs are by no means prohibitive if management's approach to DTA is sound and thorough. When that is the case, the advantages claimed by users of DTA are material and persuasive:

It focuses informal thinking on the critical elements of a decision.

It forces into the open hidden assumptions behind a decision and makes clear their logical implication.

It provides an effective vehicle for communicating the reasoning which underlies a recommendation.

Many of the executives most satisfied with DTA value it as a vehicle for communicating decision-making reasoning as well as for improving it. My own feeling is that DTA's contribution to the quality of decision making often seems to come more from forcing meaningful structure on informal reasoning than from supplementing it by formal analysis. For instance, in the Pillsbury Grocery Products Company, for every DTA pushed to its numerical conclusion, there are half a dozen cases where only a conceptual decision tree has been drawn. Such a tree is used to focus attention on the critical options and uncertainties, and is then dropped in favor of informal reasoning.

## Suggestions for Starting

After reflecting on the experiences of successful and unsuccessful users of DTA, I want to offer some suggestions for the executive intent on trying out DTA in his organization:

Ensure the sympathetic involvement of the chief executive of the company (or operating unit).

Make sure that at least a few key executives have a minimal appreciation of what DTA can do for them and what it requires of them. (This might be done by means of one of the short DTA orientation courses currently available.)

Make at least one trial run on a decision problem—preferably a live one—with the help of a DTA specialist. Use the exercise as a training vehicle for your executives and staffers, without expecting immediate pay-offs.

Plan on recruiting or developing in-house staff specialists to do the detail on subsequent analyses. The specialists should report directly to you, not to part of an organizationally distant operations research group.

Wean yourself and your staff from outside specialists as soon as possible, using them only as residual technical resources.

On any particular DTA, follow the analysis closely enough to make sure that the problem which gets solved is the problem you have, and that you accept *all* of the underlying assumptions. This will probably mean a less sophisticated analysis than would gladden the heart of the typical technician. It will also probably mean you spend more time with the analysis than you think you can afford.

## CONCLUSION

What efforts are needed to make DTA a more effective tool for the executive? It may be helpful to think of DTA as in some way analogous to an industrial product and to ask ourselves: What aspects of its "manufacture" or "marketing" stand most in need of attention?

The "fundamental research" and "product design" aspects (corresponding to statistical decision theory and the development of special analytical devices) appear to be in rather good shape. Rare are the instances in which successful use of DTA is held up through shortcomings in the purely technical state of the art. Of course, there are areas where improved DTA techniques need to be developed, such as the extraction of probability assessments, handling risk aversion and nonmonetary criteria for action, and accommodating group decision making. But, even so, it is clear that greater use of DTA does not depend on such refinements. The tools that exist are well in advance of the capacity of most companies to use them.

Improvements in "production technique"—i.e., in the ability to deliver competent DTA at an acceptable cost—appear to be somewhat harder to achieve. In one major analysis of a pricing problem, the only reason that subjective probabilities were not introduced explicitly was that the computer cost would have been too high. However, we can be confident that within a few years progress in computer technology will largely eliminate this deterrent.

The manpower costs and delays involved in performing a reasonably complete analysis are usually more intractable. With the emergence and propagation of generalized computer programs of the type developed independently by each of the leaders (notably General Electric) in the DTA field, such costs can also be expected to decline—but the improvement will be gradual during the next five to ten years.

The inadequacy of "production facilities"—that is, the ability of DTA analysts to use available methods and concepts—is another temporary obstacle. Solving this problem will take more formal education and increased awareness of the issues and techniques that others have learned. Certainly help to this end will come from university programs and professional publications. Need for access to physical facilities, such as computer services, does not seem to be a serious limiting factor.

"Promotion" and "packaging" are areas requiring serious attention because they have been more neglected. It is true that the "product awareness" needed to stimulate management demands has been created by publications and executive development programs. But willingness to *try* the product (DTA) requires communicating to a potential user the benefits he can expect. These benefits need to be ascertained and documented in a far more effective way than by incomplete testimonials from satisfied —and not so satisfied—users (as in a survey like the present one).

"Repeat buying" on the part of experimental users requires an attractive and convenient "package" so that an executive can contribute judgments and estimates with less pain and confusion, and also so that the conclusions of a DTA can be presented in a more effective, appealing manner. Confusing computer print-outs and technical reports account for many indifferent receptions to what are otherwise very adequate DTA's.

Somewhat allied to the packaging problem, and still more critical, is the question of how DTA should be *used* in the context of a company's operation. This raises the whole issue of how to organize the DTA function, how to implement recommendations, and how to identify suitable applications. Kent Quisel, a senior analyst at Du Pont, comments that he spends a third of his time on what he calls "user engineering," and that this amount is still not enough. At companies less experienced in DTA than Du Pont is, the proportion of time spent in this way is generally much less than a third, to the almost invariable detriment of DTA's effectiveness.

Possibly the most important area of all for study is "product evaluation." Just how good a product *is* DTA? How deserving is it of intensive development and promotion? The survey findings leave no doubt in my mind that many users are pleased with DTA, and with good cause. What is much less clear is just how important its impact can be on business as a whole. After all, only a very minute fraction of companies have so much as experimented with DTA. Can it really revolutionize management as mathematics has revolutionized engineering? Or will it forever be an occasionally helpful side calculation in a decision-making process that remains essentially unchanged?

The answers are clearly of major importance to businessmen and, indeed, depend in large measure on the businessmen themselves. How eager are they to improve the quality of their decision making? What scope for improvement is there? The answers to these questions are the key to many of the issues raised in this article.

## REFERENCE LIST

1. See, in particular, David B. Hertz, "Risk Analysis in Capital Investment" (January-February, 1964), p. 95; John Magee, "Decision Trees for Decision Making," (July-August, 1964), p. 126; and "How to Use Decision Trees in Capital Investment," (September-October, 1964), p. 79; Ralph O. Swalm, "Utility Theory—Insights into Risk Taking," (November-December, 1966), p. 123; and John S. Hammond, III, "Better Decisions with Preference Theory," (November-December, 1967), p. 123. Many other articles on other methods of quantitative analysis are contained in HBR's Statistical Decision Series, Parts I, II, and III.

2. See, for example, Robert O. Schlaifer, *Analysis of Decisions under Uncertainty* (New York: McGraw-Hill Book Company, Inc., 1969), and Howard Raiffa, *Decision Analysis* (Reading, Massachusetts: Addison-Wesley Publishing Company, 1968).

3. Robert O. Schlaifer, op. cit.

4. See, for example, John Magee and David B. Hertz, op. cit.

## DISCUSSION QUESTIONS

**1.** What is meant by the phrase "unprogrammed decision making"?
**2.** Generate à la Soelberg some decision making hypotheses.
**3.** Explain the GDP-I phase structure used by Soelberg as a framework for analyzing unprogrammed decision processes.
**4.** What is DTA? Can DTA be implemented within business organizations on a large scale basis?
**5.** What is the relationship between DTA and other quantitative decision making techniques such as the use of decision trees, cost-benefit analysis, indifference curves, breakeven points, payoff matrices, utility analysis, et cetera?
**6.** Give some examples of companies which are now utilizing DTA procedures. What have been some of the experienced advantages and disadvantages of DTA usage?

# Chapter 10. Communicating

George W. Porter

# NONVERBAL COMMUNICATIONS

During the past half century, social scientists of all kinds, semanticists, psychologists, etc., have been engaged in studying the relationship of people. They have analyzed their individual drives and motivations. They have studied their groups and organizations.

The purposes of these efforts have been manifold. Some of these are:

To study behavior itself.
To determine organizational makeup.
To find causes of problems arising between and among people.
To discover ways to overcoming interpersonal problems so that better quality and quantity of production can result.

Out of this mass of scientific research and study, one problem manifests itself above all others. It seems to concern itself not only with individuals but also in organizations. This problem is one of communications.

Communications can be defined as the process of transmitting and receiving a message from one individual or place to another.

There are two basic types of communications, verbal and nonverbal. Both can be found in use in organizations, by individuals and by groups. These types can be further divided as follows:

---

Used by permission of the author and publisher. *Training and Development Journal,* vol. 23, no. 6, pp. 3–8, June, 1969.

Verbal: *Expressive* communications which include both speaking and writing.

*Receptive* communications which include both listening and reading.

Nonverbal: Many types of communication indicators such as posture, facial expressions, tone of voice, etc.

In the verbal communication field, much has been written and many courses devised to develop and expand efficiency in carrying on such interpersonal and intergroup dialogue. Some of these that are familiar to many include:

Speaking: public speaking courses, Dale Carnegie course, Toastmaster clubs.

Writing: letter writing courses, speech and story writing.

Listening: Nichol's Listening Comprehension course, Xerox's Effective Listening course.

Reading: Evelyn Wood's Speed Reading course and many other courses using programmed instruction and mechanized aids.

Based on the time, money, and effort which have gone into the teaching of verbal communication skills, a person would get the feeling that nonverbal communication was comparatively unimportant. However, nonverbal communication may be more important than any one type of verbal communication because: it takes both verbal and nonverbal communication for clear communication in most cases, and probably more feelings, intentions, and emotions are communicated nonverbally than through all the verbal methods put together.

When various means of communication are used, we have situations like the following:

Singular—where either one verbal or nonverbal method is involved by each person involved.

Combination—where more than one verbal and nonverbal method are involved by each person.

Pluralistic—where two or more either verbal or nonverbal methods are involved by each person.

It would seem, therefore, that we who are interested in the total area of communication should spend more time than we do in analyzing, studying, and trying to understand meanings which are transmitted nonverbally.

Many decisions are made both in interpersonal and inter- and intra-organizational situations which are based on nonverbal cues or clues.

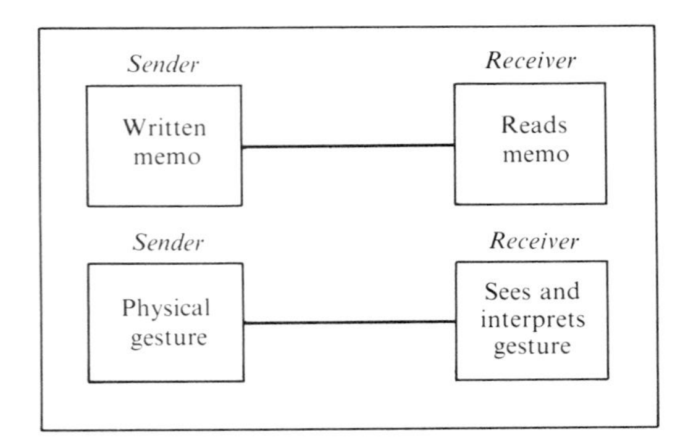


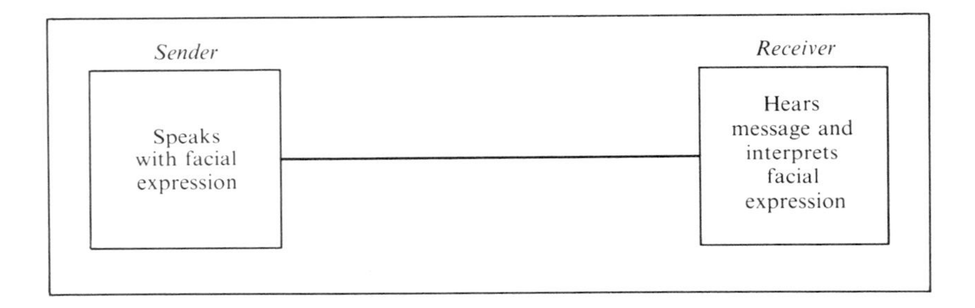


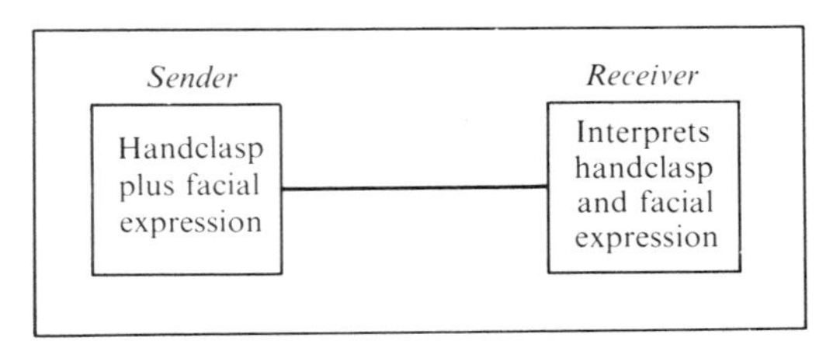


Without an accurate reading of these signs, erroneous decisions can be made. This can result in loss of time, money, and morale.

Perhaps for the sake of examination we can divide nonverbal communications into four classifications:

Physical: this covers the personal method, i.e., facial expressions, tone of voice, sense of touch, sense of smell, and body emotions.

Esthetic: this covers creative expressions such as found in instrumental music, the dance, and in other artistic structures of painting, sculpture, etc.

Symbolic: this covers those methods of conveying a message by religious, status, or ego-building symbols.

Signs: this covers more or less mechanical methods of conveying a message. Such things as signal flags, 21-gun salute, horns, sirens, etc.

## PHYSICAL COMMUNICATIONS

There seem to be five main categories of physical communications. These five are: facial expressions, tone of voice, touch, smell, and body motions.

As we think about the facial expressions and the meaning which can be conveyed by them we can readily think of the many ways we use our faces:

> Displeasure or confusion may be shown by a frown or by the sticking out of the tongue.
>
> Envy or disbelief might be displayed by the raised eyebrow.
>
> Antagonism might be shown through the tightening of the jaw muscles or by the squinting of the eyes.
>
> Anticipated pleasure or flirtation may be shown by a wink. Or a wink might be used to signify disbelief.
>
> The eyes tell stories of emotion and feeling. Watch a couple who are in love. Words need not be spoken for meaning to flow between them. Watch two people who are angry at each other. Words need not be spoken for meaning to flash like electricity from one person's eyes to the other's.

This faculty of reading each other's eyes is akin to mind reading. A case was told about a father and a daughter who had so much rapport between them that they could be sitting at opposite sides of a room and by merely looking at each other's eyes decide not only what the other was thinking but what the other's action was going to be next.

The tone of the voice may be used to signify many things also.

> Inflection of the voice may show fear, antagonism, joy, cooperation, sorrow, or complacency. If we chart inflection of voice using a center line as representing the normal voice pattern, then divergence from this norm could be indicators of the various things enumerated. See Figure 12–1.
>
> Rapidity of speech may also indicate the same feelings as inflection does. In fact the two seem, in most instances, to go along together.
>
> The tonal emphasis on various words in a sentence can also give entirely different meanings. For example: (Place emphasis on italicized word.) *Joe,* what was that? Joe, *what* was that? Joe, what *was* that? Joe, what was *that?*

In *Life Magazine* there was a short paragraph on the "Touching Game."

> It starts at twelve. Boys and girls who shunned each other's company till then start squeal-punctuated wrestling matches. Maturity brings about more subtlety to the touching game. The sun-bronzed Apollo

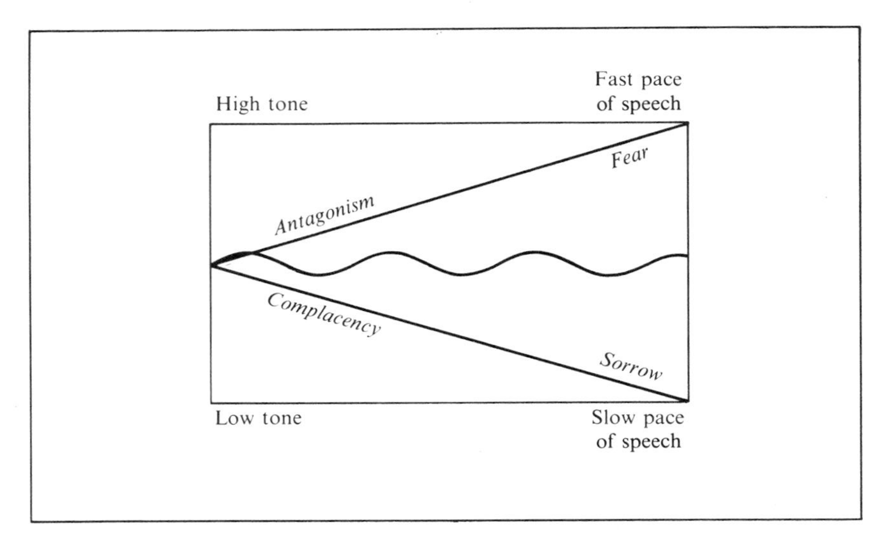


*FIGURE 12–1* Voice inflection chart.

says: "Come for a swim." She lets him lead her. But it's not the water that interests them. It's skin on skin, her against him. When they come back, they lie as close as sardines, sun-tanning although there are miles of beach to spread out upon. Guiding his hand as he lights her cigarette, gives her a chance to kindle a spark with her touch, to lower her long lashes, to lean toward him so he can breathe the fragrance of her hair. Two can play at this touch game. (From *Life* 1–10–67).

It is through this "touching game" that inmost feelings and desires are communicated by all parties concerned. We see from this that touch can be used to communicate. It is this sense that makes Braille usable for the blind.

## The Kiss

Other forms of touch are utilized besides the handholding described above. One of the most common is physical contact through osculation or kissing as a form of greeting, blessing, or farewell.

A kiss can communicate many things and can be used in many ways. Judas used it to betray Jesus. Cleopatra used it to subdue men to do her will. We can all think of many types. Each tells its own story: the motherly kiss, the sisterly kiss, the friendly kiss, the lover's kiss, the sexual kiss, the betrayal kiss, the goodbye kiss, and the "must I" kiss.

Although our culture uses the kiss in greeting, other cultures use such things as rubbing noses or the touching of foreheads.

Affection is shown not only by the kiss but also the hug or embrace.

The touching of another in a violent manner such as with a punch usually shows extreme antagonism. However, when done in a playful mood it might also show affection. These same feelings can be communicated through what is called "elbowing."

## Smell

Another sense, that of smell, may also be used to communicate needs, desires, feelings or just a state of being.

Consider the use of perfume as a means of getting a girl's message across.

> . . . A girl gets on an elevator. She is immaculately groomed. The smell of perfume and powder is enticingly strong. She is in effect communicating her desire to be noticed, admired and desired by the opposite sex. This is her need. The smell, however, may act on different people in different ways—one is attracted—another repelled—another finds it humorous—another sad. The interpretation differs for the same reasons word interpretations differ.

The smell of various foods as they are wafted on the air tells a story all its own. There is no need to call those lying in bed when bacon is frying in the pan. It communicates the fact that breakfast is ready.

The sense of smell informed a group of guests in a recent hotel incident of the fact that a fire had broken out. It didn't take long for action to ensue from this nonverbal message. Another similar incident happened in a store when a leak occurred in the ammonia system.

## Body Motion

The final physical communication in this group is that of messages transmitted through body motion.

A leader of a group meeting can usually tell who the interested people are in the group by their posture. Someone once told of a study that had been made of the motions of the lower torso and legs of a group of people attending a training laboratory session. It was said that the very motions of the buttocks, legs and feet told the story of interest and involvement in the happenings.

Even the pat of a foot can tell a story. One lady pats her foot whenever she becomes disturbed or impatient with another. Those that understand her foot message change the subject when they see the communications of her feelings.

One rather interesting motion is that of applauding. The reason for it being so interesting lies in the manner in which people do it. One person may show his extreme delight of that being presented through the exuberance of his applause. Another person may be like a little old lady who merely touches the tips of daintily gloved hands to show her sophisticated interest.

The carriage of a person may indicate to others how he feels. Is he troubled or is he joyful? The stooped shoulders usually indicate the former while the erect person usually is the healthy, vivacious, and joyful individual. The walk of the individual usually tells a similar story.

The habit of showing disdain by the thumbing of the nose is a communication which many times causes trouble.

One of the most widely used body motions is that of nodding one's head. This can be read by the viewer that the nodder understands the message being transmitted to him. However, in many instances it does not mean he understands but only that he hears. There is a vast difference between the two.

There are many other body motions which are used for communications:

The open arms as an invitation of solace.

The arms akimbo as the indication of self-satisfaction.

The kick, like one made on a flat tire, to show disgust.

The crossed fingers to say in effect, "I'm not sure."

The invitation to "come here" given by a finger or hand motion or by the jerk of the head.

## ESTHETIC COMMUNICATIONS

Moving from the physical modes of nonverbal communications we see another perhaps more nebulous method in the arts. Here are the four main areas which are used to tell a story, project feelings, etc.: music, painting, sculpture, and dancing.

In music, feelings, emotions, and even a view of life itself, are projected from the performers to the listeners by its tempo and mood. Even the choice of instruments communicates the feelings of the composers or instrumentalists.

Through music we can see change taking place in the culture of the times. From the waltz tempo to the sometimes seemingly discordant notes of such groups as the well-known Beatles, the story is told of rebellion and of change.

Almost the same type of thing has happened in the field of painting. Artists of old told the story of peace as they painted their beautiful landscapes. They projected the interest in and need for religion in the great religious murals and canvasses. They projected the style of beauty which was in vogue at the time.

Today, artists are still painting landscapes, portraits and still life themes. In addition they also are telling the story of change through "pop" art, through surrealism, through "modern" art. Here artists are communicating the story of modern life through impressions rather than tangibility.

Sculpture has been given the same treatment as painting. The treatment of the subject matter is done differently today than it was many years ago. The very use of junk in forming "sculpture" today tells the story of change.

Impinging on communication through body movements, is the art of the dance. Here the performers through body gyrations can pour out their inmost feelings to the onlookers. They can portray sadness, joy, despair, hope, fear, bravery, etc. Truly this is a creative communication medium which is not understood by everyone.

## SYMBOLIC COMMUNICATIONS

As our culture has moved from meeting survival needs to the point where we now are concerned with our ego needs, we have found a way to designate our place in society by the uses of symbols. These symbols communicate nonverbally something we are loathe to say verbally because we might be considered to be bragging and we dislike that tag.

Symbolic communications can be divided into two main categories: religious and status.

Religions all over the world have different signs and symbols to remind communicants of their beliefs.

> Prayer wheels and rosaries are used as nonverbal aids in the formation and incantation of prayers.
>
> Liturgical symbols on the paraments found in Protestant churches are used to tell of the religious time of the year or to keep the symbol for "The Christ" before the people.
>
> The Hebrews use the Ram's Horn to call the people to worship.
>
> The Sign of the Cross tells that one is a Christian while the Star of David tells that one is a Hebrew and the colored spot on the forehead of an Indian woman tells the story of her religious connection.
>
> Many hand motions are used in all the religions to give blessings, benedictions, and greetings from one to another.
>
> Even the clothing worn by the clergy, the vestments, tell the people of their particular position in the church.

### Status Symbols

Status symbols have become a way of life for us. This is the way we say to others, "We are a little better than you" or "We have had more experience than you have had" or "We are higher in the organization (pecking order) than you are."

One of the most status conscious groups is the military. Here we find that the cut and makeup of their uniforms, the service stripes they wear, the medals displayed across their chests, the braid on their caps and their sleeves all have the same story to tell—what their experience has been and what their place is in the organization.

To a great extent businesses have followed the lead of the military by the appointment of offices and the giving of service pins. The type of desk, the rug on the floor, the drapes on the windows, the water jug, the number of stars on the pin all tell the same story as the military symbols.

People carry their symbolic living over into their home life and show their affluence by the location of their homes, the choice of their automobile, the place they purchase their clothes and the clubs they belong to.

## COMMUNICATION THROUGH SIGNS

Communications through signs differ from those using symbols in the degree in which the communications are made known. Symbolic communications are more or less passive or secondary to some other function. Communications though signs is a dynamic and primary purpose of the act itself.

The two main methods of communicating through signs are: mechanical and physical.

Mechanical communications take many forms. Without them we could hardly carry on our everyday life. With them we must know what they mean so that we will not get into trouble or endanger our lives or our property.

> One of the most common forms is that found in our automobiles—the horn. Here is an instrument we use to call attention to our approach so that the other person will not be injured. This same usage is found in that of the ship's fog horn or the siren in the police and fire vehicles.
>
> Sirens have other usages though. One of the usages that we may find of utmost importance to us as time goes on is the Civil Defense siren—a warning of impending danger from an enemy of our country.
>
> Signal flags displayed from the masthead of a ship are used to spell out messages while a shot across the bow is an indication to "stop."
>
> One form of mechanical communications that we have become accustomed to is traffic signals and lights. Without them more lives would be lost in traffic accidents than there are now.
>
> We have also become dial conscious. The dials and signals of our autos,

our planes, our many machines all are used to communicate how the particular piece of equipment is operating.

Physical signs are also used in our everyday lives in many ways.

Since we use many ways of communication in the use of our cars, one of the physical signs is the hand signal for turns.

Another sign is that found in the game of baseball. The catcher gives the sign to the pitcher as to what kind of a pitch to make.

In battle, there are certain hand signals to tell the men when to move forward, when to spread out, when to take cover, etc.

The handclasp is also a physical sign of greeting. It says in effect, "I like you" or "We're friends." It can be a meaningful sign or it can be one that can transmit a lukewarmness of feeling from one to another.

The spit is a physical communication in many areas of the world. Mostly it communicates disdain. If it is done in the face, as is the custom in some countries, it communicates extreme disgust. We remember the incident of Jesus' being spat upon by the crowd as a good example of this.

## EXTRASENSORY PERCEPTION

One final method of nonverbal communication which needs to be mentioned is that of extrasensory perception or E.S.P.* E.S.P. can be defined as an awareness of, or response to, an external event or influence, not apprehended by presently known sensory means. It can be broken down into four categories:

Telepathy: direct information passing from one person's mind to another person's mind.

Clairvoyance: direct information passing from matter to mind.

Psychokinesis: mind over matter.

Precognition: the direct obtaining of information of the future.

Recently articles have appeared on this subject in the *Wall Street Journal, International Management,* and numerous newspapers and magazines. In addition, there have been E.S.P. programs on radio and television. All of this seems to point to a gain in respectability for research in this medium of communication.

---

* John Mihalasky, "Extrasensory Perception in Management," *Advanced Management Journal,* July 1967.

Results to date of experiments at the Newark College of Engineering, although preliminary, indicate that one area of utility for E.S.P. is in the area of better understanding the intuitive decision-making process and in the assistance of selection of those with superior decision-making abilities and creativeness.

## SUMMARY

In retrospect, we can summarize our examination by saying that one of the most important modes of communication is that of the nonverbal variety. It is one that can be misunderstood very easily and it takes considerable skill and practice to recognize and to interpret.

Nonverbal communications are divided into four main categories:

Physical: including such things as facial expressions, touch, smell, body motions, etc.

Esthetic: including such areas as music, painting, sculpture, dancing, etc.

Symbolic: including those involved in religion and maintaining status.

Signs: including both mechanical and physical.

The physical communication area seems to be the one which gives the most trouble since we use it every day in all of our dealings with our fellow man and therefore have more chance to misread and misinterpret the various cues and clues to the true meaning being transmitted.

Although much has been written about various aspects of this subject, there still is a great need for extensive research and testing to be done in most of the areas covered, especially in the area of extrasensory perception.

*William S. Howell*

# *A MODEL AS AN APPROACH TO INTERPERSONAL COMMUNICATION*

There are models and models. All are analogies—electronic, mechanical, anatomic. Which, if any, shall I as a teacher of speech communication choose to use? Hopefully, one which will be remembered by my student because it is helpful in his special and routine talking interactions.

What makes a model of the communication process useful to the student speaker? It must have an integrating point of view. Preferably it looks at the world through the eyes of the communicator, the source of the message. All vital decisions to be made by the speaker should be defined—and dramatized—by the model. Ideally, these decisions should appear in sequence, in the natural order of a communication event.

Every function important to the success of a unit of communication should be independently represented in the model. Phenomena of planning and implementation when possible should be separated for closer examination. The event of communicating itself should be isolated from preparation and reception yet its interaction with these elements should be represented. It should show the possibility (desirability, necessity?) of

---

Used by permission of the publisher. *Pacific Speech Quarterly,* vol. 3, no. 4, pp. 11–19, December, 1967.

occasionally (frequently, continuously?) assessing reactions of persons receiving a message *and* the utilization of that information in appropriate modification of content and delivery in the on-going communication.

Above all, the selected model must be both prescriptive and diagnostic. It should explain failures by helping us put the finger on the function at fault when speech communication breaks down. It should serve as a guide in selecting remedies for particular problems of varied communication situations.

We recognize that the useful model may become a habit. This happens because users find it sufficiently rewarding in application that following it is more satisfying than "feeling one's way" through intuitive styles of interaction.

The above criteria are empirical. The model we want is primarily practical, perhaps incidentally philosophical. It must be good in theory *because* it works, and results are its sufficient justification.[1]

The model of the process of communication (Figure 11–1) is the result of several years of evolution through class and off-campus trial and error. Let us examine it totally and part by part to see if it shows promise of satisfying our criteria and serving as an approach to the study of speech communication.

The reader is asked to remember that the model rests on three assumptions: (1) the viewpoint is that of a task-oriented source; (2) from upper left, events in the process are represented sequentially as one follows the arrows; and (3) the process is continuous without clear-cut beginning or ending. It proceeds in cycles, some short, some of considerable duration. Interactions represented don't start and stop, rather they go round and round. With these considerations in mind, let us proceed through the model by combined explanation and illustration. We will sketch in a purposeful dyadic interaction and personify it, adding, whenever appropriate, sporadic bursts of exposition.

Let us assume that I am a manager and a man called Joe carries out his work assignments under my direction. Now it happens that at the time the play begins Joe is on a wrong track. He has modified his methods of doing his job with the best of intentions but has exercised poor judgment. Consequently, he has become inefficient. As his supervisor, I have decided it will be necessary for me to modify his performance by bringing about a behavioral change, or, in the language of modern theories of management, I wish to produce in Joe "specific corrective action."[2]

The stage is set for message initiation when I, the source, am sufficiently stimulated by my everchanging universe of things, events and people to undertake purposeful communication. Having made the decision to communicate, I begin by wording my purpose, or *intent*.

*FIGURE 11–1* Model of Communication Process

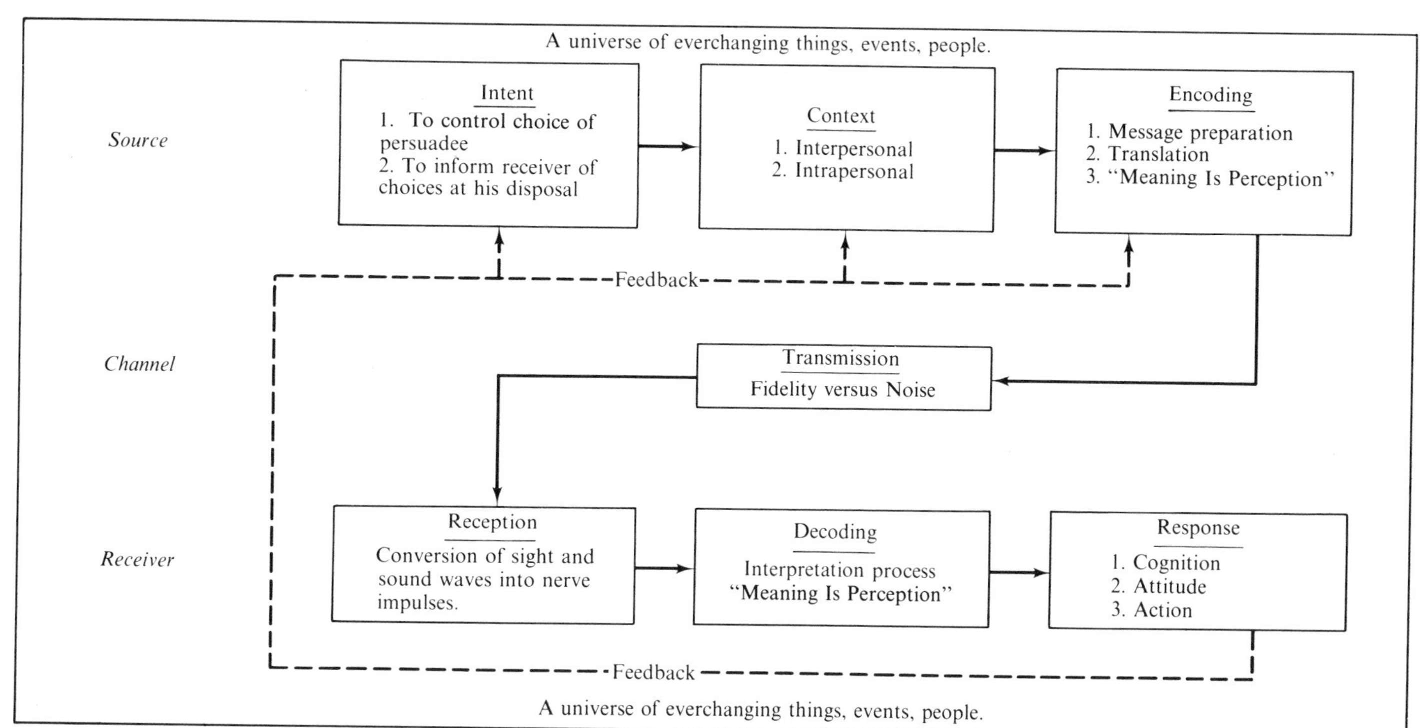


(From Bormann, Howell, Nichols, and Shapiro, *Interpersonal Communication in the Modern Organization,* Englewood Cliffs, N.J.: Prentice-Hall, 1969. The model was field-tested and subsequently improved by Dr. Sarah Sanderson, University of Hawaii.)

## INTENT

Is my intent to inform or to persuade? At this point, I am helped by a former colleague, Dr. Sarah E. Sanderson of the University of Hawaii. Here is her distinction between "informing" and "persuading." When one informs another, he attempts to *extend* the range of choices (alternatives) available to the receiver. When one persuades, his goal is to *narrow* the range of acceptable choices for the receiver. The notion of reducing the number of desirable possibilities via persuasion is a familiar one. However, the concept that the purpose of informing is necessarily to increase the range of choices for listener or reader may seem strange. It becomes concrete with a common-sense observation: "the only thing wrong with being ignorant is being able to see so few possibilities."

In my case, I wish to recommend to Joe an alternative to his present pattern of job performance. My role will be that of persuader, for I intend to narrow his options to a single preferred choice. My proposed corrective action is then formulated in a specific, clear description of the intended modification of Joe's behavior. When I know precisely what I want Joe to do, my *intent* is determined and I can consider *context*.

## CONTEXT

How will I bridge the interpersonal gap between Joe and me to best facilitate the reception of my message? I immediately dismiss the written memo as a possibility because I know I can be more efficient in telling him about the new operation if I can gesticulate and demonstrate. But when I decide to use speech communication, my planning of elements in the context of our communication is far from complete. Shall I call Joe into my office or go to visit him? Would it be more effective to be casual by taking him to lunch or coffee, or should I arrange a more formal interaction? To answer these questions I need to know about Joe.

Let us say that Joe is a sensitive, apprehensive person who is easily hurt by criticism. A formal request to report to me in my office could produce sheer terror. I decide that even a luncheon invitation might cause him concern, that the best procedure for communicating change to Joe is to be informal and casual and treat the recommendation as incidental and routine. So I decide to join him at a coffee break, thus completing my decisions concerning the interpersonal context of our interview.

To clarify the necessity of deliberating about *intrapersonal factors* we need a further diagram of the human message-receiving-and-response mechanism (Figure 11–2).

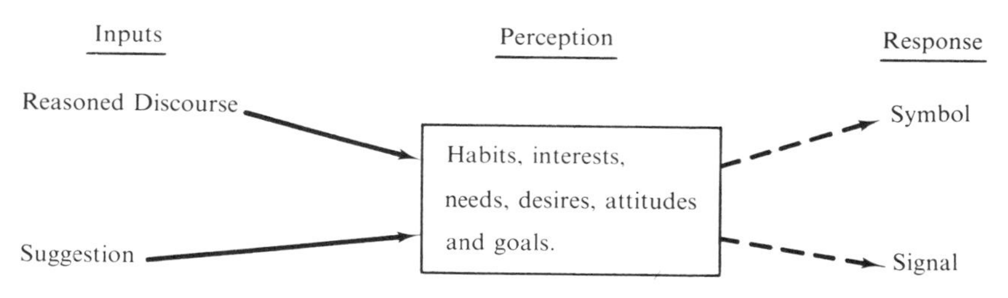


*FIGURE 11–2* Interpersonal Context of Communication

The key to predicting Joe's response is hidden in the center box. He relates to the world in terms of what he is interested in, what is important *to him.* In addition to sensitivity and apprehensiveness, let us assume that he has habits of analytical thinking and is preoccupied with process. The reason he originally revised his job methods was the fact that he finds his operation to be an intriguing thing in itself. This tells me that his thoughtful interest in his work is probably the strongest motive to which I can attach my recommendation. It further instructs me to reply upon the reasoned input with Joe rather than depending upon suggestion. If I can ask him, casually, "Joe, what do you think would happen if you did thus-and-so?" I may well set off a little two-person cooperative investigation that will lead to a solution approximating the behavioral change of my intent.

A person with major interest in what other people think of him and little concern about details of his job performance will exemplify the other input. Reliance upon reasoning about the change with him could be a major mistake. "Pete," I might say, "I think I see how you can get the 'most improved' award next month. . . ." His unthinking-signal-response might well be, "Great, what should I do?" With Pete, the choice of the "suggestion input" facilitates obtaining the desired response because his intrapersonal context is profoundly different from Joe's.

Before we leave "intrapersonal context" a word should be said about the dotted arrows leading to signal and symbol response. In most cases, symbol response, thoughtful and delayed, follows the attempt to reason with the receiver, and usually signal response, immediate and uncritical, is associated with attempted suggestion. But not always! Sometimes the source will deal with facts of the case in a most reflective fashion and the receiver will flash back a signal response. And occasionally the communicator will endeavor to use the push buttons of suggestion only to have his receiver say, "Just a doggoned minute! What's going on here?" and produce a highly critical symbol response. While most skilled communicators plan predominantly to rely upon either the input of reasoned discourse or the input of suggestion in a given instance, the dotted arrows indicate that their intended signal or symbol responses do not necessarily occur. People persist in providing surprises!

When I decide to reason with Joe about the work process, utilizing his habitual patterns of analytical thinking, the intrapersonal variables have been appraised and I am ready to take on the task of *encoding* the message.

## ENCODING

For the skilled communicator, the guide to effective encoding is a basic principle of effective communication—*meaning is perception*. In the context of human interaction, this deceptively simple little sentence becomes a hardnosed empirical criterion. It says that the only meaning which matters is that which gets into the head of the receiver. What the source *thinks* he sent produces no response. The receiver perceives a meaning that triggers his reaction. To the extent that his perceived meaning resembles the intended meaning his response will be comprehensible to the source.

Where does the receiver's meaning come from? From his experiences. He attaches his meanings to the words of the source, and these are necessarily limited to what he knows and feels. Specifically, what the communicator can convey to another person is limited by that person's knowledge and interests. These limitations are within the receiver rather than in the source.

The consequences of applying *meaning is perception* to interpersonal communication are obvious. When I structure my message to Joe, I am engaged in *translation* in just as real a sense as though I were putting it into Chinese. From my inventory of Joe's interest and knowledge, I build the message. I resist the temptation to use my words, my facts, and the things I'm interested in. The message must fit his frame of reference, not mine.

Encoding is a hazardous business, for we tend to forget that others differ from us and talk to them as though they were carbon copies of ourselves. We encode a message that is clear and of interest to us. The notion that it may be confusing and dull to the receiver doesn't enter our heads. Only reminding ourselves to "translate whenever we communicate" will prevent our failing to talk the other person's language.

## TRANSMISSION

The transmission event includes everything that happens during an interpersonal interaction through which the receiver builds a perception of a message unit. From the time I lead the "over the coffee cup" conversation with Joe to the topic of his job until we change to another topic—or part company—all items of interaction between us are part of transmission of my intended message. Not only do I play the role of sender but Joe becomes a sender also, with a fair probability that his well-motivated responses will lead him to "send" to me almost as much as I "send" to him. The dyadic transmission process thus resembles alternating current more than it does direct current.

During transmission, my primary purpose as a message source is to help Joe build a high fidelity-accurate-perception of my intended meanings. For this to occur, Joe's fair, favorable, and undivided attention must be directed to my efforts to communicate. Any incident during the time of transmission that interferes with or prevents this focusing of attention we call "noise." Noise may be actual extraneous, distracting sound such as machinery, telephones ringing, typewriters, or Muzak. It may be expressive; nervous tics, a tendency to stutter, or a lack of fluency in either source or receiver. "Noise" may be mental. Joe's sick wife may command his attention even though he wants to listen to me, and my personal predicament as the defendant in a suit resulting from an automobile accident may keep me from being sensitive to my word selection and Joe's responses.

To the skilled communicator, *transmission* offers a challenge to achieve maximum fidelity and minimum noise. Fidelity, the reader will remember, is the extent to which the perceived message resembles the one the source wanted to transmit. Reducing noise increases fidelity, hence elimination of unnecessary noise becomes of first order importance and a major concern of the source.

## RECEPTION AND DECODING

When the man with the message has done what he can with intent, context, encoding, and transmission, he switches to empathy as his modus operandi and tries to assess the ongoing processes of reception and decoding in his receiver. He somewhat artificially separates these because they pose different problems. If a difficulty is caused by poor reception, the contributing condition is physiological or neurological and is located in the receiver. Joe may have a hearing loss, and on the day we confer, the battery in his hearing aid may have run down. Any deficiency in the receptor mechanism of the receiver—visual, olfactory, tactile, auditory—requires compensatory adjustment of the means of transmission.

However, if the difficulty is in decoding and, therefore, perceptual, if Joe perceives other meanings for what I say although the words come through loud and clear, something other than transmission needs to be changed. On the spot, I must do some new encoding and revise some old, and then recheck to see if the resulting perceptions are closer to my purpose. To summarize, adjusting to faulty reception involves change of procedures of transmission, while adjusting to faulty decoding demands revision of the content of the message, new encoding, modifying context, even in some instances, redefining intent.

## RESPONSE

Throughout our illustration and explanation of the model, we have implied an important assumption—that it is possible for the source to estimate reliably the reception and perception of his message. This can be done only through interpretation of receiver response. We grant that making this estimate is difficult and imprecise but the consequences of failing to complete this step are so punishing that we must concede its absolute necessity. For example, I may take for granted that Joe understands completely the change I want him to implement because it is clear to me. If he fails to comprehend it, I will expect the change to come about, and it won't. My only chance to avoid such a catastrophe is to collect information from Joe's reactions to my transmission until I can be relatively confident that he knows what needs to be done.

The three kinds of response to a unit of communication are not mutually exclusive. *Cognition* is perceiving something previously unknown. *Attitude change* is modification of the way you feel toward something or someone in the world about. *Attitude* is a polarized predisposition, a tendency to accept or reject the object of the attitude. *Action* we define as overt, measurable change in physical behavior.

Most of us believe that everything we learn (all cognition) produces attitude change within us. Some contend that attitude change is the best measure of learning! If we remember that an attitude is toward some object, person, or situation in our environment, and that it is a *definite* tendency to reject or accept the subject of its polarization, then it becomes obvious that we can learn things which do not change attitudes. Remember, this definition makes "neutral attitude" an impossibility, a self contradiction. Certainly there are many people and situations toward which we have no definite acceptance or rejection impulse, toward which we are neutral. We are capable of learning new information about these situations and people which does not bias us *definitely* for or against them. Consequently, cognition can be accomplished without change of attitude or action. However, change of attitude or action is possible only in conjunction with cognition! To illustrate the last generalization; I can inform Joe about a possible alternative method of doing his work without necessarily producing a desire to do something about it (attitude) and without causing any change in job performance (action). But I cannot bring about either the wish to change or the change itself until he understands the nature of the change. Cognition—learning—precedes modification of attitude and/or action.

## FEEDBACK

Accomplishing feedback requires two operations: (1) interpreting visible and audible reactions of the receiver as indicators of the way the message is being received, and (2) revising one or more phases of the communication process in accordance with that interpretation.

In face-to-face dyadic interaction, the process of feedback is continuous. When Joe looks puzzled, I explain and repeat. When he leans forward and turns his good ear toward me, I talk more distinctly. When he says he disagrees, I let him talk so that I can find the cause of his dissent and counter it.

When a speaker interacts with a group, feedback is relatively intermittent and predominantly nonverbal. Its effectiveness depends upon the communicator's skill in reading facial expressions and other body movements. Feedback works better for lively speakers because through empathy their audiences move about more and provide more reactions to interpret.

The dotted feedback line in our model suggests that interpretation of receiver response may require adjustment of one or more of four elements; intent, context, encoding, and transmission. Obviously, utilizing feedback requires flexibility of the source. Any factor restricting on-the-spot adaptability of the communicator limits his benefits from feedback. For example, the person who reads his speech from a manuscript has accepted a rigidity that makes feedback almost totally unproductive.

When speech communication is remote and one-way as with radio or television, and when messages are written, only delayed feedback is possible. The on-going message unit cannot be modified, but response to it can be used to improve the next unit of communication. Information from the panel of viewers of a television program can be of value in upgrading the rest of the series or in terminating a contract.

The fact that the feedback line lies entirely within our "universe of ever-changing things, events, people" indicates that uses made of feedback must be appropriate to the situational context. Precedent, tradition, legal or other formal procedures may dictate the limits of message modification. The skilled communicator operates within extremes inherent in his universe, claiming maximum flexibility permitted under the circumstances. Most important, he never uses precedent as an excuse to avoid permissible utilization of feedback.

## THE MODEL AS A TEACHING AID

Can the present model be helpful to the teaching of speech communication? We began with this question. We specified criteria that seemed to be related to the potential usefulness of such a model in the classroom. Then, we explained and exemplified the parts of the model and their interaction.

We suggest that the reader turn back to the beginning of this article and consider which of the listed criteria the present model is likely to meet, and where it is likely to miss. If in the reader's tabulation the hits outnumber the misses, there is some possibility that the model may contribute comprehensiveness and order to the study of the process of speech communication.

## NOTES

1. A challenging variety of models of communication can be found in the literature. If the reader wishes to sample this variety, four selections will reveal a substantial range in scholarly representations of the process aspect of communication: David K. Berlo, *The Process of Communication,* New York: Holt, 1960, pp. 23–29. John T. Dorsey, Jr., "A Communication Model for Administration," in W. C. Redding and G. A. Sanborn (eds.), *Business and Industrial Communication—A Source Book,* New York: Harper & Row, 1964, pp. 75–91. H. W. Ellingsworth and T. Clevenger, Jr., *Speech and Social Action,* Englewood Cliffs, N.J.: Prentice-Hall, 1967, pp. 17–19. Susan Ervin-Tripp, "An Analysis of the Interaction of Language, Topic, and Listener," *American Anthropologist Special Publication,* The Ethnography of Communication." vol. 66, no. 6, part 2, December 1964, pp. 86–102.

2. C. H. Kepner and B. B. Tregoe, *The Rational Manager,* New York: McGraw-Hill, 1965, p. 19.

## DISCUSSION QUESTIONS

1. According to Porter, what are the four classifications into which all forms of nonverbal communication can be divided?
2. Is ESP a form or method of nonverbal communication? Into what categories can ESP be broken down?

3. Why may nonverbal communication be more important than verbal communication?
4. Present the Howell model of the communication process.
5. What is meant by and involved during the "intent" and "context" portions of the Howell communication model?
6. Define or explain the encoding and decoding segments of the Howell communication model. In which of these two communication subprocesses is error or noise most likely to be introduced?

# Part V. Environments and Implications

# Chapter 11. External Environments

*Leon C. Megginson and Kae H. Chung*

# *HUMAN ECOLOGY IN THE TWENTY-FIRST CENTURY*

Planning for human ecology is especially complex, for not only must man adapt to his physical environment, he must also adjust to the psychological, philosophical, and spiritual environments as well. If we are to plan effectively for our rapidly changing and increasingly complex ecology, we need to be able to perceive, recognize, and understand the changes that are developing in our environment.

Among the many factors which will lead to the increasingly complex economic environment are changing role of technology, expanding role of government, changing nature of unions, changing nature of organizational life, changing objectives of businessmen, changing role of work, changing composition of the work force, and changing concepts of ourselves.

## CHANGING ROLE OF TECHNOLOGY

A nation's cultural system is composed of a technological layer on the bottom, a philosophical stratum on top, and a social system in between.[1]

Used by permission of the publisher. *Personnel Administration,* vol. 33, no. 3, pp. 46–55, May-June, 1970.

The technological layer largely influences the *material* level of the cultural system, and to a certain extent the form of the social system which is superimposed upon it, and even the content of the philosophical system at the apex.

With the harnessing of the energy resources of atomic nuclei in 1945, mankind for the first time has a source of energy in a form other than solar energy. This era in man's development, with potentially unlimited power, has practically limitless possibilities for scientific developments. It is estimated that this energy source, which now accounts for only 0.1 per cent of the total power in the United States, will account for 19 per cent in 1980 and 50 per cent by the year 2000.[2]

Our unlimited supply of energy is useless unless it is harnessed, directed and controlled. In 1943, the electronic computer was developed and is now an integral part of almost all economic endeavors in this country. In 1957, the first numerically controlled machines were introduced in U.S. industry as a means of automating the production system.[3] Economic pressures from within and without the country are inevitably leading to accelerated mechanization. The increasing uses of computers and mechanization will need more people to be trained to use these machines. If a company or a country does not provide the proper environment for technological development and automation, other companies or other countries will.

Thus, we must keep pace with the Europeans in emphasizing the new technology or the United States will decline as a leading industrial nation. Most of the groups involved realize this truth rationally, but do not accept it emotionally, for nearly everyone fears change and its consequences to them. With the new source of energy and mechanization comes a sense of frustration and apprehension as to whether it is altogether good to have so much power and speed at our fingertips.

The new power source, machines, and scientific knowledge, constitute a whirling technological environment comparable to that preceding the Industrial Revolution. A huge mass in irresistible movement, which cannot be stopped or materially slowed down even if one wants to, has the force and momentum of man's total intellectual and economic heritage behind it. Some future moral philosopher will probably look back and designate this epoch of time the "Technological Revolution." This new technological environment is changing institutions, organizations, and people with great rapidity and magnitude. In order to survive, we need to live through, absorb, and deal with greater changes than ever before. We must plan to adapt and adjust to this environment; those who cannot make an orderly adjustment will not survive, but those who can shall be rewarded with a higher scale of *material* existence than ever before.

## EXPANDING ROLE OF GOVERNMENT

The role of government has also changed from passive to active participation in the American economy. At the time of the Industrial Revolution in England, the French concept of *laissez-faire* economics was given a broad and liberal interpretation, synonymous with complete economic freedom. Later, this belief in individual freedom of action was the basic assumption upon which American social and political activities were based. The American Bill of Rights provided relative freedom from Federal government interference with private property and with contract rights and encouraged industriousness, inventiveness, thrift, and business acumen. These constitutional ideals, coupled with a freedom-seeking populace, abundant natural resources, and favorable climate and geography, were conducive to the emergence of a distinctly new "American" social, economic, and political system. The new philosophy was encouraged by government, religion, and economic analysis. Under this system, the mass of people has shared more equitably and extensively in the benefits of production than under any other system in man's experience.[4] Its main *material* achievement has been the great rise in the physical standards of living; the nonmaterial benefits have included a spirit of service, personal achievement, social recognition, and freedom.

The very success of businessmen led to increased government control. The rapid consolidation of industry and capital into monolithic positions of power tended to nullify the beneficial effects of free enterprise during the period between the Civil War and World War I. The pursuit of self-interest, which Adam Smith considered the best guide for enhancing economic welfare of individuals and the society, created riches for the few who could exercise monopolistic power. But it tended to weaken the competitive positions of the majority of people. As a result of these trends and of social experiments and legislation in Europe, Americans seemed to have learned that the concept of *laissez-faire* as a method of economic operation would not produce desired results. In order to protect the rights of individuals and to insure economic freedom from the monolithic power, it was deemed necessary to bring government control into certain business activities. The passage of such Federal laws and regulations as the Interstate Commerce Act, the Sherman Antitrust Act, the Clayton Act, the Federal Trade Commission Act, and the Robinson-Patman Act are examples of how business activities are regulated to protect the public interest.

The greatest retreat from *laissez-faire* economy occurred during the "greatest depression," when a new economic doctrine emerged; namely, the government should take the responsibility for planning economic activities so that the economic system could better serve the public welfare. People now viewed the government as a partner with labor and management, each participants in the economy. The government emerged as a necessary instrument for maintaining full employment and a power balance among economic interest groups.[5] It has become a producer of goods and services that cannot be provided by profit-oriented enterprises. It finances basic research that can direct the technological changes in the economy. For these reasons, the role of government in the economy has increased tremendously during recent years. It is expected to increase in the future.

Yet, the increasing role of government is causing a problem of great magnitude. For government, far from being one among three equal power systems (business, labor, and government), constitutes the greatest power center of all, with the widest sweep of authority to compel obedience. Government alone enjoys supreme sovereign power. Govenmental intervention has made the private sector of business more dependent upon government and created a danger that a power group could dominate others. Should this trend grow in breadth and magnitude, it could destroy the pluralism in our society. It could eventually destroy our democratic way of life. If democracy is to survive, it is essential to protect the concept of pluralism in which no one power group dominates the others.[6]

## CHANGING NATURE OF UNIONS

Although unions are as old as the nation, it was only in 1914, with the passage of the Clayton Act, that they began to grow and develop into such power structures. The law declared that man's labor was a human right, not a commodity.[7] Labor unions were not to be construed as illegal combinations or conspiracies in restraint of trade, under the anti-trust laws. Union preeminance was enhanced in 1935 with the passage of the National Labor Relations Act which made collective bargaining mandatory on the part of employer and employees. World World II witnessed further improvement in the power position of labor unions with the achievement of the "union shop" and the "closed shop," requiring compulsory membership in the union which was exclusive bargaining agent for given employees. Although the latter is illegal in most industries, the unions constitute one of the great power blocs of the U.S.

The changing nature of such labor organizations should be recognized. Currently, there is a wide divergence of opinion as to the future of unions. Some authorities believe that the union movement, while its power is increasing, has lost its passion and that today unions are becoming bureaucratic institutions which are steadily weakening. The critics agree upon the lack of imaginative leadership and of fresh ideas, the need for switching from business to social unionism with an increasing emphasis upon politics, the deterioration in collective bargaining, the dilemmas raised by automation, and the alienation of the intellectuals as contributing factors to this trend.[8] In addition, improved management tactics in dealing with labor unions and complacency on the part of the workers, resulting from the high standard of living, encourage the laborers to disfavor union activities.

However, there is an equally vocal group arguing that the unions are now massing their efforts to challenge the above trends through several concerted activities. For instance, there is a move to organize the increasing numbers of white-collar workers in industry, government, and education. Some dissidents among the young labor leaders are calling for more strenuous, vocal, and active organizing drives. The authors feel that this school of thought is more accurate and that there will be a resurgence of union activities in the future.

If we accept a philosophy that the objective of industrial relations is to maximize the creative use of human resources, the following conditions need to prevail. Management must seek to maintain an environment that will preserve and nourish freedom, growth, and welfare of the individuals in the organization. Unions need to maintain the power acquired and at the same time exercise responsibility and leadership to meet the goals of the society as a whole. Government must not only maintain the power balance between management and labor but preserve an environment in which the three big powers can serve the demands of individuals in society.

## CHANGING NATURE OF ORGANIZATIONAL LIFE

Mankind has never lived, nor can it ever live as a mere struggling crowd. Society has always been made up of the family, the clan, classes, ranks, and other groupings controlled by rules, regulations, and civil contracts. Yet, with the increasing size and number of organizations, there comes the problem of living in an organized complex world. We are now passing from an age of unconsciousness of our surroundings to an acute awareness of, and dependence upon, the environment.

There are many causes for the increasing complexity in our organizational life. Among the most critical causes are the explosive growth of population, the integration and combination of business activities into the corporate form of organization, and the rapid industrialization in our culture.

The enlarged population has resulted in an increased need for economic production, with a consequent proliferation in the size and interrelationships of business enterprises, labor organizations, governmental units, and other social organisms. We need the economic production which tends to occur in cities, but it is inevitable that urban concentrations create stress. Thus, the paradox is that while the technological factors are necessary for human life, so is an environment in which it is possible to satisfy the longing for quiet, privacy, independence, initiative, and open space.

Man is in the paradoxical position of needing the organizations he has created for his survival while resenting and fearing them as usurpers of his freedom and personality. There is a sense of impotence imposed by these units; we feel unimportant, unneeded, and unwanted. Consequently, in addition to business organizations, the encircling movement of ever enlarging organizations is an environmental factor we have created in the form of government agencies and voluntary associations.

The primitive economies are noted for the personal nature of their relationships, while similar activities in a modern society are impersonal and lack individuality. Although this trend leads to conformity, there needs to be a distinction made between the debilitating conformity of thought and the rational conformity of behavior within the bounds of commonly accepted purpose and good manners. There must be a certain degree of conformity in cultural, social, and economic activities but the individual must fight to maintain his freedom of thought and *relative* freedom of action.

As industrial civilizations have grown, the problem for the individual has become serious for he has suffered a profound loss of security and certainty in his living and in the background for his thinking. He now fears becoming submerged in bigness and disappearing in anonymity until all that remains to mark him is a number in a file. He is awed by the magnitude of the institutions he has designed to serve the needs of a multiplying race, and wonders if they will crumble and crush him in the ruins. He knows that an individual can be healthy and happy only when he has meaningful intimate contacts with others, and these contacts can only occur in privacy, but there is little privacy left.

To challenge ourselves more effectively in the threatened environment, we need not only to adapt to the changes, but we also should be able to control these changes toward some desirable directions. We believe that mankind, which is in large part responsible for the changes, is able to influence the direction of changes. Especially, each individual in organizations will play a significant role in this direction. In spite of the evidence of declining individuality and man's declining perception of himself, the individual is still the critical element in the organizational endeavors, and healthy changes in organizations still result from individual initiative and creativity.

It is, therefore, strongly believed by the authors that collective action should not replace individualism in our organizational endeavors. Individualism, instead, should be reinstalled in our organizational life. Furthermore, as a group is composed of individuals, the quality of organizational activities can only be enhanced by upgrading each person who belongs to it.

## CHANGING OBJECTIVES OF BUSINESSMEN

Today's corporations, because of their size and influence are no longer strictly private organizations, but for practical purposes are quasi-public utilities, subject to control. There is also a growing separation of the role of management and ownership, resulting in a new relationship whereby the manager has "power without property," and the owners have property, but with impotence.[9]

Considerable controversy is now raging over the role and responsibility of American managers. If we view business enterprises as social organizations which involve such interested groups as stockholders, managers, employees, customers, and general public, the demand for social responsibility is as important as the profit motive for the stockholders. As a member of society who shall attempt to achieve a social goal—public welfare—a business needs to accept social responsibility. The President of General Electric stated that the job of managers was to satisfy the employees, customers, and general public, as well as the owners.[10] This is a drastic change from the philosophy of the Michigan Supreme Court in Dodge *vs.* Ford, 1919, that a business corporation is organized and carried on primarily for the profit of the stockholders.

Another reason for the trend toward such social responsibility is that the American people have accepted big business as a powerful, materialistic, generally efficient economic institution for achieving the physical requirements. A corollary development is the acceptance of the executives of big business as members of the nation's leadership, as large business enterprises are now construed to be "affected with public interest," rather than being the private affair of a group of individuals.

Yet, since the performance of the economic function is the primary characteristic differentiating business enterprises from other types of organization, the objective of profit will remain preeminent, if our objective is to improve our material well being in the twenty-first century. The profit motive performs two functions, namely: (1) serving as the stimulus to businessmen to take the risks and exert the effort, energy, time, and emotions to plan for greater material gain for the greatest number of people and (2) to serve as a measure of efficiency of how well the businessmen perform the first function.[11] The profit motive is still one of the dominant reasons for running business enterprises, and this is the prime source for meeting various demands for various parties who are concerned with the business activities.

Nevertheless, it is realistic to perceive that the objectives of managers are changing from that of profit maximization to the concept of multiple objectives which concern various interested parties. In order to achieve these new goals, managers need to compromise possible conflicts between various groups and to increase the organizational productivity which will benefit all those concerned groups. This task involves an attempt to achieve maximum potential utility and productivity of the available economic resources, human and non-human. The performance of this role will constitute the primary challenge facing managers in the future.

## CHANGING ROLE OF WORK

Historically, work has been viewed as performing one of four roles. First, it was considered to have intrinsic value and man worked because he enjoyed it. Second, it had moral, spiritual, or ethical value and man received purpose, challenge, and responsibility from hard work, thrift, and frugality. Third, it was a necessary evil to be performed in order to get enough money to have pleasure while not depriving the worker of too much leisure. Fourth, while it is a source of material existence, it also satisfied man's spiritual, social, and psychological needs, for research has shown that work regulates the life of individuals and binds them to reality.[12] While men find their productive role important in relating themselves to the social system and maintaining their sense of well being in the economic order, today, most workers seem to have difficulty in perceiving their jobs as being important except as these jobs improve their standards of living.

The nature of work in our industrial system has lost intrinsic job values which were usually found under the older economic system, especially to the jobs at the lower levels in organizations. Under the older economic systems, production was divided into complete jobs with one worker performing the entire task, which was marked by creativity, control over the process of production, and a knowledge of the "meaning" of the job. Under our industrial system, work is divided into smaller parts with each worker producing one minute portion of it. The satisfaction derived from performing a whole job has been smothered under the minuscule, functional division of labor. While the work of professional, managerial, and technical groups tends to possess meaningful job contents, these contents are usually lacking, at least by a matter of degree, in lower level jobs. For example, one study showed that 68 percent of the professional, and 59 percent of sales personnel would continue the same kind of work if they had enough money to live comfortably, as opposed to 33 percent of service, and 16 percent of unskilled workers.[13]

Among other factors, this growing sense of low status and the inability to achieve a position of prestige in his job has frustrated employee individuality and creativity, resulting in boredom, lack of interest, a sense of inferiority and unrest, and a search for other means of obtaining status, especially the heroic struggles for professional identification. A more serious consequence of the previous tendency is social stratification of industry, for as the complexities of the new technology make technical education a prerequisite for the operating executive, the prospect of workers rising through the ranks becomes progressively dimmed. One great need as we approach the twenty-first century is an upgrading of the social status of manual type work, by reorganizing the job contents to generate some intrinsic job satisfaction or by providing effective economic motives, for we must find sufficient workers to replace those now performing these jobs. This is not feasible as long as young people shun preparation for skilled manual jobs.

Improving technology tends to lessen the need for work. It is now possible for a person to produce more in a shorter period of time, resulting in more time for leisure pursuits. We have estimated that the average American employee of the nineteenth century worked 3,700 hours per year. Now, with the 8-hour day, 5-day week, and with around three weeks paid vacation and eight paid holidays, he works only around 1,800 hours annually. It has also been estimated that *all* Americans spent 13 percent of all available time working in 1900, 10 percent in 1950, and will spend only 7 percent in 2000.[14] If this prediction is correct, most people have to adjust their way of life from the work-oriented to the leisure-oriented. If we are not successful in this change, we will be bored to death or will try to discharge our energies into possibly undesirable activities.

We believe that through this institution of work men will ultimately find the answer to their sense of impotence caused by the tremendous growth and complexity of the organizational world in which they live and work. The individual employee may eventually look upon work as the link between himself and society, offering him economic and psychological stability in the swirling processes of change. Work is an ego-satisfying institution through which we fulfill many of our needs such as economic, socio-psychological balance and a sense of importance which are necessary to counterbalance the feeling of being overwhelmed by the giant organizations. Therefore, we predict that more leisure with less work will not be the best substitute for toil.[15]

## CHANGING COMPOSITION OF WORK FORCE

We must plan for a radically changed work force for the twenty-first century. Now, only around 57 percent of all persons 14 years of age and older are employed.[16] It is estimated that only about 45 percent will be employed at that time. The others will be in various types of institutions and educational establishments, unemployed, or unemployable. Those employed will be younger, because of earlier retirement, and more highly educated. In 1964, the average employed person had 12.2 years of schooling.[17] We forecast this will probably increase to 18 years by the end of this century, assuming that most people will pursue a graduate degree.

The work force will have a significantly higher proportion of Negroes employed. Out of every 1,000 workers in the U.S. in 1963 only 65 were Negroes.[18] This is expected to be closer to 110 or the same ratio as the Negro to total population in three more decades. There will also be higher proportions of female workers. While only 35 percent of employed persons now are females, it is expected that this figure will approach 50 percent as women achieve greater equality, and as a smaller proportion of the population is employed.[19]

Changes have occurred in the occupational patterns of the work force. Prior to 1870, we were an agricultural nation, as more workers were engaged in agriculture and extractive industries than any other. From then until 1966, we were an industrial nation, as more workers were producing manufactured products than were farming. Since then, we have become a service type economy, for more people are now employed in nonmanufacturing activities, and this trend should accelerate. This trend indicates that we need to develop skilled and white-collar personnel who will man the service industries.

As the work force will be composed of higher caliber personnel, especially service, technical, scientific, and professional employees, the style of supervision of these individuals must be different from those previously utilized with lower level personnel. Consequently, the traditional motivational factors must be changed. Increased emphasis should be given to the full utilization of the employee's talents and training, his status, and his opportunities for development with his professional career.

## CHANGING NATURE OF MAN

Most of the great systems of human thought have contained in them some concept of what man is. While the eternal question of what he really is has never been answered, it is known that man's *economic* position has seen a phenomenal improvement, while his *philosophical* and *psychological* perception of his role in the economic and cultural *milieu* has declined. His economic improvement has resulted in the employee having a sense of independence and freedom; his philosophical perception has caused a sense of insecurity and frustration that results in a craving for meaning, worth, and dignity in his ecology. These two trends have affected man's position in two ways.

First, the employee's economic position has improved to the point where he is no longer dependent upon one particular firm or management for his survival, and no longer can managers rely upon authority as the primary motivational method, but they must make new assumptions about the basic nature, beliefs, and motivation of employees. Earlier, the employee was viewed as an "economic man" who behaved in a rational, analytical, and reasoning manner in response to purely economic factors of costs, prices, and profits. However, as the employee has improved his economic position, his needs for personal dignity, security, recognition, achievement, and other socio-psychological reasons demand actions for satisfaction. Therefore, the problem is not a question of whether man desires the economic benefits *or* the more intangible benefits, but that he demands them *both* in order to make bearable an otherwise unbearable existence in the economic environment.

Second, while man's economic position has grown, his philosophical and psychological perception of himself has declined. Man sees himself as a cog in a machine which functions in the complex and impersonal organizational life. Especially, when he sees himself a mere reactor whose responses are largely determined by outside forces, he downgrades himself from philosophical and psychological standpoints. There have been two great movements in mankind's history as far as his philosophical and psychological perception of himself is conceived. The first tended to glorify his perception of himself, while the second downgraded it.[20]

The glorification of man, which began in prehistoric times, continued until the Renaissance. It was manifest from a religious, philosophical, aesthetic, literary, and scientific point of view. From a religious point of view, the human aggrandizement has recurred in most of the world's religions, including the Judeo-Christian faiths. From a philosophical point of view, mankind has also been exalted as a higher form of intellectual being. Most of the philosophical writings tended to glorify the human race and its relationship to the universe.

From an aesthetic point of view, the Greek, Roman, and Renaissance artists and sculptors glorified humanity in their paintings, statuary, and other artistic forms. The Greek sculpture especially personified the beauty and dignity of man. From a literary point of view, humanity reached its apex of grandeur and glory, as far as man's perception of himself and his fellow man was concerned, during the Renaissance. Man was construed to be so important that his body was considered as a microcosm of the universe.

From a scientific point of view, the Homo sapiens was also glorified, for a number of major achievements were necessary in the development of life before he could exist. For example, our grasping, manipulating forelimb hands and our big brain which makes it possible for us to produce and use tools and machines distinguish us from the lower order of beings and make us superior to them.

While the downgrading of man's perception of himself continues until the present, it began roughly with the end of the Renaissance. The destructive process has taken many forms, but essentially it involves challenges to the aforementioned factors.

Mankind's relationship to the universe was first challenged. Under the Ptolemaic system of astronomy, the earth was the stationary center of the universe and the sun, moon, and stars revolve about it. As the universe was the macrocosm and man was the microcosm, he was the center of the universe. However, Copernicus showed that the sun was the center of our solar system, and the earth moved around it and man was no longer the center.

Our relationship to the social order was questioned by Machiavelli who said that we are morally evil and therefore incapable of good action. Whoever desires to organize a government and give it laws must start by "assuming that all men are bad and ever ready to display their vicious nature, whenever they may find occasion for it."[21]

Man's relationship to the economic order lowered by the Industrial Revolution, which, with all its material benefits, tended to transfer skills from the worker to the machine so that he became an adjunct to it; labor was degraded and the workers became dependent upon the job and its wages. The systematic devaluation of our perception of ourselves was furthered by Karl Marx's contention that values are not derived from man's soul but of ideology shaped by his economic environment.

Charles Darwin's theory of organic evolution diminished man's perception of his dignity and worth by saying that man is not the apex of spiritual beings but is merely the latest link in the evolutionary chain of organisms. Freud tried to deny us the illusion of self determination by theorizing that we are not even rational, reasoning, analytical beings but are creatures driven by unconscious processes. Yet, research shows that one of our important needs is to enlarge those areas of our lives in which our own decisions determine the outcome of our efforts.[22] It has even stated that we cannot conclude that the metal "brains" of computers possess less capacity for creature leadership than the human brain.[23]

## SUMMARY AND CONCLUSION

In view of these trends there are some problems that need resolving in planning for the twenty-first century. While the results of the encroaching interaction of people discussed in this paper are manifold, the most significant ones are the increasing number and size of organizations, with their consequent impersonality, and a lessening of individualism. Any planning for human ecology must come to grips with these problems, for the extreme alternatives—virtual utopia or serious, perhaps irreversible, disasters for man—have become real. In fact, the course of future events may be decisively set in this and a few succeeding generations.[24]

There are several courses of action available to us if we desire to enhance the quality of our life in the changing environment. First, we can focus on the individual development through education and training so as to place the individuals in positions where they can realize their potentials. Thereby, each individual can be an effective user of organizations and master of technological machinery rather than a servant of them. Second, we can focus on the individual situations by manipulating the environment in order to counteract the forces toward overconformity. Thereby, each individual can be allowed the opportunity to exercise individual initiative in a positive way. Third, our society apparently is placing too much emphasis upon natural sciences and economic value and overlooking the philosophy that moral and spiritual values are also basic to our developmental process. We need to value the role of man as an individual person in society, and protect human dignity, personal integrity, and freedom, because we know man is the highest earthly being and, hence, the ultimate decision-making unit in a complex world.[25] Finally, as the population grows and organizational life becomes more complex and impersonal, we need to learn to live together harmoniously, for conflict will only threaten our existence. The ever-expanding knowledge of behavioral sciences should play a significant role in this endeavor.

## REFERENCE LIST

1. Leslie A. White, *The Science of Culture: A Study of Man and Civilization* (New York: Farrar, Straus and Co., 1949), p. 393.

2. "Power Plan for the Future—One System to Serve Whole U.S.," *U.S. News and World Report,* December 28, 1964, p. 64.

3. "Spotlight on Business: The Challenge of Automation," *Newsweek,* January 25, 1965, p. 73.

4. "Declaration of the 51st National Foreign Trade Convention," *National Foreign Trade Council,* New York, November 16–18, 1964, p. 6.

5. See Eli Ginzberg, Dale L. Hiestand, and B. G. Reubens, *The Pluralistic Economy* (New York: McGraw-Hill, 1965); and Joseph W. McGuire, *Business and Society* (New York: McGraw-Hill, 1963), pp. 87–94.

6. McGuire, *ibid.,* p. 131.

7. It is interesting to note that this concept is diametrically opposed to that of Karl Marx who emphasized that the value of a product was the value of the embodied labor, and therefore, the value of labor tended to equate the value of goods.

8. Albert A. Blum, "Labor at the Crossroads," *Harvard Business Review,* Vol. 42, No. 4 (July-August, 1964), pp. 6–19, 172.

9. Adolf A. Berle, Jr., *Power Without Property* (New York: Harcourt, Brace and Co., 1959), p. 59.

10. C. E. Wilson of General Electric, in *Hearings on Profits, Sub-Committee of the Joint Committee on the Economic Report,* 80th Congress, December, 1949.

11. Even the Socialist countries of Eastern Europe now recognize the necessity of these two functions. Following a speech at the Joint European Conference of the Econometrics Society and The Institute of Management Sciences in Warsaw, Poland in September, 1966, the senior author spent one hour answering questions from Socialist teachers and managers from Eastern Europe on how to make a profit. This was the result of mentioning the word "profit" only once in the speech.

12. Eli Ginzberg, "Man and His Work," *California Management Review,* Vol. V, No. 2 (Winter, 1962), pp. 21–28; Elaine Michelson, "Volunteer Work Aids Mental Patients," *Journal of Rehabilitation,* Vol. XXX, No. 1 (January-February, 1964), pp. 14–16.

13. Robert Blauner, "Extent of Satisfaction: A Review of General Research," in T. W. Costello and S. S. Zalkind (eds.), *Psychology in Administration: A Research Orientation* (Englewood Cliffs, New Jersey: Prentice-Hall, 1963), p. 82.

14. Marion Clawson, "How Much Leisure, Now and in the Future?", in J. C. Charlesworth (ed.), *Leisure in America: Blessing or Curse?* (Philadelphia: American Academy of Political and Social Science, 1964), pp. 1–20.

15. John Kenneth Galbraith, *The New Industrial State* (Boston: Houghton Mifflin, 1967), p. 365.

16. Sophia Cooper and Dennis F. Johnston, "Labor Force Projections for 1970–80," *Monthly Labor Review,* Vol. 88, No. 2 (February, 1965), pp. 129–40.

17. Dennis F. Johnston, "Educational Attainment of Workers," *Monthly Labor Review,* Vol. 88, No. 5 (May, 1965). p. 519.

18. Joseph A. Brackett, "Employment of Negroes by Government Contractors," *Monthly Labor Review,* Vol. 87, No. 7 (July, 1964), p. 791.

19. Cooper and Johnston, *ibid.,* p. 130.

20. See Leon C. Megginson, *Personnel: A Behavioral Approach to Administration* (Homewood: Richard D. Irwin, 1967), pp. 608–11.

21. Count Carle Sforza, *The Living Thoughts of Machiavelli* (New York: Fawcett World Library, 1958), p. 41.

22. Chris Argyris, "Individual Actualization in Complex Organizations," in G. D. Bell (ed.), *Organizations and Human Behavior* (Englewood Cliffs, N.J.: Prentice-Hall, 1967), pp. 208–17.

23. Stanley Stark, "Management in Perspective: Creative Leadership: Human vs. Metal Brain," *Academy of Management Journal,* Vol. VI, No. 2 (June, 1963), pp. 160–69.

24. Demitri B. Shimkin, "Adaptive Strategies: A Basic Problem in Human Ecology," in *Three Papers on Human Ecology,* Mills College, 1966, pp. 37–52.

25. Keith Davis, "Individual Needs and Automation," *Academy of Management Journal,* Vol. 6. No. 3 (December, 1963), pp. 278–83.

*Endel J. Kolde*

# *THE INTERNATIONAL BUSINESS SYSTEM*

Business is modern society's means of subsistence. In industrial countries it determines not only the material standards of life but also the modes of production, consumption, work, and leisure, and to an increasing degree the influence and power structure of the society. Business has replaced the traditional elites—the landed aristocracy, the ecclesiastics, and the military—in the industrial countries and is forcing reform in the semi-industrial and even the primitive areas. Thus, business is more than the workshop of the society. Besides goods and services, it provides the stage on which most of modern life's drama is played; and besides being the main fountain of wealth and power, it is a source of both economic and social progress. Indeed, modernity in a social sense is synonymous with a business-dependent industrial society such as is found in the United States and Western Europe, where business is a way of life.

## The National Business System

A system is a set of interrelated elements. In simple systems the elements are individual components or factors which have cause-and-effect rela-

---

Used by permission of the author and publisher. From *International Business Enterprise,* copyright 1968, chapter 1, pp. 3–12, Prentice-Hall, Englewood Cliffs, New Jersey, 1968.

tionships to one another. In complex systems the elements are interacting subsystems, which themselves may contain several orders of subsystems as well as nonsystem components. The business system is exactly such a complex hierarchy of subsystems of different order and character.

The components of this complex are, first, the different enterprises—both private and public—created to produce goods and services. They, in turn, consist of internal subsystems such as subsidiaries, branches, divisions, departments, cost centers, and work groups. A second category of components of the business system consists of industry associations of various kinds; they range from intraindustry trade associations (often with limited purposes) to interindustry and community-wide bodies such as Chambers of Commerce, development associations, and industrial planning boards. A third set of components comprises labor, vocational, and professional groupings, which are self-explanatory. A fourth category embraces subsystems which function simultaneously as components in the business system and in one or more of the political, legal, governmental, educational, and other social systems of the country. These elements link the business system functionally to most other important systems of the society. And through such links the interactions between the business system and the society as a whole, the inputs and the outputs, manifest themselves.

As a methodological clarification it might be added that, for any one of the subsystems in a complex hierarchy such as the international business system, the next smaller subsystems are its components and the larger systems to which it belongs constitute its environment. The impacts of the environment upon the system (effects of the system on a subsystem) are inputs, and the impacts of the system upon its environment (effects of a subsystem on the system) are its outputs, positive or negative. The impacts among the components, the interactions within the system, constitute the behavior of the system.

## The International Business System

The national business systems combine into the international or multinational business system. Its components are basically of five types:

(1) the national business systems of individual countries
(2) the various intermediary institutions designed to serve as channels for interaction among them
(3) multinational enterprises
(4) intergovernmental agencies and arrangements
(5) supranational entities and bodies

Categories (2) and (3) are peculiar to international business in the sense that they do not exist in the domestic business scene. They have evolved in response to multinational business requirements, and in the absence of such business they would at best have a tangential impact on the domestic system. As intercountry links, they transmit and often generate many of the interactions among the different national business systems. For this reason, the study of international business tends to polarize around intercountry links and to treat the internal workings of the national business systems in only a limited way.

The international business system has no fixed geographic boundaries but varies with one's objective. Unlike the national system, which, by definition, has concrete territorial scope and which, in turn, is composed of relatively easily defined subdivisions—regions, provinces, and municipalities—the international business system may be delineated in any way from only two countries up to the global totality. Between these extremes one can conceive, at least in theory, as many different systems as there are combinations of countries. In practice, the boundaries of the system should be chosen to facilitate the study or analysis of particular aspects or particular behavior. Thus, different geographical boundaries are appropriate for different purposes.

### The Business System Contrasted to the Economic System

For clarity, it is important to note that the concept of the business system as used here is not synonymous with that of the economic system. As defined above, the business system embraces all of society's productive organization and its behavior. The economic system is a much narrower concept, best delineated in terms of the areas to which modern economics as a field of knowledge is confined. They are three: the theory of price (microeconomics), the measurement of the aggregate production and income of a country (macroeconomics), and more recently the development of mathematical tools to improve economic analysis. But the science of economics has very little to do with the concrete processes of producing or distributing goods, not to mention organizing and directing enterprises. In recent years attempts have been made to bring into the purview of economics organizational, technological, and behavioral problems which traditionally have been beyond its scope. However, such "transboundary" knowledge has been accumulated primarily by scholars in business administration and its supporting disciplines—operations research, management science, and quantitative methods—rather than by those in economics. Therefore, it is not likely that the concepts of economics and of the economic system will in the future be expanded to coincide in scope with those of the business system.

Although the study of both economics and business must be based on the scientific method, the values, the criteria, and the frames of reference are different. Business is reality centered. For it the overriding requirement is to understand, explain, and reform reality. Economics is theory centered. Its main concern is with abstract principles and concepts, which may or may not explain reality. Since the economic system, as usually defined, is a narrower concept, it must be viewed as a special component of the business system. As a whole, it is more useful to classify economics and the economic system with other specialized disciplines, such as communication, psychology, anthropology, political science, law, and mathematics, which can all serve as tools for the study of business administration.

## INTERNATIONAL BUSINESS ADMINISTRATION

Business administration deals with the organization, operation, and behavior of business enterprise. It has two main objectives: to explore the ideas, institutions, and processes which control and condition business activity; and to cultivate the knowledge and skills which can enhance the productive efficiency of business from both an economic and a social standpoint. Thus business administration is an unusually diverse and complex subject; indeed, it might be argued that, instead of being one discipline, business administration is a composite of many related but different subjects—production, finance, marketing, transportation, personnel, management science, operations research, etc.—which all focus on the study of business enterprise. Many other academic disciplines have similar branches or subdisciplines. Physics, for example, consists of optics, acoustics, mechanics, thermodynamics, etc.; biology of botany, zoology, bacteriology, etc. As the systematized knowledge of business administration grows and matures, its branching into subfields is likely to continue, and, as in other fields, some of these branch disciplines will become relatively, if not entirely, independent of business administration itself. Such a branching process has been the beginning of practically all the disciplines, except philosophy, that we know today. Business administration itself started as an offshoot of economics in the beginning of this century, and, because of this, it is often confused with applied economics.

None of the foregoing is meant to imply that business administration is independent of other fields. In fact, it draws on many disciplines, especially economics, social sciences, law, and quantitative methods. The degree to which these various subjects enter into business administration varies from subfield to subfield. Since the study of the environments and the functioning of enterprise in different societies involves many cross-cultural and other "nonbusiness" problems, international business is particularly dependent on the knowledge and analytical tools of other fields. The more important disciplines for international business are economics, area studies, cultural anthropology, law, political science, and social psychology. Geography, history, languages, regional science, and comparative literature also make important contributions. From the subdisciplines of business administration itself the most important areas for international business are finance, marketing, and business policy. Others such as production, industrial relations, organization theory, and social environment including government-business relations grow in importance as one's studies of international business progress.

## Transferability of Knowledge

The applicability of American business learning to international and especially to foreign business situations is much more limited than is generally recognized because business administration deals to a great extent with phenomena which either are products of or are conditioned by the culture of the society involved. The business knowledge which has been developed in the United States treats many culture-determined factors as universal knowledge. This practice may be dangerously misleading in the international field for only pure theories, techniques, and principles are universal knowledge and, as such, have applicability irrespective of the cultural setting. As in other social sciences, much of business administration is not theory, technique, or principle; instead, it deals with culture-determined phenomena such as institutions, behavior, motivation, regulation, and control, which cannot be transplanted from one country to another without some adaptation.

Consider, for instance, fields such as finance, marketing, and personnel. What part of them has international applicability? Only that which is left after one plucks from them all the elements that are purely American: the laws; the public policies; the size and linguistic unity of the American market; the labor organization; the American consumer with his particular economic, social, and psychological makeup; the American ideas of competition, fair play, and acceptable conduct; the specialized services such as marketing research, advertising, labor relations, investments, and counseling.

Only after all the elements of Americana have been removed can one talk about the universal and thus the internationally transferable portion of business administration. Obviously, the scope of transferable knowledge varies with the intercultural heterogeneities which any particular group of countries presents. Close cultural kinship such as between Canada and the United States or Ceylon and India permits a much greater carryover of business knowledge and experience from one to the other than would be possible between Canada and Ceylon or India and the United States. The carryover varies inversely with the number of countries and cultures involved: the greater the number, the greater the intercountry differences and the smaller the body of system-wide business knowledge; and conversely the fewer the countries, the greater the chances for internal similarities as well as for adaptations.

Since neither the multiformities nor the uniformities of the international business environments follow any consistent pattern and since the fabric of cross-cultural influences continuously changes, it is futile to endeavor to distinguish the aspects of business administration which have international applicability from those which do not. Our concept of universality must be based not on a *catalogue raisonné* but on analytical comparisons of business realities at specific points in time in different countries. The elements of thought and practice which are congruent to the different environments can emerge only after the observer becomes aware of the value of comparative analysis. The lack of such awareness together with cultural inertia —having exclusively American ways of viewing and doing things—seem to be the most common obstacles keeping U.S. businessmen and scholars from a more rational and productive utilization of business administration in the international field.

## PROBLEM AREAS

A general outline of the main areas with which international business must cope is in Figure 1–1. In the center lie the objectives of the enterprise (usually either profit maximization or the fulfillment of norms prescribed in a national plan). To achieve the objectives, management must formulate and implement appropriate strategies, programs, and policies. From a functional standpoint, the managerial responsibilities fall into four main categories: finance, production, marketing, and the organizational and institutional structure within which the enterprise is to function. Each of the four contains subareas, of which three main ones are shown in the figure. An explanation of how these, in turn, proliferate into clusters of component fields will occupy much of this book. However, they all represent only the internal view of an enterprise.

From the outside the company encounters both positive and negative elements which must be identified, understood, and anticipated before rational choices can be made among the alternatives available in different parts of the world. The environmental effects on business enterprise are among the most subtle and complex influences in an international context. As the scope of an enterprise transcends a single country and extends successively to more countries, the environmental diversity grows progressively in countless respects. From such diversity arise new opportunities, uncertainties, incentives, impediments, and necessities for the enterprise

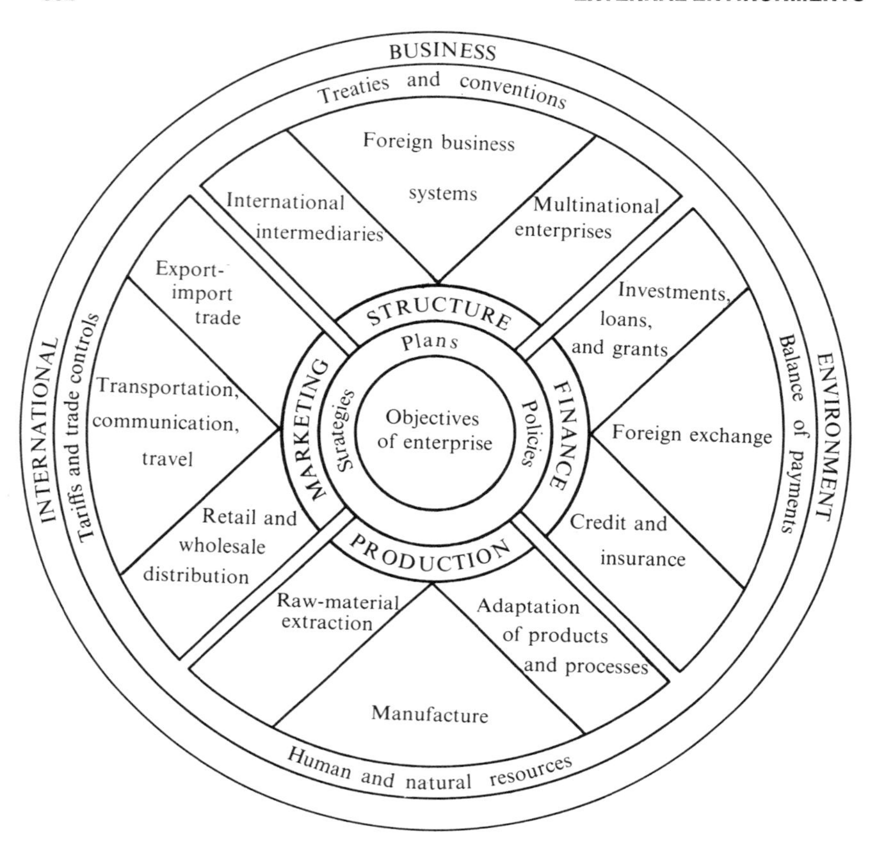


*FIGURE 1–1* The Scope and Composition of International Business

and its management. Multinational diversity may also transmute the previous norms, the managerial conduct, the executive action, and the corporate behavior as a whole. The multinational environmental framework, within which international enterprise must function and in reference to which its administrative decisions must be made, is, therefore, of paramount importance in the study and the understanding of international business.

Some have argued that the need for international business as a field could be obviated if only the traditional areas of business administration would broaden their coverage to the international aspects of their respective subjects. Although the advocates of this view have been dwindling in number and the experience of multinational companies has strongly discredited this view, the point may still be worth making that no amount of "internationalization" of the specialized subfields of business administration can take the place of international business per se. Technical and functional disciplines such as finance, marketing, and production are often helpful and sometimes vital for the study of international business. But, since none of them deals with the multinational frameworks as such, they can neither singly nor collectively cope with the basic problems of international business administration. Not only is the sum of the parts smaller than the whole, but also many of the parts, including the most important ones, would never be included if the environmental framework of international business were not subjected to thorough analysis and study. It goes without saying that the problems peculiar to foreign societies lie far beyond the purview of the traditional subfields of business administration as we know them today and as they are taught by collegiate schools in this country.

The growth of multinational business operations and the increasing interdependence of world economies are exerting growing pressures upon business educators to go beyond the American experience. There is little doubt that sooner or later all fields of business administration will cover some international subjects. The sooner this happens the better. International business is not a substitute for but a supplement to the other fields of business administration. It is not, and should not be permitted to become, a technique-oriented or functionally confined subject. Its basic pedagogical task is to broaden the executive's perspective by giving him a wider and a structurally more flexible frame of reference and a more diversified conceptual grasp than he otherwise would possess. This knowledge will increase his powers to perceive, compare, and adapt. International work done in the base subjects such as finance, marketing, and production is a direct benefit to international business since it contributes to the total store of relevant knowledge and enables more sophisticated, higher-level treatment in the integrative and behavioral analyses which international business must pursue.

Conversely, a solid international business program benefits all other fields of business administration by providing the frame of reference in which they can more effectively pursue international objectives of their own. Thus the fear of faculties in some business schools to allocate the necessary resources to international business lest it displace some subareas is quite unfounded, except where some of the existing course offerings are outdated or otherwise unable to withstand an objective reappraisal of their educational merits in comparison with those of international business. As the problems and needs in the business world change so must the courses and research efforts of universities. Certain courses and entire subject fields may decline in importance, and they should in the interest of maximizing the return on the scarce educational resources be replaced by those of relatively greater relevance to the contemporary business scene. It is only in this context that international business represents a "threat" to some other subjects in the business school curricula. It is not alone in this role; others—operations research, simulation, computer technology, and management science—challenge the position of the older and more traditional areas of business administration. This is as it should be.

## INTERNATIONAL BUSINESS, TRADE, AND ECONOMICS

International business is a new concept. It was first accepted as a distinct field by two or three universities in the mid 1950's. Since then it has replaced its academic predecessors—foreign trade and international economics—progressively at more and more collegiate schools of business administration. Outside the business schools, especially in the departments of economics, the older concepts continue to be used. Although the three fields—foreign trade, international economics, and international business—overlap, they are essentially different concepts.

Foreign trade is the oldest of the three. It has had several connotations in economic and business literature. For the classical and neoclassical writers it was synonymous with international economic relations. Much of this aspect of it was later transferred to international economics. In contemporary usage *foreign trade* refers to export and import activities, i.e., selling to or buying from residents of other countries. Whether we concentrate upon the theory of these activities or upon the practical operations of enterprises engaged in them, the scope of the field remains narrow.

International economics is a newer concept and covers a wider range. Although no two economists may agree on the precise delineations of international economics any more than they agree on those of economics per se, the field is essentially confined to those transactions which give rise to international financial obligations. In addition to import and export activities, international economics thus covers cultural, political, diplomatic, and all other transboundary transactions if they result in international payments.

International business, as already indicated, goes beyond both the older concepts by encompassing not only international transactions but also the structural framework of the institutions and organizations which produce the transactions. Although international economics identifies some international institutions, such as the International Monetary Fund, the World Bank, and notably cartels, it has nothing to say about multinational companies, joint ventures, foreign-based affiliates, or even the

European Common Market. It is in the area of international institutions, especially in their motivation, functioning, and behavior, that international business makes its unique contribution. These entities have most of the capacity for carrying out transboundary activities and in relation to one another they produce the structural framework to which international transactions must conform.

What has been said so far refers to binational or multinational transactions and institutions. However, international business, quite unlike international economics, also embraces certain uninational activities. Transactions between a French subsidiary of an American company and a French firm are a simple illustration. In the same way, international business includes the study of entities and organizations which may be uninational but which function primarily in the international realm.

### International Operations

The change in academic concepts which was discussed above was antedated by analogous changes in business practice. For many generations international business activity was confined to foreign trade. Accordingly management concepts as well as business organizations provided for an entity to perform exporting or importing functions or both. It was typical to find an export department, an import department, or a foreign trade department. Although such functionally narrow units still exist, they have been incorporated into or entirely replaced by broader entities usually called *international operations, foreign operations,* or *overseas operations.* This is not just a play on words. Indeed the words do not adequately reflect the nature and magnitude of the real changes which have occurred in the shift from foreign trade to international operations. As will be shown in Chapters 14 through 22, the new terminology hides more than it reveals. The shift involves not only organizational adjustments but also a fundamental change in the objectives of and the approaches to international business enterprise.

## THE CENTRAL THEME

Instead of trying to summarize these introductory notions, it might be appropriate to state the focal concern of this new field. The central objective of international business as an academic field is to study the problems which arise when business operations and organizations cross national boundaries and become multinational in structure and scope. In recent years, international expansion has become commonplace in U.S. business, making international problems an organic aspect of management. As a result, there is an increasing need to understand foreign environments, business methods, and the techniques of adapting management processes and organizational behavior to new and different conditions. The rest of the book is addressed to this growing need.

## DISCUSSION QUESTIONS

1. Identify some of the changes and trends which are today taking place within society in general that are of particular interest to the business community.
2. Is the concept or role of work changing within the American culture? If so, in what manner?
3. Explain how and why the objectives of businessmen are changing today.
4. According to Kolde, what are the five components of the international business system?
5. By means of the Kolde model, present and discuss "the scope and composition of international business."
6. Compare and contrast the "business system" and the "economic system."

# Chapter 12. Management Principles and Transferability

*Harold Koontz*

# A MODEL FOR ANALYZING THE UNIVERSALITY AND TRANSFERABILITY OF MANAGEMENT

As the area of management has increasingly commanded world wide interest and recognition, the question whether management is a science with universal application has concerned scholars and practitioners alike. It is now fairly generally recognized that effective management is the critical element in national economic growth and enterprise success. But it is far from generally agreed that management, as an emerging science, has universal application.

Obviously, if it does not, it is hardly even an embryonic science. For the role of science is to organize basic knowledge. A real science should explain phenomena regardless of national or cultural environments. Thus, the science of mechanics knows no boundaries providing it applies to the reality being considered. Principles of the building sciences are no different if applied to a small house or a large building and whether these structures are built in the tropics or the arctic.

Moreover, unless basic management science can be useful for practitioners in varying circumstances, it is certainly suspect. For the task of an *operational* science is so to organize pertinent knowledge as to make it applicable, and thereby useful, to those who would utilize it for accomplishing real results.

---

Used by permission of the author and publisher. *Academy of Management Journal,* vol. 12, no. 4, pp. 415–430, December, 1969.

Certainly, if managing is the critical element in economic success, the best possible and most widely useful underlying science is a social "must." Nor should it be forgotten that effective management goes beyond what is usually regarded as the economic, or business, sphere. It is my firm conviction that it really does not matter what is being managed, whether business, governments, charitable or religious organizations, or even universities, the task of every manager at every level is so to manage as to accomplish group purposes with the least expenditure of material or human resources.

## MANAGEMENT: THE CRITICAL ELEMENT IN ECONOMIC SUCCESS

It is a striking fact of life that per capita income varies widely in countries. In 1966, for example, only 18 countries were found to have Gross National Product per capita of more than $1,000 per year, while 33 had GNP per capita of $201–$1,000 per year, and 66 had GNP per capita of less than $200 per year.[1]

Because of these wide differences in per capita national incomes and product, attention of world leaders and development economists has naturally turned to the need for increasing productivity. One author has even referred to this concern and the many programs undertaken in the past quarter century as "one of the great world crusades of our time."[2] Until fairly recently, assuring development was thought to be one of transferring capital, technology, and education from the developed to the underdeveloped countries. But, as important as these are, it has come to be widely recognized now that managerial know-how is almost certainly the most critical ingredient for growth.[3] As one Chilean executive has put it:

> Perhaps it is time to alter our concept of underdevelopment and think in terms of management. This would focus our attention on helping mismanaged areas to improve their organizations and knowledge. No amount of capital investment will succeed in furthering human progress if such wealth producing resources are mishandled or undermined through lack of fundamental concepts. This lack of knowledge exists and the modern tools of finance, marketing, etc. are not common knowledge in underdeveloped areas and their absence prevents the rapid and successful expansion of areas. Capital alone will not replace this information, but likewise the lack of such capital will make it impossible to bring about the looked for development.[4]

Many who have worked with and studied the problems of economic development have come to similar conclusions. Rostow clearly had this in mind when he noted that "A small professional elite [of entrepreneurs and executives] can go a long way toward initiating economic growth."[5] Sayles has expressed the same viewpoint even more strongly when he concludes that "In the world race for economic growth and for the allegiance and stability of lesser-developed sections of the globe, United States management 'know-how' is a crucial factor."[6]

Conclusions such as these are not difficult for a person knowledgeable in management to understand. As pointed out above, the goal and *raison d'etre* of managing is to make it possible for people operating in groups to cooperate most effectively and gain the most in terms of goals sought with resources available. In other words, resources—whether human or material—will almost surely be wasted without effective management.

While emphasizing the critical role of managing, the importance of having technical knowledge, capital, and needed natural, physical and human resources should not be overlooked. But note that these are usually relatively easily transferred. No nation holds a monopoly on technical knowledge. Even so sophisticated a technology as the atomic bomb whose secrecy was so carefully protected by the United States did not remain a monopoly possession long. Most advances in technology, which are not nearly as complex or well-guarded, can be transferred from one country to another without great difficulty since only a few people need to have this knowledge to make it available for general use. Even capital can be fairly easily transferred, as can many other natural resources. Moreover, there are few underdeveloped areas of the world where the basic shortage is one of natural physical resources.

On the other hand, a cultural factor such as the level of education, particularly knowledge of skills, has an important impact on economic progress. Constraining on economic progress may be a large number of political factors, such as labor regulations, fiscal policy, business restrictions, and foreign policy. These and many other constraints in the environment where an enterprise must operate will necessarily influence management effectiveness. However, qualified managers can do much to bring economic progress by identifying them and by designing a managerial approach or technique to take them into account. This is the essence of "design" as engineers have found who must design a "black box" to operate in difficult environments.

This point was well identified by two specialists on international management when they said:

> We view management as the single most critical activity in connection with economic progress. Physical, financial, and manpower resources are by themselves but passive agents; they must be effectively combined and coordinated through sound, active management if a country is to experience a level of economic growth and development. A country can

have sizeable natural and manpower resources including plentiful skilled labor and substantial capital but still be relatively poor because very few competent managers are available to put these resources efficiently together in the production and distribution of useful goods and services.[7]

In speaking of the critical role of management, there is no implication that one is referring to *American* management. It is true that the United States has a much higher per-capita Gross National Product than any other country. It is also true that Americans are generally credited with having the most advanced management competence. It is likewise believed that there is some correlation between these two developments, although non-managerial environment factors have also played a part. But the essential point is that competent management is a basic phenomenon and, as any scholar and international practitioner knows, the underlying knowledge of management is international and many countries in the world have and are producing knowledgeable managerial practitioners.

## IS MANAGEMENT CULTURE BOUND?

A considerable amount of difference has been expressed on the question whether management is culture bound. Those who take the position that management is culture bound reason that, since management practices differ and people and their cultural environments vary, management theory and principle—the framework by which management knowledge can be organized—that apply to a developed economy like the United States are not applicable in materially different cultural environments. It is even sometimes argued that within the same national culture, the fundamentals of management may apply to business, but not to government or universities, or between different sizes of business, or businesses in different industries.

The findings of Gonzalez and McMillan are among those that are often quoted to the effect that management is culture bound. These scholars, on the basis of a two-year study in Brazil, concluded that "American management experience abroad provides evidence that our uniquely American philosophy of management is not universally applicable but is a rather special case."[8] It is worth noting that these authors refer to "philosophy" and not to "science" or "theory" or "principles." They also point out that "that aspect of management which lacks universality has to do with interpersonal relationships, including those between management and workers, management and suppliers, management and the customer, the community, competition and government."[9]

On the basis of similar research, Oberg appears to agree with Gonzalez and McMillan. He doubts that the "game" of management in Brazil, being so different from that played in the United States, would permit application of management principles successfully employed in the United States to Brazil.[10] Oberg even expresses the belief that management principles may not only be inapplicable between cultures, but also between subcultures, such as those between rural businesses and large corporations in the United States.[11] From these observations he concludes that, since the applicability of management principles is limited to a particular culture or situation, it may be fruitless to search for a common set of principles or "determinate solutions."

However, even those who question the transferability of managerial knowledge and the universality of management principles admit that the application of American management knowledge in other countries has often been successful. Gonzalez and McMillan, for example, while concluding that the American philosophy of management is culture bound, admitted that:

> Transferred abroad, this know-how is first viewed with skepticism. Foreign national employees and partners are slow to respond and understand the American scientific approach to management problems. However, once fully indoctrinated, they accept and support this way of doing things. The superiority of this more objective, systematic, orderly and controlled approach to problems is seen and appreciated. For the host country, for American international relations, and for the American parent firm itself the export of American managerial know-how as well as technological know-how has yielded great dividends.[12]

Similar conclusions have been reached by Harbison and Myers in their study of management in a number of countries around the world. They not only found a common "logic of industrialization" but also that "organization building has its logic, too, which rests upon the development of management" and that "there is a general logic of management development which has applicability both to advanced and industrializing companies in the modern world."[13]

Interesting and consistent findings were made in another study in which the behavior of some 3600 managers in 14 countries was probed. This study, undertaken by Haire, Ghiselli and Porter, found a high degree of similarity in managerial behavior patterns and that many of the variations disclosed were due to identifiable cultural differences.[14] It is interesting, also, that Richman, in reporting on the developing interest in management in the Soviet Union in 1965, found that the evolving Soviet approach to management utilized the functions of managers—planning, organizing, coordination, control, direction, leadership, motivation, and staffing—which were essentially the same as long-held American concepts.[15] Other evidence pointing to universality has been found in various studies.[16]

## THE IMPORTANCE OF DISTINGUISHING BETWEEN THE SCIENCE AND ART OF MANAGEMENT

It has often been argued whether managing is an art or a science. This is, of course, a fruitless and an absurd line of argument. Managing is an art, but so are engineering, medicine, accounting, and baseball. For art is the application of knowledge to reality with a view to accomplishing some concrete results, ordinarily with compromise, blend, or design to get the best total results. As can be readily recognized, the best art arises where the artist possesses a store of organized and applicable knowledge and understands how to apply it to reality. Thus, engineers have long understood that the best designers are those who are well grounded in the underlying sciences and who have an ability to conceptualize a problem in the light of goals sought and the further ability to *design* a solution to the problem to accomplish goals at the lowest system cost.

The same can be said of the task of managing. As an art, there is every reason to believe that it will succeed best if the practitioner has a store of applicable and organized knowledge to serve him. This knowledge, when organized, is science. When it is organized in such a way as to serve practice best, it becomes a truly *operational* science. It is the job of theory to act, as Homans has said so well, as "a classification, it provides a set of pigeonholes, a filing cabinet, in which fact can accumulate. For nothing is more lost than a loose fact. The empty folders of the file demand filling. In time the accumulation makes necessary a more economical filing system, with more cross references, and a new theory is born."[17]

In order to develop a theory, clear concepts are imperative. Likewise, the task of principles is to help in organizing knowledge by explaining relationships between two or more sets of variables, relationships believed to be generally true and, therefore, to have a predictive value. But, as every scientist knows, principles only describe and predict. They do not become normative (i.e., state or imply what "ought" to be) until the user applies them with a system of values (for example efficiency or effectiveness of a group effort) in mind. Moreover, no one should be surprised to see principles apparently disregarded in practice. The fact that, for example, many cases of disunity of command exist in practice does not mean that this practice has not tended to lead to confusion and splitting of responsibility. It is only to be hoped that the designer has taken into account the costs of disunity in creating his system. To say that existence of disunity of command in practice proves the invalidity of the principle is like saying that a space satellite invalidates the law of gravity.

It is exactly in the failure to distinguish between science and art where many of those who doubt the universality of management, as an organized body of knowledge, make their mistake. In a very real sense, one might say that there is a *practice* of managing and a *science* (no matter how crude it may be) of management.

Moreover, many who have written and studied managing in various cultures have erred on the very first requirement of science, the utilization of clear concepts or definitions. In reviewing the research and analysis that have been made in the field of comparative management, one is struck with how many of the differing conclusions as to the transferability of management are due to problems of semantics. The concepts of "management philosophy," "management know-how," "management theory," "management principles," and "management knowledge" are usually left either undefined or not clearly defined. One of the most widely used concepts, "management philosophy," almost defies clear definition. Strictly speaking, philosophy is the love, study, or pursuit of knowledge and is sometimes used as the equivalent of science. On the other hand, looking at studies of comparative management, one finds such definitions of "management philosophy" as "the expressed and implied attitude or relationships of a firm with some of its external and internal agents" such as consumers, stockholders, suppliers, distributors, employee unions, community, and local, state, and federal governments.[18]

In other places the term "management philosophy" is taken to mean a combination of management theory and principles, along with cultural attitudes and beliefs. Obviously, if philosophy includes such cultural beliefs as attitudes toward property rights and individuals, actual management *practice* would be expected to vary between certain cultures. Indeed, concepts such as this, particularly if they represent a composite of management fundamentals and cultural factors, can hardly have any universality. No one can argue that cultural differences exist between various societies, sometimes to a marked degree. There are even subcultural differences of an important nature in the same country or society.

It is clear then, by making the distinction between science and art, that the only generally comparative and transferable aspects of management are those which can be classified as science. When the distinction is made between management fundamentals, as expressed in basic concepts, theory and principles, and management practice—the application of management fundamentals to a given situation—progress can be made in determining the extent of management universality and the transferability of management fundamentals.

However, this does not necessarily mean that a given management technique or approach successful in one society may not work with few, if any, modifications in another. But it does mean that, if a manager borrows a technique from one society where it has worked well, he should be aware that some change may be required to make it workable in another cultural environment. At the same time, some management techniques can be surprisingly easily transferred from a well developed economy to a much less developed one. The author has found this possible, for example, with such techniques as variable budgeting, utilization of rate-of-return-on-investment, and network planning, even though less sophisticated applications of these techniques were often necessary. This is really not too surprising. These and other management techniques are so completely reflections of underlying proved principles that cultural differences often have little effect on their applicability, although they may not permit a very sophisticated approach because of limitations of information and understanding.

## MANAGING AND ITS ENVIRONMENT

The above distinction between science and art necessarily means certain things that any perceptive practicing manager has long recognized. In the first place, while the principal task of the manager is to design an *internal* environment for performance, he must necessarily do so within the constraints and influences of the enterprise's external environment—whether economic, technological, social, political, or ethical. Thus, managing as an art has never assumed a closed system. It would certainly come as a surprise to practitioners to find recent writers accusing "traditional" (whoever they are) managers of having managed without recognizing interchange of influences between the enterprise and its environment. Obviously, anyone who has utilized human and material resources or who has ever attempted to engineer and market a product understands well the openness of the system in which he is operating.

However, it is true that recent researches have clarified the science, as well as the practice, of management by placing increasing emphasis on the environment. This has been particularly noteworthy in the increasing recognition of cultural factors. Many are the American multinational companies that have found they must vary their managerial approaches and techniques when they move to the management of an operation in a foreign country where they are forced to take into account different sets of customs and mores, as well as more obvious differences in government and labor rules, capital and equipment availability, and levels of learning of available workers.

But, as differences in cultural environments are better understood and considered by the intelligent manager, this does not mean that the fundamentals of management are different. However, it does mean that, in studying the universality of management or undertaking comparative management analyses, the researcher must carefully distinguish between these fundamentals and their application.

## ATTEMPTS AT SEPARATING ENVIRONMENTAL FACTORS FROM MANAGEMENT FUNDAMENTALS: THE FARMER-RICHMAN MODEL

The meaningful study of comparative management may be regarded as starting from several important attempts to separate environmental factors from management fundamentals. One of the pioneering approaches for doing so is the model developed by Professors Farmer and Richman.[19] In this model, the approach is, first, to identify the critical elements in the management process and attempt to evaluate their operation in individual firms in varying cultures. A second feature of the model is to identify various environmental factors that have been found to have a significant impact on the operations and effectiveness of managers; these factors have been classified among (1) educational variables, (2) sociological-cultural variables, (3) political and legal variables, and (4) economic variables.

As may be noted, what these scholars have done is to postulate that environmental factors affect the elements of the management process, the way in which managing is done, and its effectiveness. They thus attempt to segregate environmental factors from the basics of management.[20] But they do not do so entirely. By including actual policies with the basics of the managerial functions, the authors have, unfortunately, not made their model as useful as it might have been for distilling from different environments the universals of management. In other words, while the fundamental concept of a policy as a guide to action in decision making is universal, as are the roles of policies in planning and the relationship of policies to delegation, an actual policy may differ considerably in varying environments. Thus, a make-or-buy production policy would be heavily dependent on national import regulations or on the availability of suppliers in a country. And policies with respect to sources of capital and distribution of earnings would be completely different in a socialized economy and a private-enterprise economy.

The Farmer-Richman model is graphically shown on page 367.

But, despite this mixing of environmentally resultant policy considerations with the basics of management in the Farmer-Richman model, these scholars have made an exceptionally important contribution to the separation of environmental and management factors. If those policies so dependent on environmental factors were separated from the fundamentals

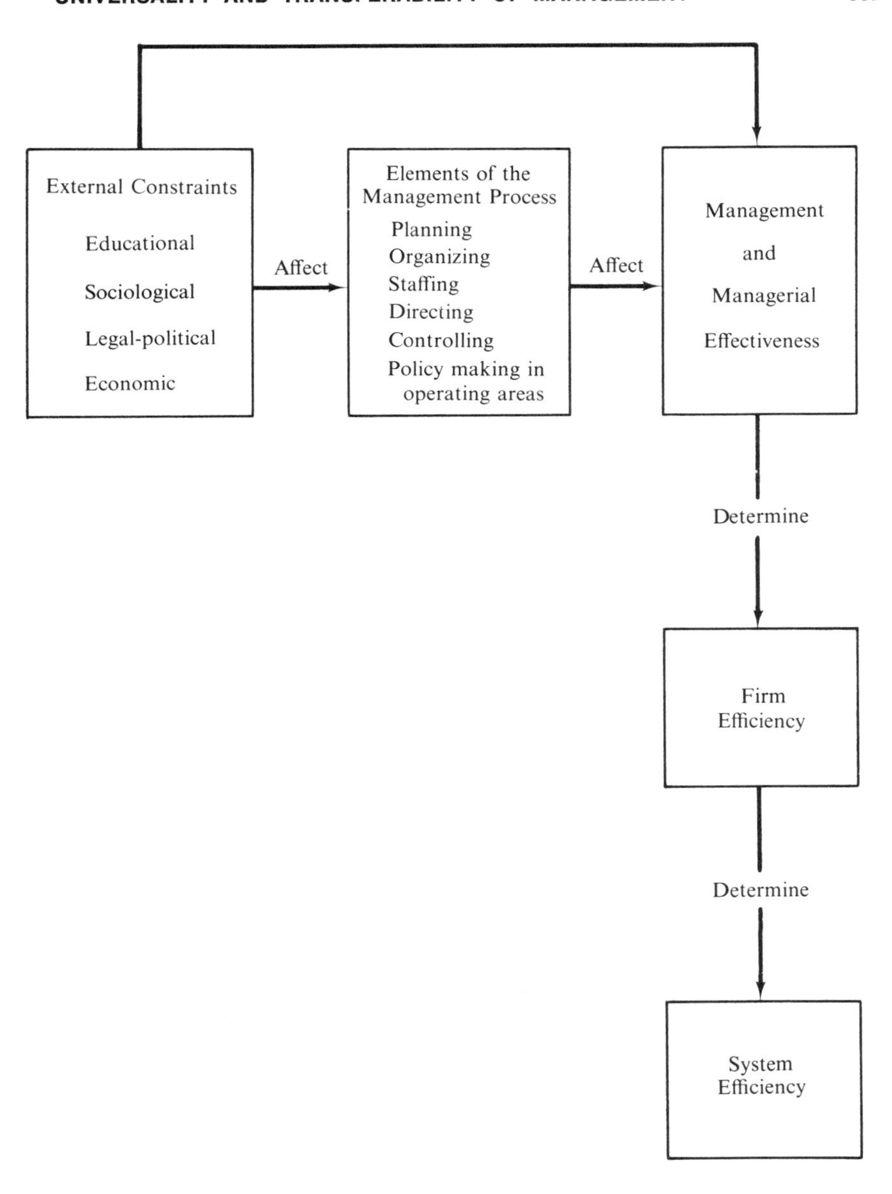


of policy making and other elements of management, we could then have a model which would be very useful in distilling the transferable universals of management.

## ATTEMPTS AT SEPARATING ENVIRONMENTAL FACTORS FROM MANAGEMENT FUNDAMENTALS: THE NEGANDHI-ESTAFEN MODEL

Another model designed to separate the influence of the external environment from an analysis of the basics of management is the model first offered by Professors Negandhi and Estafen in 1965[21] and somewhat modified since and used as a research device by the senior author.[22] This model differs somewhat from the Farmer-Richman model although it does focus on the task of separating environmental variables from managerial practice. The major difference in the Negandhi-Estafen model is the introduction of a major independent (or at least mostly so) variable in the form of management philosophy—an expressed or implied attitude of the firm toward such important internal and external agents as consumers, employees, distributors, stockholders, government, and the community.

The Negandhi-Estafen model is graphically depicted below (p. 368). As can be seen, in this model, both management philosophy and environmental factors are seen as having influence on the practice of management and environmental factors are seen as also independently affecting management and enterprise effectiveness. Thus, the Negandhi-Estafen model does not make the error, from the standpoint of separating management universals, that the Richman-Farmer model does. However, one

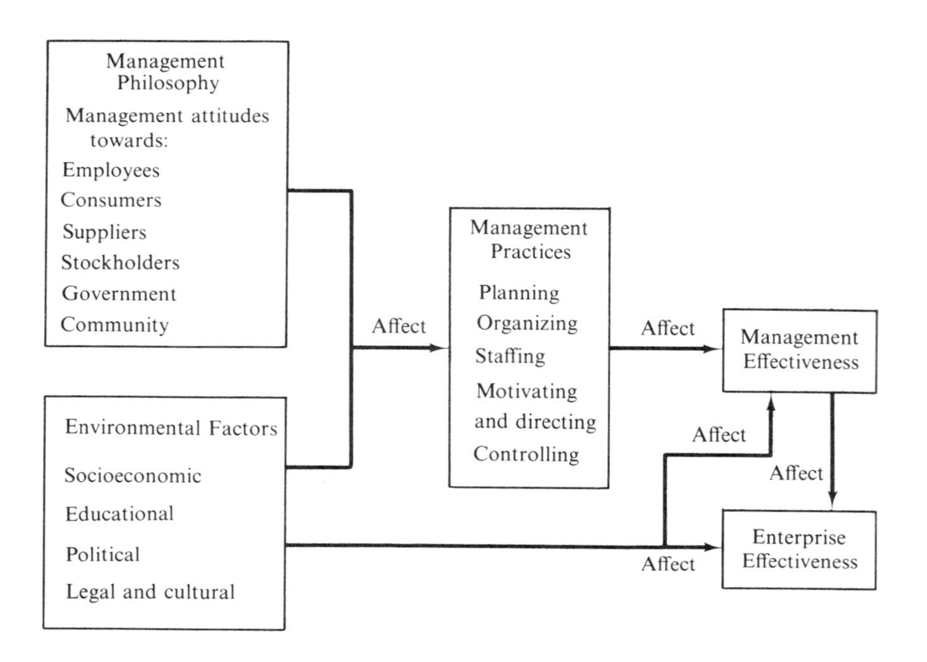

does have difficulty in seeing the area of management philosophy (attitudes and beliefs) as being independent of environmental factors. Also, the model itself does not make sure that management techniques or approaches can be separated between basics and environmentally influenced practices.

## SEPARATING ENVIRONMENTAL FACTORS FROM MANAGEMENT FUNDAMENTALS: A PROPOSED MODEL

From the point of view of studying comparative management to determine the universality and transferability of the basics of management and thus to make a start in separating science from practice in this field, neither of the above models seems to be suitable. Both make major contributions in recognizing the importance of environmental factors and in attempting to show how they affect the practice of management, but both are not as useful as they might be in dealing with the problem of transferability. Likewise, many other studies that have contributed much to an understanding of comparative management suffer from similar disabilities.

There are several difficulties with the generally used models. The problem of separating the art and science of management has been noted. Also, the effectiveness of an enterprise's operation not only depends upon management but on other factors. An obvious additional factor is the availability of human and material resources. While these are naturally products of an environment, it is still possible in the same environment—indeed common—for different enterprises, for many reasons, to have varying degrees of access to and availability of such resources.

Furthermore, management knowledge does not by any means encompass all the knowledge that is utilized in an enterprise. The specialized knowledge, or science, in such basic areas of enterprise operation as marketing, engineering, production, and finance, is essential to enterprise operation. As is well known, many are the enterprises that have been successful (and, therefore, at least apparently effective) despite poor management, because of brilliant marketing, strong engineering, well organized and operated production, or astute financing. Even though it is the writer's firm judgment, based on an analysis of the histories of many companies, that effectiveness of management will ultimately make the difference between continued success and decline, at least in a competitive economy, it is still true that enterprises have for a time succeeded entirely through nonmanagerial factors. It is also probably true that, if an enterprise has excellent capabilities in nonmanagerial areas, effective managing would greatly enhance and would surely assure this success.

In total, then, if we look at enterprise activities, they fall into two broad categories, managerial and nonmanagerial. Either or both can be the causal factors for at least some degree of enterprise effectiveness. Also, nonmanagerial activities will be affected by underlying science or knowledge in these areas, just as managerial activities will be affected by underlying basic management science. And both types of activities will be affected by the availability of human and material resources and by the constraints and influences of the external environment, whether these are educational, political-legal, economic, technological, or sociological-ethical.

If the factors affecting enterprise effectiveness and the role of underlying management science are to be brought to light more clearly than has been done, it would appear that we need a model as shown on p. 371.

As can be seen, the above model is far more complex than those used by previous researchers in the field of comparative management. It is also believed to be far more accurate and realistic. If our purpose is to study comparative *management,* we must do something like this. Only by so doing can we understand and see the elements of universality in management.

The real problem is not only to separate the influence of environmental factors but also the importance of managerial, rather than nonmanagerial, factors in determining enterprise effectiveness. This is obviously difficult. If we could put an enterprise in a laboratory where we could control all input variables except managerial, it would then be possible to ascribe effectiveness to the quality of managing. But we know that this is impossible. However, if comparative management researchers would try to introduce into their analyses the same kind of attempt to identify enterprise function factors as they have done so well with the external environment variables, a closer, even though crude, recognition of *managerial* effectiveness could be made.

This may not be as difficult as it appears. If we could take enterprises (whether business, government, or other) operating in essentially the same external environment and trace their primary causes of effectiveness to managerial and nonmanagerial factors, we might be surprised at what would be disclosed. The author has had the occasion to analyze several companies in the United States that had had a profitable growth only to find in some instances the quality of managing was rather poor and the success—often erroneously ascribed to astute managing—was really due to genius in marketing or in engineering, or in clever financial manipulation.

## EVIDENCES OF UNIVERSALITY

Despite the difficulties in separating the variables involved in enterprise effectiveness or ineffectiveness, there has been persuasive evidence that

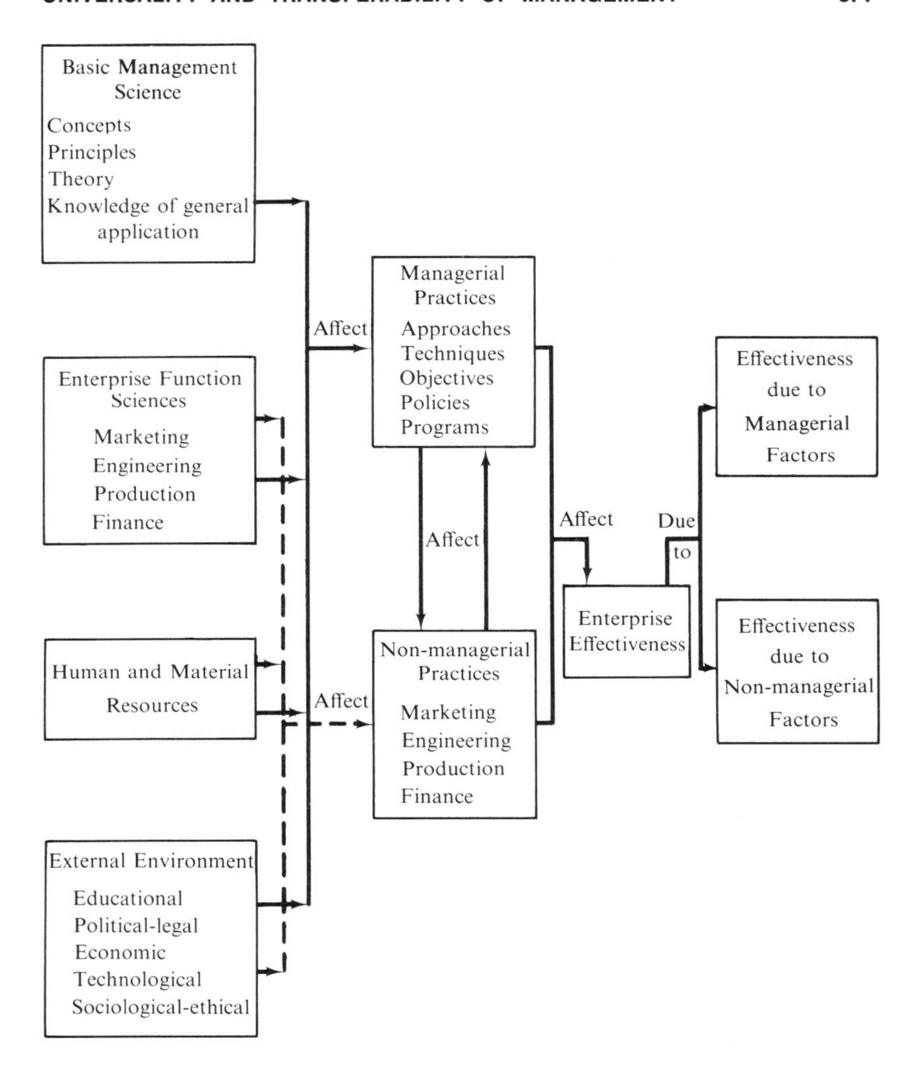


the fundamentals of managing are universal. While much of this represents conclusions and opinions, it has arisen from studies and analyses of well qualified scholars. While the studies are too numerous to be summarized in this paper, some references can be noted. The conclusion of Harbison and Myers that "organization building has its logic" has been noted.[23] The work of Farmer and Richman[24] covering a number of different cultures is particularly noteworthy and indicates the universality of basic management theory and principles. Likewise, the work of Negandhi points in the same direction.[25] The same kind of inferences can clearly be drawn from the work of Fayerweather on Mexico,[26] the various publications of the National Planning Association,[27] the work of Abegglen on Japan,[28] the studies of Prasad,[29] and many others.

Also, a number of studies on comparative management have been made in recent years by doctoral students. Most of these have indicated a high degree of universality in the application of management concepts and principles. For example, a series of studies undertaken at the University of California, Los Angeles, indicate pretty persuasively that well-managed American-owned companies, operating in less developed countries, have generally shown superiority in management and economic effectiveness.[30]

The universal nature of management fundamentals has also been apparent by examination of specialized books on administration for business, government, and other types of enterprises. While semantic differences may exist, one finds that, at the fundamental level, authors are talking about the same phenomena.

Persons like the author who have led management seminars for various types of enterprises find that the identical concepts, theory, and principles, often the same techniques (such as variable budgeting or management by objectives) apply with equal force in widely different enterprise environments. Also, it is interesting that most of the basic propositions inventoried from the behavioral sciences have universal application where relevant to managerial situations.[31]

## THE SIGNIFICANCE OF UNIVERSALITY FOR MANAGEMENT RESEARCH, TEACHING, AND PRACTICE

It is hoped that increasing effort will be made to separate underlying science of management from the art of managing. By so doing, we should then become increasingly able to recognize fundamentals of universal application and transferability. And, in doing so, many of the clouds that have obscured the analysis, teaching, and practice of management may be lifted and the jungle of management theory made into orderly rows of trees at last.

Managing as a science and practice is complex enough. But when it is put in the operating framework of enterprise functions and surrounded by a myriad of environmental influences, its complexity becomes virtually incomprehensible. With growing recognition of the importance of competent managing for effectively and efficiently reaching group and social goals, those whose role is to research, teach, or practice in the field have an obligation at least to clarify the field.

Much research has been done. Teaching of basic management has greatly expanded in the past 15 years. Management practice has become far more sophisticated and capable. But only the surface of this important field has been touched. Meanwhile, a great waste of human and material resources continues through inept research, ineffective teaching, and too much seat-of-the-pants managing. It is believed that much can be accomplished through the simple, but largely unaccomplished, approach of clearly and purposively separating underlying science from its artful application to reality. Early attempts to do so may be crude, but they, at least, should not be confusing.

## REFERENCE LIST

1. R. N. Farmer and B. M. Richman, *International Business: An Operational Theory* (Homewood, Ill.: Richard D. Irwin, 1966), p. 39.

2. M. D. Bryce, *Industrial Development* (New York: McGraw-Hill, 1960), p. 3.

3. "Know-how" is defined here as the ability to apply knowledge to practice; it therefore includes the knowledge of underlying science and the ability to apply it to reality to gain desired results.

4. J. Ross, "The Profit Motive and Its Potential for New Economics," *Proceedings, International Management Congress,* CIOS, XIII (New York: Council for International Progress in Management (U.S.A.), Inc., 1963).

5. W. W. Rostow, *The Stages of Economic Growth* (Cambridge, Mass.: Harvard University Press, 1962), p. 52.

6. L. R. Sayles, *Managerial Behavior* (New York: McGraw-Hill, 1964), p. 17.

7. R. N. Farmer and B. M. Richman, *Comparative Management and Economic Progress* (Homewood, Ill.: Richard D. Irwin, 1965), p. 1.

8. R. F. Gonzalez and C. McMillan, Jr., "The Universality of American Management Philosophy," *Journal of the Academy of Management,* IV, No. 1 (April, 1961), 41.

9. *Ibid.,* p. 39.

10. W. Oberg, "Cross-Cultural Perspectives on Management Principles," *Academy of Management Journal,* VI, No. 2 (June, 1963), 120.

11. *Ibid.,* pp. 142–143.

12. Gonzales and McMillan, p. 39.

13. F. Harbison and C. A. Myers, *Management in the Industrial World* (New York: McGraw-Hill, 1959), p. 117.

14. M. Haire, E. E. Ghiselli, and L. W. Porter, *Managerial Thinking: An International Study* (New York: John Wiley and Sons, 1966).

15. B. M. Richman, "The Soviet Educational and Research Revolution: Implications for Management Development," *California Management Review,* IX, No. 4 (Summer, 1967), 12.

16. See studies referred to in footnotes 22–30.

17. G. C. Homans, *The Human Group* (New York: Harcourt, Brace & World, 1950), p. 5.

18. A. R. Negandhi and B. D. Estafen, "A Research Model to Determine the Applicability of American Know-How in Differing Cultures and/or Environments," *Academy of Management Journal,* VIII, No. 4 (December, 1965), 312.

19. R. N. Farmer and B. M. Richman, *Comparative Management and Economic Progress* (Homewood, Ill.: Richard D. Irwin, 1965). See also "A Model for Research in Comparative Management," *California Management Review,* VII, No. 2 (Winter, 1964), 58–68.

20. The authors break down educational-cultural variables into 6 variables (such as literacy level and attitude toward education), the sociological-cultural variables into 9 items (such as attitude toward achievement and work and attitude toward change), the political and legal variables into 6 items (such as political stability and type of political organization), and the economic variables into 8 classes (such as fiscal policy and social overhead capital). Likewise, the elements of the management process are broken down into a number of basic factors under both the process items (planning, organizing, staffing, directing, and controlling) and various policy areas (marketing policies pursued, production and procurement policies, research and development policies, financial policies, and policies with respect to public and external relations). For a complete description of these factors, see *Comparative Management and Economic Progress,* pp. 20–21, 29–30.

21. A. R. Negandhi and B. D. Estafen, *op. cit.*

22. See A. R. Negandhi, "A Model for Analyzing Organizations in Cross-Cultural Settings: A Conceptual Scheme and Some Research Findings," in Negandhi *et al., Comparative Administration and Management Conference* (Kent, Ohio: Bureau of Economic and Business Research, Kent State University, 1969.)

23. *op. cit.,* p. 117.

24. *Comparative Management and Economic Progress, loc. cit.* See also many other publications by the same authors, either jointly or individually presented.

25. See, for example, his paper on "A Model for Organizations in Cross-Cultural Settings: A Conceptual Scheme and Some Research Findings," *loc. cit.*

26. J. Fayerweather, *The Executive Overseas* (Syracuse: Syracuse University Press, 1959).

27. See, for example, F. Brandenberg, *The Development of Latin American Private Enterprise* (1964); T. Geiger, *The General Electric Company in Brazil* (1961); T. Geiger and W. Armstrong, *The Development of African Private Enterprise* (1961); and S. Kannappan and E. Burgess, *Aluminum Ltd. in India* (1967).

28. *The Japanese Factory* (New York: The Free Press of Glencoe, 1958).

29. See, for example, "New Managerialism in Czechoslovakia and the Soviet Union," *Academy of Management Journal,* IX, No. 4 (December, 1966), 328–336.

30. These include such unpublished dissertations as B. D. Estafen, "An Empirical Experiment in Comparative Management: A Study of the Transferability of American Management Policies and Practices into Firms Operating in Chile" (1967); A. J. Papageorge, "Transferability of Management: A Case Study of the United States and Greece" (1967); F. C. Flores, Jr., "Applicability of American Management Know-How to Developing Countries: Case Studies of U. S. Firms Operating Both in the United States and the Philippines in Comparison with Domestic Firms in the Philippines" (1967); John Jaeger, "A Comparative Management Study: Organization Patterns and Processes of Hotels in Four Countries" (1965).

31. See, for example, the inventory of propositions in J. L. Pierce, *Organizational Effectiveness: An Inventory of Propositions* (Homewood, Ill.: Richard D. Irwin, 1968) and B. Berelson and G. A. Steiner, *Human Behavior: An Inventory of Scientific Findings* (New York: Harcourt, Brace & World, 1964).

*Rollin H. Simonds*

# *ARE ORGANIZATIONAL PRINCIPLES A THING OF THE PAST?*

The main texts used in many undergraduate business courses are "principles of management" books focusing on organization structure and administrative practice in business concerns. As a rule, these books contain a good deal of descriptive and analytical material, and they sometimes cover the traditional "principles of organization" in a relatively small part of the total. Yet these particular principles come in for a disproportionate amount of criticism.

Organizational principles—often with a considerable "behavioral" emphasis—include such recommendations as: clear-cut lines of authority and responsibility, coextensive authority and accountability, unity of command, limited span of control, the precept that a unit checking performance of another should not report to the department it is to check, appropriate delegation of authority, and no bypassing in the chain of command.

Among the modern writers who take a rather dim view of these principles, March and Simon say in their book *Organization,* "The great bulk of this wisdom and lore has never been subjected to the rigorous scrutiny of scientific method. The literature contains many assertions but little evidence to determine—by the usual scientific standards of public testability

---

and reproducibility—whether these assertions really hold up in the world of fact."

In *Modern Organizations Theory,* Mason Haire wrote that organization theory was by then (1959) drawing on "game theory and decision theory, information theory and communication theory, group theory, and developments in motivation theory," but he also commented that "we have virtually no studies of what management actually does."

## "THE WORLD OF FACT"

In an effort to find out what actually was going on in the areas of organization and administrative practice, a study was made of 75 manufacturing concerns, ranging in size from 40 to 600 employees. Teams of two researchers visited each plant from one to four times, interviewing from two to ten executives. The earliest interviews were in 1958 and the most recent in 1967.

In addition to a conventional chart of authority relationships, as part of the study procedure a function and duty chart was prepared for each company, calling for a much more precise and detailed knowledge of operating practice than the usual charts.

How did the traditional principles of management fare in the companies studied? First, there were many violations, but the business concerns in general did reflect the principles, or the principles reflected the company practices. In the great majority of concerns the structure was basically in line with the principles, with perhaps one or two deviations, although in a few cases there appeared to be a high degree of general confusion.

It is perhaps not surprising that in no instance did any of the executives interviewed complain of an organizational feature that conformed to the principles. No manager expressed a wish to report to more than one boss, or indicated that he felt effectiveness was being damaged by too clear an understanding and agreement as to each person's duties, authority, and responsibility. No one felt he or anyone else should be held accountable for things outside their authority, or objected to being held responsible for anything he had the authority and power to control.

When it came to violations of the principles, there were mixed reports. Some people involved said things were going well, that everyone cooperated to achieve the common goals, and such statements may have been entirely sincere, because often the "deviating" feature of the organization seemed to be causing no trouble whatever. Sometimes, however, when the "big boss" liked the structure the way it was, the explanation may have been that his subordinates tried hard to make it work and judged it prudent not to criticize.

### Trouble from the Top

As a matter of fact, several executives told the investigators frankly that the company's internal difficulties stemmed from the chief executive. Some instances of principle violation apparently reflected an unwillingness on the part of the chief executive to delegate authority. It is a familiar story—the man who started his company believes (perhaps correctly) that he can handle each one of the necessary functions better than any man he has working for him, and so tries to run the show single-handed. What he fails to realize is that, as the company grows, he cannot continue to manage all the functions without slighting some, and is actually doing a poorer job than his subordinates could do if they had the authority.

The confused organization, the one with obvious bypassing, sometimes suits the top man because he feels he has his hands on everything. Usually, this system finally breaks down, but it is possible that, in very small companies, a state of some confusion as to precisely who has responsibility for what may contribute to a feeling of cooperation and identification with the goals of the company. In a few of the companies surveyed whose managers acknowledged they did not really know who was supposed to take care of what, they nevertheless claimed morale was good and things were going smoothly.

### What Price Confusion?

It is hard to tell whether the morale and results were pretty good because of or in spite of the confused organization. In a relatively small group where all are well-acquainted and have been with the company a long time, when a need appears whoever is at hand and not busy may pitch in and do the job. However, strong morale and good results were also found where there was clear demarcation of duties. All in all, risks of inefficiency, of overlooking important matters, of conflicting orders or plans would be a high price to pay for a *possible* gain in morale or employee identification with the company.

In one company that was notable for lack of unity of command, with a great deal of bypassing or ignoring of supposed authority relationships, the morale was apparently the worst of all the concerns studied. Costs were high. People worked at cross purposes. The only person not expressing dissatisfaction was the president, and he did not appear to trust his subordinates.

## THE HUMAN TESTIMONY

It would be much easier if we had only to run correlations between types of organization and administration on the one hand and profit on the other, but profit is affected by so many things that such analyses would be useless. In the studies reported here, one concern seemed to be poorly organized and administered from almost any point of view, but it had made substantial profits in its ten years of existence, apparently because it had made a good choice of product and introduced some good design features, and had an advantageous location for raw materials, labor, and markets.

It appears that for the present, at least, we shall have to try to evaluate particular organizational practices largely on the basis of what we can learn from the people involved.

Now we might consider some specific instances where organization was not in line with the principles.

## A Problem of Nepotism

Company A employed 150 people, manufacturing metal products. The problem of unity of command appeared in every interview conducted; the secretary-treasurer, the chief engineer, and the vice-presidents, particularly, were gravely concerned about it. A vice-president stated, "The company has an absentee president. It is an excellent example of disorganization. Everyone tries to operate it."

In fairness, it should be pointed out that much of this confusion may have been of a temporary nature. The president had retired from full control, and his two sons as vice-presidents, as well as other officers, were attempting to make the decisions without a clear division of responsibility. The president was in his office part of each day and employees did not know whether to report to him, to a vice-president or to another executive. The company had no organization chart and although the managerial group knew their titles, they differed considerably in the way they saw the structure. The sons recognized the problem, however, and expressed a belief that in six months they could make some improvements.

Not all of the departures from traditional principles in Company A were attributable to transfer of control from the father to the two sons, however. For example, the purchasing agent reported to both the chief engineer and the plant manager. It is not uncommon, particularly in small companies, for one man to report to two bosses for two different kinds of work, and if each boss requires only about half a man's time, the arrangement may be appropriate. In this case, there was not complete division in the work of the purchasing agent, but it was nevertheless reported that the dual subordination was working satisfactorily.

At one time there had been a vice-president of engineering to whom the chief engineer reported. Half of the officers queried said that the position was still in existence but did not know whether it was currently filled, the other half were uncertain about the existence of the position. One of the vice-presidents told the interviewers that the chief engineer reported to the executive vice-president, a statement that puzzled other officers because of the extensive traveling done by the executive vice-president. The chief engineer himself stated that he had taken the position of vice-president of engineering but did not have the title.

The officers—most of them in their thirties or early forties—had taken a cut in salary two years earlier without reducing the pay of any other employees. There seemed to be a general desire to cooperate and contribute to company goals, but there also seemed to be some glaring inadequacies in downward communication. Some of the executives indicated that lack of clear structure reduced efficiency and contributed to poor decisions at times.

### Friendly Informality

Company B employed 125 people, producing and selling a line of metal products. There appeared to be little respect for the chain of command; except for employees on the assembly line, the established procedure was to go to whoever was in charge of a particular matter without bothering one's immediate superior. This bypassing did not seem to cause any trouble, perhaps because all but one of the officers and other managers lived in a very small city, had worked together for years, and, as one of the foremen said, were hunting and fishing buddies.

Two violations of unity of command stood out: A foreman had been taking orders of one kind or another from seven different people, but finally refused to do it any longer; everyone agreed that he was right and the situation was rectified. In the other instance, the assistant engineer took orders from both the chief engineer and the vice-president. If the vice-president's orders could be carried out in no more than 30 minutes, he would stop what he was doing and comply, but otherwise the order would "have to wait until he could get to it." Neither of this man's bosses seemed to object.

### Reluctance to Delegate

Company C was a jobbing company employing 275 people. The top officers were the owners of the company and were relatives. While its organization chart was reasonably clear-cut, middle management explained that almost no decisions were made by second-level executives, even in their own functional areas. Moreover, the executive vice-president frequently went directly to the person he thought was the source of any problem, without first asking for information from that person's superior.

While the investigators found no objective evidence of loss of profit due to the failure to delegate fully the authority apparently conveyed by titles, the vehemence with which middle management commented on it implied considerable dissatisfaction at that level.

### Democratic and Orderly

Company D had just under 200 people producing a fiber product. It was family-owned, and apparently some of the younger generation were being groomed for key positions, but nonfamily executives had bought a moderate number of shares.

The investigators got the impression of a friendly atmosphere throughout the organization. The president talked informally with employees about company policy or problems in departmental group meetings, and also held a monthly staff meeting in which current operating problems of the business were discussed. He had established a rotating chairmanship pattern at those meetings for two reasons, to give all members of the group a chance to prepare and lead a group discussion, and to foster freer discussion.

The organization chart indicated a clear assignment of authority and responsibility, and nothing was said to indicate that the principles were not consistently followed, but an example of dual subordination was noted —one man was assistant to both the purchasing agent and the production manager. Apparently, though, his duties in the two roles were quite different in nature, so the likelihood of conflicting orders was minimal, except, perhaps, in terms of demands on his time.

### Overburdened Foreman

Company E was also family-owned, employing 130 people. The chief engineer, sales manager, and superintendent all said they reported to and received orders from both the vice-president and the president, depending on who happened to be around at the time. All of these men except the president (who was not interviewed) agreed that this situation sometimes led to conflicting orders and confusion.

Here, the function and duty chart showed that one foreman performed more and higher-level functions than the other foremen. His chief job was foreman over the "second operations" department. In addition, however, all inspectors reported to him and he did all the planning and scheduling of production in both his own department and in the "first operations" department. He was also frequently called in to deal with problems in the shipping department. Other management members agreed that he was overloaded, but added that something would be done about it in the near future.

The investigators believe that these circumstances resulted from the family owners' desire to have all high-level positions occupied by family members and all close family members employed to have high positions. Hence the creation of the position of vice-president, thus providing three levels of management above the foremen, whereas if the vice-president had remained a superintendent, he would have carried some of the duties of the overloaded foreman and the dual reporting of engineering, sales, and production would not have come about.

## One Weak Link . . .

Company F was a tool and die company with employees varying in number from 40 to 90. Here we found an example of violation of the principles tied in with periods of transition or conditions that were not expected to continue indefinitely. At the time of the interviews the superintendent was considered inadequate for his job. He had been appointed not long before to fill a vacancy caused by a death, but what was needed for this position was a man who not only understood the operations and could direct the men under him, but also was good at controlling and estimating costs. The company had been unsuccessfully seeking a replacement, but meanwhile the president, the office manager, and the assistant superintendent had been working with the superintendent to make cost estimates, and there was no clear understanding as to just whose responsibility this was.

There was further confusion among the diemakers (who, themselves, directed less skilled workers), some of whom said they reported directly to the president, while he thought they were directed by either the superintendent or the assistant superintendent.

A capable and respected superintendent presumably would straighten out these tangles, particularly if the position of assistant superintendent were cleared up. According to organizational principles, he should eventually be slotted in a staff capacity, rather than between the superintendent and the diemakers, or else some division of responsibilities should be found so the assistant superintendent would not simply add another level with no reduction in span of control.

## Multiple Jobs and Bosses

Company G was a metal manufacturer with 60 employees. The president said they used to have an organization chart, but he could not find it. Yet he went on record that he felt organization to be important and that each man's responsibilities and authority should be clearly defined.

There was one function being carried out in conflict with the principles: Inspection was the responsibility of one of the foremen, who reported to the superintendent in both his capacities and, to some degree, to the president when wearing his chief inspector's hat. Thus, not only was one man reporting to two bosses, but a function (inspection) intended to check on another function (production) was largely under the control of the function being checked. The president expressed dissatisfaction with the arrangement and said that in the interest of tighter quality control he intended later to relieve the man of his foreman duties and have him report solely to the president.

Because there were only 60 employees, it should be remembered that less-than-ideal divisions and combinations of duties are almost inevitable in the very small business.

## Juggling Jobs

Company H, with 100 employees, also illustrated this point in two examples of apparent violation. First, all 60 day production workers reported to one foreman. This is a rather large span of control, particularly in view of the fact that the shipping and receiving foreman and the chief inspector also reported to this man, and even the night foreman to some degree was under his direction. The day foreman himself was the only person reporting to the plant superintendent.

Actually, though, the responsibilities of the day foreman were not quite so onerous as might appear, since the employees for the most part were skilled workers, some of them group leaders. Still, the day foreman and the plant superintendent represented two levels with no reduction in span of control.

Having the chief inspector report to the day foreman was the second departure from organizational principles, in that a function intended to check on another was subordinate to the function that it checked.

The company structure would have been more in line with the principles if the chief inspector had reported to the superintendent and if the shipping and receiving foreman had, too, at least partially narrowing the day foreman's span of control. The function and duty chart revealed that supervisory responsibility in connection with inspection was shared by the day foreman with the superintendent, so that in fact inspection wasn't totally controlled by the function it inspected, but, at the same time, duality of command was introduced.

The function and duty chart also showed that the superintendent carried out production planning and control and did most of the hiring. Thus, it seems likely that in cases where the span of control resides in only one man, there are some understood divisions of labor between superior and subordinate that do not show up clearly in the conventional chart of authority relationships.

As a matter of fact, in this company the president himself performed some of the inspection functions in heavy-machine orders, and the chief inspector was also the top mechanic of the plant, doing something of the work of a millwright. All these factors emphasize again that the smaller the company, especially in the under-150-employee category, the more various members of management will perform functions and "bend" organizational principles.

In summary, despite these deviations, the principles of organization came out rather well in this survey; the various violations, numerous though they were, appeared as significant exceptions, rather than the rule. There was abundant evidence that activities could be carried on very successfully despite failure to conform to the principles, but there is no proof that those successes were not in spite of deviations from traditional management, rather than because of them.

Further, it is significant that a considerable number of the instances of nonconformity to the principles were accompanied by signs of serious dissatisfaction and/or inefficiencies. In all 75 companies, the only complaints voiced to the investigators were about situations of which traditional management would have disapproved. It should be noted, too, that a leading cause for complaint—failure to delegate authortiy—is a weakness that would be deplored not only by traditionalists, but by many critics of traditional-principles literature as well.

It should also be pointed out that this study was carried out by interviews with various members of management; employees at the bottom of the hierarchies were not polled. So, while no managers or staff specialists voiced dissatisfaction over structure or tactics in line with traditional principles, it is entirely possible that nonsupervisory employees might feel differently. They present a wholly separate area to be explored in evaluating organizational principles.

## DISCUSSION QUESTIONS

1. How important is managerial ability as a variable affecting the economic development of nations? Defend your answer.
2. Compare and contrast the Farmer-Richman, Negandhi-Estafen and Koontz models which relate management fundamentals and environmental factors.
3. Are principles or fundamentals of management universal in nature? Defend your answer.

4. Give examples of "principles of management" which seem to be in use in many organizational settings.

5. What specific instances often occur or exist where organizations are not operated by means of management principles (theories or fundamentals)?

6. Can international business (comparative management) be considered to be a unique and separate discipline or academic field? Defend your answer.